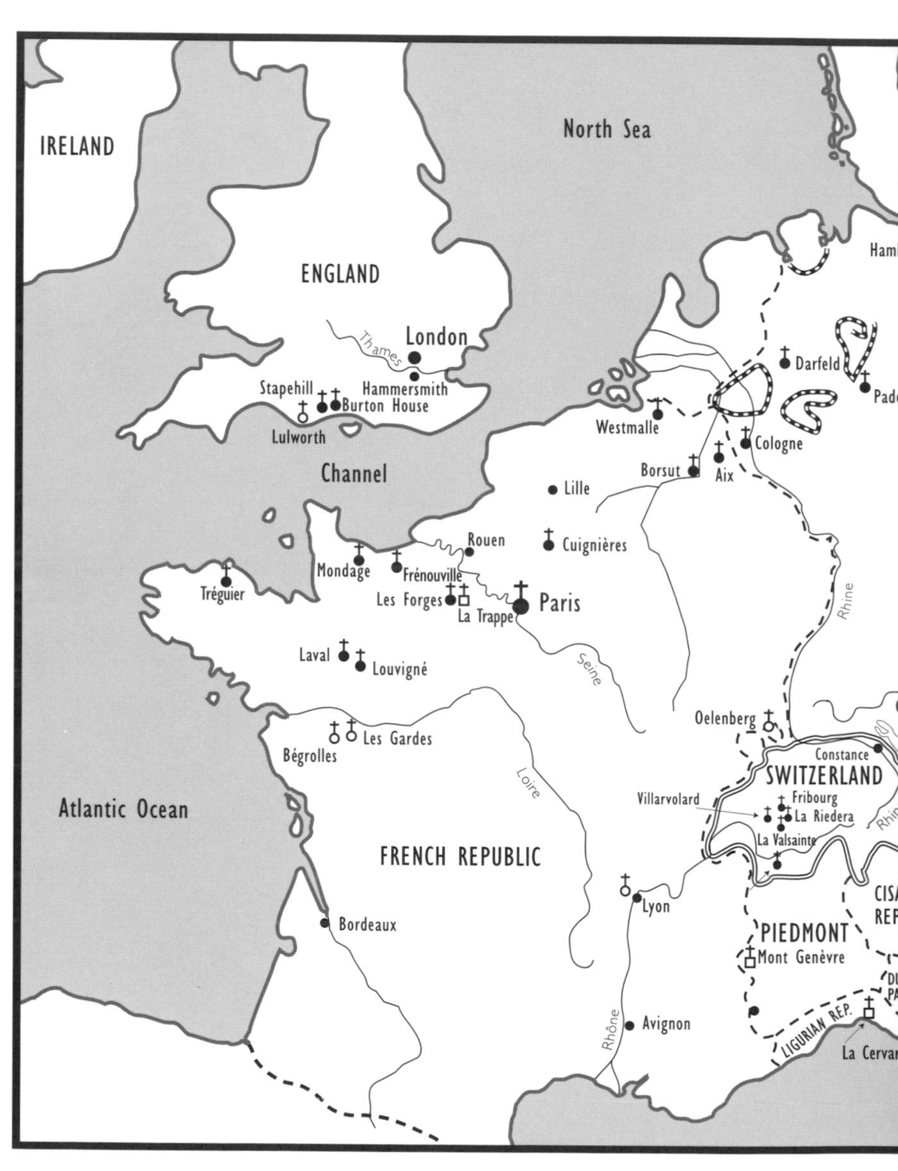

IRELAND
North Sea
ENGLAND
London
Thames
Hammersmith
Stapehill
Burton House
Lulworth
Channel
Westmalle
Darfeld
Cologne
Borsut
Aix
Lille
Rouen
Cuignières
Mondage
Frénouville
Tréguier
Les Forges
La Trappe
Paris
Laval
Louvigné
Seine
Rhine
Oelenberg
Les Gardes
Bégrolles
Loire
Constance
SWITZERLAND
Villarvolard
Fribourg
La Riedera
La Valsainte
Atlantic Ocean
FRENCH REPUBLIC
Lyon
PIEDMONT
Mont Genèvre
Bordeaux
Avignon
Rhône
LIGURIAN REP.

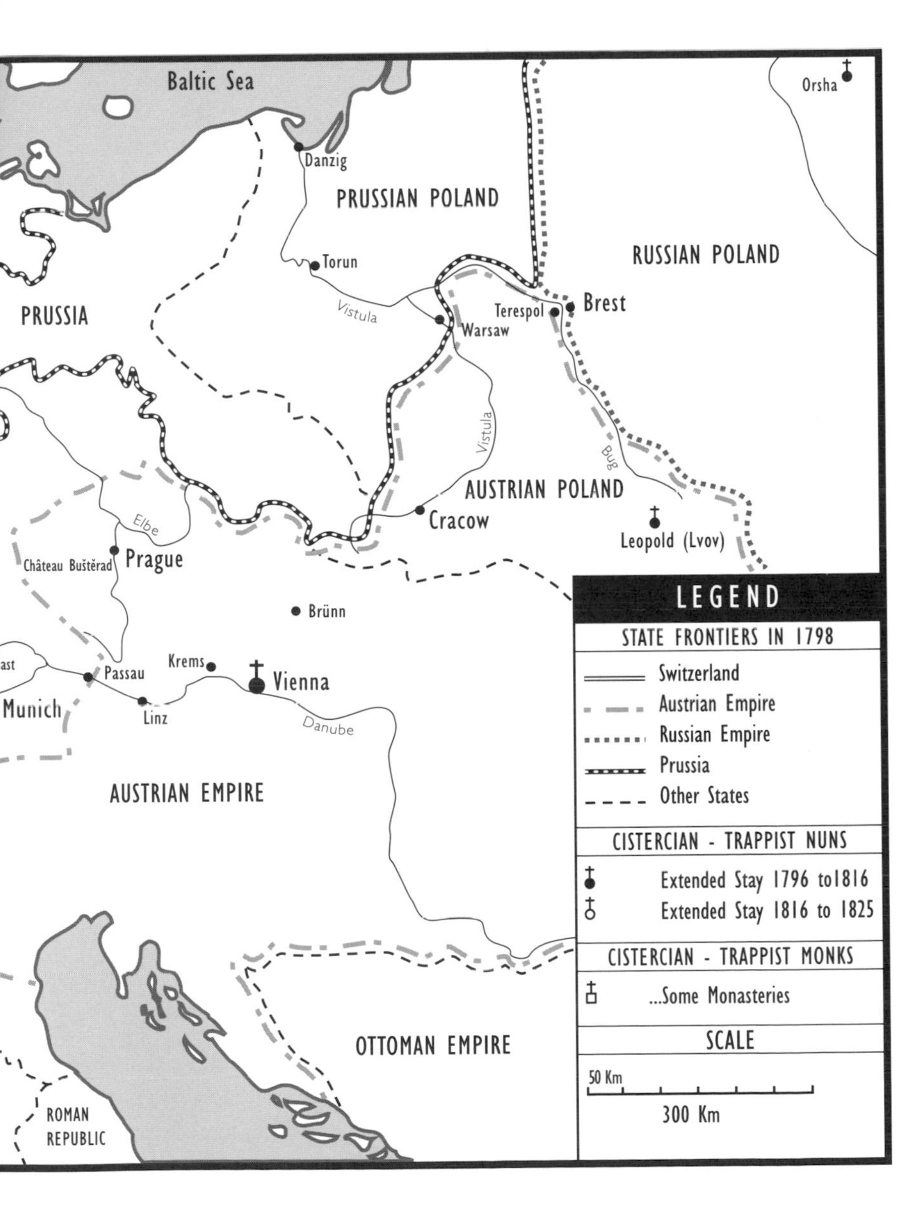

Baltic Sea
Danzig
PRUSSIAN POLAND
Orsha
RUSSIAN POLAND
Torun
PRUSSIA
Vistula
Warsaw
Terespol
Brest
Vistula
Bug
AUSTRIAN POLAND
Cracow
Leopold (Lvov)
Elbe
Château Buštěrad
Prague
Brünn
ast
Passau
Krems
Vienna
Munich
Linz
Danube
AUSTRIAN EMPIRE
OTTOMAN EMPIRE
ROMAN
REPUBLIC
LEGEND
STATE FRONTIERS IN 1798
Switzerland
Austrian Empire
Russian Empire
Prussia
Other States
CISTERCIAN - TRAPPIST NUNS
Extended Stay 1796 to1816
Extended Stay 1816 to 1825
CISTERCIAN - TRAPPIST MONKS
...Some Monasteries
SCALE
50 Km
300 Km

CISTERCIAN STUDIES SERIES: NUMBER ONE-HUNDRED SEVENTY-ONE

A MONASTIC ODYSSEY

by

Marie de la Trinité Kervingant OCSO

Translated by Jean Holman OCSO

CISTERCIAN STUDIES SERIES: NUMBER ONE HUNDRED SEVENTY-ONE

A MONASTIC ODYSSEY

by

Marie de la Trinité Kervingant OCSO

Translated by Jean Holman OCSO

Cistercian Publications
Kalamazoo, Michigan – Spencer, Massachusetts
1999

Original title:
Des Moniales face à La Révolution Française. Paris: Beauchesne, 1989

The work of Cistercian publications is made possible in part
by support from Western Michigan University to
The Institute of Cistercian Studies

Library of Congress Cataloguing-in-Publication Data available on request

TABLE OF CONTENTS

Scenes illustrating the Trappistines' journey across Europe were painted by Sister Clare Nash OCSO, a nun of Holy Cross Abbey, Stapehill. Born on 15 July 1900 at Crick, near Matlock, in Derbyshire, England, she was received into the Roman Catholic Church in 1930 and entered monastic life seven years later. The scenes are part of an illustrated map of the long and arduous journey which had brought her community's foundresses to Stapehill. She entitled it 'A Monastic Odyssey. A Refugee Cistercian Community in Search of a Home'. Color reproductions of all her illustrations are available, with captions in both French and English, in a small book *Une Odyssée Monastique*, from Editions Beauchesne, 72 rue des Saints-Pères, 75007 Paris. Used with permission of the Abbess and Community of Holy Cross Abbey, Whitland.

PREFACE

NUMEROUS PUBLICATIONS have been devoted to telling the story of Dom Augustin Lestrange and the monks associated with him in an astonishing journey through Eastern Europe. Hitherto, however, no detailed account has been published about the nuns involved in this monastic odyssey of unbelievable hardship and courage. Mother Marie de la Trinité has done a great service in painstakingly researching the history of these nuns. To do so she had to examine many scattered archives and piece together a great number of intricate details. She herself was the first to admit that all is not certain and that gaps still remain in our knowledge of this period. And yet her work has provided pointers for further research.

The courage and tenacious fidelity shown by the nuns portrayed in this book are astonishing. There were exaggerations, as the author judiciously points out, but they were caused mainly by the strange times in which these nuns had to live. Their fervour and fidelity has surely been rewarded by the remarkable growth of their foundations once the political climate permitted it.

We owe a great debt of thanks to Mother Marie de la Trinité for enabling us to know more about this somewhat neglected chapter of monastic history and to have done it in such a competent way.

21 March 1988 Dom Ambrose Southey
Abbot General, OCSO

TRANSLATOR'S PREFACE

THIS FASCINATING STORY, stranger than any fiction, is set in eighteenth-century France and begins during the French Revolution. All the 'useless' monasteries and religious houses were to be closed and the property sold. What became of the monks and nuns so ruthlessly put outside their monasteries?

The story we have here tells of the extraordinary adventures of these religious and their determination to retain their 'holy state' (*saint état*), as they called their vocation. A monk of la Trappe in Normandy, Dom Augustin de Lestrange, zealous for the glory of God, had a single ideal: to keep the monks and nuns of the Order thriving, no matter where. Providence sent him a novice who was to be of great assistance to him, helping him to obtain lodging and houses in which to settle during their wanderings about central Europe. This was Princess Marie-Louise de Condé, in religion Sister Marie-Joseph. Her letters and accounts have been preserved and have supplied the author of this book with many details hitherto unknown. Other monks and nuns have also left accounts of their adventures and journeys, each in his or her own way. The author lets them speak for themselves. By this means we have here a first-hand account of an unbelievable odyssey. Not only do the letters and journals add great charm to the story but they let us meet, so to speak, face to face the very human qualities of the religious who undertook this journey.

Translating these eighteenth-century documents into readable English has not been without its problems. There are many terms that have no present-day equivalents. The names of unfamiliar and often local religious Orders have simply been left in French. Means of transport, and distinctions between them important at the time, have been rendered as carriages or coaches. Monastic jargon and customs have been explained in the text or with a brief note. Proper names of persons and places have been left in the original to facilitate further research; but countries, towns, and rivers have been cast in their modern english spelling. Empires and their borders in the eighteenth century have been set out in the maps with english nomenclature.

None of this undertaking would have been concluded without the patient work of the abbot of Mount Saint Bernard, Dom John Moakler, and of Father Paul Diemer, both of whom looked through the translation, made many suggestions, removed gallicisms, misunderstandings and misspellings, in the process spending many hours re-typing whole paragraphs, doing research on geographical and historical problems, and supplying me with english maps.

Mother Anne Morin, the abbess of Ubexy, encouraged me from the beginning to undertake this work, providing me with time and place, and the use of a computer. I wish here to convey my gratitude to the members of the community at Ubexy for providing me with the necessary equipment. Sister Marie-Vincent Hemmer very skillfully typed into the computer all the Tables contained in this book; may she be assured of my gratitude for this patient work.

Any remaining errors and misinterpretations must be attributed to the translator, often at a loss when faced with difficult definitions and decisions on how to construe mysterious archaisms.

It is my hope that this strange story be a source of inspiration for all who have followed these men and women in their cistercian vocation.

Jean Holman OCSO

FOREWORD

The living search out their origins
this is why the tales
that they tell among themselves
have something of the 'mythical' about them,
in other words,
their meaning is found
by referring to their beginnings

Philippe Lécrivain

THE HISTORY of the Trappist monks during the French Revolution, told at length in the course of the nineteenth century, is sprinkled with passing allusions to the presence of nuns who followed them from exile to exile. Intrigued, and at the same time conquered, by the courage of these women, I have wanted for a long time to know more about them.

The best way seemed to be an assiduous search of original documents concerning the nuns. The abbey of La Trappe at Soligny, where the whole story started, was the first source to dip into. The Father Archivist there obligingly acquired for me, among other documents, a photocopy of two unpretentious notebooks marked 55–13 and 55–13 *bis*. The two texts were almost identical, so much so that one ended with this note: 'I have re-copied this account in a notebook written by the venerable Mother Stanislaus, Subprioress, who died at La Riedera'.

By this note the account can be dated between 1806 and 1813, the year of the author's death. It is a brief and precise narrative of a long and strange adventure which lead a large group of nuns from France to Switzerland, then into Bavaria, Austria, Bohemia, Poland, Russia, and finally back to Switzerland. During these years they travelled about 6000 kilometers. Their aim, expressed many times, was to find a place where they could be settled permanently, peacefully to live in common the monastic life which brought meaning to their lives; what they called *conserver notre saint état*, preserving our holy way of life.[1]

Encouraged on many sides to pursue my research, I was invited by the oldest monasteries of nuns to be established to see their archives. The resulting harvest was sufficiently abundant in the form of anecdotes, letters, registers, profession schedules, and obituaries to prompt me to sketch a rough draft of this astonishing history: an appearance on the ancient Cistercian tree of a vigorous feminine branch of the Order, at the very hour when every vestige of monastic life was disappearing in France. So I thought I would write some articles on the subject.

The first two provoked great interest and an influx of new documents arrived from Switzerland, Bavaria, Austria, Westphalia, and England. Poised at the dawn of the second centenary of the French Revolution, why not use this great wealth of material to write a book? It could trace the major developments and stimulate further work which would deepen the meaning of this odyssey and/or its repercussions and consequences. In fact, the history of these nuns has never been written. The odyssey of the monks has been described in several nineteenth-century books, but nothing has been written about the nuns.

My purpose therefore has been to write this history *au*

[1] This document seemed to me to be of primary importance; it needed only to be used. I was advised to publish this text, as yet unedited, in the historical review of the Order, *Cîteaux* with an introduction and some notes. This work obliged me to do yet more research. See *Cîteaux* 35 (1984) 185–214.

féminin, without neglecting to show how the nuns benefitted from the spiritual and material help of their brother monks and how this entire experience built solid bonds between the two branches of the Order. In the course of the following pages, as much as possible, I have allowed the sisters to speak for themselves through their letters and narratives. These last, even though they were written down later, retain a spontaneity and vivacity which well conveys the facts presented and allows us to visualise what the nuns had to live through from day to day. The other documents; in particular the registers and profession schedules, are a mine of information of all sorts, giving precise details of places and dates which are often missing elsewhere. Many gaps still remain, and fragile hypotheses which are far from being confirmed because of a lack of evidence in the archives. The field is open for further research.

Let me here express my appreciation for all those who have helped me in my research and in putting together this book. They are numerous and my debt is great. Such collaboration and friendly help have been stimulating and encouraging. May each be assured of my gratitude.

PART ONE

The Monastic World at the End of the Eighteenth Century

Abbeys of Cistercian Nuns at the Time of the French Revolution

Map showing the *Departements* established on 26 February 1790, with Avignon and the Comtat Venaissin annexed on 14 September 1791.
Savoy was occupied on 27 November 1792.
The Alpes Maritimes were occupied on 31 January 1793.
The Rhône and the Loire were divided on 19 November 1793.

A dot • marks an abbey not always juridically linked with the Order, but observing the 'rule' of Cîteaux.

Figure 1

Abbeys of nuns following cistercian observances on the eve of the French Revolution. After a late eighteenth-century map by a monk of Clairvaux, now at the Archives Nationale, Paris, NN179(71).

MONASTIC COMMUNITIES were a realm apart. They were separated from the world by their vocation yet nevertheless immersed in it; molded by it without their knowledge. They let the outside world in through a thousand fissures, offering in spite of themselves the two-sided face of ritualism and adaptability. They were marked by the evolution of society, yet kept the outward customs of another age. This was a contrast which too often gave them a distorted image.[1]

Endowed with privileges, the right to collect tithes, and, like the nobles who ruled the land, exempt from taxes, monks gave the appearance of being so well provided for that they could dispense themselves from work because of the vast properties they owned. In Paris alone religious houses occupied a quarter of the surface area of the city. In France as a whole they occupied six to ten percent of the country, and in some regions fifteen to twenty percent of the country was monastic or conventual property, while the number of their beneficiaries barely reached a two-thousandth of the french population. For the most part these lands were gifts received and accumulated over the course of centuries in exchange for spiritual favors in the form of perpetual

[1] See G. Reynes. *Couvents de femmes. La vie des religieuses cloîtres dans la France des XVII et XVIII siècle* (Paris, 1987).

prayers to be said for the donors or Mass intentions to be said for the living and dead members of their families, or again for the care of the poor in the name of those who willed benefactions to be continued after their death.

All this is recorded in charters carefully preserved in archives. Tithes and benefices were also revenues, guaranteed not by the labor of the monks, but by the poor peasants deprived of land who, having paid their taxes, had to scrape together what they could to avoid dying of hunger.

After 1517, when a Concordat was concluded between the king of France, Francis I, and the pope, Leo X, the practice of commendatory abbots and abbesses added a serious difficulty to the life of the monasteries. The king himself could appoint the abbots and abbesses of the monastic communities, and could nominate to these offices lay persons and even children. These commendatory abbots were usually satisfied with having the revenues of an abbey, without bothering about the responsibility. Theoretically, the revenues of these properties were divided into three parts: that of of the 'abbot', that of the monks, and that of the poor. Often, however, the 'abbot' helped himself to the lion's share, took no interest in the upkeep of the buildings, and never even went to see the place. Consequently the monks, reduced to subsistence living, tended to diminish in numbers, leaving the portion for the poor barely adequate.

Even more lamentable than material poverty under the guise of opulence was the spiritual crisis that for long years severely undermined the monasteries in spite of some exceptions and attempts at reform.

Wars, in particular the Hundred Years War, famines, severe epidemics such as the Black Death and cholera, decimated the civilian populations as well as the religious houses in the fourteenth and fifteenth centuries. That morale plummeted was only inevitable. Worse, all christendom was shocked and disturbed by the great western schism. The renaissance and reformation followed, transforming the whole social order. Yet by the end of the sixteenth and the beginning of the seventeenth century, there were some signs of regeneration. Austere reforms, represented by a mystical movement in the French school of spirituality, and a growing vitality in the Church in France. But at the same time a tumult of new ideas and controversies was causing bitter conflicts. Here, I am thinking firstly of Port Royal and the crisis which ensued. Division and opposition were prevalent among the foremost men of the day—Rancé and Mabillon, Bossuet and Fénelon—as were currents of thought developed from the cartesian philosophy of enlightenment which dominated the entire eighteenth century.

While the social environment was imperceptibly infiltrated by these ideas, the monastic world was also infected in some areas, for in the mind of 'enlightened' critics, this medieval institution was simply inadequate for a society on the brink of total transformation. The population could no longer support the monastic institution as it had in the twelfth century. There was no co-operation and no sympathy between the monks and those around them. How then could they hope to survive without adapting? How could they sustain indefinitely a way of life which was held in contempt by society?

This explains why in the second half of the eighteenth century, monks seriously examined their way of life 'in the spirit of the times'. An angevin monk of Montreuil-Bellay in 1769 published the *Lettres sur l'esprit du siècle*, in which he developed the idea of an egalitarian utopia completely centered on the idea of happiness. He questioned whether the clergy, morality, or even God were necessary. This did not seem to prevent him from leading the regular life. Others went further and put ideas into action. How then can we be surprised at the decadence found by the 'Commission of Regulars' instituted in 1764 by Louis XV to do away with the religious Orders and abbeys, and assign their property to the State. A breach was open which could not fail to hasten the French Revolution already in preparation.[2]

[2] For all this see J. Leflon, 'La crise révolutionnaire', in A. Fliche and V. Martin, *Histoire de l'Eglise*, 20:23–27; F. Bluche, *La vie quotidienne au temps de Louis XVI*, 163–168; L. Lekai, *The Cistercians. Ideals and Reality*, 162–168; B. Plongeron, *Théologie et politique au siècle des Lumières, 1770–1820* (Genève, 1973), and *La vie quotidienne du clergé français au XVIII siècle* (Paris, 1974, 1988). See also M. Vovelle, *Religion et révolution. La déchristianisation de l'an II* (Paris, 1976); T. Tackett, *La Révolution, L'Eglise, La France* (Paris, 1986) trans, A. Spiess (Princetown University Press, 1985).

CHAPTER ONE

CISTERCIAN ABBEYS OF MONKS AND NUNS

ABBEYS OF MONKS

AT THE TIME OF THE REVOLUTION in France, abbeys of cistercian monks were still quite numerous. Louis Lekai has drawn up a comprehensive table with statistics in the appendix of his book, *The Cistercians: Ideals and Reality*. He lists two hundred thirty-seven abbeys, and gives the number of persons in each monastery, separating choir monks and lay brothers, in the year 1790. These are the official statistics required by the government when the monasteries were dissolved.

Threats of Extinction

For many decades an atmosphere of apprehension had already invaded the communities. The Commission of Regulars instituted by Louis XV under the presidency of the Archbishop of Toulouse, Loménie de Brienne, had suppressed nine religious Orders and closed more than four hundred fifty monasteries between 1764 and 1768. Those that remained feared for their survival. The Cistercians had so far been spared. 'The President of the Commission has noted himself that the business of Cîteaux will be one of the most difficult to deal with . . . by reason of the importance of the Order, extended over all of Europe, their extensive possessions and their close connections with the lords of the land.'[1] For a long time monks had been more and more considered useless idlers, dreamers, and relics of an age that must disappear.

The General Chapter at Cîteaux in 1786 sought a remedy for their perilous situation. The Abbot General, François Trouvé, during this Chapter set up a special commission called 'The Service Bureau'. Thought was given to reviving the College of Saint Bernard in Paris, which by then had only one monk. With the goods and the revenues of monasteries with only a few monks, scholarships could be founded for students. Professors would then be trained for other, more flourishing monasteries, capable of creating colleges for young boys. Teaching had long been considered a legitimate field of monastic activity. Other abbeys could take on pastoral and parish work. None of these projects had time to materialize.

The Monastic Situation

What sort of picture, then, did the Cistercian Order present in France at the time the Revolution was planning a new society that eliminated useless members?

Among the two hundred thirty-seven monasteries of monks of the Cistercian Order, one hundred seventy-three were of the Common Observance and sixty-four were grouped as Cistercians of the Strict Observance. Among the latter, two had been reformed in the seventeenth century, La Trappe by the Abbot de Rancé, and Sept-Fons by Dom Eustache de Beaufort. Some abbeys in both Observances were still under the *commend*. The commendatory abbots, appointed by royal decree, did not live in the abbeys and the communities were governed by claustral priors. Many of the elected abbots lived much as did great Lords. Of the one hundred seventy-three monasteries of the Common

[1] J. M. Canivez, in *DHGE*, art. 'Cîteaux', col. 993.

Observance, only twenty-six numbered ten or more monks; among these six abbeys had more than twenty monks: Cîteaux had fifty-five, which included eight lay brothers.[2] Lucelle had forty-seven, which included five lay brothers; Loos had thirty-nine, including one lay brother; Clairvaux had thirty-three, which included ten lay brothers; Vaucelles had thirty-one and no lay brothers; Morimond had twenty-five monks, and this included nine lay brothers. Twenty other abbeys had between ten and twenty monks. The other one hundred forty-seven abbeys not included in this fifteen percent of the monasteries, had fewer than ten monks, just enough to maintain the Divine Office. Fourteen abbeys had only one monk, living sometimes in huge buildings.

An examination of the Strict Observance shows that twenty-nine percent of the abbeys had ten monks or more. The largest community was La Trappe, which counted ninety-one monks, including thirty-six lay brothers. After it came Sept-Fons with seventy monks, including twenty-six lay brothers. Fifteen other monasteries had between ten and twenty monks. Among the forty-six abbeys counting fewer than ten monks, one only had a single monk.

The overall situation then was rather poor, except for the nine abbeys having a large community and the thirty-five others with more than ten monks. With such a picture it is difficult to imagine an authentic monastic life in these buildings, now too large for their communities. This was the case in one hundred ninety-eight abbeys of the Order in France, that is eighty percent of the monasteries.

[2] Twenty-eight of these monks came from other abbeys. The abbot of Cîteaux welcomed them for reasons of charity.

THE ABBEYS OF NUNS

What then was the situation of the nuns?

To the best of my knowledge we have no overall statistics for the monasteries of nuns. Apart from some monographs and a few documents in archives, for example that of the abbey of Saint-Antoine in Paris, I have had to depend on the *Dictionnaire des monastères cisterciens* by Father Maur Cocheril, and by 1976 only one tome had appeared: *Cartes géographiques*. I have had to fill in with the short accounts found in the *Atlas cistercien* by Frédéric Van Der Meer, published in 1965. In spite of some uncertainties, these provided what seemed adequate information for a brief introduction for a history of cistercian nuns at the dawn of the Revolution.

Geographical Survey and Population Statistics

In 1789 there were between one hundred and one hundred-five monasteries of nuns in France, rather unevenly distributed over the country. A look at the maps shows that entire regions had very few or no monasteries of Cistercian nuns. Curiously these are, with some exceptions, mostly on the coastal regions bordering the Mediterranean, the Atlantic, and the English Channel, in Brittany and lower Normandy, and also in some central regions of France. On the other hand, Paris alone counted four abbeys; Flanders and Picardy had fourteen; the region around Avignon five; the diocese of Langres seven, Besançon four; and Puy-en-Velay four, all within a few miles from each other.

Were all these abbeys populated? Various historians have noted in passing that the nuns were generally more fervent and more attached to their vocation, and that their monasteries were clearly better populated than those of the monks. Jean Leflon, in his book *La Crise révolutionnaire*, gives a good summary of the situation:

> If in spite of restrictions imposed on some Orders, houses or regions, the situation for the monasteries of monks remained less than brilliant, and sometimes lamentable; on the other hand, the situation for the monasteries of nuns seemed to be quite satisfactory. Here the exceptions are in the reverse, and on the whole there was no laxity. Except for the Chapters of Canonesses, which was a noble institution, half religious and half lay, the nuns were a credit to their vocation.[3]

The nuns were then, on the whole, better able to face the coming ordeals, even though their material resources were more limited and their sphere of action as women more restricted.

In various books on the history of the religious life and in a few monographs I have turned up some statistics on the Cistercian abbeys of nuns. Here are a few figures gleaned here and there on abbeys situated in various regions of France.

In the North, Marqette numbered sixty-nine nuns, choir and lay; La Woestine thirty-one nuns; Flines nearly a hundred; Notre-Dame-des-Prés thirty-eight choir nuns and eighteen lay sisters. In Pas-des-Calais, the Abbey of La Brayelle d'Annay had twenty-six choir nuns and sixteen lay sisters. Le Paraclet in the Somme had thirty-nine nuns. In Paris, the three official lists preserved in the National Archives, for the abbey of Sainte-Antoine-des-Champs, show the signature of twenty-five choir nuns and twelve lay sisters. In the first list of 1790, each sister is given her religious and her family name, some have their employment added, and the age of each sister is also given. In the two lists dated 1792, the religious name has not been noted and the family name of the nuns of the nobility has been deprived of the particle *de*.[4] In Avignon the monastery of Sainte-Catherine numbered

[3] Leflon, 'La crise révolutionnaire', page 26.

[4] National Archives, section légale du Royaume, leg. n° 102, 26 March 1790 and May-July 1792. Abbess Gabrielle-Charlotte de Beauvau was

twenty-two choir nuns, five lay sisters and two externs. The oldest nun was eighty-seven and the youngest nineteen years old.

A monastery in Lozère, Mercoire in Gévaudan, only had seven nuns in 1790. But we must realize that the number of nuns was limited by the revenues from the property and that Lozère was a poor county. As the revenues of an abbey often varied quite considerably, royal authority could send a sealed letter forbidding the future reception of new members. So in the archives of the abbey of Annay, Notre-Dame-de-la-Brayelle (North), we find a request dated 1765, addressed to 'Our Lords the Commissioners of the Office for Religious Communities' giving all the reasons why the *Dames religieuses* hope that a sealed letter of 4 May will be revoked. This sealed letter, in effect, forbade them thenceforth to receive any novices without the express permission of His Majesty. The petitions concluded by adding: 'How fortunate we shall be if these observations (*all the rights that they have to remain*) would allow them the freedom to choose other sisters who could help and support them in their various undertakings; and who would continue after them the regularity and the glory of the house . . .'. In fact, they gained little after the withdrawal of the interdiction. We note in passing that these nuns placed at the forefront the 'zeal for religion and for the good of the State while giving ourselves to the instruction of youth'. We shall see later that the monks also were very anxious to prove their social utility, a characteristic of this period.[5] It is important to remember how much this criterion of usefulness

sixty-five years old, two nuns were ninety and eighty years old, nine between sixty and seventy years old, six between fifty and sixty years old, eleven between forty and fifty years old, two between thirty and forty years old, five between twenty and thirty years old.

[5] Archives dép. North, QH Cumulus 6602. In the same admonition it is said of the lay sisters: 'They will hardly venture to put themselves on the same level as the choir religious, who nevertheless treat them with kindness and charity, as they are religious of the same house, even if inferior in rank'.

influenced the lives of the monasteries of nuns in the eighteenth century.

THE BOARDERS

Almost all the monasteries took in boarders, both children to educate and elderly ladies with no family. The historian Bonnardot has given us some concrete details of these activities in his study of the abbey Sainte-Antoine-des-Champs-lès-Paris:

> The religious of the Abbey of Sainte-Antoine take in boarders. In 1760, the usual cost of boarding was 400 *livres*. Each boarder had to provide a bed, a trousseau and *une voie de bois*.[6] The heavy laundry was taken care of by the Abbey, and the lighter laundry by the parents. At this period they only had room for 21 boarders.[7]

In 1787 the cost of boarding was between four hundred and five hundred *livres*. The number of boarders was fixed at twenty-one, the same as in 1760. The Dauphin Almanac or the Royal Tablettes on the true worth of Artists adds, with regard to the convents for women and young ladies of which the abbey of Sainte-Antoine was one example: 'Private establishments where religious women devote themselves to the education of young girls who are entrusted to them by their parents: in these houses they learn reading, writing, embroidery, dancing, music, and all that is required for an elegant education'.[8] Of these lady boarders, Bonnardot adds: 'For those who wish to enter the abbey and live retired

[6] E. Littre, *Dictionnaire de langue française*: *Voie de bois*. *Une voie* is something that can be carried on one journey, or at one time, by carriage or other transport. In Paris the *voie de bois* was about two *stères* (1 *stère* 9 *dixièmes*). The *voie de bois* weighed roughly 754 kg' (Coulomb, Inst. Mem. SC, t.II, p. 389).

[7] H. Bonnardot, *L'Abbaye rouale de Saint-Antoine-des-Champs-lez-Paris*, p. 78.

[8] *Ibid.*, p. 79

from the world, the cost of boarding during this period was fixed at five hundred fifty *livres*'. To this the Almanac adds: 'These women enjoyed the freedom to go out whenever they pleased'.

RECEPTION INTO THE COMMUNITY

Some of the young boarders, after finishing their education, would ask to enter the community as religious. This was the case for Marie-Rosalie de Vergèses at Sainte-Antoine in 1784, when she was only fifteen years old. We will meet her again in this history under the name Sister Augustin de Vergèses de Chabannes. Bonnardot tells us that as a rule the postulancy lasted six months and the novitiate one year. 'With the reception of the habit this period cost eight-hundred *livres*. The dowry was fixed between four thousand and six thousand *livres* according to the means of those who wished to enter.' But Marie-Rosalie, on account of her youth made a three-year novitiate before pronouncing her vows at eighteen; this in spite of a civil law which since 1768 had forbidden the taking of vows before the twenty-first year. Another cistercian nun whom we will meet later in this book, is Sister Stanislaus Michel, who entered the abbey of Sainte-Catherine in Avignon 5 September 1774, at the age of twenty-two years. She made her profession the following year on 29 September.

So it seems that the rules on this question and others, like the dowry, were rather flexible and varied according to each monastery and the regions.

Community Life

This diversity was due also perhaps to the fact that each abbey of nuns was especially entrusted to an abbot of the Order who was called the 'Father Immediate'. As the abbots rarely assembled for a General Chapter to discuss procedures for the direction of their communities, different interpretations, especially when unforeseen situations occurred were bound to arise, such as attempts at new constitutions required by the Royal Commission of Regulars, a project that was never concluded.

In fact, for a long time royal power had interfered with the governance of the abbeys, just as it had with the Church following the Concordat of 1517. The majority of the monastic communities, especially the royal abbeys, had lost the right to elect their own abbess. Abbesses were appointed by 'Royal Warrant', without consulting the community; some of these selected abbesses were strangers to the community and even to the Order. Several abbesses of the Royal Abbey of Sainte-Antoine-des-Champs for example came from Benedictine abbeys or from Fontevrand, or even from a Dominican convent. The king's choice was frequently determined by the need to recompense a noble family or obtain a favor. The title of abbess designated not a service but an honor.

In this way the monasteries reflected their social surroundings, and a very clear hierarchy was established within the communities according to the social classes of the period. The abbess, as we have seen, usually came from the nobility. The choir nuns were nearly all of the nobility or bourgeoisie. Manual work and the upkeep of the house, the garden and the farmyard was assigned to the lay sisters, who were usually illiterate and lived separately from the choir nuns. All of this was taken for granted and does not seem to have caused any problems in the community.

During the eighteenth century this class distinction was even demonstrated in the frequency of reception of the sacraments. The abbot of Vaucelles, when making the Regular Visitation at the Abbey of La Brayelle in July 1765, left an admonition for the nuns which we today find quite astonishing. After having invited the choir nuns to 'frequent the sacraments, which are a channel of the graces and merits of our Redeemer', the Father Visitor specifies the manner and times when the choir religious and the lay sisters should participate at the Eucharist:

> The choir religious approach the Eucharist at least on Sundays and Feasts of Sermon, and the days when an indulgence is granted, and the other days fixed in the ritual . . . . These days of communion being for us days of conversation with our Saviour, and of confidence and love with our Spouse, we will abstain from all that could trouble or diminish the fruit and growth of our affection. On these happy days we will take care to enjoy His caresses and benefit from His graces. We will never be allowed to profane these days with useless amusements to the detriment of our progress. As for our dear lay sisters they will receive communion every two weeks according to the Usages of the Order . . . . They can, however, receive communion on days when a plenary indulgence is granted and when these days are Feasts of Sermon.[9]

Discrimination between choir nuns and lay sisters was practised, quite officially, even with regard to the sacraments. Perhaps we can see here a hint of Jansenism, which considered the material occupations of the lay sisters incompatible with the reverence which should surround the reception of the Eucharist and the spirit of thanksgiving which should follow it throughout the day. It was an aberration generated by the lack of esteem allotted to the work of the poor and a far cry from the worth of each person proclaimed by Saint Paul and insisted on so forcefully in the Rule of Saint Benedict.

We shall see a small change take place, however, in new foundations of nuns, those to be re-born from the ashes of the Revolution. All members were called Sister, and the distinctions between choir and lay sisters re-appeared only gradually when it became clear that some of the aspirants were quite incapable of reading Latin or standing for long periods in choir to sing the Office. Others had difficulty

[9] Document quoted, n. 5.

with the diet, which was more coarse than frugal. But social dinstinction seems no longer to have had any influence, and some discrimination had been eliminated by the hardships and privations shared together.

THE UNITY OF THE MONKS AND NUNS IN THE CISTERCIAN ORDER

Another aspect of life in communities of nuns in the eighteenth century, was the steadfast and persistent bonds established since the twelfth century between the monks and nuns of Cîteaux. The abbeys of nuns are an integral part of the Order, except for those who separated by choice to form independent Congregations of reformed Bernardines under the jurisdiction of the bishops. All legislation for the nuns of the Cistercian Order was established and modified by the General Chapter of the monks. The abbots, the Fathers Immediate[10] in charge of one or more of these communities, served as intermediaries between the nuns and the General Chapters, because the nuns were strictly enclosed, a *sine qua non* condition of their belonging to the Order. In addition, their chaplains always had to be Cistercian monks. All this was in general rendered more effective by the institution of the Regular Visitations which could, if necessary, correct any irregularities or conflicts and bring the case before the judgement of the General Chapter of abbots, the supreme authority in the Order.

The spiritual zeal which animated the community of the Father Abbot could have happy repercussions in the life of the nuns' community, as was also true of the reverse. It happened in the last decade of the seventeenth century,

[10] In the Cistercian Order, the abbot, as Father Immediate of the nuns, is in the same catergory as the ecclesiastical superior for non-clerical religious institutes. He has the duty of observing how the community keeps the Rule and the customs of the Order and, he is also ordinarily the counsellor of the abbess.

that a community of nuns wanting to reform asked Abbot de Rancé to become their Father Immediate.

The Visitor who conscientiously fulfilled his duties had to send a report to the abbot of Cîteaux with a view to the forthcoming General Chapter. For example, we have extant the report of the abbot of Vaucelles who made the Visitation of the abbey of Annay in 1768. Besides the exhortation we have already seen given at the abbey of Brayelle, there was a sort of official report giving information on the areas of the monastery visited and his impressions. The abbot of Vaucelles tells us that after having visited the cells of the sisters he found them 'clean, modest, practical, reflecting religious poverty and simplicity, according to our rules'. He also examined 'the accounts of expenses and receipts', and 'praised the good administration and economy of this house'. He ends by 'praising the Mother Abbess and the Mistress of the boarders for the zeal they show in instructing their pupils in piety, religion, and the sciences, as is fitting for these young people'.

From this overall picture we can conclude that this community of cistercian nuns was well managed and seriously lived the Rule that each had vowed on the day of her profession. Probably the great majority of nuns' monasteries throughout the country were similiarly well-managed.

In this atmosphere of peace and regularity did they have any presentiment of the menace hanging over them? Perhaps some, the superiors particularly, could sense more than others the rumors coming from outside the monastery; but in the spring of 1789, no one could really foresee the sufferings and troubles which would besiege the country in the following ten years. Successive blows which struck at the deepest aspirations of the monks and nuns developed in an unplanned manner. What began as a generous proposal for liberty and equality ended by becoming an ideology which repeatedly led to dictatorships which were ruthless and destructive of genuine liberty.

CHAPTER TWO

REVOLUTION

THE PERIOD OF POLITICAL and social fever which preceded the beginning of the Estates General began in a sort of unspoken collusion, a tacit agreement and even a quasi-harmony between the Church and the State. The most convinced 'patriots' felt the need to lean on the authority which the Church still held over the great majority of the French population. This was the case even when records of grievances of the Third Estate show a pronounced hostility against the privileges, tax exemptions, and tithes accorded to the clergy and nobility. André Latreille wrote that, 'With regard to the monks, hostility was more vague or at least less radical than the attacks of philosophers would lead us to believe. Rarely was it a question of their suppression, but innumerable claims for reform showed that public feeling was not happy with the decadence of the monasteries and could not accept the purely contemplative Orders without some directly useful social mission'.[1]

THE FIRST REVOLUTIONARY DEMONSTRATIONS

The Estates General opened at Versailles on May 1789. Representatives from each of the three Orders—clergy, nobility, ordinary folk—sat in separate rooms, and their first task was

[1] A. Latreille, *L'Eglise catholique et la Révolution française* (Paris, 1970) 1:82.

to verify the powers of the delegates present. But conflicting currents of opinions emerged within the assemblies. While the nobles swiftly united to preserve the *status quo*, notable divergences appeared between the high and low clergy and even within the two parts of the first Order. The Third Estate, impatient with these endless discussions, rallied a few dissidents from both chambers and on 17 June declared itself the National Assembly. On 20 May the National Assembly decided to meet in Versailles, at the usual place of assembly for the Third Estate, but the premises were closed. The representatives of the people went to the nearby hall of the Jeu de Paume, and there 'took a solemn oath never to separate and to reassemble anywhere when the circumstances required, until the Constitution of the kingdom was established'.

Two days later, taking refuge in the large nave of the Church of Saint Louis at Versailles, they gained one hundred fifty members from among the clergy. On 7 July, the rest of the other Orders joined them in spite of the contrary decision formulated by the king on 23 June. The National Assembly then established a 'Constitutional Committee'. From then on this body became the Constituent Assembly. It was prepared to share its powers with the king and to govern with the liberal aristocracy.

The king responded on 11 July by exiling Necker and dismissing the liberal ministers. In the eyes of the people of Paris, who had been in ferment for two weeks, this was the proof of an aristocratic plot which provoked the beginning of what was called the 'The Reign of Terror'. Insurrection flared and on the 14 July the Bastille was captured, with all the horrors that followed.

THE SUPPRESSION OF PRIVILEGES

Two days later, an uneasy Louis XVI recalled Necker and the dismissed Ministers, while the Reign of Terror ran like a brush fire throughout France. Next, the nobility began to emigrate, and in the economic crisis which followed, the peasants revolted and armed themselves with guns, scythes, and sticks. The Assembly faced a difficult choice. During the celebrated night of 4 August, they voted for the abolition of the last traces of the feudal system and of some of the privileges accorded to the nobility. Renunciation of these privileges was freely given by the nobility and clergy in a kind of general euphoria. During the next few days, however, they found themselves facing the reality of such a generous gesture and the difficulties of putting it into practice. Drawing up the Constitutions was therefore not without hardships, or without attempts to regress, but on 12 August the new legislation was ready.

The Assembly then prepared its great task, the definition of its general political plan. This was promulgated on 26 August under the name The Declaration of the Rights of Man and of the Citizen. It began with this specific statement: 'All men are born free and have equal rights', which are then enumerated: the right to property, to security, to freedom from oppression, and in consequence, civil and tax equality, individual freedom, and the right to all employments.

The Constituent Assembly, in the course of the same month of August 1789, set up an Ecclesiastical Committee composed of fifteen members, and presided over by a chairman, Jean-Baptiste Treilhard, a lawyer of integrity, a demon for work, and a free thinker, who henceforth put all his influence at the service of the civil Constitution on the clergy.

TRANSFERRING CHURCH PROPERTY TO THE NATION

Thirteen monks from the Cluniac Abbey of Saint-Martin-des-Champs in Paris, discontented with their lot, provided Treillard and his followers with an opportunity to interfere directly in monastic affairs. On 25 September, these monks wrote a letter to the Assembly, putting their monastery at the disposition of the nation in exchange for annual pensions and expressing their desire to enjoy the liberty offered to all French citizens.[2] The Assembly responded on 28 October with a decree releasing them from their religious vows.

This same week in October saw other serious problems: famine threatened and the government was in desperate straits. Talleyrand, the bishop of Autun, on 10 October had put forward a motion to transfer to the nation all ecclesiastical beneficies and foundations as a natural resource to annul the growing debts of the State. Some of the deputies of the Right Wing began to desert the Assembly during October. The proposition of Talleyrand was debated until 2 November. That day, by a vote of 568 against and 386 in favor, all ecclesiastical benefices were put at the disposition of the nation. The State would henceforth be responsible for all Church expenses, the support of its ministers and the care of the poor. A stroke of irony! It was within the very premises of the archbishop of Paris that the vote was taken on the law despoiling the Church of France.

THE ABOLITION OF MONASTIC VOWS

While the Assembly put up for sale the first allocation of four hundred millions in 'national goods', the Ecclesiastical Committee did not remain idle. Treilhard, on 17 December, presented a report on the reform of the Congregations, which he concluded by the following affirmation: 'The civil law no longer recognizes religious commitments and in consequence declares free all those who wish to leave their communities'.

The Ecclesiastical Committee was reshuffled in January 1790, and fifteen new members were admitted in order

[2] L. Lekai, *Cistercians, Ideals and Reality*, p. 166.

to provide a majority favorable to Treilhard's propositions. These were not debated by the Assembly until February, but on the 13th of that month a decree was passed forbidding the taking of all religious vows and requiring the dissolution of Orders with solemn vows not having any teaching or nursing activities. This was, in effect, the death blow for all contemplative monasteries. An inquiry was to be made into each of them and monks and nuns were to be given a choice, to stay or to leave. Those who left were to receive a personal pension; the others could live in common provided there were at least twenty in each house. Smaller communities were to be grouped together into one house.

Already these measures filled Catholics with anxiety. The bishop of Clermont, de Bonal, who had been the first president of the Ecclesiastical Committee, expressed his fear that civil authority had overstepped the limits of its jurisdiction, when he declared:

> What I do not consider lawful in the exercise of this authority is that they have broken down barriers which they did not put up. Without the agreement of the Church they have granted liberty to men who have freely promised under the seal of religion to live and die in the cloister and whom the Church has promised to maintain in all the terms of their commitment. That this civil authority has permitted them to break this commitment . . . and all that, before the only authority in the spiritual order which has the power to bind or loose on earth has been able to declare a decision.

André Latreille, who quotes this text, adds: 'This declaration touched the heart of the religious problems'.[3]

On the whole these procedures were implemented by the commissioners in a relatively kindly manner, at least in the beginning of the year 1790. The majority of the nuns refused the 'gift' of the Assembly, but defections were more

[3] Latreille, p. 93.

numerous among the monks. Even so, a good many monasteries continued to survive even after their possessions had passed into the hands of the civil administration. Certainly rumors were circulating in monastic communities about all these matters well before the actual promulgation of the law, especially in the Parisian abbeys. An indication of the anxiety level can be discerned in the petition that the abbess and nuns of Saint-Antoine in Paris sent to the Assembly at the beginning of February. There were still twenty-seven nuns in the abbey and they proposed that their house receive communities which were too few in numbers legally to continue. They also explained how beneficial they were to the poor in the neighborhood of Saint-Antoine whom they regularly assisted. Therefore may they be allowed to retain their monastery?[4] No trace of any reply to their petition has come down to us, but in the following chapter we will see what became of the abbey.

THE OATH AND THE CIVIL CONSTITUTION OF THE CLERGY

In the following months misgivings grew during the debates in the Assembly as it tried to work out a statute which would put the Church at the service of the new order of society about to be born. The old institutions had been swept away but had not yet been replaced by new ones. For two months the Assembly deliberated, while the population in different regions of France existed in a state of ferment. Pressure came from all sides. Moderate prelates tried to find means of conciliation, but mutual defiance grew between the Revolution and the Church. The projects of the Ecclesiatical Committee to integrate the Church into the State Constitution were discussed article by article and

[4] See the complete text of the petition at the end of this chapter, which is preserved in the National Archives: 'Comité ecclésiastique - E: XIX, n°237 - 2ePa. vingtièmme, reçu le 11 fevrier'.

the vote finally passed on 12 July 1790. The combined laws formed the Civil Constitution of the clergy. In itself this reform might have been accepted by the Roman Church, as the reforms of Joseph II of Austria had been. But for the Church there was one indispensable condition: this legislation could not be promulgated by one party alone. It must be ratified by pontifical authority, and without doubt it would be modified somewhat in talks with the French government. If a new distribution of the dioceses—eighty-five instead of one hundred thirty-five, which coincided with the new administrative division of the departments in France—was acceptable, the clause that all the citizens, even non-catholics or atheists, could elect bishops and pastors could raise a problem.

The reaction of Pius VI was to wait for eight months, eight long months during which the Assembly continued to promulgate one law after another in terms applicable to the Constitution. There were protestations from all the bishops except Talleyrand and de Gobel, the bishop of Lydda and the future constitutional bishop of Paris.

Then on 27 November, the decree was promulgated which was to split the Church in France and bring about schism. The members of the Assembly 'Call upon all the bishops, the former archbishops, the priests and other public civil servants, to swear an oath to be faithful to the Nation, the Law and the King, and to uphold with all their power the Constitution decreed by the Assembly and approved by the king'. Only seven bishops and about half of the priests took the oath. As early as the third of January, the clergy who had not taken the oath were relieved of their duties. Before the verdict of the Pope had arrived, the new Church was being organized, with its bishops and priests selected by the people. On 21 February 1791, Talleyrand who had just resigned as bishop of Autun, presided at the consecration of the first two constitutional bishops.

On 10 March, Pope Pius VI vehemently denounced not only the Civil Constitution of the clergy, but also the principles of the Revolution, by the Brief *Quod aliquantum*. In the light of the pope's condemnation, a trend towards retractation appeared among the clergy in the summer of 1791.

Another event both serious and political complicated the religious and political situation in France. On 20 June 1791, the king and the royal family fled towards the eastern frontier. Their carriage was stopped at Varennes and brought back to Paris under heavy escort. From then on, the king and royalty were considered enemies of the Revolution, like the Church which had refused the Civil Constitution of the clergy. In the minds of the people these events caused more confusion: religion and royalty were bound together in common opposition to the Constitution. For many of the simple folk, attacking or defending royalty was attacking or defending religion. The revolutionaries wanted royalty and religion exterminated. In the following year this became, in their eyes, an accomplished fact.

The Constitutional Assembly concluded its work. On 13 September 1791, the revised Constitution was sanctioned by the King, and on 30 September the Constituency gave place to the legislative Assembly, which took its seats on 1 October. On 29 November, it declared 'suspect' all clergy who had not taken the Oath, and on 27 May 1792, it passed a decree which expelled all refractors from France, by simple denunciation. On 27 July the Legislative Assembly confiscated all the goods of the emigrants. Riots broke out almost everywhere. On 10 August the 'Insurrectionary Commune' was set up, the Tuileries was invaded and royal power suspended. The Commune interned the king and his family in the Temple.

THE ABOLITION OF ALL RELIGIOUS ORDERS

On 18 August a new decree of the legislative Assembly was passed abolishing all religious Orders. Then teachers and hospitallers joined the monks in public reprobation. By October all the convents were to be cleared of their occupants. At the end of August, the threat from foreign armies became clear increasing the unrest among the people. On 26 August the Assembly decided to order the deportation or exile of all refractory persons.

There were then about two thousand six hundred prisoners in the nine prisons of Paris: non-juring priests, political suspects, and common law criminals. A transfer of prisoners from the Town Hall to the abbey prison on 2 September provoked a panic; a mob assembled and put the condemned to death, the crowd broke lose and massacred prisoners even in the jails; at the prison of the Carmelites, then at the abbey and at La Force. These riots lasted until 6 September. Murders of the same type occurred in the provinces.

Some refinements of cruelty were exhibited during these demonstrations, as was reported by Bonnardot in his history of the abbey of Saint-Antoine.

> The Princess de Lamballe, who in 1778, had stayed a year at the abbey after the death of her husband and fifteen months of marriage, was murdered in the prison of La Force on 5 September. About midday they decided to cut off her head and display it in the streets of Paris. Her other limbs were distributed to a troup of cannibals who also dragged them about the streets. Her head was first of all brought to the Abbey of Saint-Antoine . . . and presented to Madame de Beauvau, the former abbess of this Abbey and close friend of Madame de Lamballe.[5]

THE OATH OF LIBERTY AND EQUALITY

On 3 September the Assembly decided to impose on all the citizens an oath, formulated as follows:

[5] Bonnardot, p. 81, which gives as reference J. Peltier, *Dernier tableau de Paris* . . . (London, 1794).

> I swear to be faithful to the nation, to maintain with all my power the liberty, equality, and the safe-keeping of persons and properties, and to die if necesary for the enforcement of the law.

This oath of so-called 'liberty and equality' was to replace all previous oaths. In particular, it would enable the Revolutionaries to reach all those priests who thought they could escape deportation because they had no parishes or public function,and therefore had not been obliged to take the oath of 1790.[6] This new oath, while it appeared neutral, must again have aroused many problems of conscience to more than one Christian who questioned the act.

On 20 September, the final act of the Legislative Assembly before dispersing was to establish civil Registers to replace the ecclesiastical Registers kept by the parish priests. These proceedings were to solve a practical problem, because many Christians refused to register for the principal events in their lives—baptism, marriage and burial with a constitutional priest—the municipalities waited! This law would end the confusion between the temporal and spiritual which had existed since the Middle Ages, and pave the way for the separation of Church and State.

On 21 September the Convention assembled and in their first act the same day abolished the monarchy. The next day, 22 September 1792, the New Era was inaugurated with the Republican calendar. This calendar was designed to eradicate all traces of Christianity in the sequence of days, months, and years.

We can stop here. This rapid outline of the main events of the French Revolution is indispensable to an understanding of the monastic history which follows. After the law of 18 August 1792, monks and nuns were no longer legal in France. Six weeks later, all convents were cleared of

[6] Cf. A. Latreille, 1:133. See also the works of B. Plongeron quoted above, Introduction, no. 2.

their inhabitants or should have been. The buildings and properties were entirely at the disposition of the nation.

In the following chapter we will study briefly some of the consequences of laws, and especially look at how the nuns reacted to the legal dispositions which concerned them. Some will speak for themselves and give a general idea of the way these events marked in a particularly perceptible manner the Order of Cîteaux in France.

Comité Ecclesiastique F. XIX. N° 237 - 2e D. Vingt quieme

Reçu 11 fevrier N° 843.

N° 110

A Nos Seigneurs de L'assemblée nationale

600
1000

Nos Seigneurs

Puisque le bonheur général et individuel est le but de vos glorieux travaux, souffrés que Les abbesse, Prieure et Religieuses de St. Antoine des champs lés Paris, réclament aujourd'huy l'unique moyen qu'elles ont pour y participer.

Pénétrées de la Sagesse de vos décrets, elles sacrifient sans peine, leurs interets personnels au bien public; mais le seul objet qui les interesse réellement a coeur, c'est celuy d'être conservées dans la demeure qu'elles occupent, qu'elles ont choisi et qui leur est chere a tant de titres.

Une Maison de chaque ordre doit etre exceptée de La Suppression que vous avés prononcée, elles demandent cette exception en leur faveur, elles l'attendent de votre Justice, et voici les moyens sur lesquels elles se fondent.

Leur local suffit pour la réunion des autres maisons a la leur et ce local est aëré, salubre, absolument hors du tumulte et tel qu'il convient a des religieuses; Mais, par cela même, par son

26

Plates 46, 47, 48

Decree of the Ecclesiastical Committee dissolving religious orders.

eloignement de la ville, par la stérilité de son sol, il est d'une valeur très modique et bien au dessous de celle des autres maisons religieuses de la capitale; il est, d'ailleurs, d'une vente si difficile qu'il n'offre aucune spéculation avantageuse pour les besoins actuels de l'état: un fait suffit pour prouver cette assertion.

Le Marché St Antoine est situé au centre du faubourg, bien plus avantageusement placé que l'abbaye, ouvert de tous côtés par des rües que l'on a percées à grands frais, et malgré toutes ces prérogatives, les adjudicataires qui, depuis 14 ans l'ont mis en vente n'ont pû se procurer des acquereurs pour la troisième partie du terrein qui le compose, le reste leur demeure en pure perte.

Aucune autre maison ne présentera, sans doute des motifs aussi déterminans, et si quelqu'une pouvoit entrer en concurrence avec l'abbaye pour la solidité des raisons; toutes choses egales; l'abbaye employeroit, alors, des moyens de considération qui luy sont particuliers.

Elle vous diroit, Messieurs, que c'est à elle à qui le faubourg St Antoine doit son existence, que c'est sur ses terres qu'il s'est édiffié, que c'est sous sa sauvegarde qu'il s'est si prodigieusement peuplé d'artistes en tous genres, à la faveur d'une franchise dont elle avoit la propriété, et dont elle leur a laissé très gratuitement l'exercice; franchise que l'abbaye a deffendue tant de fois, à ses frais contre les attaques multipliées des Communautés et maitrises de Paris; elle vous diroit enfin que, par ce moyen et par des aumônes journalières elle est parvenue à soutenir un nombre infini de familles et à les sauver des horreurs de l'indigence.

elle ne vous dissimuleroit pas non plus l'attachement extrême qu'elle a pour ces pauvres habitans et qui est tel que, quelque puisse etre leur existence future, si les Religieuses restent parmi ces infortunés, elles sauront encor leur tendre une main secourable. Ces Considérations leur mériteroient, sans doute, la préference et leur conservation; c'est le seul bien, le seul avantage auxquels elles puissent etre sensibles; fixées par la vocation la plus décidée, même par goût, à leur profession, à leurs devoirs, à leur demeure, elles attendent de votre equité, de votre humanité une décision favorable et votre sagesse leur est un sûr garant qu'elles ne seront point trompées dans leur attente.

Sr G. Ch. de Beauvau Abbesse

Sr Catherine Robines Prieure,

Sr Louise D'Elbrémons Sr Elizabeth Lecoq,

Sr J Catherine Soullanger Sr Marguerite Ruion

Sr Benoite Nouvaux Desfinces

Sr Louise de St Varand Sr Marie gagneraux

Sr Louise Beauquet de Monville Sr Olympe Charlotte Baltazard Sr Marie de vergasso. Sr G. Demilly

Sr C. J. des Verges. Sr B. Ch. Estard Sr H. E. Verges.

L Boulanger pensioner age de 80 ans agrege

Sr J. S. G. Villot Dépositaire

CHAPTER THREE

THE FATE OF CISTERCIAN ABBEYS AND THEIR MEMBERS

INVENTORIES AND RECORDS OF THE COMMUNITIES

THE FIRST PHASE of the enforcement of the laws of 1789 and 1790 for nuns was rapidly put into practice. A decree of 13 November 1789 ordered that:

> All the holders of benefices, of whatsoever nature they be, and all the Superiors of ecclestiastical Houses and Establishments without any exception, will be bound to draw up on unstamped paper, free of charge, within two months of the publication of this decree before royal judges or municipal officers of the place, a detailed declaration of all personal estate and real estate dependent on the said benefices, houses and establishments, also that of their revenues, and to produce within the same allotted time a detailed account of the taxes to which these goods could be subject .[1]

We have some inventories more or less complete, from various cistercian monasteries, situated in various places around the country. These give us an overall view of the material situation, also varied, of some hundred abbeys of nuns that existed in France at the end of the eighteenth century.

[1] Bonnardot, p. 80.

THE ABBEY OF SAINT-ANTOINE

One of the most important abbeys in Paris was the Royal Abbey of Saint-Antoine-des-Champs-lès-Paris, from which was to come a pioneer of the restoration: the young nun, Marie-Vergèses du Mazel, later known as Mother Augustin de Chabannes.

In 1789, the abbey of Saint-Antoine was governed by Madame Gabrielle Charlotte de Beauvau-Craon, forty-second and last abbess of this renowned abbey. In a study made of her in the nineteenth century, Hippolyte Bonnardot wrote:

> The Abbess of Saint-Antoine in Paris conferred on André Guibout, a dealer, particular and special powers of attorney, to declare on 28 February 1790, before Barthélémi Jean Louis Le Couteulx de la Moraye, Lieutenant Mayor of the City of Paris, in execution of the aforementioned decree that the revenues of the abbey were shown to be 75,285 *livres*, fifteen *sols*, and two *deniers*: deriving from the rents of houses in Paris, meat sales, dues on grains, taxes and sales in Paris and at Montreuil, and life annuities, and that the expenses of the abbey amounted to 32,119 *livres*, twelve *sols*, and ten *deniers*. But the total debt is 78,195 *livres*, ten *sols*.[2]

A second process soon followed in consequence of the law of 13 February 1790 which suppressed all monastic vows. The new plan was to take a census of all persons in religious communities and to examine their intentions regarding the freedom offered them by the National Assembly. A document conserved in the National Archives, very carefully recorded, has preserved for us the census made at Saint-Antoine on 25 March 1790. It was confirmed and signed by the abbess.[3] The community numbered twenty-

[2] *Ibid.*

[3] Archives Nationales section légale du Royaume, leg. n°102.

five choir nuns, of whom five were absent: one with her family, two in the suburb of Saint-Denis n°77, another at the abbey of Andrecy-en-Brie, the fifth with the community of Grand-Charonne. There were twelve lay sisters, including an eighty-eight and a half year old 'family sister'. Three of the lay sisters were with their families.

The abbess was sixty-six. The oldest of the choir nuns eighty-two and a half, the youngest, Sister Augustin de Vergèses, was twenty-one. Two of her blood sisters were also on the list, Marie-Marguerite de Vergèses, twenty-eight, and Catherine Justine, twenty-five. The ages of the community are distributed as: six sisters between twenty and thirty, five between forty and fifty, three between sixty and seventy years. Those absent were between forty six and sixty-five years. The lay sisters on the whole were older; the youngest was thirty-nine and the eldest sixty-five.

Two other censuses were made two years later:on 1 May and on 11 July 1792. The 'familiar' had died in June of that year, over ninety. One choir nun had left 10 March 1792. All the others had signed, but it was noted that the lay sisters 'for the most part' could not write.

Obviously these lists tell us nothing directly of the nuns' intentions regarding the freedom offered them, but we can believe that they wished to continue their common life, since all, except one sister of seventy-one, stayed together during these years of uncertitude.

THE ABBEY OF MERCOIRE

Documents on the Royal Abbey of Gévaudan, in the diocese of Mende, allow us to glimpse some brief periods of history six centuries old. The abbey of Mercoire was founded in 1207 in the heart of the Cévennes, in a context altogether different from that of Saint-Antoine. It had very prosperous beginnings, and numbered up to fifty nuns in the thirteenth century. At the end of the fifteenth century, however, wars, burning and looting, and also the harshness of the area, reduced the community to about fifteen. There were periods of discouragement, then recoveries, but by the beginning of the Revolution there were only seven nuns in the abbey and two of them were absent.

On 11 August 1790, the commissioners of the district of Langogne arrived to make an inventory of the personal effects and securities of the community. The different sources of revenue amounted to 9,781 *livres* four *sols*. There was no mention of expenses. Once the inventory had been concluded, the nuns were questioned and required to declare 'if they have the intention to live in their house with the vows they promised or if they wish to take advantage of the liberty the law offered them'. The responses recorded are unanimous. Madame de Treilles, the abbess, and the four other sisters present declared that we 'wish to live and to die in the community if it can continue under the vows that they have contracted'. Two sisters, Françoise and Rosalie du Fayet de Chabannes, were among those present. On 11 November 1790, one of the absent nuns, Marie-Anne de Vergèses du Mazel,[4] thirty years old, wrote to the district of Langogne and declared that she wished to live and die in

[4] Among their twelve children, the family of Antoine Vergèses du Mazel and of Marianne Clavel counted five Cistercians: Marie, the eldest, born in 1751, entered Saint-Antoine in Paris; (there as Mistress of the boarders, her youngest sister, aged 5, Marie-Rosalie in 1744 (See *La Trappe in England,* p. 72); three others were also nuns at Saint-Antoine in 1790: Marguerite, born in 1763, Catherine-Justine, born in 1764, and Marie-Rosalie, born in 1769. Another daughter, Marie-Anne, born in 1761, was a Cistercian at Mercoire. Another, Adélaïde, born in 1762, was a Benedictine at the abbey of Yerres, where she made her profession. Later she found refuge in the cistercian abbey of Bellecombe in Haute-Loire, where her sister Marie-Anne had also gone at the end of 1789. One of their brothers, Charles, born in 1755, was the parish priest at Blavignac (Lozère); he died in 1828. Another brother, Michel, married a grand-daughter of Magdeleine de Fayet de Chabannes. This information has been supplied by Monsieur Bernard Grenié, a descendant of the family of Vergèses du Mazel, who has also done research for me in the National Archives on the abbey of Saint-Antoine in Paris.

the state she had embraced. 'I remain always', she said, 'as a member of the Abbey of Mercoire. I left the Abbey the 19 November 1789, with the full permission of my Superiors.' The other sister absent, Anne de la Tour de Clamouse, declared that she left Mercoire 'with the permission of her Superiors and by express order of the doctor . . . to have the necessary remedies for her health' (25 January 1791).[5]

The *Directoire* of the district of Langogne was in no hurry to supply the pension promised to the nuns of Mercoire. No longer able to use their revenues, the sisters lived in extreme poverty without complaining, but some common reports notified the administration department of their distress. On 14 July 1791, the magistrates deliberated together and granted them a provision of eighteen hundred *livres*, and on 6 August they fixed the pension of the abbess at fifteen hundred *livres* with seven hundred *livres* for the other nuns, a pension payable every three months by the district commissioner.

The nuns were still at Mercoire on 15 July 1792. On that date there was a thorough search of the premises, owing to an informer, a 'patriot' of Langogne, who had described the place as a hideout of dangerous suspects. But the investigators found only 'the ladies and domestics' and no weapons, so the nuns were left alone to manage their house. But not for long, for on 29 December the same year 1792, the nuns were no longer there, because of the law passed on 18 August.[6]

The Abbey of Saint Catherine at Avignon

The archives in Avignon have not preserved any detailed accounts of the dispersion of the religious. On 1 September 1792, it was again the abbess who received the municipal

[5] F. André, *L'Abbaye de Mercoire* (Mende, 1868) p. 49.
[6] *Ibid*., pp. 52–53.

commissioners who had come to draw up an inventory. The community was composed of twenty-two choir nuns, five lay sisters and two *tourières*. Apparently four of the nuns had blood sisters in the same community. An annual payment was proposed to any sisters who would agree to take the Oath. This varied from five hundred to seven hundred *livres* according to age. The oldest was then eighty-seven and the youngest nineteen. A list of those eligible to receive this ecclesiastical pension between 14 and 29 September contains no name of any nun of Saint-Catherine.[7] Therefore none of the sisters took the Oath. Later we will see that two of the sisters from Saint-Catherine, blood sisters, Marguerite-Eléonore and Madeleine-Françoise de Justamond, were guillotined at Orange in July 1794.

The Abbey of Koenigsbruck (Alsace)

We know very little about this abbey not far from Haguenau, northeast of Strasbourg; the ruins have completely disappeared. A brick inscribed with the name of the monastery was found at the depth of one metre by some hard-working amateur archeologists. In 1792 it was ransacked by peasants and the abbey real estate was sold as national property.[8] We know even less about the nuns who lived at Koenigsbruck, except that in 1791 there were thirty-one nuns with an average age above middle age.[9] One nun has escaped total oblivion, the last professed, Sister Edmond-Paul de Barth, who later entered the refuge monastery in Switzerland in 1797, and revived the cistercian life in Westphalia.

[7] Information kindly supplied by M. Hayez (Archives départementale of Avignon).

[8] According to an article which appeared in *L'Alsace*, a daily paper printed in Mulhouse, 3 December 1968.

[9] See Claude Muller, '*Les Cisterciennes de Koenigsbruck* en 1791', *Outre-Forêt* (n° 51, 1985) 44–47.

The Abbey of La Brayelle at Annay

Towards the northwest of France we find the abbey of La Brayelle at Annay in the diocese of Arras, already mentioned in the preceding chapter. Some interesting documents on it have been collected and published, particularly those dealing with the period of the French Revolution.[10] All that remains today is an inventory enumerating the possessions of the abbey, and another rather curious document confiding to the care of the abbess and of the trustee, the titles and papers concerning the goods of the abbey.[11]

On 8 December 1790, a list of the personnel of the monastery was drawn up, with the declaration of each nun on her future intentions. The abbess, Dame Eléonore Hennecart de Briffoeil, was sixty-two years old, the prioress seventy, the sub-prioress fifty-eight. The community counted twenty-six choir nuns and seventeen lay sisters. All decided (with some subtle differences) to stay in their monastery. A chart dated 1 January 1791, shows the pension allotted to each religious. Two thousand *livres* annually for the Abbess, seven hundred *livres* for each choir nun whatever her age (the oldest was seventy-eight and the youngest twenty-two) and three hundred *livres* for the lay sisters, (the oldest of whom was seventy-four and the youngest twenty-eight). The

[10] Numerous documents on the history of this abbey have been put together by Father Buquet (a typed volume, Arras 1982.) I owe this information to the kindness of the Bernadine-Cistercians of Esquermes who originally came from this abbey.

[11] Here is the text. The statements of the commissioners and of the two nuns who signed it, are mingled: 'All the titles and papers of the above inventory, remain in their place, locked in our cupboards in the archives, in which place we have found a table and two chairs, the which titles have been represented by the said Dames, the which have declared to us that they have not altered directly or indirectly, and the which titles and papers have been left in the keeping and possession of the said Dames who have willingly taken responsibility being Madame the Abbess de Briffoeil and Dame Flavie Cavalier, trustee.' Signed E. Hennecart de Briffoeil and Flavie Cavalier (Arch. dép. du P.-de-C., 1790, 8 November).

chaplain, a monk of Vaucelles, received one thousand *livres* on 3 August 1791, in payment of his salary of that year.[12] On 12 September 1792, the nuns settled their accounts. Since Martinmas (11 November) 1789, they had received in income 29,150 *livres*, eighteen *sols*, two *deniers*. In expenses 32,435 *livres*, eighteen *sols*, ten *deniers*. The Public Treasury was to pay the difference since the monastery was now their property.

On 15 September a certain Rohart was appointed administrator of the house of these *ci-devant Dames d'Annay* [*ci-devant Dames* denotes that before the Revolution they came from the nobility, now no longer recognized —trans. note]. The nuns do not seem to have left the house until the end of September, the time limit set by the law.

On 26 September, the administrators of the district were instructed to move all the monastery furnishings. The sale was fixed for 10 October, but immediately an organized looting took place; windows, doors, and floor boards were removed as were the mantlepieces from fire places and tiled flooring. The looters took lead and iron, and much more. The Justice of the Peace of the canton said that sixty carriages were loaded with stolen furniture and woodwork, three or four of iron, two of lead. He added that there still remained a fine grille of iron which adorned the nuns' choir [the *ms* reads *coeur*: adorned the *heart* of the nuns! — trans.] and also a set of organ stops, all broken, which were not sold.

They sent fifty men to stand guard over what remained. About twenty of the culprits were arrested, including the Justice of the Peace, but no case was made against them. During the following months, the sale of the land and property went ahead.[13]

[12] Extract from the Register of the deliberations of the Directoire of the district of Béthune (12 March 1791 to 22 February 1793).

[13] See the documents collected by Father Buquet (above n. 10).

THE FATE OF THE EXILED NUNS

In general we have very little information of what befell the nuns who were expelled from their monasteries, but some details gleaned here and there can give us a glimpse of what happened.

Returning to Their Families

At first, those who still had a family home found shelter there. This was the case of the abbess of Saint-Antoine, Madame de Beauvau, who retired to the home of her brother, the Marshal de Beauvau. Other nuns assembled in a private house, wishing to live the common life together. Madame de Treilles, the abbess of Mercoire and her nuns went to their relations, one to Mende, another to Langogne and other places. They corresponded with each other until the day they were imprisoned. A decree of the General Committee of Police on 24*frimaire*, year II (14 December 1794) granted them their liberty. Madame de Treilles died at Mende on 22 February 1810.[14]

Re-Assembling in Secret

The superior of the Ursulines of Bollène, having rented several houses in the small town, welcomed nuns from anywhere to join them. Among these were two Carmelites from Sainte-Catherine in Avignon, the sisters de Justamond, who had an aunt and another sister in the Ursulines of Bollène. From the community of Koenigsbruck, we only know of one sister who escaped and made her way to Switzerland to find the monastic life there.

[14] André, p. 54.

The abbess of La Brayelle at Annay, Madame Hennecart de Briffoeil,retired to Arras, while the abbess of Notre-Dame-des-Prés, daughter house of La Brayelle, Madame Henriette de Maes, went into exile in England with most of her community.

Dame Hombeline Le Couvreur, a nun of Annay, went to Belgium with Marie-Ghislaine Defontaine, the prioress, aged seventy-two. Welcomed at first at Audenarde among the Cistercians, they had to flee again before the revolutionary armies. They reached another cistercian monastery at Himmel-Pforten in Westphalia, where they stayed until 1796. They were joined by Dame Hyacinthe Devisme from the abbey of Woestine, another daughter house of La Brayelle.

Imprisonment

Meanwhile the nuns of Saint-Antoine of Paris, who had reassembled in Paris itself, were arrested and put in one of the prisons of the capital. There they awaited sentence before the revolutionary tribunal. During the month of July 1794, these Cistercians, like the Carmelites of Compèigne, the nuns of Orange, and many others in various places, were preparing themselves to be called at any moment to the guillotine, the usual result of a judgement of the tribunal. They encouraged each other to die valiantly. The 27th of that month, (the 9 *thermidor*), all the prisoners in the gaols in Paris thought they would be massacred, as they could hear cannons and rioting during the night. But on the morning of 28 July, the prisons were opened and they found themselves free.

At Bollène, however, it was not the same. There the two Cistercians had found a refuge in the private houses rented by the Ursulines. They were arrested along with sixteen Ursulines, thirteen Sacramentines, one Benedictine and some others. The order for their arrest had come from Paris in

April. All the sisters were invited to take the oath of liberty and equality; when they refused they were transported on 2 May to Orange in five carts and interned in the *prison de la Cure*. From the first day of their detention, these religious, who numbered more than forty, organized their common life in prison as if they were living in their convents. Each one gave for the common use all that she had brought with her. A life of great charity united them all. For three weeks from the 6th to the 26th of July, interrogations, summary judgements and executions followed in rapid succession. On the 12th Sister Marguerite de Justamond and on the 16th her sister Madeleine and three Ursulines were judged and guillotined. The last executions took place on the 26th of July. About ten sisters, among them four who had already been judged and condemned, escaped the massacre, while thirty-two of their companions had already won the palm of martydom. These last were beatified in 1925.

Those who escaped brought back memories of those three months of common life in the prison of Orange. Among the flashes of humor which sprinkle the recital was this short dialogue at the foot of the scaffold. A young lay sister, a Sacramentine known as Soeur du Bon Ange (Sister Good Angel), Marie Cluse, twenty-two years old, was so beautiful that the executioner, struck by her beauty, offered to save her if she would marry him. Marie Cluse, indignant, alluding to her name in religion, replied: 'Executioner, get on with your job, I want to go this evening and dine with the angels'.[15]

The abbess of La Brayelle at Annay, living in refuge at Annay, signed the oath of liberty and equality, but a short time later was denounced as an aristocrat and accused of fanaticism. Found guilty by the jury of having removed from the abbey furnishings and other objects (among which 'happily removed', was the body of Saint Juste, martyr,

[15] See C. Arnemann, *Les bienheureuses Soeurs de Bollène martyrisées à Orange* (Fribourg, 1965).

venerated in the abbey since 1680), she declared that she would not leave a single nail to the nation. This occurred on the 7 *messidor* year II, 25 June 1794.[16]

Emigration

What happened to the nuns who escaped the guillotine? We would like to know much more about their lives between 1794 and 1796. What happened to Sister Augustin de Vergèses and her companions of Saint-Antoine after their liberation? On this point our research and enquiries have yielded only one little piece of information. To avoid another imprisonment under the double defamatory accusation of being of noble birth and a religious, they found it more prudent to go about in disguise, to pass as unnoticed as possible, and to elude being denounced as a suspect and fanatic. It seems that this is the solution Sister Augustin adopted. A little notebook belonging to her has been preserved in the Stapehill archives. It is headed 'Account of Small Expenses'. Begun in October 1796, it ended in June 1797, when the owner entered the monastery of La Sainte-Volonté-de-Dieu in Switzerland. Was this how long it took her to travel to this haven of peace? Each month she noted the price of the laundry for the preceding month, the ironing of bonnets, shawls, small haberdashery needs, braid for a dress, black thread and so on, so it seems obvious that during this period she dressed as a peasant.

Why was it that she made her way to Switzerland? A scrap of a letter written in the hand of Dom Augustin de Lestrange almost thirty years later tells us that he had had some brochures printed in Paris.[17] Actually, the former

[16] See documents collected by Father Buquet (Above n°10).

[17] Arch. SH, catalogue, p.2, n°1. *Memorandum by Madame de Chabannes on the establishment of the Monastery of La Sainte-Volonté-de-Dieu.*

novice master of La Trappe in Normandy had been entreated by some nuns to help them live together not far from his refuge monastery of La Valsainte, in the canton of Fribourg.

To one of his friends, a Sulpician living in Paris, the abbot of La Valsainte had suggested this publication, which provided a glimmer of hope for these nuns whose hearts remained so attached to their *saint état*. Thus it came about, thanks to this printed leaflet, that many were able to find their way to Switzerland.

Among these nuns were a Sister Sainte-Marie Bigaux from Dreux and a Benedictine of the Blessed Sacrament from the same place who wrote to Father Jean-Baptiste La Sausse, a Sulpician, who had directed her towards Switzerland. She gave him an account of her journey, written 21 September 1796:

> Sir,
> For two days I walked along the edge of Lake Geneva . . . From Saint-Maurice to La Sainte-Volonté-de-Dieu it is about six leagues which I did on foot. Before this I would not have believed I could walk one league, so it is true that you can do much more than you would have thought possible. You in France cannot imagine the great charity they have here for the french nuns, and there are so many of us in our holy house. Two of them have come from France on foot (the two sisters of Dom Augustin) with their belongings on their back. More courageous than myself, because I made the journey easily enough.[18]

Another travel account, written in 1798, at the time of the Directoire Wars, when Germany and Switzerland had already been, or were about to be invaded, was kept by Sister Saint-Maur Miel, a Benedictine of the Petit-Calvaire

[18] Sister Sainte-Marie Bigaux, Benedictine of Perpetual Adoration of the Blessed Sacrament at Dreux, in *Les Nouveaux Trapistes* [sic] *ou Recueil de pièces* (Paris, 1797), a copy preserved in the Arch. SH. J.-B. La Sausse (1740–1826) was the Parisian correspondent of Dom Augustin and author of *Nouveaux Trapistes*.

in Paris. We will meet her again further on. She found a companion, another Benedictine of the Blessed Sacrament at Arcies, in the diocese of Chartres, where Sister Saint-Maur herself had been born. Armed with the authorization of the Vicar General of Chartres, a Father Osier, they both set out for La Trappe in Switzerland at the beginning of Lent 1798. But let us allow her to give her own account.

> Provided with passports to go only as far as Strasbourg, we arrived in Paris and made our way to a chemist whose address we had been given, and who had helped several priests to pass into Germany. Supplied with a letter from our chemist we left Paris during Lent in the year 1798 and took a coach for Strasbourg. I was then twenty-eight years old. We arrived at Strasbourg in the evening, and asked the innkeeper for one room, a bed, and supper, as we had only had light snacks on the journey. During the meal, the others who had travelled with us spoke to the innkeeper about us; although a protestant, he was very touched by our misfortunes and the next day, when we wanted to pay him, he made signs we could not understand, because he did not speak French. We left our luggage there and took our letter from the chemist to the person who would allow us to pass into Germany. We asked him to speak to the innkeeper so we could pay him, but the innkeeper replied that he would not take anything, we had enough troubles and he was only too happy to help us. The carriage driver in collaboration with the protestant chemist who had already helped so many priests over the border had already gone, so we were obliged to wait four or five days. Then this gentleman, knowing that we knew nobody in the town, offered us lodgings with two ladies of our religion, if we could just pay for our food, because they were not at all wealthy. We accepted this gracious offer and we were made most welcome. We also found in addition all the consolations of our religion, because these two ladies knew of some nuns who had hidden a priest in their house, so they were able to have a Mass every day, which we had the joy of attending. The day

of our departure arrived, and the gentleman who was helping us spoke to the carriage driver, because he had not been able to renew our passports; he said that we would just have to take our chances, seeing that we had no alternative. The best thing to do was to seal our luggage, then it would not be searched going across the Rhine. To go through the town to the first custom office was a good league, then two or three more before crossing the bridge, but the first was the decisive one. The good gentleman again had the kindness to see that we were accompanied by a trustworthy person, who would bring us back if we did not succeed in crossing. Arriving at the first post, we were asked for our passports, and, as soon as they were checked, immediately we were told; 'Ladies you cannot pass, you need other passports'. As we expected this, we were not surprised, but as the man seemed to be an honest sort, we had recourse to prayer, without, however, gaining anything for two or three hours. It was not that he was unmoved by our sad situation, but he said; 'My head is at stake, I am the father of a family and must think of them; anyway if I let you pass you will certainly be arrested at the other posts'. Finally, he thought of a solution: we could pass as soldier's wives. He knew a colonel who would not make any difficulties, so he wrote and asked him to send us new passports to enable us to join our husbands. Like this we were able to pass without any trouble; and our driver having told us that we had nothing else to fear, we were able to say the *Te Deum* with all our heart in thanksgiving for our deliverance'.[19]

All did not end there, however. They had to get to Augsburg in Bavaria. From stage to stage, recommendation to recommendation, refuge to refuge, the two nuns finally arrived in Augsburg soon after Palm Sunday. The following

[19] *Relation des voyages de la vénérable Mère Saint- Maur, religieuse du Calvaire de Paris pendant son émigration*, MS (Paris, 1829) copy preserved in the archives of the Benedictines of Calvaire, Angers, pp. 1, 2, 3, 4.

Wednesday they met Abbot de Lestrange. We will meet them again in the following chapters.

Already we can see the same ideals converging among these nuns: to preserve at all costs for themselves and for the Church the form of religious life which had attracted them in their youth and which they desired to live in spite of thousands of obstacles.

This does not mean to say that they all found in the new La Trappe the means of realizing their aspirations, but they did make an effort, and God sometimes led them along other paths. One among them was able to recover her first vocation and her Petit-Calvaire in Paris, while another was to be the foundress of a new benedictine monastery, also in Paris, after the Restoration. A third, who entered later, and on the advice of the abbot himself, would become the foundress of a remarkable missionary Institute which still keeps the motto *La Sainte-Volonté-de-Dieu* (God's Holy Will). Thus God works out his plans in the midst of apparant failure using the deepest aspirations of these women of character.

PART TWO

New Seeds

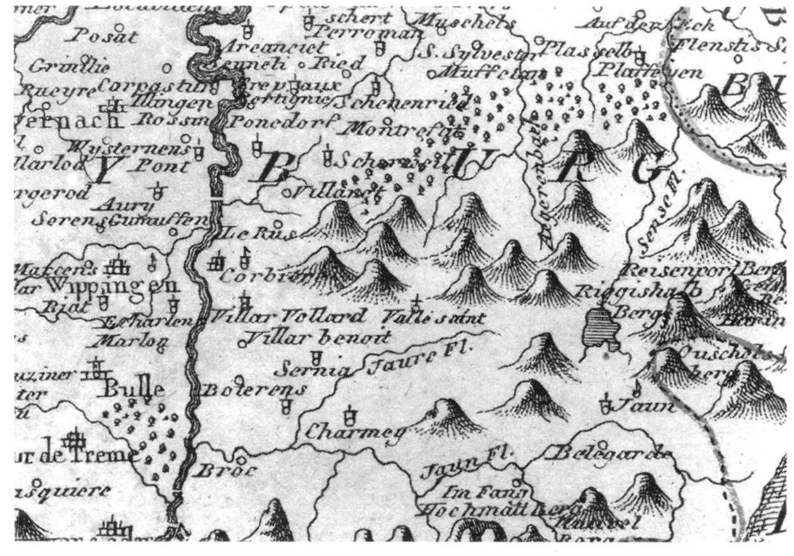

Figure 2

Switzerland in 1791. Center: La Val-Saint. Left: Villar Vollard. Right: Ried (= La Riedera). After Franz J.J. von Reilly, *Universal-Atlas*, Theil 2, Band 2 (Vienna, 1791).

'GOD HAS STRANGE WAYS of sweeping his threshing floor', was how the Curé of Ars, Saint John Vianney, once summed up the French Revolution. This thought has haunted all my readings about the Revolutionary period, and I have come to realize just how profound is the truth of this saying. The threshing floor of the Lord, the whole of Christendom, needed this long ordeal to be purified of the accumulated dross of centuries of routine, struggles for influence, battles of ideas, compromises with civil authorities, unbridled luxury of the wealthy, exploitation of the poor, and—long-endured blatant social inequalities, in a word, the general neglect of the demands of the Gospel.

The monastic threshing floor, as we have seen, had not escaped this decline. The time had come for it to be cleansed radically. It was easy to believe that monasticism no longer had any useful purpose and would be wiped off the map forever. In its place would be built a free and just society which the architects were already planning in this Age of Enlightenment. The Ideal or Utopia always has its prophets and apostles. They forget that human beings are not born upright by nature, and that it is not easy for them to refrain from pleasures and the money that procures them. People forget that they are possessed by a *spiritual* hunger: 'Man does not live by bread alone'. He yearns to give meaning to his life.

Yet on this devasted threshing floor a few grains were preserved. A few seeds, as if kept for a new harvest, escaped destruction. It is the survival of these seeds which we are going to follow in the next chapters. After being thrown on ground broken by trials, they looked as if they would die. 'Unless the grain of wheat falls into the ground and dies . . .' But these scattered grains had living germs within them, and these were to produce the harvest. The floor on which they were to be threshed would find itself beaten hard by the constancy and fidelity of these women, whose love carried them far beyond the capacities of their physical strength. They held on, they drew others, they died, and they were renewed. In them life conquered death. In the centuries which followed, many new barns were to be built to house the abundant harvest.

CHAPTER ONE

THE FOUNDATION OF TRAPPISTS AT LA VALSAINTE

A FEW GRAINS WERE STILL preserved in most of the abbeys. Even Voltaire admitted that, 'There is hardly any monastery which does not still harbor admirable souls who do honor to human nature'.[1] Certainly there were some in the abbey of La Trappe, reformed by the abbé de Rancé in the last thirty years of the seventeenth century. In 1790, as we have seen, there were ninety-one monks, fifty-five of whom were choir monks; its very fervor brought the confidence that it would be spared by the menacing Revolution.

ANXIETIES AND PROJECTS

So it was in the Spring of 1790, when the Novice Master, Dom Augustin de Lestrange, spoke to the prior (the abbot, Dom Pierre Ollivier had died on 7 February that year) about the menaces weighing in on the abbey, as on all the monasteries in France. He was hardly listened to. He had proposed finding a refuge abroad, to preserve the religious state. The prior, Dom Gervais Brunel, was absolutely opposed to splitting up the community, and denounced the novice master to the Father Immediate, the abbot of Clairvaux, saying he was a trouble maker and caused division in the community, especially among the younger monks. The Father

[1] Cited by A. Latreille, p. 34.

Immediate, who had full authority over the abbot-less La Trappe, made the decision to relieve the novice master of his duties. Lestrange accepted the reprimand as an occasion to entrust himself even more to Providence and remained at peace.

In the preceding months he had received from the bishop of Lausanne a quasi-assurance of being welcomed in the canton of Fribourg in Switzerland, on the condition that he come in person to present his request to the Senate of Fribourg. But Dom Augustin had hesitated at the time, not wishing to leave the novices of whom he had charge to carry out this mission. The penalty now imposed gave him the freedom to act, even if he could not act immediately.

Two months went by in uncertainty, but the situation deteriorated in spite of the sympathy the monks enjoyed in the neighborhood. The General Council of Orne, had in fact, decided that there was no reason why the community of La Trappe should be exempted from the law, conceding, however, that the monastery would be kept under the legal title of 'Communal Departmental House', for the monks who wished to live and die in the observance of their Rule, because most of them had expressed this desire.

Initial Proceedings

The prior announced this news to the community and Dom Augustin, having consulted with his Superior, was given leave to go to Fribourg and in person present to the Senate the request he had kept ready. He also had permission to have it signed by six more monks who were in favor of his project. Dom Augustin departed without delay. He passed through Sées to receive the blessing of his bishop and letters of recommendation. He then went on to Paris, where he hoped to receive help from influential friends. They advised him to go to Clairvaux to see his Father Immediate.

Dom Augustin, trusting in God, followed this advice and set out for Clairvaux. Contrary to all expectations, Dom Rocourt was very much in favor of the project and gave his obedient son an official authorization to do all that was necessary to accomplish his plans to emigrate with some of his community in order to preserve the monastic life, threatened with extinction in France. This document, signed by the abbot of Clairvaux and bearing his seal, is dated 12 March 1791.[2]

Dom Augustin then left Clairvaux and made his way to Cîteaux, to meet the Abbot General of the Order, Dom François Trouvé, already an octogenarian. He was received kindly and given every encouragement and the powers required by the political situation. Much reassured, Dom Augustin set out for Fribourg. His meeting with the Senate was crowned with success: the commission appointed to study the case and report back to the competent authorities was expressed in these terms: 'The Illustrious Lords of Fribourg give permission to the religious of La Trappe to establish themselves in their State, in order to live therein according to their Rule and, to observe it with exactitude, and they will take them under their august protection'.

This authorisation was given for twenty-four monks. The Senate put at the monks disposition the former Charterhouse of La Valsainte, near Cerniat, left vacant fifteen years earlier by the Carthusians.

Dom Augustin, considerably comforted by this document, given him in writing, returned without delay to La Trappe, but he stopped on the way again at Clairvaux to see his Father Immediate and explain the outcome of his mission and obtain some directives about the transfer to Switzerland. Dom Rocourt wrote a letter to the prior of La Trappe so that the foundation could be made without further difficulties.

[2] Archives of La Trappe, cote 1, n°4.

Preparations for Departure

Dom Augustin brought the good news back to his brothers at La Trappe, and the seven who had signed previously were joined by seventeen others to make up the number allowed to go and live in Switzerland. These twenty-four monks assembled together in a solemn meeting on 26 April 1791, and signed a deed in which they agreed on the conditions imposed by the Senate of Fribourg. They were sixteen choir monks and eight lay brothers. At the same meeting they decided there and then to vote for a superior, as time was short. The former novice master received all the votes except his own. On 3 May Dom Rocourt gave his formal consent to all the arrangements of this memorable meeting and by an official act he gave to the elected Superior 'all the authority, the full and entire powers which are attached to this Office, to govern and administer in spiritual and temporal matters this new monastery according to the customs of our Order, the decrees of our General Chapters and our Apostolic Constitutions'.

With everything regularized under obedience, the monks prepared to depart without much delay. Twenty professed, with Dom Augustin at their head, set out on the journey. For various reasons, four monks who had signed at the Meeting on 26 April were not able to go, so three novices took their place.

The journey into Switzerland was accomplished in several stages in a large covered carriage which could not fail to attract attention from either well-wishers or suspicious police. Four stops were envisaged; at Saint-Cyr near Versailles with the Lazarists, and then at Paris with the Carthusians. From there the travellers took the stage coach to Besançon. To pass the frontier together (for they had a common passport) they all got into a wagon again. The border guards, pitying the lot of these unfortunates, never even asked to see their passports.

Finally, the fugitives reached the cistercian abbey of

Hauterive, not far from Fribourg. Here they received a cordial and fraternal welcome, and stayed for eight days. During this time Dom Augustin and his monks went to greet the bishop of Fribourg and thank the *Avoyers*, the two sovereign magistrates who presided in turn over the Senate of the canton.

On 1 June 1791 the founders entered the Charterhouse of La Valsainte; where for seven years they were to find asylum.

LA VALSAINTE

The buildings of this ancient charterhouse had retained something of their former beauty, but, uninhabited for long years and not kept in repair, they did not offer the arrivals anything but a depressing place for refuge. What was worse, there was absolutely no furniture at all. The first refectory tables were planks placed on tree trunks. The monks, without being disheartened, set to work to make the place habitable. Sympathetic neighbors came to their rescue now and again but could not be counted on. Even in the midst of all this destitution, the newcomers did not lose sight of the promise they had made at La Trappe 'to continue in their profession and to live according to their Rule and follow it precisely'. To preserve their *saint état* was the perspective they never lost sight of in their daily labors to earn their living by the work of their hands. From the soil which was allotted them they were able to procure all they needed. This constant physical effort, sustained by up to ten or twelve hours a day by the strongest, did not let them forget the essentials of fidelity to the Rule.

New Regulations

The Rule of Saint Benedict does not go into small details of daily life. It can be adapted to the place and the circumstances where the monks live. In the seventeenth century abbot de Rancé had composed some Regulations (*Règlements*) for his monastery that gave more specific details on some of the observances: silence, fasting, conduct in the Church, how things should be done in particular circumstances.

The monks of La Trappe now had to live in a different locality and under very different circumstances. They asked their Superior to re-read with them the Rule of Saint Benedict, so they could all decide how, practically, they could best live the Rule. During the following months, they re-read chapter after chapter of the Rule, each monk giving his opinions on the best means of being faithful in the new context of their life. The conclusions were noted down by a secretary and then submitted to the conventual chapter.

This first 'Constituent Assembly' took place 19 July 1791. Others followed. The entire Rule of Saint Benedict was examined in this way. A concise report of the meeting appears in *L'Histoire abrégée de l'établissement des Religieux de La Trappe en Suisse,* printed at the beginning of the two large volumes of the famous *Règlements de la Maison-Dieu de Notre Dame-de-la- Trappe par Mr l'Abbé de Rancé, son digne Réformateur, mis en ordre et augmentés des usages particuliers de la Maison Dieu de La Valsainte de N.-D.-de- la-Trappe au canton de Fribourg en Suisse, choisis et tirés par les premiers religieux de ce monastère*.[3]

If the report of these community discussions is succinct, their redaction in the form of Regulations is prolix. There are no less than nine hundred twenty-nine pages in two large volumes. Clearly several secretaries had worked on the composition and did the research for the numerous

[3] The recital of all these events with the supporting documents has been printed on seventy-eight pages of volume one of *The Regulations of La Trappe*, under the title: 'Histoire abrégée de l'etablissement des religieux de La Trappe en Suisse'. It follows after thirty-six pages of introduction to the volume. This is only a summary of a much longer text found in a manuscript in the archives at La Trappe.

references which adorn the margins. There are references to the Rule of Saint Benedict, to the *Nomasticon*, to the Usages and Rituals of Cîteaux, to the Regulations of Rancé, to decisions of ancient General Chapters[4]—in short an impressive arsenal overburdened with numerous innovations and a multiplicity of details strongly marked by declarations of principle in which one finds neither the discretion of Saint Benedict nor the sobriety of de Rancé.

Here is one example among many: Part 1, chapter XII, referring to the employment of a physician whose function it is to examine the sick religious and prescribe the necessary remedies for the infirmarian to administer:

> This duty (i.e. infirmarian) is not one of minor importance in the house. This is not because of its object—the health of the religious—since the solitaries must profess to make little of this, as of life itself, but because of the influence it can have on the regular observance of the monastery.[5]

This excessive language goes far beyond the already austere Regulations of Rancé; but Dom Augustin thought that Rancé was not able to do all that he wished. That was why he wanted to go further. Hence the chilling impression one experiences when reading these pages. The Regulations, which abound in excesses of this kind, were never to be approved by the Church, and they were to become the occasion of painful crises at the heart of the Order when it was in the process of being reborn.

Why These Excesses?

We can offer excuses for the man we rightly call 'The Savior of La Trappe', who made it possible for the cistercian

[4] This research was done Father Colomban Moroge.

[5] *Règlements*, I:191.

monastic life to be transmitted, without break, to future generations,

The troubled times in which the monks were living was in itself a justification for these excessive penances, and few were astonished to see them revived. Some were anxious for even more. A tragic situation employs tragic means. The whole of the nineteenth century was to be branded by this contempt for the body, with the idea of penance at any price and redemptive flagellations, forgetting perhaps in this perspective the person of our Redeemer. Yet in spite of these extreme ideas, it is only fair to point out that these men had honorable intentions, and that God can write straight with crooked lines, even where there are optical illusions.

In this chapter it is not possible to study the contents of some thousand pages of the Regulations. I mention them only because they influenced the lives of the nuns who adopted them, entrusting themselves to the man who providentially helped them 'preserve their holy way of life'.

The daily life lived in the monastery of La Sainte-Volonté-de-Dieu, as we shall see later, was bathed in an atmosphere of absolute silence imposed by the Regulations. This created an ambiance of peace and joy that everyone was grateful to have experienced and deeply appreciated.

EXPANSION

As in the past at La Trappe with the abbot de Rancé, so now, the community of La Valsainte attracted many candidates to the monastic life. The first twenty-three founders were soon joined by many others—monks, priests, or lay men in search of God. In order not to break the restrictions laid down by the Senate of Fribourg—twenty-four monks only—Dom Augustin saw that he was obliged to think about making some foundations. These premature and hastily arranged establishments were often rendered unstable and short lived by external circumstances. Moreover all had to be arranged and provided for as soon as possible to prevent suspicions in the locality of the canton.

As the superior of La Valsainte was substantially supported by the Cistercians in Spain, who often sent him sums of money, he thought in April 1793 of trying a foundation there to take care of the influx of postulants. Two monks took the road for Spain and were joined by five others the following year. After many delays and evasive promises they were able to found the monastery of Santa Susanna in Aragon. This house, which enjoyed some prosperity, was soon separated from La Valsainte for reasons of civil administration, and then dissolved by the Spanish Revolution in 1831.

In August 1793, three other monks were sent in the direction of Canada. They were supposed to take a ship at Amsterdam, but the port was closed because of war. The travellers were then invited by the bishop of Antwerp to settle in a house not far away at Westmalle. Here they embarked on a true foundation, which had its ups and downs but survived by moving to Darfeld in Westphalia. We will meet them again in 1800.

The following year, on 22 April 1794, another group was designated to go to Canada. They were to go to Westmalle and there change places with some of the other monks. This done, the group embarked at Amsterdam, arriving in London in July. There they were offered property in England. After obtaining the approval of their superior at La Valsainte, the colony settled at Lulworth in Dorset, not far from the south coast. Here the community prospered, but it returned to France in 1817 to the former Cistercian monastery of Melleray in South Brittany.

A fourth group was sent to the Piedmont about the same time. Their fate was to be more complicated. We shall see them again, but nothing remains of this foundation.

La Trappe

While the Swiss foundation of La Trappe flourished, the monks who had stayed behind in France were all turned out of their monastery in June 1792. The prior, Dom Gervais Brunel, went with two brothers to Luneville, where they stayed some time. One day they were denounced as non-juring priests and sent to the prison ships at Rochefort. Here they died in destitution, true confessors of the faith. A lay brother fought in the war at Vendée, was taken prisoner and guillotined at Angers. Other monks emigrated towards Switzerland, reuniting in small temporary communities. Others used the dispersion as an occasion to marry.

Dom Augustin, no doubt knowing about all these events, put ferocious energy into keeping as many monks together as possible throughout the long years of exile. This tenacious will of his was to make of him the true savior of La Trappe.

The Elevation of La Valsainte Into an Abbey

The foundation originating from La Trappe three years earlier, now no longer had any canonical support from the motherhouse. The abbey of Clairvaux, which had the paternity of La Trappe, had suffered the same fate. Dom Augustin therefore planned to have his community canonically erected. He applied to Rome, and received a favorable reply through the intermediary of the nuncio at Lucerne. Dom Augustin was then elected abbot by the unanimous vote of his brothers and received the abbatial blessing in Lucerne from the Nuncio on 8 December 1794. In this way the trappist foundation of La Valsainte was canonically erected as an abbey. It was from this branch of trappist exiles that a long road would be taken. During the next two hundred years they were to be the source of some ninety monasteries of cistercian monks now living under the name of the Cistercian Order of the Strict Observance, and today established on five continents.

LE R. P. DOM AUGUSTIN DE LESTRANGE

DOM AUGUSTIN DE LESTRANGE (1754–1827)

Who was this monk whose intrepid undertakings would make him become for posterity the 'Saviour of La Trappe'? Promoter of an authorized regular foundation, he also became in the course of dramatic circumstances, the founder and organizer of a group of nuns gathered together with deep conviction and a strong desire to preserve their *saint état*.

It is interesting to see how Providence prepared this man for such responsibilities by temperament and education. Louis-Henri de Lestrange belonged to a noble family of Vivarais. His father was an officer in the guard of Louis XV, but after the battle of Fontenoy left uniform and Court behind, to avoid what he considered a life that was too luxurious and hardly in conformity with the Gospel. In the autumn of 1745, he retired to his manor of Bosas in the

Ardèche. There, to facilitate attendance at daily Mass in the winter months, his custom was to go with his wife and children to live in the large presbytery of his brother, the parish priest at Colombier-le-Vieux. It was at Colombier that Louis-Henri was born on 19 January 1754, the fourteenth child in a family that would number twenty-two children. His mother, Jeanne-Pierrette Lawlor, was the daughter of an Irish gentleman who had followed King James II of England into exile in France. The family lived evangelical poverty in a very concrete manner. Louis did his primary studies at Clamecy with a near relative who was fond of him, then at the college of Tournon. In his fifteenth year he passed out of the sixth form and went to the seminary of Saint-Irénée at Lyon for philosophy. His parents hoped he would go into the navy as an officer, but he had set his heart on being a priest. With this end in view, he went to Paris to the seminary of Saint-Sulpice for his theology. There he had as a fellow student, Talleyrand. They both received the sub-diaconate the same day. Lestrange was ordained in 1778 and stayed on in the parish of Saint-Sulpice for a short time. Here they called him 'the little saint'.

Returning to see his family he was noticed by the archbishop of Vienne, who made him his Vicar General and then secured him as his coadjutor. This news so upset the young priest, who felt himself far too young at twenty-six to accept so much responsibility, that without any advance notice he went to La Trappe which he had already been thinking of entering, and asked for the novice's habit. He received the name Augustin, and from that momen on wanted only to make his vows. After his profession it was soon realized that he was well suited to guide newcomers in the monastic life, and thus, without their suspecting it, to prepare them to follow him into an exile totally divested of everything.

It seems certain that he was gifted with charm and attractiveness, and he used these qualities with complete self-detachment for the glory and service of God. When he spoke of his project of a foundation, he had, as we have seen, his admirers and detractors. But he trusted in God's help and sought his will with all sincerity. 'The Will of God' (*La Volonté de Dieu*) became his motto; and to those who consented to follow him he transmitted the value and purpose of this maxim. This they did willingly, so appealing was his own way of living.

A monk, whom we will meet again in this story, Father François de Paule Dargnies, joined La Valsainte in 1793. In the *Mémoires en forme de lettres* which he wrote, he says of Dom Augustin

> The Reverend Father lived in the monastery with the greatest exactitude, but if some indispensable business obliged him to be absent, it was always for only a few days. He always travelled on foot, accompanied by one of his monks. When in the monastery, he followed all the exercises with care. You could see him in the cloister doing his reading with the brothers . . . If he was not in the cloister, he was in his office, which was only a small place near the chapter room, very damp,with no fire or any other amenity whatsoever. It was here during all the free intervals that he listened to anyone who wished to speak with him. He himself distributed the work and led the community out to the fields. You could see him out there working with the brothers. After working some considerable time he would go through the different workshops in the monastery. He attended to some business, then went back to where the community was working . . . He neglected nothing for the well-being and advancement of his Reform (Letter 4).

This devotion of the superior to the common life was in large part responsible for the fervor which animated the community. It was truly magnetic.

Nuns from various religious Orders and Congregations were also drawn by his exemplary reputation. They entreated this eminent superior for his counsel and clear guidance; they too wished to live in community together and find again what they had known, loved and chosen in the past.

That is why we will find on almost every page of this book the name of Dom Augustin de Lestrange. The abbot of La Valsainte directed all the initiatives taken by the nuns, who put themselves into his hands with complete confidence. Nothing seemed to be impossible to their generosity, because of both the end in view and the prestigious guide who directed them.

CHAPTER TWO

THE FIRST COMMUNITY OF CISTERCIAN-TRAPPISTINES

THE UNDERTAKING OF the monks at La Trappe in making a foundation abroad under the firm guidance of Dom Augustin de Lestrange soon became well known among the general public in France, and the nuns who had been dispersed in September 1792 were not the last to be very interested indeed. Deprived of the means of action open to the monks, they refused to be discouraged by the long wait. In their hearts was the desire to resume the community life they had professed in their younger days, and they were always on the watch to seize the least sign of hope. So, as we have already seen, some of them took the road to Switzerland.

From this beginning was born a new community of cistercian nuns. Called at first 'trappistes' because of their relationship with the foundation of La Valsainte, these cistercian nuns were soon known as 'Trappistines', to distinguish them from their brother monks. Unfortunately their history suffered from various stories about the 'Monastic Odyssey' which appeared in the nineteenth century. Two recently discovered documents are behind this more systematic research in the archives of our monasteries. These investigations have allowed me to give more precise details on the place of the foundation and the personnel in the first community of Cistercian-Trappistines.

THE TWO DOCUMENTS

The first, the oldest, is an account written by Sister Stanislaus Michel. In December 1797, she entered the new monastery of Sembrancher in Switzerland, after ten years of cistercian life at the abbey of Sainte-Catherine in Avignon. In 1805 at La Riedra, in her joy at having found a place where she could live peacefully as she desired, she invited her sisters to give thanks to God who had sustained them all during their long wanderings which she describes with some restraint. Of the foundation, she wrote:

> It was in the year 1796 that this house was founded. The Reverend Dom Augustin de Lestrange, abbot of La Valsainte, a holy man of whom the world was not worthy, had by his care and zeal established after the Revolution in France, a community of religious of La Trappe in the monastery of La Valsainte, in the canton of Fribourg in Switzerland; as you can see in the first book of our Regulations.
>
> But the ardor of his zeal for the glory of God and the salvation of souls urged him, in the year 1796, to establish a house for women, where they kept exactly the same observances as in the monastery of La Valsainte. To accomplish this project and open a place of refuge for so many souls who were languishing in the world, he chose a place near St-Brancer in the Bas-Valais, where he had a house built and brought in some nuns of good will who were willing to adhere to his plans.
>
> This was on 14 September, the day of the Exaltation of the Cross, that our first foundresses made their entrance, embraced the [foundation] cross, and then placed themselves under this divine Standard to combat with courage the enemies of their salvation. On this first day there were eight nuns.
>
> The Reverend Mother Sainte-Marie, a very worthy religious, forever memorable in our Order for the great example of her virtue and zeal for the observance, was chosen by our Reverend Father to be their Superior. He

was not mistaken in the choice he made of this worthy nun. The fervor of this new community was soon seen by the great care she took to see that the regular discipline was observed.[1]

The second document, written some twenty years later, is in the hand of Mother Augustin de Chabannes, the foundress of the monastery at Stapehill. It is a reply to a letter written by the foundress and first abbess of Saint-Catherine at Laval, Mother Elisabeth Piette, and dated 3 December 1824:

> Allow me to have recourse to you so that I may be enlightened as to the origins and year that the trappistine religious were established. I have only a very confused idea; and do not know who installed the first superior, nor even who was the first Mother, although I think that it is you yourself who are our common Mother, of whom we have the happiness to be your children. It is very interesting and even rather important for me at this moment to have some exact ideas on this subject . . . .[2]

Here is part of a rough draft of the reply, discovered at Stapehill:

> A short time after the foundation of our Fathers at La Val Sainte, some religious and other pious persons implored the Reverend Dom Augustin to found a similiar place for women (*personnes du sex*). Full of zeal to help so many nuns forced by the miseries of the Revolution to live in the world, he worked at this good project and had some leaflets printed in Paris. In 1796, three benedictine nuns and some lay people went to Switzerland and there they

[1] Cf. Kervingant, TR cote 55, n° 13 *bis*, 'Aux origines des Cisterciennes-Trappistines. Un document inédit', *Cîteaux*, 35 (1984) 185–214.

[2] Archives of Stapehill: correspondence with the monastery of Laval. *La Trappe in England*, p. 118, remarks that 'unfortunately' the letters of Mother de Chabannes have not been preserved at Laval. Mother Elizabeth entered Darfeld in 1806 and made her profession there in 1808.

> entreated him to accomplish this project. On 13 September of the same year, they entered their own simple monastery; there were seven of them. It was Father Augustin who appointed a superior. She was a Benedictine before the Revolution, a simple religious in her monastery. The first profession took place on 17 September 1797, all this into the hands and by the sole authority (*sic*) of Dom Augustin. However, I firmly believe that Mgr the Bishop of Sion knew all about our establishment and it had his approval, at least tacitly.[3] In the space of one year our numbers rose to more than sixty.

Here the narrative breaks off.

THE FIRST FOUNDATION

Sembrancher, about which Sister Stanislaus spoke, is a small village in Valais, not far from Saint-Maurice, to which six months previously the Father Abbot had already sent a colony of monks. Here they had built a very modest house. When the Father Abbot decided to establish a foundation of nuns, the monks moved to a grange on some property, bought by Dom Augustin on the Ile-Bernard leaving the house empty for the sisters. They built a cloister wall around the house and Father Abbot came and blessed the place called La Sainte-Volonté-de-Dieu (the Holy Will of God), after the motto so dear to him. He always did everything in the name of this Holy Will.

In the spring of 1796, the Princess de Condé, who was to become a novice with the name Marie-Joseph, came to see where the foundation for women was to be. A little later she wrote to the Princess of Piedmont:

[3] This supposition appears to be confirmed by a testimony of the bishop of Sion, the Ordinary of Sembrancher, dated 14 December 1797. I will be referring to this document later. (Archives of La Trappe, cote 13, n°11).

> After leaving you . . . I found a lodging right in the neighborhood of the place where a cloister wall is being built around a sort of poky little house (*bicoque*), which will become the first monastery of trappist nuns. Only the building was there and as yet no sign of anyone living there.[4]

Between this first visit to Sembrancher and her entrance into the monastery in September 1797, she lived in Vienna (Austria) with the Visitation nuns. We will see later that this stay would prove to be providential, as it enabled her to direct Dom Augustin and 'his flock' to a place of welcome during their journey into exile in the East. After a trial period of one year, she obtained the authorization to enter La Sainte-Volonté-de-Dieu. In a letter written some days later to a friend, a princess, she gives a vivid picture of what she found on her arrival:

> I was admitted into this house some days ago and tomorrow I have the privilege of being given the white veil to start my novitiate . . . Forty or fifty women live in this little house, the four walls are divided inside by partitions of pine, which form the principal regular places of a convent.
>
> Among other things, the choir is so cramped for room that soon it will be physically impossible to turn round and perform the Office in a fitting manner. A grille divides the choir from the altar, and it is so poor that the chapel has the advantage of reminding one of the stable at Bethlehem. All this, it is true, harmonizes with the holy religious who live in this place, and nobody complains. But what is really painful at the moment is to see that we are forced to refuse so many who arrive in great numbers, because of the smallness of the house. Not only is what we call the dormitory full, but already the tables of the refectory are used as beds, and the inconveniences that these holy souls put up with in order to be able to find a place for those who come to serve God with them are

[4]*Lettres*, ed. Rabory, p. 102.

> so many causes of joy and happiness in their eyes. For the rest, an atmosphere of peace and contentment reigns here reflected on their faces in a way you could never begin to imagine . . . [5]

The candidates were indeed numerous. We find sixty-two inscriptions in the Register of Admissions between September 1796 and December 1797. In spite of two deaths and seventeen departures, there was still lack of space in the *bicoque*; each evening they had to improvise dormitories. This must have been a great trial for most of them who had known conditions materially very different.

The First Nuns

According to the first extant Register, seven women[6] were present that evening of 13 September to start the regular monastic life on 14 September, the feast of the Exaltation of the Cross, the official date of the foundation.

On this day too Dom Augustin gave the cistercian habit to Sister Sainte-Marie Laignier, whom he immediately named prioress of the young community. She was then forty-six years old, having been born in Paris to Martin Laignier, gold and silver smith and Marianne Labutte, living in Paris at the Pont Notre-Dame. She had entered the Benedictines of the Blessed Sacrament at the priory of Charneton in the Val-d'Osne.

The next week the Father Abbot gave the habit to another Benedictine, Sister Sainte-Marie Bigaux, whom he promptly named as sub-prioress and novice mistress. Born in 1762 at Dreux, in the diocese of Chartres, to Charles

[5] *Ibid.*, p. 160.

[6] Cf. Kervingant, 'Aux origines des Cisterciennes-Trappistines.' Pp. 63–80. The register is preserved at Abbaye de L'Assomption, Rogersville (Canada), archives Lyon-Vaise.

Bigaux, royal attorney of the bailiff's court at Dreux, and Angélique Le Vaigneur, she entered the Benedictines of the Blessed Sacrament at Dreux (the first priory founded by the monastery in Rouen during the time of Mother Catherine de Bar). She made her solemn profession on 30 January 1788. When her monastery closed, she went back to her own family. Then, with the help of a Sulpician priest in Paris who was a friend of Dom Augustin, she managed to get into Switzerland in 1796.

The other five aspirants all received the habit before the end of the month:

— Sister Suzanne de Valois, a Poor Clare for ten years from Alençon, was not able to endure the austere life in her new religious family and left the following 8 January.

— Sister Madeleine Guyot, the widow of a copper-plate engraver, aged thirty- six, received the habit on 21 September, but did not make her profession until three years later in Russia.

— Sister Bernard de Lestrange, the eldest sister of Dom Augustin was a nun of Saint-Pierre-les-Nonnains at Lyon. Aged forty-six at the time of the foundation, she died two months later, on 19 November 1796.

— Sister M. de la Croix, Louise de Lestrange, another sister of the Father Abbot and twentieth child of the de Lestrange family. She never made her profession but was the first teacher of the Third Order, and looked after the children. She stayed on until about 1820.

— A young girl of twenty-one, Marie-Françoise Beaubiller, stayed only two months in the community.

There were eight other entries spread out over the months of October, November and December. They all persevered in the Order until death. One died the following May. She was a nun of Saint Francis who had come from Amiens. Aged thirty-four on her arrival in Switzerland, she had already been a professed nun for ten years.

Her seven companions were a Capuchin from Armentières, a Poor Clare from Besançon, a Carmelite from Dôle and four other young girls, all of whom made their profession the following year accepting the Trappist way of life for a long road ahead which would lead them into Bavaria, Poland, Russia, Westphalia, England, Switzerland and into France, a journey of many years.

In three and a half months the young community had grown to fifteen members, in spite of one death and one sister leaving during this period. We can say that the thirteen present at the end of 1796 had already established a consistent stable community. The austere Regulations of La Valsainte, which the nuns begged Dom Augustin to allow them to follow, were to be, in a political context which remained disquieting, a sure unifying force of minds and hearts. In these first months the abbot was often there himself to form the sisters in the spirit of the Regulations. The former novice master felt at ease in this task; he gave instructions every day and presided over the chapter of faults, heard their confessions or gave spiritual direction, following each in her progress, ascertaining her background to discover her aspirations and aptitudes. He stayed with the young community so often that the monks at La Valsainte began to complain of his long absences.

THE GEOGRAPHICAL ORIGINS OF THE POSTULANTS

In spite of the humble living conditions and material poverty at La Sainte-Volonté-de-Dieu, postulants poured in, and it is interesting to note where all the candidates came from.

Of the sixty-two postulants who entered La Sainte-Volonté-de-Dieu and are listed in the register, four came from Paris, one from the Parisian region, nine from Lyon, twelve from Franche-Comté, three from Bourgogne, four from Flanders and Picardy, three from the northeast of France, four from Normandy, one from Alsace, three from the Massif Central, one from Avignon, one from Savoy and eight from Switzerland. For five others there is no mention of where they came from.

Many arrived on the same day, sometimes two or three coming from the same place or from the same religious community. Some blood sisters arrived together or were re-united there. All this information makes it possible to appreciate how natural affinities or friendships helped to cement the fraternal charity of this community.

The presence of the first community of monks at La Valsainte in the canton of Fribourg and the new foundation for nuns at Sembrancher (Bas-Valais) influenced young swiss girls to enter; four came from Fribourg and four from Saint-Maurice or Sembrancher itself.

SOCIAL ORIGINS

Another aspect of the sisters' backgrounds is shown in the register by their family and social standing. Usually the father's profession is noted after his name. Alongside the daughter of the Prince de Condé (whom a new arrival one day mistook for a swiss farm girl), there are twelve daughters of laborers, farmers and agricultural people. There are also twelve daughters of various merchants; four are noted simply as merchants or tradesmen, but five have a descriptive adjective—goldsmith, tanner, hatter, grocer, butcher. Three others were merchants of wood, wine, and fish. Craftsmen were also well represented: two bakers, a locksmith, a tailor, a wax chandler, a carpenter, a cloth shearer, a silk worker, a simple workman. We find as well a silk weaver and some 'masters' in their crafts: a master cobbler, master saddler, master harness maker, and a school master. We find as well a valet from the household of the Duchess de Choiseul appears next to a royal bailiff, a secretary of the king, and some five 'bourgeois' of Paris, Lyon and elsewhere. A landlord, a gentleman usher and a sculptor—all levels of society were represented in this small world, this microcosm, the first trappistine community.

From the beginning all the women were called sister with no distinction made between choir and lay, Third Order or oblate sisters, categories which were introduced only later depending on individual aptitudes for choir, Latin Office and the austerities of the Regulations.

We can only marvel at the flexibility and charity of these first nuns, who were able to build a real community from persons of very diverse backgrounds and ages, as we shall see. This is particularly amazing when we consider how rapidly the community received new recruits, the sort of life each had been accustomed to, and the fact that many of them had belonged to different religious Orders and Congregations.

The age of entry varied from nineteen to seventy-one. The following table of the age groups of entries and how many persevered in each age group indicates this graphically.

Age	*Under 20 years*	*21–30 years*	*31–40 years*	*41–50 years*	*51–60 years*	*61–70 years*	*Over 70 years*	*Unknown*	*Total*
Admissions	4	22	17	13	1	1	1	3	62
Persevered	0	12	9	8	0	1	1	0	31

Apart from the two extremes—those under twenty-one and those of unknown age, of whom none persevered—a little more than half the women in each age group went on to profession.

Altogether, thirty-four aspirants came directly from their families. Thirty two were single women but of these only fourteen made profession; two widows both persevered. This comes to a total of forty-seven percent who persevered.

Of the other twenty-eight aspirants who had already lived some time in the religious life, fifteen died as Cistercian Trappistines: one sister of the Annunciation out of two, one Benedictine out of two, two Benedictines of the Blessed Sacrament out of three, two Capuchins out of two, one Carmelite out of three, three Cistercians out of three, four Poor Clares out of eight, and one Franciscan. Three Canonesses and an Ursuline all left. Fifty-three percent of the religious who entered died in the Order.

INTEGRATION INTO THE COMMUNITY

Integration into the community was made in three stages, postulancy, novitiate, profession. After the date of a sister's entry, the *Register* notes the day she took the habit, which marked the beginning of her novitiate. By this we can calculate the length of the postulancy. Usually it was quite short, but sometimes it extended to six months or over without any particular reason being noted. Because it is difficult to calculate the average time for the postulancy, we can only surmise from this that on this point there was no fixed rule. The bare facts given can be sumarized as following: clothing, the beginning of the novitiate, could take place on the day of entry, or after two, five, or ten days, two weeks or three months. One religious waited four months before taking the habit; three young girls all left at the end of six months without being clothed. It would be difficult to find a rule with more flexibility!

The length of the novitiate was more regular, mostly at least one year and sometimes a little longer.

The first profession was that of Mother Sainte-Marie Laignier, the prioress, on 17 September 1797, one year and three days after she received the habit on the day of the foundation. The following month, on 24 October, that is one year and five weeks after their clothing, five novices made their vows. They were one Benedictine from Dreux, one

Capuchin from Armentières, one Poor Clare from Besançon and two girls. Eight days later, on 1 November, there was a ceremony of profession for a Carmelite from Dôle and a young girl from Besançon, who had made a novitiate of one year and twenty days.

Two professions made at La Sainte-Volonté-de-Dieu were exceptions to this rule of a one-year novitiate. These were two Cistercians who had already lived for some time under the Rule of Saint Benedict before their arrival at Sembrancher. The first was Mother Augustin de Chabannes, a nun of the abbey of Saint-Antoine in Paris from 1784–1792. When she entered at Sembrancher on 21 June 1797, she was twenty-eight years old, and she made her profession the same year on 29 October. The second was Mother Edmond-Paul de Barth a nun of Koenigsbruck (Pont-du-Roi) near Haguenau (Alsace). She entered on 30 September 1797, when she was forty-three years old, and made her profession on 24 December 1797, after a two month's novitiate.

Two reasons may explain why these two novitiates were cut short. The first is that entry at Sembrancher for both novices was only a change of stability, and there did not seem to be anything in the *Regulations* of La Valsainte to cover such cases. The second reason was urgency. Dom Augustin wanted to assure that there was a least a permanent nucleus for the exile already foreseen as the Revolutionary armies advanced towards Switzerland.

THE ACT OF PROFESSION

Two profession schedules[7] from this period, in the archives at Stapehill, show us various formulae for profession: one in the case of a change of stability as with Mother Augustin

[7] The schedule is the paper or parchment on which the novice wrote the formula of her vows. She read it aloud herself, then signed it in the presence of the community, and then placed it on the altar during the Mass of profession.

de Chabannes; another at a new profession in a different Order, made by Sister M.-Joséphine de Montron, a former Carmelite who entered the Order of Cîteaux.

It is worthwhile examining closely these two schedules, pronounced within three days of each other. The wording is far from identical in several places. I have placed in italics the difference in the texts. Both were written in the hand of the signatory.

> I, Sister Augustin de Vergèses, religious *of the Order of Cîteaux*, promise my stability and obedience according to the Rule of Saint Benedict, Abbot, before God and the saints whose relics are here in this place *which* is called the monastery of La Volonté de Dieu, *of the same Order*, in the presence of the Reverend Father Augustine, Abbot of the house of God of La Valsainte de Notre-Dame-de-la-Trappe.
>
> I, Sister Marie-Joséphine de Montron, promise my stability *under perpetual enclosure*, *the conversion of my manners*, and obedience according to the Rule of Saint Benedict, Abbot, before God and all the saints whose relics are here in this place called the monastery of La Saint-Volonté-de-Dieu *of the Order of Cîteaux*, in the presence of the Reverend Father Augustin, Abbot of the House of God of La Valsainte de Notre Dame-de-la-Trappe.

We can see immediately that the first nun omitted any mention of perpetual enclosure and the conversion of manners (which means living according to the monastic way of Saint Benedict), because she mentions explicitly that she is a 'religious of the Order of Cîteaux': there is no need to mention these two points again. But having changed the place and the superior, she affirms her resolution of stability and obedience.

Another point stands out in the wording in these two schedules; the prioress is not named, only the Father Abbot, who always called himself 'abbot of the monks and nuns of La Trappe'. Gradually the name of the superior of the house will be mentioned.

A final difference with the traditional formula of the Order of Cîteaux: the monastery of La Sainte-Volonté-de-Dieu is not declared to be 'constructed in the honor of the Blessed Mother of God, Mary ever virgin'. The tradition was taken up again later and is today still in use.

THE CANONICAL STATUS OF THESE PROFESSIONS

What exactly did the professions of the nuns signify? They were made under the Rule of Saint Benedict, but without any mention of the legislation which formulated them. At La Sainte-Volonté-de-Dieu the religious did not follow either the Regulations of the Reform of de Rancé which had been approved by the Church, or those of the primitive Cistercian Order.

In his article in *Revue Mabillon* (1934) Dom Alexis Presse has studied the question of the validity of these vows as solemn vows, and he concluded, to my mind rather hastily, in the affirmative. The canonical situation of the monastery of La Sainte-Volonté-de-Dieu is not, it seems, sufficiently clear to be able to be judged. The document of the Bishop of Sion which I referred to at the beginning of this chapter, however, allows us to think that the foundation was recognized and authorized by the local Ordinary. An official letter approving a new foundation of the Third Order in the diocese[8] reads in translation from the Latin:

> We, Joseph, Antoine Blatter, Bishop of Sion by the grace of God and of the Apostolic See, to those who will read the aforesaid document, eternal salvation in the Lord.
>
> By a touching display of Divine Providence we *esteem that at the side of the double colony of monks and nuns of this same Cistercian Order of La Valsainte, erected in*

[8] Archives of La Trappe, cote 13, n°11.

> *our diocese under the name of La Sainte-Volonté-de-Dieu near Sembrancher*: in the same manner another more recently, Agaune, called the Third Order of La Trappe, has been erected by the zeal for our Savior, Jesus Christ, by the R. Father Augustin de Lestrange, Abbot of the same Order. It has been received with our approbation and to the satisfaction of all those who think as honest citizens etc.
>
> We have all confidence in our Savior, but experience has already proved it. In witness whereof we have signed and sealed this present document.
>
> Sion in Valais, 14 December 1797

This act of approval for a house of the Third Order[9] shows us, with utter certitude, that the Bishop of Sion had earlier approved the foundation of Sembrancher, monks and nuns, and appreciated the benefits of their presence.

Whether the vows taken at this period were simple or solemn seems to us rather secondary. The important fact is that this commitment was binding for life and had been accepted by God in a community recognized by the Church in the person of its local representative.

[9] On 1 May 1794, a child was entrusted to the monks of La Valsainte, probably the child of a political refugee. The zeal of Dom Augustin knowing no limits, he seized every occasion to demonstrate it. 'Other children soon followed, because Dom Augustin offered to train and educate the children in a christian manner (those between six and ten years of age was the rule) whose families wished to give them into his care. Soon the requests were so numerous that by the end of 1794, a distinct community had to be organized, with monks as teachers, those whose health prevented them from following the Rule in its full austerity. Dom Augustin grouped these monks and children (who numbered over a hundred), into an institution called the Third Order of La Trappe. Their Rule was greatly mitigated. The habit was that of the monks without the cowl, a brown scapular and a heart sewn on it in red cloth with the inscription 'La Sainte Volonté de Dieu'. (Bouton, *Histoire de l'Ordre*, fiches cisterciennes, n°104, p. 14.) Parallel with the Third Order of La Valsainte, Dom Augustin founded at Agaune a Third Order of Trappistines for the education of small girls.

DEATHS AND DEPARTURES

Not all who entered the community bound themselves for life to the Order. Two sisters died rather suddenly during this first period of the foundation. The first, Sister Bernard de Lestrange, a former Benedictine of Lyon, died at forty-six, two months after her entry on 19 November 1796. The second, Sister Marie du Saint-Sacrement de Lassus, a Franciscan from Amiens, died on 25 May 1797 at thirty-five, after a six-months novitiate. Seventeen others were not able to persevere and left of their own volition on the advice of their superior. The *Register* nearly always noted briefly the reason for the departure: lack of vocation, simple-mindedness, uncompromising, unstable, neurotic and so on. Five of these departures were religious not able to adapt to a new form of claustral life: three Poor Clares, one Carmelite and one Ursuline.

Most of the departures took place between December 1796 and December 1797. One each left in January, March, April, and June; three in September, one in November, two in December and five at an unknown date. An eighteenth left on 13 February 1798, just as the last members of the community were about to close the house.

How then was this austere form of life capable of retaining more than two thirds of the candidates who flocked to the monastery of La Sainte-Volonté-de-Dieu? What was it that attracted them, stimulated them and brought them peace and joy in mutual charity? Certainly it was not an easy life, as we shall see in the next chapter; but a will anchored by a desire to be faithful to God can laugh at all obstacles. What the woman wants, as we well know, God wants.

CHAPTER THREE

DAILY LIFE UNDER THE REGULATIONS OF LA VALSAINTE

IN THEIR GENEROSITY, the first arrivals at Sembrancher had asked to follow in totality the Rules adopted by the monks at La Valsainte. At first Dom Augustin seems to have hesitated a little, but inwardly he was delighted with their fervor and consented. Apparently it did not occur to him to question the consequences of these austerities on women whose constitutions were more fragile and who were less inclined than their brother monks to deviate in practical matters from the letter of the law.

The decision made, the Rules were accepted in all their vigor, and it seems that at the beginning of the foundation there were no great difficulties.

THE SPIRIT OF THE REGULATIONS

As we have already seen, the *Regulations* were composed of abundant minute prescriptions, presumably to clarify the Rule of Saint Benedict in the spirit of early Cîteaux. The accent was definitely on penance, austerities, manual work and poverty. The Reform of de Rancé in the seventeenth century had taken up these themes, which had been somewhat forgotten during the previous three centuries of civil war and invasion. Furthermore, the reformer had taken his inspiration from the Fathers of the Desert, whose writings had just been translated by Arnauld d'Andilly. For the abbot de Rancé the monk was a penitent shedding tears over his sins, giving himself to prayer, manual work and *lectio divina*; and someone who had definitely broken with the world. Asceticism was of the first order for all conversion and the way to God.

Dom de Lestrange, a monk of de Rancé's La Trappe, faced with the excesses of the Revolution, thought it his duty to invite his brothers to still more rigorous asceticism and penance, thus perfecting the work of de Rancé. The equilibrium established by Saint Benedict and early Cîteaux, and the relative sobriety of de Rancé, was shattered. For the new reformer, penance was the *raison d'être* of the observances, which, consequently, had to be as penitential as possible. Hence the multiplicity and lengthening of prayers in common, the emphasis on humiliations, the absolute silence, the increased manual work at the expense of *lectio divina*, the reduction of the time for sleep, and the dietary restrictions.

VARIATIONS IN THE DAILY HORARIUM[1]

In the third book of the Regulations we find the *horarium*, complex and detailed, which governed the monastic day during the different seasons of the year. Each liturgical season, Advent, Christmas, Lent, Pascal, and the seasons of summer and winter, all had their own particular time table. Even within these periods the days did not always follow the same rhythm, because Sundays and Feastdays according to the various rites, broke the monotony of the ferial days, not to offer a respite or some rest, but to lengthen the time of prayer. The Offices were a good deal longer and more solemn, extra prayers were recited in common: litanies, rosaries and other devotions, or processions with chants replaced work times.

[1] *Les Règlements*, volume two, p. 5–24.

In general, three principal occupations make up the monastic day. The Divine Office chanted with psalms at the different liturgical hours, *lectio divina* (spiritual reading and private prayer), and manual work. A certain balance between these three elements is required for a harmonious monastic life, conducive to the monk's or nun's relationship with God. It is a balance which always has to be watched, because it is not invariable and has in fact changed over the centuries and in accordance with the needs of the communities. Meals, sleep, care for the body, should all be given their due place in the *horarium*, without having to be mentioned explicitly in the rules. We must keep this perspective in mind in order to follow the nuns in their monastic day in the monastery at Sembrancher according to the Regulations of La Valsainte.

A TYPICAL DAY AT SEMBRANCHER

We will follow a typical day in winter, noting any modifications for other times of the year.

On work days the hour for rising was a few minutes before 1:30 am allowing enough time for the nuns to arrive in the Chapel where the Canonical Office started exactly at 1:30 am; on Sundays it was 1:00 am and on principal feast days at midnight. The Offices followed one another: Matins, Matins and Lauds of the Dead on ferial days, then Matins and Lauds of the Blessed Virgin, followed by the Angelus, then the canonical Office of Lauds. All this lasted until 4 am.

One hour of *lectio divina* followed. From 5:15 until 5:30 there was time for prayer, and, then the Office of Prime. This ended, the community filed into the chapter room where they heard a passage from the Rule of Saint Benedict, then a commentary by the superior or the abbot if he was present. Chapter was terminated by the chapter of faults, at which the sisters accused themselves of breaches against the Regulations or were 'proclaimed' for faults they had not noticed, either by the superior or by another more vigilant sister!

After Chapter there was more time for reading, before a first bell rang for the Mass (this was rung half an hour before the service. The time varied). During this time the sisters could go to tidy their cells and make their beds. This was soon done since the bed consisted of a wooden plank, a blanket and probably a bed cover as prescribed in the Rule of Saint Benedict.

We cannot be sure of the exact time the Mass began; this seemed to vary. What we can be sure of is when the Mass ended, at 8:30 precisely! At this moment Terce started, and it was followed immediately by work. The end of work was signalled by the first bell for Sext at 11:30 am. At the second bell the community sang Sext, then made an examination of conscience and recited the *Angelus*. Then work was resumed until 2 pm. At 2:15 None was sung and at 2:30 the community went to the refectory for the only meal of the day. In Lent the meal was deferred until 4:15. But on the other hand, from Easter Day and throughout the summer, except Wednesdays and Fridays not in Paschaltide, dinner was at 11:30 am and an evening collation was served at 6 pm.

During the winter season, on coming out of the refectory, the sisters had a singing lesson which lasted in principle until 4 pm. Then a brief interval for a respite and a little exercise was followed by Vespers at 4:15. This was concluded by some private prayer until 5pm. *Lectio divina* followed until 6 pm when the community assembled for the short reading in common which preceded the Office of Compline. Compline ended, the *Salve Regina* was sung very slowly and majestically, and was separated into three parts by full prostrations. This chant to the Virgin Mary lasted a good quarter of an hour. An examination of conscience brought to an end the day in choir. At 7 pm the nuns retired to the dormitory for some well-earned rest, but not for long. The longest night was six hours and the shortest a bare five hours.

As we can see, the number and length of the Offices took up a considerable amount of time, about nine hours a day. *Lectio divina* was notably reduced, as was work time, only four hours. Where, we can ask ourselves is the equilibrium of this horarium?

The order of these exercises I have just summarized took up about twenty pages, this is followed immediately by paragraphs indicating the manner of comportment in choir, refectory, chapter, everywhere and at all times and in all circumstances. The Regulations for sleeping in the dormitory took one page; those for the refectory needed twenty-eight pages and for the Night Office forty-six pages. Not a detail, not a gesture, not a movement escaped comment, but was explained and regulated in the minutest detail. Everything in all the ceremonials could be the occasion for an accusation or proclamation at the chapter of faults every morning. All this maintained and kept awake the fervor and desire for penance which animated these women in their joy at having found the lost coin.

Silence

The entire day was spent in absolute silence. The procedure was laid down in Chapter Eight of the third part of the Regulations. In paragraph 4 on page 110, we read:

> 1. Silence is looked upon as the foundation of all the regularity of this house, and the slightest infringement will be considered a grave fault. By transgressions we mean not words pronounced, because such a disorder is not even to be considered, but signs accompanied by movement of the lips to assist some understanding of the signs, or unspoken sounds; all that leads to a breach of the silence, which would soon be broken altogether.
> 2. It will also be considered culpable, under the clause on silence, that those who have authority to speak, say

> things that have nothing to do with the reason for which they have permission to speak.

Paragraph 4 goes on for three more pages, enumerating the cases when one can speak to a superior and a brother (or a sister). It then expounds the precaution to be taken for every word spoken 'that is be under the spirit of God'. In all there were fourteen recommendations to be remembered. The ninth is amusing: 'One does not gesticulate with the hands and the feet, nor sway the body about when speaking'.

Manual Work

A good dozen pages of Chapter Eleven are devoted to manual work. From the first, it is emphasized that work is penitential. 'The monk will recall that work is the first penance imposed on man . . . .' There follows the quotation from the book of Genesis: 'Man will eat his bread in the sweat of his brow', and that of the Rule of Saint Benedict, 'Idleness is the enemy of the soul'.

The first article contains a multitude of rules on monastic decorum, all explained at great length, while article two is devoted to the nature of the work. The first paragraph distinguishes two sorts of work, that done in the field and that done in the monastery. Only this latter applied to the nuns. At Sembrancher they had no fields to cultivate, and even if they had, their enclosure would not have permitted them to do the work themselves.

Work inside the monastery that had not yet been invaded by electrical household appliances was quite abundant and absorbing. The paragraph on indoor work gives us some idea of the different activities and the spirit in which work had to be done, with obedience and humility:

> The work of the nuns is first of all that which has to be done in the house. This they will do following the order

> of the Superiors. They will themselves prepare whatever food is necessary, weave their own cloth, make their habits and mend their worn clothing, etc. With their own hands they will cultivate their gardens, do their own polishing, sweeping, washing etc. They will do their own laundry, clean out the stables and cart the manure to the garden, and, in a word, they will do all the meanest and most humiliating tasks.[2]

The nuns were kept busy according to their age and strength, growing vegetables, peeling them, cooking them, spinning wool, weaving it, making it into habits, washing and mending them. A real bee hive from nine in the morning until two in the afternoon, with a pause around mid-time.

In the recommendations that follow, a small mortification is mentioned on passing:

> Those who work in the wardrobe (a common sewing room) should never be inquisitive as to what goes on in another *boutique* (*sic*) other than where one is.

At the end of the seventeenth century there was no question of nuns earning their own living in the strict sense of the word, that is being paid for work, other than, as we have seen, the education of young girls. Income usually came from lands owned by the abbey, rents from tenants, dowries of the nuns, or donations freely given. Having lost all assured income, however, the immigrant nuns had to rely on Providence, the charity of their brother monks, and the benevolence of those, near and far, who took an interest in their plight. Thus they had to live in extreme poverty. From about the middle to the end of the nineteenth century, workshops began to appear for outside customers, such as needlework, small commercial enterprises, the making of altar breads, chocolate or cheese. It was the beginning of an evolution that developed in the twentieth century. It was

[2] *Ibid*., p. 133.

at the same time and for another two centuries domestic tasks had capital importance in the lives of communities. Often these everyday labors needed a considerable output of physical energy which was not always sustained by a substantial diet. Let us see what the Regulations say on this subject.

Meals

From the long chapter 'On the Meals' we will mention only about bread, drink and the dishes that were to be served. There are three pages on bread, distinguishing three different kinds; brown bread made of sifted whole wheat for the community; white bread of an ordinary kind for guests and the sick; and the 'indulgence bread' which was given only under certain conditions to those for whom 'a good pound of bread' (Rule of Saint Benedict) was not sufficient for the day. 'This is made with the lowest quality grain in the country in the simplest and poorest manner . . . potatoes or other similiar fare may be added.'

There are four pages on beverages. At the beginning the principle was laid down: 'We never drink wine, beer, cider or any other intoxicating drink, only pure water'. The text goes on to demonstrate how throughout the times of monastic history, Anthony, Pachomius, Basil, and through the centuries to Rancé, this was the practice of the true monk.

As to the nature and quality of the rest of the food, we read in paragraph 3, n°5:

> Meat, fish, eggs and butter are forbidden to all who are in good health. Such was the practice from the beginnings of our Order, of this we have no doubt, so this is what we too will follow. Never, under any pretext or on any occasion whatever, will anything like this be served in the refectory, unless to an invalid.

In n°7 of the same paragraph more details are given:

> Never may we add in our food any seasoning such as butter, sugar, honey or any sort of spices; all these things have only one object, to flatter sensuality. We will be content with the herbs that can be found in the garden, or in the countries where we live. In general the portions will be served and cooked in the simplest manner possible.

Quoting Saint Bernard, the paragraph continues with a diatribe against things like spices and ends by saying: 'According to Saint Bernard the salt of appetite is the only seasoning that monks are allowed.' A small condescension is added in n°7: 'Sometimes butter may be added to the portion for invalids and honey may be served to guests'.[3]

What could these monks and nuns eat, who saw themselves deprived of all that was necessary to maintain good health? They simply took the same fare as the poorest people. Other than the bread and water, which we have mentioned, they had only one meal a day. This principal meal consisted of vegetables cooked in salt and water—two cooked dishes of which one might be a sort of soup—and also on certain days and periods of the year, milk dishes or cheese. This more substantial diet was never to be served in Advent, Lent or on the Fridays outside Paschaltide, or on the fast days of the Church.

When there was an evening meal it was cold and consisted of salad, some raw or cooked vegetables served cold; a dessert of fruit or cheese was added in a measured portion.

If the work was longer or harder than usual, the portions could be more substantial but never the quality. No food added to the usual menu was allowed.

At the beginning of article two in this chapter on meals, the author of the Regulations—and here no one can doubt that the text was written by Dom Augustin himself—declares openly:

[3] *Ibid.*, p. 159.

> Of all our practices, fasting and abstinence seem to be what most strikes people in the world, and against which they revolt even more, although we keep these practices in such a modest manner [!]. You hear them say with a sort of horror; 'to live as a Trappist, never eating meat, nor fish, nor eggs, nor butter—only eating once a day during more than half the year . . . . If to this reflexion if you add our idea of silence, this is quite enough for most of them to consider themselves dispensed from examining whether God is calling them to live among us. Such a life is at once judged as going beyond the powers of nature, and it would be tempting God even to attempt it. Such is the pretext that the enemy of our salvation uses the most successfully and frequently to prevent souls from following their interior aspirations to live a life of penitence; or to make them turn back after having taken some steps towards a calling which formerly one could hardly even give the name 'strict'.[4]

This discourse continues along the same lines for four more pages, to the end of article two.

Certainly to follow Dom Augustin in all these excesses, which were not without disastrous consequences on the health and equilibrium of the communities, would be painful, especially for women who had accepted and wanted to follow the Regulations. We shall look into this in the next pages.

Charity

This excessive austerity beyond the means of ordinary human strength, was to some degree alleviated by the intention which governed its exercise; it expressed a delicate and constant charity. If their minds and hearts were turned towards love in its two dimensions, of God and of neighbour,

[4] *Ibid.*, p.145.

then the nuns were not so concerned with what they ate and their physical well-being. We find in the Regulations some real pearls on this subject, and I would like to draw attention to these before we see how the nuns of La Sainte-Volonté-de-Dieu understood this encouragement to go ahead with their project.

> The perfection of monks, as of all Christians, consists in charity, so we can look at this virtue which begins this Article [*III*]. Whatever resides principally in the heart should be shown exteriorly in such a way as not to be misunderstood; because nothing contributes so much to strengthening the interior [life] as the outward practices by which it is deeply expressed.[5]

Then follow some indications of a practical nature on what the monks were to do when they met one another in the cloisters where they did their reading, and the marks of politeness that should be observed. Then follow some other recommendations:

> All the monks should take great care not to give the least offence against charity. If by weakness it happens that someone gives a sign of discontent, irritability or ill humor, he will at once acknowledge his fault and kneel before his brother, who in his turn will also kneel down, reproaching himself for having troubled the peace of his brother; witnessing by his openness and affection that the small offence had in no way wounded him, making the other get up immediately.

A little further on there is a caution: 'However we must avoid multiplying these sorts of satisfactions in a way which could become troublesome, making them at any time and without a real reason.

On a more positive note, the directory continues:

[5] *Ibid.*, p. 102 ff.

> As nothing contributes more to the preservation of charity than the mutual services we do for one another, we will not fail to help a brother when we see him in difficulties, such as carrying too heavy a load; and for the most part we will always be ready to sacrifice our own leisure, convenience and self-interest for the well-being of our brother.
>
> In general, we will welcome all the services offered us, because they can hardly be refused without offending our brother. However, if it is altogether unnecessary, one can always refuse with careful consideration.[6]

It is particularly comforting to find in these lines a sign of considerable benevolence on brotherly relations, and at the same time a good deal of common sense in the measure with which it is warmly recommended.

TESTIMONIALS

Without doubt this charity was the secret behind the peace and joy visible on the faces of the nuns, and in their daily manner of living in the heart of this young community. We have found some witnesses in letters written from day to day which have come down to us.

From the pen of Sister Sainte-Marie Bigaux, the sub prioress and novice mistress during the beginnings at Sembrancher we read:

> Having obtained from God the grace to live again my *saint état*, I cannot without ingratitude abstain from making it known how great is his mercy . . . I am not alone in sensing this peace . . . More than twenty-six novices for whom I am responsible will also bear me witness that they too, when they entered here, began to sense the peace and the joy, and in a word, the happiness that until now they have never known . . . I must admit that it is

[6] *Ibid.*, p. 104

very surprising, in a novitiate made up of persons of all ages and all conditions, nuns and lay women, that they are all so happy. But when faith is so firmly fixed in the direction of the eternity we hope to gain, the acquisition of the virtues is worth any discomfort. This is so true that we would willingly support the desires of most of the novices, who want to add to our practices several kinds of mortifications which our rules do not oblige us to do.[7]

In another place the same sister writes:

By themselves our exterior practices detatched from any supernatural motives which should animate them, are nothing and lead to nowhere, since Saint Paul assures us that without charity, in vain do we give our bodies to the flames etc. We shall receive no recompense whatever. Indeed would God agree with our kind of life if we did not have his holy love in our hearts, and if the charity which must unite us together did not reign among us? Yes, by the mercy of the God of charity, this divine virtue, the sacred bond which so closely unites so many persons of different nationalities, age and condition; so contrasting, that it is true to say that only charity could accomplish all the good that one finds in this house . . . . The depths of our solitude provide us with so many means to fulfil my obligations, without any obstacles, other than my weaknesses.[8]

She writes again—and this may seem surprising at the end of a century in which many historians have pointed out the disappearance of the Christocentricism which had animated the spirituality of the seventeenth century.[9]

[7] Archives St, Letters or declarations, 1797.

[8] *Ibid.*, another declaration, Archives St.

[9] See, for example, François Bluche, *La Vie quotidinne au temps de Louis XVI*, especially chapter V: 'La religion de l'Etre suprême', particularly pp. 163–166.

> I am not unaware that the enemies of the cross of Jesus Christ storm against those who have the obligation to follow this Divine Savior in the capacity of Christians, and are doubly obliged in the capacity of religious to accept gladly his maxims and to follow his examples. Alas! I am forced to confess to my confusion that after fulfilling all my duties in the holy state of La Trappe, I am still far from imitating totally the life of the God-Man. He is however the way that we must follow, the truth that we must believe, and the life that must be the model of our own.[10]
>
> Sleeping on planks, fully clothed, is done for the purpose of afflicting nature they say. No doubt, but do you think Sir, that the body does not easily get used to this practice? Look, for a whole year now I have slept like that, I have practiced the fasts prescribed at La Trappe, and thanks be to God my health bears up well, and I have seen more novices surprised at how little it costs to lead our kind of life than I have met who found it harder than they had anticipated.[11]

These declarations of the novice mistress are confirmed by the statistics found in the first *Register of Admissions*. Of the sixty-two women who entered La Sainte-Volonté-de-Dieu in fifteen months, only eighteen left the community before the departure into exile: 70% went on the long exodus.

The Sentiments of a Novice

Even more spontaneous and freely expressed are the letters of Sister Marie-Joseph, Princess de Condé.[12] The recipients

[10] See note 7.

[11] *Ibid.*

[12] Princess Louis de Condé on 22 August 1786, had been elected abbess of a former benedictine abbey, transformed at the end of the thirteenth century into a chapter of canonesses. The superior kept the title abbess. To be part of this chapter, sixteen quarterings of nobility were required, to prove nine generations of knighthood. Madame Elizabeth,

of these letters varied, but she says the same to everyone—with some subtle differences—about the atmosphere that she found at La Sainte Volonté-de-Dieu and her own reactions to the kind of life she led there. I will quote here some passages from these letters she wrote during the four months she lived at Sembrancher before they all left for the East.

She was forty years old when, on 26 September 1797, she entered the monastery founded by Dom Augustin de Lestrange. As early as October first the Father Abbot allowed her to take the cistercian habit. On the 28 September she wrote to Father de Bouzonville, who had been her spiritual director for the previous three years:[13]

> Ah! my Father, thank him, this good and admirable God, to whose feet you have directed me . . . I can say that the Lord has now opened to me the entrance into his sanctuary! Yes, this place is holy, God is truly here. At last I have found a religious life which my heart so profoundly desired . . . I write to you in the joy of my soul; I have asked of our Reverend Father the grace to receive the habit on Sunday with some other sisters who have this blessing . . . This place is hardly what so many people think; everything here is delightful. I do not know what this austerity is of which they paint such a terrible picture. I see faces in the best of health, rosy and white, but better still, faces at peace, happy and holy.

---

sister of Louis XVI, was proposed for this Office, but she deferred to the Princess de Condé, who accepted the election on 26 August. Madame de Condé took to heart the interests of her Chapter. She stayed with them several times and was very much loved by the canonesses. Cf. B. Hours, *Madame Louise, princesse au Carmel* (Paris, 1987).

[13] Armand-Louis Le Juge de Bouzonville, a former field-marshal in the army who was widowed after eight years of marriage, devoted his life to God. He was Vicar General at Nancy when the Revolution broke out. Arriving in Fribourg in May 1791, he tried his vocation at La Valsainte, then retired to Fribourg. In 1793 he met Louise de Bourbon-Condé and was her director for three years. He witnessed her very perceptible spiritual growth.

The letter continues in this tone but finishes with a more matter of fact postscript:

> I am very well, I eat and sleep well; I am hungry enough only for dinner, and I am really amazed that I thought for so long one was obliged to take breakfast and supper. All the same I eat very moderately at dinner, as from the beginning I realized that I must reduce the amount of bread, because of its quality. As for the vegetable fricassee, I find this very good, and not at all unwholesome; those who complain are making false accusations. Altogether, my very good Father, in body and spirit, for time and eternity, it is on Jesus Christ alone that I count, on whom I lean, and to whom I abandon myself entirely and without reserve, through his great grace and mercy.[14]

On 30 September the eve of her clothing, she wrote to the archduchess Marie-Anne:[15]

> I cannot express the happiness that I have found at La Trappe, which is very noticeable on the faces of the sisters. The day is so well regulated that it seems to fly in an instant. One does not know what it is to be bored. As to the austerity that is believed so repellant, I do not know where it is to be found. It seems to me that I enjoy complete comfort, at least all that is necessary for christian souls who have as their Master and Model Jesus crucified. The silence, the recollection, and the peace is what I find the most moving in this holy house, which is so regular and fervent. Even if we are always together it is easy to practice interior solitude because of the general example of the community; also without speaking to one

[14] Dom Jean Rabory, OSB, *Correspondance de la princesse de Condé* (Paris, 1889) p. 152.

[15] The archduchess Marie-Anne belonged to the family Habsbourg-Lorraine, and was the youngest sister of the Emperor of Austria and of Marie-Antoinette. We will meet her again during the travels in exile through Europe. She was very helpful and welcoming to a group of nuns at one of her châteaux in Bohemia.

another the charity which reigns here is apparent in all their hearts.[16]

The following 2 November, one month after her clothing, she was still writing with the same enthusiasm to Father de Bouzonville:

> I must admit that sometimes the silence is hard, only for the reason that I would like to say how happy I am and that everything here is delightful; sometimes I feel like climbing to the top of a mountain and calling everyone to come to our little desert . . . With great joy I see *our community* increasing daily and becoming more established by [new] professions. We have had several in a short space of time, among them an old friend of yours, the good Tinturier. Today we had two professions and four clothings. Among these last was a Poor Clare of seventy, who has come in the joy of her heart to begin her novitiate, after having been herself for many years the novice mistress in her convent. Nobody has any worry about dying at La Trappe.[17]

We cannot positively say that the sixty persons gathered at La Saint-Volonté-de-Dieu all had the same sentiments as did Sister Marie-Joseph in her first months at Sembrancher. If eighteen sisters left the house before the departure into exile, perhaps it was because the novelty had worn off and only solid vocations, joined to a well-balanced humanity, could withstand the nervous exhaustion generated by the continual effort required by such a life.

Another ordeal was soon to be added to it: the exodus towards safety. Switzerland was no longer a haven of peace. Sister Marie-Joseph wrote on Christmas Day to her father, the Prince de Condé, then in exile in Russia:

> Switzerland will not escape the French persecutions. Even now, the *Directoire* has insisted, in a high-handed manner

[16] *Correspondance*, p. 158.

[17] *Ibid.*, p. 169.

> and with appalling despotism, on the expulsion of all immigrants, and it even appears that he honors the Trappists particularly, marking them out by name.[18]

Soon the community would plan its departure towards the East.

[18] *Ibid.*, p. 172, a letter of 25 December 1797.

PART THREE

On the Roads of Europe

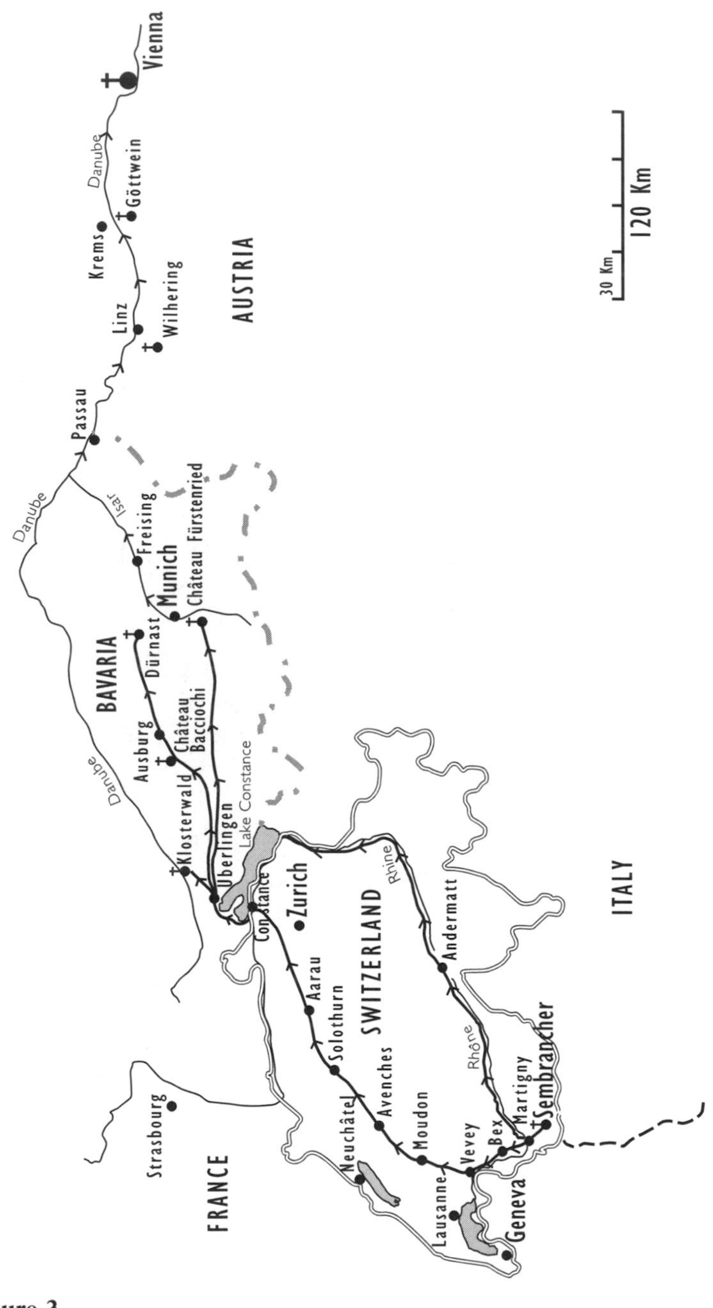

Figure 3

The journey through Switzerland, Bavaria and Austria.

AS EARLY AS THE FINAL MONTHS of 1797, Dom Augustin de Lestrange, who had been closely following political and military actions of the *Directoire* in France,[1] sensed the peril approaching Switzerland. He took stock of his responsibilities, more than two hundred people who had found refuge in the various houses opened by him in Switzerland: monks, nuns, religious of the Third Order, and children. It was up to him to ensure the safety of all these people.

In an unfinished account written much later and left on a scrap of paper, Dom Augustin himself tells what he asked of Sister Marie-Joseph:

> It was Sister Marie-Joseph, formerly the Princess de Condé, whom God wished to use to protect us from our enemies and give a shining example of his admirable Providence. As I knew that, before entering the monastery, she had sometimes had some connections by correspondence

[1] The Coup d'Etat of 18 *fructidor* year V (3 September 1797) had reacted against the movement to the right in the Assembly, by some exceptional measures which touched the refugees, their families and their goods. Some priests, both constitutional and refractory were imprisoned then deported. Worse, the revolutionary armies were on the frontiers, ranged along the Alps and the Rhine in such force that the treaty of Campo Formio on 18 October, the legalized presence of the conquerors in the north of Italy. Altogether these events could only harbor forebodings and provoke panic among the french immigrants.

> with the Emperor Paul I, I said to her, 'You must write to him to see if he will receive us in his States'.[2]

In reality Princess Louise had more than 'connections by correspondence' with Tsar Paul. When he was still the Tsarevitch, this son of Catherine II and a passionate admirer of Frederick II, had quarrelled with his mother. To occupy his leisure he left in 1781, with his wife, for a tour of Western Europe, under the name of the 'Count of the North'. He was received at Chantilly in the house of the Prince de Condé, where the motherless Louise, then twenty four years old, acted as hostess at the reception. She had enchanted the future Tsar.

Sister Marie-Joseph did not hesitate when the abbot asked her to write a letter. In fact, she wrote, not directly to the Tsar, but to the Empress Marie, her 'cousin', who received the letter through the hands of the Prince de Condé, then stationed at Saint Petersburg at the head of his troops. With the grace that characterized her, Madame Louise asked the Empress to transmit her request to the Tsar in these terms: 'I ask the gracious "Count of the North" to intercede for me with the Emperor Paul'. The pleasant recollections of the Tsarevitch should dispose the Tsar to a warm welcome.

This happened in December 1797. Some traces of this appeal are found in a letter from Sister Marie-Joseph to Father de Bouzonville, dated 7 December.

> You were right as usual, to advise me to take my seal with my coat of arms; I beg you to send them to me as soon as possible. The Reverend sub-prior has written to the Post Master asking him to do all he can to see they reach us; so would you see he gets them?[3]

[2] Arch. TR, cote 217, pièce 28, p. 3.

[3] *Lettres de piété ou correspondance intime . . . de Louise Adélaïde de Bourbon-Condé*. t.II, p. 186. The sub-prior to whom she refers was Father Benoït Rabier. He accompanied the group which included Sister Marie-Joseph during the first part of their journey as far as Bavaria.

Evidently this seal was indispensable to authenticate the message sent to the Empress of Russia through the care of the Prince de Condé.

Even before receiving a favorable response from the Tsar, Dom Augustine started organizing the departures. These were spread out from mid January until 17 February 1798.

Closely comparing the different accounts that have come down to us, we can conclude that the nuns left in three groups or colonies. The first group to leave departed on 19 January, the second was arranged for the next day according to a letter of Sister Marie-Joseph, and the third group left at the beginning of February but no other details are known. On 10 February, General Berthier entered Rome and over the following days plundered the city, while the pope, by order of Berthier, left the city on 20 February.[4] Between these two dates Switzerland was invaded.[5]

It was then more than time to leave the country. The house at Sembracher, where the nuns had lived for sixteen months was sold at the same time as the neighboring property of Ile-Bernard, where the monks lived. 'Dom Urbain Guillet [the prior] stayed behind with one lay brother to see the sale through . . . for the sum of one hundred gold *louis*. This sum was payable "this evening or tomorrow morning before I leave,'" (deed of 16 February 1798) . . . The next day 17 February, the deed was authenticated, and at the same time the sale of the house and the end of these two monasteries at Sembrancher was ratified.[6]

[4] Latreille, p. 289.

[5] 'During the night of 13 to 14 February 1798, the Directoire ordered a march on Berne, most probably at the instigation of Bonaparte. Brune advanced from Lausanne and Schauenbourg from the Jura; the city fell after a lively resistance . . . They seized the treasury at Berne, the contents of which had partly motivated the whole enterprise, and which also served to finance the expedition to Egypt'. (G. Lefebvre, *La Révolution française* (Paris, 1968) 522.

[6] *Helvetia Sacra*, 1982, Jean de la Croix Bouton and Patrick Braun, 'Les Trappistes et les Trappistines en Suisse', p. 1068.

If the monastery of La Sainte-Volonté-de-Dieu was no more, the community which had lived there survived. They continued to survive for several years on the roads of Europe, unsettled, destitute and suffering hardships without number; they persisted in their purpose, fidelity to God and the monastic state.

CHAPTER ONE

FROM SWITZERLAND TO BAVARIA

FROM THIS POINT ON we must follow the exiles along the roadways of Europe. While we have some specific details of the composition and itinerary of the first and third groups; of the second, we know practically nothing other than scant information gleaned among the various accounts which have come down to us.

For the purpose of clarity, I think it preferable to accompany each of the three groups from the date they left until they were all reunited for the first time in Bavaria.

THE FIRST GROUP

We can follow the first group easily, at least in the initial stages of their journey, through the letters of Sister Marie-Joseph de Condé, a novice of four months. On 20 January 1798, she wrote to Father de Bouzonville, an *emigré* living in Fribourg:[1]

> We left yesterday morning in *charabancs*: the good God had withheld the cold. We travelled like this as far as Martigny, the Reverend Father accompanying us on foot in the mud and manure. At Martigny we found some large and handsome coaches, in which we felt more like

[1] The following quotations are extracts from this letter, written 20 January and printed in the two collections of the letters of the Princess de Condé.

> princesses than Trappists. The Reverend Father accompanied us on a mule as far as Bex where we stayed the night. He took great care to see that we had food and blankets (because, as you well know, there was no question of beds). All we could do was marvel. I can assure you that he was solicitous for each and every one of us. This morning we started off again in the same comfortable coaches. The Reverend Father left us a little before we reached Vevey, to our great regret. At the inn, he had put us into the care of Reverend Father Benoît, sub-prior of Valsainte, a man very dignified and gentle; and also Father Joseph our chaplain. They had with them several children, a brother of the Third Order and one or two lay brothers. I think that there were also one or two monks. They had a nice looking carriage and also a sort of little covered wagon.

These monks had left La Valsainte at the same time as the nuns; the two groups, monks and nuns, could travel this way quite rapidly and in good condition as far as Constance. Sister Marie-Joseph continues:

> As for us, we are eleven in our coaches. I am with our Reverend Mother, (who had been our novice mistress),[2] another professed and a young novice, who is seventeen years old; she received the habit yesterday before we left; she was baptised and made her abjuration the evening before, after having spent some time with us.[3] We have with us also the little de Rougé (twelve years old) surprisingly mature for her age and very edifying. Her father had hesitated somewhat to leave her with us, but her mother (between you and me) asked me to write a letter assuring her that whatever befell us, her daughter would always be with me personally. This produced the desired effect.

[2] Mother Sainte-Marie Bigaux (See Part 2, Chapter 2).

[3] The *Register* preserved at Rivet notes the entrance of this young girl of seventeen as follows: 'Caroline-Philippe Sévère, daughter of Jean-Philippe Sévère and of Suzanne Balan, farmer, entered our monastery 30 November 1797, aged seventeen years. Departed.

> The child, it is true, would have been very distressed to return to the world.

We shall see later how Madame de Condé kept her promise when she left La Trappe.

> In the other coach, there are three black veils, not yet professed with us, but we give the black veil to those who were professed in their own convents,[4] above all for travelling to avoid a lot of white veils in public. Sister Jean-Baptiste (Chassaignon) is one of them. We also have a young professed lay sister, a sister of the Third Order (she is the sister of our Reverend Father, a secret I know), and a little girl of three or four years old.

Five novices, three professed, a sister of the Third Order and two very young girls formed the first group. After having described her companions, Sister Marie-Joseph adds with spiritual enthusiasm:

> So far everything has gone marvellously and the good God never ceases to treat us like spoilt children. Today, as an encouragement, God gave us a really beautiful spring day, sunny without clouds, and quite a magnificent sky, mild weather and almost hot.

The cheerful personality of Madame de Condé did not, however, conceal the difficulties of the enterprise as a whole. 'Where will our hopes and desires for a foundation lead us in the midst of all this wretched destruction? God only knows; he knows also my complete confidence in him.' She then adds in brackets 'Again this morning eleven of us had to leave.' Nevertheless she goes on to reassure her spiritual father, always very concerned about his illustrious religious daughter:

[4] Other than Sister Jean-Baptiste Chassaignon, seven former religious, still novices, could have been one of the two novices in black veils. We cannot identify with certainty the companions of Sister Marie-Joseph.

> I forgot to tell you also how attentive and charitable our Reverend Mother is for her daughters: in a word, my Father, everything is arranged so you may be at peace about my situtation, which I would not change for anything else, I assure you. If you knew how I feel, not only happy, but really proud to travel and show myself to the eyes of Europe clothed in God's holy habit, this God to whom you have dedicated me. You know how many times I told you at Fribourg that I prefer to be consecrated to the Lord, doing the job of a drum major, than living an elegant style of life in a convent without vows. I still feel the same. I much prefer to be a Trappist, even running around the world as I am forced to do today.

A postscript adds:

> In the Inn at Moudon, 21 January.
> P.S. I do not think it possible to receive a reply from you until we reach Augsburg. Address it to me in the envelope going to M. Bacciochi, at whose place we will be stopping and perhaps staying.

There follows a request for some spiritual books, in particular those of Father Berthier,[5] for the use of the travelling community, which wanted as far as possible to live the monastic life they had all come looking for at Sembrancher. In the same letter, Sister Marie-Joseph notes in fact:

> We follow our exercises as much as possible. However they are mitigated, of course. For example, we do not get up in the middle of the night, but the Office is divided between the evening and the morning. The reason for this is that we do not wish to disturb other people in the inns; accordingly the feeble human nature of the Trappists benefits. For myself, I am vexed, you know how I love the night Office. As for our food, we maintain our regular

[5] Guillaume Joseph Berthier, celebrated Jesuit and author of a commentary on the psalms in 8 volumes (1704–1782).

> routine (and God be blessed for it!) but it is not too severe for real needs.

This colorful description of their first two days of travel could leave us with the impression that they were leaving on vacation: the *charabancs*, the coaches, the sun, the cheerful atmosphere. But anxiety comes through. They must reach Augsburg, and then may not be certain of a place to lodge. What does the future hold? 'M. Bacciochi at whose place we will be stopping and perhaps staying.' Refugees were travelling along all the roads of Switzerland, and could not expect a particularly warm welcome in Bavaria.[6]

Before arriving at the place of M. Bacciochi, they still had several days' journey. They had to pass through Constance, where Dom Augustin had arranged a meeting place for the different groups leaving Switzerland.

According to Dom Rabory, this is the itinerary followed by the first group: Bex, Vevey, Moudon, Avenches on the southern shore of Lake Neuchâtel, then Soleure and Aarau. Avoiding large towns as much as possible, in particular Berne, they arrived at Constance on Saturday 27 January. Two days later the group travelled to Augsburg.[7]

Sister Marie-Joseph described the departure from Switzerland in a letter written to her father on 14 April, giving some details:

> I was happy enough to find a decent place of refuge near Augsburg, which was only allowed us for a fixed length

[6] Old Bavaria comprised the electoral principality: Upper and Lower Bavaria, the Upper Palatinate and some territories in the west of Germany. The rest of Bavaria was still independent: the territories of the Prince-Bishops of Bamberg, Wurtzburg, Augsburg, Passau, and Eichstadt. Those of Regensburg and Freising were quite small. Finally there were the protestant marquisates of Ansbach and Bayreuth, then governed by Prussia, and a multitude of free towns, princely abbeys, principalities, and lordly domains. These political groupings manifested varying reactions towards the refugees. See Norbert Baeckmund, O. Prae., 'Les Cisterciens français émigrés en Bavière', *Cîteaux* (1982) 138–143.

[7] Cf. J. Robory, *Vie de la princesse de Condé* (Paris, 1889) p. 257.

> of time.[8] However, I asked the Elector of Bavaria[9] if we could stay until a reply came from Russia. This he granted me,[10] because Providence has for some time now given me credit with the sovereigns, which I did not have in the days of my glory, now dead and gone![11]

It is hardly necessary to underline in passing the good humor of the Princess, which helped her to see everything with a certain optimism yet, at the same time, with a shrewd and supernatural outlook. We shall see further proof of this later in the narrative.

Various Places of Hospitality

From the same letter, we learn that Dom Augustin had established his general headquarters at Überlingen, on the Bavarian side of Lake Constance, formerly the headquarters of the army of Condé. From this strategic point, the Father Abbot directed the movements of his flock as they left Switzerland. He had already sent a group of monks to Klosterwald, an abbey of Cistercian nuns not far from Überlingen.[12] Among

[8] Only for two months. 'It was promised me until Easter.' Having arrived early in February, she had to leave the place by Easter, which fell that year on 8 April.

[9] Charles-Théodore de Deux-Ponts-Neubourg, Elector Palatine of Bavaria (1724–1799), 'while fearing an infiltration of subversive ideas, received the refugees with a better disposition than the Princes of the Church. All the refugees had to be registered, and to avoid undesirables, the certificate of admission was nearly always restricted', (Baeckmund, p. 138).

[10] This was the castle of Fürstenried, situated seven km southwest of Munich. This castle, constructed in 1717, was the residence of King Otto of Bavaria.

[11] Letter dated 14 April to the Prince de Condé.

[12] The abbey of Klosterwald or Wald, in the diocese of Constance, was founded between 1200–1212. It reached the height of its fame around 1500. The church was rebuilt in 1725 in the baroque style, and is today the parish church. The monastery was suppressed in 1806.

the monks sheltering there was a Father François de Paule Dargnies whose *Mémoires en forme de lettres* gives precise, sometimes well-salted, details on this *odyssée monastique*. He remembered this stay at Wald, allowing us to follow the nuns who passed through Überlingen.

> I can only recall [he says] that some days before I fell ill, the Reverend Father had me mount a horse and ride with him to a small village about four leagues from Klosterwald, to visit a group of nuns from Valais who had been lodged in a private house. The others, I heard, had taken the road to Bavaria.[13]

The nuns resting at Überlingen were probably those who were disabled or exhausted from the difficult journey of the third group, whose ordeals we will learn about further on. Father Dargnies was the head infirmarian—a sort of physician—who gave prudent advice on restoring the health of the others and was very devoted to them in spite of his own infirmities, of which the memoirs speak abundantly.

Already the first group and no doubt the second had reached Augsburg and found shelter at the small castle Bacciochi at the gates of the town, before moving on to the castle Fürstenried. On 24 March, Sister Marie-Joseph sent word to Father de Bouzonville:

> A word on our worldly situation. The asylum near the town of Augsburg having been promised us only until Easter, the Elector of Bavaria allowed us a place two leagues from Munich to await the response from Russia, which seems never to arrive! Some of our group came here rather suddenly owing to the age and delicate health of the Prince, and it is a good thing to be here in case of emergency. We already have passports to go across the Empire, *if* we can go into Russia. Up to now I have been

[13] Mémoire Dargnies, letter 13.

> granted most of what I asked for, but only for a specific number of persons.[14]

She added with a sigh of uneasiness:

> And I must admit that to see the *entire flock* of the Reverend Father Abbot going along *altogether, this side of the border*, frightens me somewhat about the future of all these procedures.

Speaking of the place where she stayed with the sisters, although at the time she did not know its name, she added in postscript:

> The good M. Marduel and M. Dictriez have both been very kind to us in all manner of ways. We are quite well; the Elector gave us a little money for a feastday treat. We have used your permission and taken some of your books, and also those which had belonged to me. While on the subject of books, if you could ever get a copy of *Le chrétien par sentiment*, three volumes in twelve°, dedicated to M. the Count de Clermont, read them and have them read to your parishoners.[15]

THE SECOND GROUP

The second group, which left Sembrancher on 20 January, probably followed the same route as the first, because the way was still open in that part of Switzerland, which was no longer the case three weeks later. Who made up the group and how they journeyed we cannot know for certain; but what we know of the third group permits us to think that it was directed by Mother Sainte-Marie Laignier, the first superior of La Sainte-Volonté-de-Dieu, probably

[14] Letter of 24 March 1798, written at Fürstenried (*correspondance intime*, p.207).

[15] *Ibid*.

accompanied by Mother Edmond-Paul de Barth, because she spoke German.

How many were in this second group is difficult to say with exactitude. There must have been fifteen or seventeen sisters, even though Sister Marie-Joseph wrote in her letter on 20 January that 'Again this morning eleven of us had to leave'. The house would not have been emptied of all its inhabitants if the number of those leaving had been this small. Mother Stanislaus in her account says of her own group, the third, that there were seventeen sisters. According to the extant Register, the community counted forty-two religious in the month of January, plus some children. So the two last groups must have been about equal.

Before hospitality was assured them at Fürstenried, the two first groups, leaving at one day's interval, probably found shelter in the house of M. Bacciochi, a rich patron of the arts. We do not know at this point the composition of the groups which seemed to vary. It seems nevertheless that by the beginning of April most of the immigrants had reached the château of the Elector of Bavaria at Fürstenried.

The Arrival of New Recruits

At Augsburg the first two postulants were welcomed during the journey. These were two French Benedictines who had been in contact with Dom Augustin about entering at Sembrancher. The abbot had warned them that he must escape from Switzerland with both his communities, but would await them at Augsburg.

On their arrival in the town on Palm Sunday (1 April), these two Benedictines, Sister Saint-Maur Miel from the Petit-Calvaire in Paris, and Sister Thérèse Janis from the abbey at Arcis in the diocese of Chartres, were lodged with the English Dames, a community of teaching sisters who kept a boarding school in the town. There they found a novice who had just left La Trappe. But let us allow Sister Maur herself to tell us of the sequence of events:

> The superior of the house treated us with all kinds of goodness and charity until the Wednesday in Holy Week, when she took us to meet the Father Abbot, who received us with great kindness. He spoke very little and asked us only if we were really resolved to be faithful to the customs of his Order. He also asked us how we had managed to cross the Rhine, and if we had any money. We recounted our journey and told him we had very little money left, as I had no more than eighty francs and my companion had only three hundred. He told us to give it to the Mother Prioress, to whom he conducted us straightaway.[16]

This Prioress must have been either Mother Sainte-Marie Laignier or Mother Edmond-Paul de Barth.

> We found her in a village Inn[17] outside the town, with only two novices, because all the religious could not be together for fear of being recognized by the French who occupied the whole of Switzerland. They received us warmly and made us eat with them at midday contrary to the custom of La Trappe where in Lent the meal was not taken until 4.15 pm. The Mother Prioress, knowing that we were religious, began at once to cut out two habits, which we could only tack together, not having the time to sew them properly.[18]

It is interesting to compare these facts written thirty years after the events, with the Register of 'admissions during the journeys'. There we read:

[16] *Relation*, p. 8.

[17] It may seem surprising that a *brasserie* was offered to the religious as a lodging, but here it means the country house of M. Bacciochi. In Bavaria all the country houses or castles belonging to the wealthy classes included a little village and nearly always a farm, gardens and an inn.

[18] *Relation*, p. 8.

> Madeleine-Renée Miel, daughter of Pierre Miel, innkeeper of Champeron, and of Marie Renaud his wife, entered our monastery [!] on 3 April 1798, aged twenty-nine years; being a religious of the Petit-Calvaire in Paris, she has been clothed in our holy habit on 6 April the same year under the name Sister Maur.
>
> Madeleine Janis, daughter of Robert-Philippe Janis, citizen of the town of Rouen, and of Catherine Renaud his wife, entered our monastery, aged forty-three years on the 3 April 1798; being a religious of the Abbey of Arcis in the diocese of Chartres, she has been clothed in our holy habit the 7th day of the same month under the name Sister Thérèse".[19]

Neither of these novices, who seem to have been first cousins on their mother's side, were to make their profession at La Trappe. The second soon left; the first, the younger, did not leave La Trappe until after two years of hardships and journeys. Then she was able to rejoin her 'Petit-Calvaire' in Paris with great joy, having had many numerous adventures.

We shall be meeting Sister Maur again in these pages. Explict details adorn her accounts, which she presented in a lively and picturesque way. On several occasions we find two traits characteristic of her: the extraordinary fascination she had for the Princess de Condé, whom she never called Sister Marie-Joseph, but often referred to Madame Louise; and the thousand remarks to do with the menu and the food, not for the attraction or repulsion it might have had for her, but as the most ordinary daily subject to fill the horizon. I cannot resist the pleasure of quoting one of these passages where these two traits are found together.

Sister Maur had just arrived at La Trappe and as soon as she had received the habit was placed in charge of the novice cook, and also of seeing to the cleaning of and service in the refectory.

[19] *Register* preserved at L. R. (Rivet).

> I asked the Superior if it was true, as I had heard, that Madame the Princess de Condé had entered La Trappe. She told me it was true and moreover that in a few days time the Princess would be here with several other sisters. I expressed my great desire to see her and this was promised. So the day they were to arrive, the Superior came in the morning asking me to prepare a more abundant dinner, not in quality but in quantity, because it was always thin soup and the same dish.
>
> When it was time for dinner, I served it round, but I forgot the Princess. The Mother Prioress noticed, got up from the table and came to make me realize my careless mistake. To tell the truth, I was not in the least upset as this was a good chance to see her. When I came to serve her her portion, I was not at all modest or mortified enough not to look at her. Then I had to prostrate before her, and when I got up, I could again see her face much better, because she was standing up, and as is the custom in that Order, the veil is lowered all the time, even at table and work. But that day I saw her so well that ever since I have never been mistaken.[20]

This little episode informs us that between the sisters living at Fürstenried and those lodging at Augsburg, there was some communication and exchanges, provoked no doubt by administrative processes. Less than fifteen days later, however, the group at Augsburg joined up with those at Fürstenried to prepare for the journey to Austria with all the groups travelling together, before another separation.

THE THIRD GROUP

We can now join the third group who had to close up the first Cistercian-Trappist monastery. The 'shanty' (*bicoque*) was how the Princess de Condé had described it on her first visit to Sembrancher. There is now no trace of it.

[20] *Relation*, p. 9.

There was about a three week interval between the first and the last departures. Time was short as the invaders were already over the border. This last exodus was the most painful. Some years later, it was written down by one of the members of the third group, a forty-year old nun, a former Cistercian from the Abbey of Sainte-Catherine in Avignon, Sister Stanislaus Michel. Her account is lucid, moderate, well-balanced, exact, and always attentive to the reality.

From the beginning the narrator's aim is very clear: to invite her sisters to thanksgiving and fervor. By then she was Sub–prioress at La Riedera, and the community seemed to have found a place where they could settle down.

> We were the last group who left the house of Valais at the beginning of the month of February 1798. We were seventeen, having as superior the Reverend Mother Augustin [de Chabannes]. Mother Sainte-Marie [Laignier] had already left at the head of another group. Here my sisters I will speak only of what happened in our coach; although the charity and unity which reigned among us made our distresses common to all, I can speak more truthfully if I confine myself to those things of which I myself was an eyewitness.[21]

We are informed from the beginning that there will be no fantasies in this recital, but that it will be clear and that the facts put before us will contain few personal commentaries other than some pious suggestions underlining the goodness of God for his erring and shorn sheep and the charity which united them.

> We were destined to go to Germany, but as the French were already spreading terror in the country of Valais,[22] to

[21] The complete text of the account cited here in extract is printed in *Cïteaux* 35 (1984) 199- 214. It is taken from Arch.TR, cote 55, 13 bis.

[22] We have seen that under the instigation of Bonaparte, but also under the pressure of Swiss *émigrés* in France who were fleeing the

> avoid their ferocity, we were obliged to go by remote and roundabout ways and to cross the mountains of Switzerland over some rocky heights which were enough to intimidate even the most intrepid.

We should not be unduly surprised at the terror the revolutionary armies could arouse in these religious, hunted down as they were by the laws which had forced them to leave their monasteries, not to mention the memories of the prisons where one or more of them had been held, and the scaffolds which had not spared some of their sisters. Mother Stanislaus in Avignon, was at the gates of Orange where thirty-two religious (among them two nuns from Sainte-Catherine) had been guillotined in July 1794. They could not forget these horrors and moreover, it was common knowledge that the Revolutionary soldiers had to subsist by looting,and that they did not deprive themselves of anything.

Berne had been surrounded and taken, so the third group of nuns could not follow the same route as the first two groups. The monks and nuns of Sembrancher having reached Martigny, instead of going again towards Lake Neuchâtel, entered the valley of the Rhône as far as the Furka and Andermatt Pass. After that point two routes were possible: the more direct over Altdorf; the longer by way of the Oberalp Pass and the Rhine Valley. The narrative does not give any clearer details. Such a roundabout trek represented between four hundred and five hundred km, caused by climbing and descending with the obvious detours and indecisions about which way to go—all this in February

---

aristocracy in power in certain cantons, the *Directoire* itself decided to intervene in Switzerland. 'The French troops were led to make a double expedition against Berne, the principal aristocratic canton and the principal element of the confederation, and imposed on it a new constitution on 6 March . . . The Swiss Republic was created 12 April 1798'. (C. Pouthas, *Le mouvement des nationalités en Europe*, fasc.II (Paris: CDU, 1946) p. 76.

and March, at altitudes where the cold can bite severely. We can believe Mother Stanislaus when she describes this long month of peregrinations over the mountains:

> The carriages were not able to make the grade, so some of us were obliged to travel on foot, others on mules. I leave you to imagine the tribulations we went through on this first journey; women little accustomed to walking or riding, did one hundred-forty leagues over steep mountains, covered in snow and ice, bordered by hair-raising chasms the sight of which alone was terrifying; for if one fell, there was no way out, and long tracks so narrow that often there was only just room for the mule. We had to walk more than a month like this, always with death before our eyes because of the obvious dangers of where we were, suffering a great deal from the cold, the rigors of the season and hunger, not finding anywhere to stop during the day and often walking quite late before arriving at unpleasant inns. However, thanks be to Providence we never wanted for necessities and even several times we met charitable people who kindly received and helped us.
>
> Finally in the middle of March we arrived in the town of Constance . . . On arriving we found our Reverend Father, who had been waiting for us a long time. This meeting compensated for all our ills and fatigue, filling us with consolations. After having stayed several days with him, our confidence and hope was renewed of preserving our '*saint état*'. We then left him to go to a castle 'near Augsburg' [another hand has crossed out Augsburg on the manuscript and put above it: Munich].

We can ask whether this refers to the castle of Bacciochi or Fürstenried? I think the last, because M. Stanislaus added: 'where we found some of our sisters who had left before us. We were all reunited with great joy, and *we stayed there for Holy Week and Easter*'. As we saw above, when Sister Maur and her companion asked to be admitted at Augsburg, it was the beginning of Holy Week, and only the prioress of the place and two novices were there.

Last Weeks in Bavaria

About this time the long-awaited reply arrived from Russia. Sister Marie-Joseph wrote and told her father of it in a letter dated 14 April:

> I forgot to tell you that, being near Augsburg (castle Bacciochi) and knowing on the whole that political affairs were getting more and more entangled, and that these countries were not without anxiety, I thought it my duty to write again to the Empress of Russia, thinking that perhaps my letter had not reached you where I addressed it. It is only now that she had replied to my last letter (of 15 February), telling me that she did not receive the first letter. She was good enough to send an express messenger, a young officer, with orders to accompany me and take good care of me—of a Trappist—Imagine!
>
> Well, no matter, this man (the Baron de Stoose) had brought me the help of some money, passports and the permission to take into Russian Poland fifteen monks and fifteen nuns, to Orsha, where his Majesty the Emperor willingly allows us a refuge in a former convent of the Trinitarians.

Further on she adds: 'We shall leave without delay, embarking on the Danube with the Reverend Father Abbot at our head'.

Actually they had to wait a good three weeks because Sister Marie-Joseph was still at Fürstenried on 7 May, as we can see from an important document drafted at the request of Dom Augustin, dated and signed by the Princess, and countersigned by the Father Abbot. This document explains that even though she has a refuge in Russia for thirty members of her Order, there still remained in Bavaria seven or eight times as many of their brothers and sisters in religion whose situation was far from being resolved. Dom Augustin hoped that all could eventually find a refuge in Russia. Meanwhile he had to arrange some sort of security for them, and we know how precarious this was in Bavaria.

On May sixth, Prince Charles-Théodore, who had put his castle at Fürstenried at the disposition of the daughter of the Prince de Condé, wrote her the following letter:[23]

Madame,

I am charmed to have been able to oblige Your Highness by facilitating the Means to continue your projected Journey and cooperate in your religious purpose which does Honor to your Virtues and way of thinking. I would like at the same time to find a favorable Occasion, so that I can assure you, Madame, of the subsequent marks of my Desire to be useful to your Designs, and I will not fail to prove to those whom you leave behind and for whom you are solicitous, the Sentiments of Consideration that I hold for your Recommendation.

In reiterating my wishes for your happy journey, I have the honor to be,

Madame De V.A. Munich 6 May 1798.

Your very affectionate Cousin and Servant
Charles Théodore

The last three lines and the signature are in the handwriting of the Prince Elector himself.

Taking advantage of the evident good will of her host, the Princess wrote out the document to which I alluded above:

We Louise-Adelaide de Bourbon-Condé, in religion Sister Marie-Joseph, having given and hereby giving, if the case arises; to M. le Chevalier de Lamorte[24] titular *aide de*

[23] Original in the archives of the Benedictines of Limon-Vauhallan. We have respected the expressions, spelling, punctuation and capitals of the original.

[24] In the article 'Les Cisterciens français émigrés en Bavière, 1793–1802' we find mention of 'de la Morte, Chevalier, Trappiste. In September 1795 his admission for Dürnast is extended. Perhaps he is the one who, generously fulfilling the wishes of Madame de Condé, founded this refuge

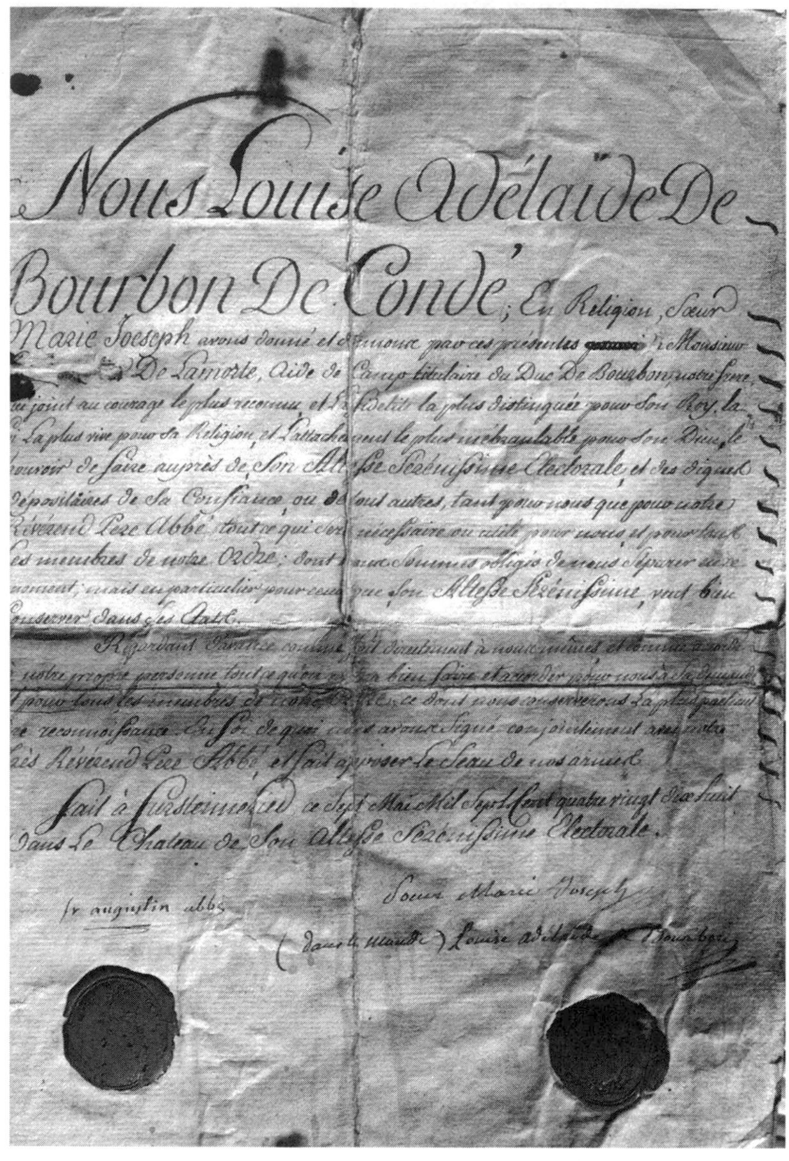

Nous Louise Adélaïde De Bourbon De Condé; En Religion, Sœur Marie Joseph avons donné et donnons par ces présentes [illegible] Monsieur De Lamorte, Aide de Camp titulaire du Duc De Bourbon notre frère qui joint au courage le plus reconnu et la fidelité la plus distinguée pour son Roy, la [illegible] la plus vive pour sa Religion, et l'attachement le plus inébranlable pour son Dieu, le pouvoir de faire auprès de Son Altesse Sérénissime Electorale, et des dignes dépositaires de sa Confiance, ou de tout autres, tant pour nous que pour notre Révérend Père Abbé tout ce qui est nécessaire ou utile pour nous, et pour tous les membres de notre Ordre; dont [illegible] religieux [illegible] moment, mais en particulier pour ceux que Son Altesse Sérénissime veut bien conserver dans ses Etats.

Regardant comme fait directement à nous mêmes et comme rendu à notre propre personne tout ce qu'on [illegible] bien faire et accorder pour nous [illegible] et pour tous les membres de notre Ordre, ce dont nous conserverons la plus parfaite reconnoissance. En foi de quoi nous avons signé conjointement avec notre très Révérend Père Abbé, et fait apposer le sceau de nos armes.

Fait à Furstenried ce sept Mai Mil Sept Cent quatre vingt dix huit dans le Château de Son Altesse Sérénissime Electorale.

Sœur Marie Joseph

fr augustin abbé

(dans le monde) Louise Adélaïde de Bourbon

Figure 4

Document by Louise Adelaide de Bourbon de Condé

camp of the Duke of Bourbon our brother, who unites the greatest courage and most distinguished fidelity for his King, the most lively faith for his Religion and the most unshakable attachment for his God; the power to act for His Most Serene Highness the Elector and some worthy depositories of His confidence, or all others, for us as for our Reverend Father Abbot, all that is necessary or useful for us and for all the members of our Order, from whom we are obliged to be separated at present, but in particular for those whom His Serene Highness wishes to keep in His States.

Considering as done directly to Ourselves and for our own person all that one would like well to do and grant for us at His command and for all the members of our Order, for which we will retain most particularly our gratitude. In witness thereof we have signed conjointly with our Very Reverend Father Abbot and affixed the seal of our coat of arms.

Given at Fürstenried this seventh day of May in the year one thousand seven hundred and ninety eight in the Château of His Serene Highness the Elector.

Fr. Augustin, Abbot Sister Marie-Joseph
(in the world) Louise-Adélaïde de Bourbon[26]

THE SPIRITUAL LIFE DURING EMIGRATION

In the midst of recounting the many arrangements to ensure the material life and security of these itinerant communities outside their normal environment, it is interesting to capture something of the depth of spirit which animated them.

---

at Dürnast for the monks and nuns of which we will have occasion to speak in the following chapter. In the same article, there is mentioned a Nicolas-Jean Villot, trappist of the Diocese of Dijon. Provided with a medical certificate he went to Passau in August 1798. This stay was lengthened twice, in October 1798 and in March 1799. In October 1798 he obtained the jurisdiction to hear the confessions of the nuns.

[26] The signature is entirely in the hand of Sister Marie-Joseph.

A letter of Sister Marie-Joseph to Father de Bouzonville allows us a quick look at their spiritual sharing which was not interrupted by outward circumstances. The candor and vigor of the exchanges between the novice and the excellent counsellor, who was a Father Rabier, the young sub-prior of La Valsainte, was remarkable:

> Since I have been on the road, my vocation (and I would not have thought it possible) has intensified with even more determination. My God, *as ever infinitely good*, has permitted that we be given a superior whose fervent piety, combined with an honest character, inspires me with respect and confidence. *However, knowing and esteeming his* saint état *he did not conceal from me either the inconveniences or the consequences, which can be feared for certain souls*, and, believe me, I know much more about that now, than all that you told me. I have been acutely struck by what I have learned, and even a little *frightened*, but by no means shaken, (by *frightened*, I mean only in the interior, and not of the austerities which are always such a normal feature of my life). This very feeling of *dread* was caused only by a sort of *involuntary obligation* that I felt *in the center of my soul*, to continue in a way of life which seemed for him the only *one* for me. I said: "But, Reverend Father, you frighten me"; yet I could not take it upon myself to renounce my way of life; *it is the only one . . . where I have found all that my heart desired since the first moment of my religious vocation*. After that I asked him, having made known the merciful ways in which God has *drawn* me to him, *if I could possibly not have been resolved* to give myself to Him without any reservation. He came to the same conclusion on the above as yourself.

And a little further on:

> He especially recommended recollection, prayer, union with God, and above all his holy love. Everything must tend towards this end, he told me. It does not count to be a religious, to be a Trappist, or to practice this or

> that virtue; all that is good, excellent, but only because it all leads to union with God, to his holy love . . . You can sense, Father, by these few words I have quoted, the high-minded conduct taught me, which entails details that are useful and binding . . . I will *never forget* anything of what has been said to me and consequently I will try to act accordingly.[27]

This quotation, perhaps over-long, seems to me to mirror the spiritual climate which these women maintained on their way to a place where, in peace of heart as in a favorable environment, they could continue their assiduous search of God. This letter was written 24 March 1798, hardly two months after their arrival in Bavaria. In another two months the entire flock of the Father Abbot would come together to move towards the Danube.

[27] Lettres de piété ou correspondance intime de Louise-Adelaïde de Bourbon-Condé, t.II, (Paris, 1845) 205–207.

CHAPTER TWO

BAVARIA, AUSTRIA, BOHEMIA, AND RUSSIA

THE REFUGEES WERE RECEIVED in most of the Austrian Empire for only a short stay, particularly in Catholic Bavaria, where the infiltration of revolutionary ideas was feared. The Prince-Elector, Charles Théodore, welcomed monks and nuns in his territories at the request of the Princess de Condé, as we have seen but this was only a provisional refuge. At the time Bavaria was not totally unified. Some estates enclosing private properties still remain; such as the territory of Freising, governed by a Prince-Bishop. On this territory there was an important benedictine abbey, Weihenstephan, which owned, not far from Freising, a summer residence, the castle at Dürnast.[1]

BAVARIA

Dom Augustin discovered that the Chevalier de la Morte had lived in Bavaria for some time, so he considered asking the Prince-Bishop of Freising for a 'temporary residence' for some monks and nuns in poor health who could not undertake the long journey to Russia. In the archives of the archbishop's house in Munich-Freising a letter of Dom Augustin is preserved in which he excuses himself for not

[1] Anton Mayer, *Statistische Beschreibung der Erzbisthums* (Munich-Freising) t. I, ed. Manz (Munich, 1874) points out that there was formerly at Dürnast a palace with a chapel dedicated to Saint Benedict. This two storey palace was sold at auction in 1803.

being able to honor an appointment granted by the Prince-Bishop, because he was called away urgently to Souabe.

The Monks and Nuns who Stayed in Bavaria

The request was granted, as other documents preserved in Munich testify. They are listed as follows by the archivist, Sigmund Benker:[2]

> In file 58 in the Bishop's House in Freising, there is a bundle of letters. The first letter is from the subprior of the benedictine monastery of Weihenstephan, a Brother Raphael Thaller, dated 22 May 1798. It transmits the request of the prioress of the Trappistines still at Dürnast (the others had left by the river Isar). It concerned eight persons, four monks and four nuns, most of them ill.
>
> These members of the Order ask permission to reserve the Blessed Sacrament in the castle where Holy Mass is daily celebrated, also the other Offices as circumstances allow. This request was made in view of the liturgical feasts of Pentecost and Corpus Christi, because it was impossible to have a Corpus Christi procession at Hohenbachern. The Bishop's House granted the request.
>
> On 9 June 1798, the superior Father Bernard,[3] and the prioress, Sister Augustin, presented a petition in French to the Prince-Bishop. The former referred to himself as being from "the Maison-Dieu, La Valsainte, at N.D. de-laTrappe". The prioress, from "the monastery of La Sainte-Volonté-de-Dieu at N.D. de-la-Trappe". Again they asked permission to reserve the Blessed Sacrament.

[2] Archives of the house of the Archbishop of Munich and Freising, file 58, communicated in 1985 by the very obliging archivist Mgr Dr Sigmund Benker to one of the sisters at the abbey of Altbronn. All the following information comes from this source.

[3] Father Bernard Fleury, a monk of La Valsainte. Later, about 1808, he was chaplain of the nuns at Valenta, and he was to be their faithful companion during the hours of dispersion in 1811. He died at La Trappe.

This time the response was negative, because the neighboring parish priest at Vötting, consulted by the bishop, did not think it advisable for various reasons (3 July 1798).

On 24 July, permission was again requested by the Chevalier de la Morte. The file does not contain a reply. It is probable however that the bishop relented, because the refugees had to stay there until April of the following year, and the four nuns received quite a number of postulants.

At first their extreme poverty did not permit them to have chalices or candles, or even a tabernacle which the Chapel of Saint-Benoît lacked. But thanks to the activities of the monks, who wanted to have the Blessed Sacrament reserved as much as the nuns did, their circumstances seem to have improved gradually.

Little by little their life became organized in spite of afflictions within the community. One of the sick sisters died on 3 July, a scant two months after their arrival. Sister Marie-Thérèse Tinturier was twenty-seven years old when she entered La Sainte-Volonté-de-Dieu on 18 September 1796. Professed the following year on 24 October, she did not hesitate to undertake the great adventure towards the East with her sisters. Nevertheless her physical strength was not sufficient and she soon died. The death Register at the parish of Weihenstephan at Vötting, has preserved the record of this premature death.[4]

[4] Here is the translation of the notice about her found in the parish register of Vötting, not far from Dürnast (archives of the archbishop's house at Munich-Freising):

> The Reverend Mother, Dame Marie-Thérèse, of the Congregation of Cistercians, *émigrée* from Seligen Thal [here the writer has misunderstood; he thought that the sisters came from La Valsainte, which he has translated into German as SeligenThal [blessed Valley], and on her way through Bavaria, was at the castle of Dürnast, and has been called from this world by God our Savior after a long illness of her lungs and consumption. After having received the holy sacraments for the dying in this place some time ago, she expired on the 4 July 1798, at 5 o'clock in the morning, at the age of twenty-seven. She

It was the young superior, Mother Augustin de Chabannes, twenty-nine, who bore this shock. During the course of her long life she was to endure many more. She was to be the last survivor of the Trappistines who had gone to Russia when she left this world some fifty years later. We do not know the names of their two other companions.

The sisters were helped by four monks, one probably a lay brother. The superior was Father Bernard Fleury, already mentioned: the other two were a Father François-Joseph, who died 23 March 1799, and almost certainly a Father Nicholas-Jean Villot, who in October 1798 received from the Prince-Bishop the authorization to hear the nuns' confessions and, then in March 1799 an extension of their stay.[5]

Admissions of the Postulants

Under the rubric *entrées en voyage*, the Register tells us that twenty-nine postulants entered at Dürnast between 3 July 1798 and 3 April 1799. The first seven came from the immediate area. From Bavaria itself came three postulants, and two more from Vienna, where they must have seen the arrival of the principal group in the Austrian capital city at the end of May. Two others arrived from Bohemia-Moravia. Only one of these made her profession, Véronique Müller, who came from Olmutz, and entered when she was twenty-eight. She died in Westphalia in 1821.

---

has been buried in the habit of her Order alongside the cross in the cemetery of Saint-Ulrich at Hohenbachern. P. Corbinian Zaubzer. I am grateful for this translation to Sister Jean-Baptiste Moshenross].

In the same register the death of a child of the Third Order is noted: Brother Bruno, age seven years, on the first of June 1798, and of Franciscus Joseph Letoudal, religious of the monastery of N.D.-de-La-Valsainte, on the 23 March 1799, buried in the same place.

[5] See D. Norbert Baeckmund, O.Prae., 'Les Cisterciens français émigrés en Bavière', p.143.

The twenty-two other postulants were emigrants from various regions of France: Lille, Bergures, Amiens, Rouen, Paris, Gisors, Sens, Dijon, Dôle, Besançon, Reiningue, Grenoble. Nine of them were already religious. Three sisters of the Annunciation (*Annonciades célestes*) arrived together; one Ursuline and one Carmelite came from Amiens. All five died as Trappistines. One other Carmelite, two Benedictines and a Capuchin withdrew, either at Dürnast or during the journey back towards the west.

The Register does not note the former situation of the other thirteen. Only three made profession in the Order, after a time of probation which varied in length. Others left at Dürnast. Despite all this, some eighteen or twenty sisters took the road for Russia in April 1799. We will catch up with them again at the Lithuanian castle near Brest-Litvosk.

AUSTRIA AND BOHEMIA

The Departure

The eight monks and nuns taking refuge at Dürnast were only a very small part from the 'flock' of the Father Abbot. There were more than two-hundred others, divided into groups spread out across Bavaria. We must now bring them together. In fact, some approaches made under the protection of the Princess de Condé had succeeded in obtaining a collective passport which authorized all the monks and nuns to enter the Austrian Empire.

We left nearly all the nuns at the castle of Fürstenried, expecting Russia to be the first place to welcome them, a welcome mixed with reserve and giving much matter for reflection. And this was just what Sister Marie-Joseph was doing. She revealed her anxieties to her best friend and confident outside the Order, Father de Bouzonville. She wrote to him from Fürstenried on 18 April:

> The longed for responses have arrived at last by an express messenger, who has been instructed to take my *orders* for the whole journey. These sovereigns have only a vague idea who this Sister Marie-Joseph might be. We have been granted, but only as a refuge, a former convent of Trinitarians in the town of Orsha on the frontiers of Galicia in Russian Poland (White Russia) for fifteen monks and fifteen nuns. The Reverend Father flatters himself that when we are there, it will be a great success, but we must wait and abandon ourselves to Providence.
>
> I myself feel a great need for resignation at the moment, because I shall be separated from the help and support of the respected Superior of whom I spoke about in my last letter, and whom the Reverend Father will not take with us. Ah! yes my Father, it is a great loss for me and I feel it deeply. In spite of everything however, I do not cease to have confidence in Jesus Christ. In Jesus Christ is all my hope. Pray much for me, I beg you.[6]

After recalling her letter of 24 March, quoted in the preceding chapter, and expressing the gratitude she had in her heart for her correspondent, she added a postscript: 'We will leave immediately after the return of our Reverend Father.

Actually, Dom Augustin was busily trying to get the groups altogether, indicating the place and time to assemble, so that everyone would be ready to cross the frontier between Bavaria and Austria in a single group. In theory, this was to be at Passau on the Danube.

On 14 April, Sister Marie-Joseph wrote to her father, the Prince de Condé:

> Only a fixed number (as one might expect) will go to the Russian States, but the actual situation obliges us to try to benefit from all the rest of the passports I received from Vienna. These allow the Trappists, with the Princess Louise de Condé, to pass through the States of the Empire, and if need be to reside there. We know very well that this

[6] *Lettres de piété*, p. 210.

only refers to short stays, but Providence will provide. I am also relying on it for our stay in Russia, because, just between us, I do not have all I desire, even though I truly realise the goodness of their Majesties in all this. What I want is an establishment, something very different from a simple refuge for a fixed number, which does not admit any possibility of receiving new members, or of receiving valid professions; but for the moment we can only be grateful.

A little further on she adds:

> I will send this letter to you by the Russian envoy at Regensburg, the Comte d'Alopeus, whom I cannot praise enough. Faithful to the intention in his heart and full of goodness towards me since my stay near Augsburg, this minister will charge someone, with all the delicacy that one used to call French, to watch and see whether events could place me in such circumstances that he would be able to make me some offers of assistance, awaiting the outcome of the most unmistakable and noble intentions of his Sovereign. Upon my reply, as sincere as it was grateful, he made me a gift of three thousand florins.[7]

In this way 'the poor of Jesus Christ' were to have something to complement the largesse of their host, Charles-Théodore. Because the aged Elector and his entourage could see they were obliged to aid the departure of these refugees whom the population wished to see gone, he ordered two flat-bottomed boats to be constructed in haste. Each had a cabin, destined to convey the monks and nuns then lodging at Fürstenried towards the Danube. Carriages took the travellers seven kilometres to Munich. There they embarked on the Isar, which flows into the Danube a little above Passau, and continued to navigate towards Passau, Linz, and Vienna.

[7] *Correspondance*, éd. Rabory, p. 186.

On the Danube

We possess several original accounts of this voyage but not all the statements agree. It seems difficult and even useless to try to harmonize them, because these various accounts were drawn from memory, some eight, ten or thirty years later, and the facts observed did not necessarily come from the same point of view, or from the same group on the same boat; the whole fleet on this part of the voyage numbered at least seven boats.

Mother Stanislaus Michel says of their trip down the Danube:

> Some time after [Easter], we left [Fürstenried] to go to the town of Linz [corrected in another hand to Passau], where all the groups of monks and nuns were gathered together. This was when our joy equalled our sadness, the charity which united hearts gave us so much consolation at being together again. It was a most edifying spectacle and quite remarkable to see so many monks and nuns; because we were, according to what the Reverend Father said to me, about two hundred persons[8] who undertook the long voyage to Russia, without any resources or help other than that of Providence.
>
> As we were on our boats, some in one, some in another, we went along singing the Office, the monks in their boat formed one choir and we in ours made up the other. There was nothing more touching than this novel sight. Astonished crowds gathered along the banks of the river, and what they saw caused various reactions: for some,

[8] The number varies with the documents and the places. Two hundred appears to be the minimum. We know only that the constant changing of persons in the groups made it very difficult to have an exact census, most of all during the period of exile when there was the grief of leaving the sick behind at various stopping points, and deaths. On the other hand, new members joined the first groups leaving Switzerland: monks, nuns, lay people and even children. More than one person dropped out along the way, leaving the pitiable caravan to continue on its way.

compassion, being very upset to see so many religious in exile, obliged to flee like this to foreign countries to avoid persecution and *conserver son état*; others made fun of us or held us in contempt. This is what we had to endure in the various places we went through.[9]

In quite another vein is the account of Sister Maur. The circumstances and details are different, and some of them are not without relish and explicit, so we can more closely participate in this rather out of the ordinary adventure.

When all the monks and nuns of La Trappe were reunited, about a hundred of us at least, we left in carriages with all our luggage, not knowing where we were going. After several days on the road, we were put into seven or eight boats. I cannot remember the name of the river, but it seemed to me to be the Danube. We sang the Office in our boats, except for Matins, which was said in a low tone.

For our meals, the boats were drawn closely together and our pittances could be passed over in buckets. When we would arrive at a town in the evening, we passed the night in some religious house if there was one, or at the inn. In spite of our large number, we did not create much trouble, because we slept on the floor. We had each brought with us a blanket and workbag which served as a pillow; we put half our blanket under our habits which were white, and thus slept perfectly well. Madame the Princess was always very active and very vigilant. Next morning, the Father Abbot said Holy Mass in some Church, during which we would sing the litanies of the Sacred Heart and at the end of the Mass the *Salve Regina*. When we arrived in a village, we slept in some barns. Often it happened that at the time for our meal we could not find a place, so then the good Fathers had to walk around a village buying something to make a dinner for all of us, and this was no small undertaking. After that it all had to be prepared and cooked. This could make us four or five

[9] *Relation* in the article in *Cîteaux* 34, pp. 202–203.

hours late. Also the Father Abbot sent us to have a siesta. I forgot to mention that he heard our confessions even in the boats.[10]

As for Father François de Paule Dargnies, he seems to have lived these days on the river as a dilettante and a poet; for once it does not matter, because there is a certain pleasure in reading these lines and perhaps hearing within us the murmur of the melody of the *Blue Danube*.

I had the satisfaction of contemplating at leisure the delightful spectacle that was afforded us along the enchanting banks of the Danube. I have never seen anything so pleasant or more picturesque, from Passau to Vienna. I do not speak of the artificial beauty of these sumptuous and magnificent buildings, of these classic parks, of these pleasure gardens, of these well-laid out plantations which form the precincts of a town more than a league away; but I speak of the simple beauties of nature. We were in the month of May, all the trees were in flower, the green leaves just starting to unfurl, the twittering of birds could be heard everywhere, the sky was pure and calm during the day, and the night agreeably fresh, compensating for the scorching sun. Sometimes we boated between two chains of steep rocks completely covered with thousands of flowering bushes; sometimes on one side these perpendicular rocks seemed to threaten to fall on us, while on the other side a vast plain offered us a view of the most splendid open countryside. But, I am exhausting in vain, my little bag of eloquence . . . to paint for you the various scenes that nature seems to take pleasure in offering to our gaze. All I can say is that I would like to be there again to relish and savor the pleasure I experienced: and if there was something I missed most about our journeys, it is particularly the banks of the Danube.[11]

[10] *Relation* S.M., p. 10–11.

[11] Mémoires D., letter 17, p. 92. Nicolas-Claude Dargnies, son of Jacques-Antoine, barrister-at-law in Parliament, and of Henriette-Vic-

The letter continues, but this time in another tone. It mentions the incident of the boats of monks and nuns drawing close together to sing in two choirs at the time of the Office, as Mother Stanislaus had noted. It seems that this custom was not continued. At least this is the account of our friend Dargnies, which is not without humor and a hint of misogyny.

> The Father Abbot, having assembled everyone on rafts, the monks and nuns separately, thought that we could sing the Office in two choirs, one composed of monks, the other of nuns. For this reason he had their barge tied to ours, and made us all come out of our cabin.[12] We started to sing the psalms alternatively in a loud voice. This was, I believe, the first time the banks of the Danube had echoed the praises of the Lord in this place. Happily the multitude of faults made in the course of the Office was a cause of far more distraction than edification, so this first time was also the last. The Reverend Father did not judge it fit to continue, which gave me a great deal of pleasure. Because in addition to making our burden much harder to bear, the arrangement was not without certain inconveniences caused by bringing together the two sexes, even though there was a little distance between them. The sirens, even though they sang from afar, were no less fatal to the sailor!

Daily Life Going Downstream

Still following our narrator, who expands the sparing description of our first documents with some lively details of

---

toire Bouteillier his wife, native to the parish Saint-André of Abbeville in Picardy, diocese of Amiens. At the time of the Revolution, he had retired to La Trappe in Switzerland about six years before, and had been a professed monk for four years. He had weak health and was subject to severe pains in the chest (from the chronicle of the Visitandines at Vienna).

[12] The boats were equipped with a cabin, where the sick and the weakest were usually cared for, and of which Father François de Paule had particular charge as infirmarian of the 'colony'.

life on this 'mobile monastery', 'because', he said, 'this is what we can call our barges, since we could observe exactly the same regularities as in the monastery.'

> As we were provided with all the necessities of life, we went ashore only very rarely, even for sleeping, and almost always we had our meals on board. We travelled on Sundays and feast days as on other days, except that on these days we always tried to arrange to find some Church near the banks if we could, to go and to say Mass, which we did sometimes even during the week. This is approximately the order we followed.
>
> Arriving at the place indicated, the Reverend Father went ashore to go to see the parish priest, or he delegated two monks who were priests, to ask permission to celebrate Mass. This was never refused, which is something well worth remarking, since we will never know how to thank God enough. For in all our travels, even in Protestant countries, the priests were never deprived of the happiness of saying holy Mass, at least on Sundays and feasts, and the community with him, to partake of holy Communion. Also at the same time we have never wanted, for one single day, the necessary bread for our moderate subsistence.
>
> The Reverend Father informed us shortly ahead of time that we were going to disembark, so that at the signal everyone was ready. Then according to rank, we went ashore. The Reverend Father at the head, we progressed sedately two by two, first the monks, the lay brothers, and then the children, followed by the nuns in the same order. As we went along, the novelty of such a spectacle attracted an incredibly large crowd. When we arrived at the Church we often had trouble entering as it was already full. After having satisfied our devotion, we came out in the same order and went back to our barges, always accompanied by a huge crowd of people. Something that I cannot refrain from admiring and attributing to the particular protection of the Blessed Virgin, in whose honor we have never for a single day missed singing the *Salve*, is that, in the large towns where often there was very little religion, even

> among the Protestants, we were exposed to a considerable crowd of the populace, but never have we been insulted. Rather, on the contrary most of the people have shown us a great deal of compassion, and the children have always returned to the boats laden with bread and money. I have indeed, it is true, heard some talk which implies that our manner of travelling invites abuse; and again that these rumors were said half jokingly *sotto voce* without loud laughter.[13]

We do not know exactly how long the journey as far as Passau took. The barrier at the frontier did not open easily to a collective passport. The police had misgiving at seeing such a crowd of unidentifiable refugees. Suspicious, they sent a Commissary to Vienna to verify the authenticity of the passport. The travellers had to wait about twelve days. They did, however, get permission to go on as far as Wilhering, nine km upstream from Linz, where there was a cistercian monastery. Here they found hospitality until the return of the Commissary.

Branching off Towards Bohemia

Doubtless it was there that arrangements were made for another division of the nuns .We come back again to the account of Sister Stanislaus Michel, always succinct and usually accurate:

> We were then landed like this at Linz on the eve of Pentecost [26 May 1798]. We went straight into a church where we sang the *Salve*, the most beautiful and solemn

[13] Mémoires D., letter 17. These 'jokes' were aimed at the processions. Some people found it very peculiar to see men, women and children in uniform. In their minds this could only suggest a family relationship. Dom Augustin, having learned of this, had only the monks and children march in procession. The nuns were hidden from view and taken to their destination in carriages.

I ever heard. From there we were conducted to an inn where we spent the feast. Here we were separated into groups again with many tears. The Reverend Father had obtained permission to establish his Order in Russia, but they had fixed the number of persons who could go there. Consequently, we had to form three groups again, and Mother Sainte-Marie [Laignier] was among those destined to go to Orsha in White Russia, to a monastery which had been granted them; the two other groups were bound for Bavaria[14] and Bohemia. Our group was destined to go to Bohemia, to a castle near Prague belonging to the Prince de Deux-Ponts. We were about fourteen or fifteen with Mother Sainte-Marie as superior.

This was the castle of Buštěrhad, in the borough of Kladmo, northwest of Prague. It was the personal property of the emperor of Austria, with a castle and large inn.[15] A colony of monks with a Father Urbain Guillet at their head was sent a little later to Kladno, leaving for Krems and going by road, whereas the group of nuns travelled by water on the Moldau. Sister Stanislaus recounts briefly the journey, giving a lot of space to a very popular saint in Bohemia:

We embarked on the Mulde (*Moldau*), a river remarkable for the martydom of Saint John Nepomuck.[16] It was into

[14] In reality the 'colony' destined for Bavaria stayed at Dürnast, as I have already indicated, but there were still three 'colonies': those destined for Bohemia and then Russia, and the rest who had to stay on in Vienna, awaiting another destination. We shall be seeing them again later on.

[15] *Herder Konversation Lexicon* (1903) t. II: col. 389. It seems that Sister Stanislaus was mistaken in attributing the possession of this castle to the Prince de Deux-Ponts, who owned the castle of Fürstenried in Bavaria, as we saw above.

[16] The narrator was impressed by the legends which supported popular devotion to this saint, whose very existence has sometimes been contested. This was a holy priest John, confessor of the Empress Jeanne, who steadfastly refused to reveal the contents of her confession to the Emperor Wenceslas. The exasperated Emperor, after putting him in prison, had him tied up and thrown at night into the river which supplied water to the city of Prague.

these waters that his holy body was thrown and after his death he appeared above the waters, brilliant with light. I can tell you that this recollection animated my devotion for this great saint; and nearing Prague, where his holy body rests and is held in great veneration, I prayed to him with all my heart. This great saint is very much honored in Germany, Bohemia, and Poland, and it was consoling to see his image so often along the roads. It was in the month of May that we arrived at this place. We stayed here for five months, overwhelmed with the generosity of the prince and the archduchess.[17]

Two months after their arrival they experienced a very sad incident that Sister Stanislaus does not mention, but which we know about from records in two Registers. Sister Anne (Claudine Petit), from Seurre in the diocese of Besançon, who had entered Sembrancer on the 8 July 1797, aged twenty-seven, fell ill and made her profession on her deathbed 26 July 1798. She was laid on straw and ashes according to old monastic custom. And on the 10th of August she went to God. It is very moving to look at the Register *Des professions qui ont été faites dans les voyages en danger de mort depuis le 26 juillet 1798*, and see the trembling signature of Sister Marie-Anne Petit on her profession, which had been written by another hand. This Register was kept by a Father Fayt, who accompanied the group. He was a priest who had associated with the Trappists of La Trappe without joining the monastic Order, but by his experience and wisdom he had won the confidence of the Father Abbot. The superior of the group, Mother Sainte-Marie Bigaux,

[17] The Archduchess Marie-Anne, who received the group of Mother Sainte-Marie Bigaux at Busterhad, was a Habsbourg-Lorraine, the youngest sister of the Emperor of Austria, Francis II, and of Marie-Antoinette. Furthermore, we know by the *Vie de la princesse de Condé* that the Princess de Condé and the Archduchess met in Vienna in 1796, whence the affectionate interest lavished on the trappistine sisters by the Archduchess during their stay at Busterhad. [It is probable that this refuge was obtained by the mediation of Sister Marie-Joseph].

signed the schedule with him, as did a Brother Louis. We shall meet them again in the next chapter.

Arrival in Vienna

While Bohemia welcomed them for a time, Austria also received temporarily the 'colony' destined for Russia and about twelve other nuns who would not be going East just yet. Two days after Pentecost, on 29 May 1798, after the stop at Linz, the boats again drifted down the Danube and arrived without delay in Vienna. From the village where the boats moored, not far from town, Dom Augustin, accompanied by Sister Marie-Joseph, went to the convent of the Visitation by coach to request the hospitality of the nuns for his communities.

'After having travelled many days by water,' Sister Maur tells us, 'we took some coaches and arrived in Vienna in Austria . . . and we went to the monastery of the Visitation in this city, a very large and very beautiful monastery where the princesses of Austria are educated.'

Dom Augustin, in fact, came back with several carriages and made the nuns get inside to guard them from public view. During this time, the monks, lay brothers, the Third Order, and children filed in procession along the boulevards, going like this through part of the city to reach the Visitation monastery. In this stronghold of the philosopy of enlightenment, the sight caused a sensation.

The Reception at the Monastery of the Visitation

Two letters of Sister Marie-Joseph—one to her father on 6 June, the other to Father de Bouzonville on 25 July, allow us to reconstruct the stages of the emigrants' arrival and stay in Vienna of the whole group of emigrants on the way to Russia. To Father de Bouzonville she gives some details on their choice of lodgings.

> No doubt you will be astonished that once again I am at the Visitation.[18] I am not less astonished than you; but on approaching Vienna, we had to find someone we knew. I was not able to suggest to our Reverend Father anyone but Madame de Fossière. She offered us a shelter for the three or four days we had thought to stay, and instead of that we have stayed until now, but we leave the day after tomorrow for the famous Orsha in White Russia. We stayed some time in a suburban house, rented since to the Princess de Lorraine, and then with your good friend Mademoiselle Joseph. I saw these ladies only twice and I would not have been sorry to see them more often so that I could say all over again that I prefer to be a Trappist than a Visitandine. We have much to thank them for, except that they put butter in our food, which seemed to me now like eating pure grease. I much prefer our vegetable fricassees. In all, I am happy with what we are doing, to the point that I pretend, and it is very true, that I lead a very pleasant life and that I enjoy myself. This statement is definitely ridiculous, I know, but my own father has always said to me that I was a little ridiculous and not like the others.[19]

Sister Maur, however, was not of the same opinion about the food:

> Father Abbot told the Mother Superior that we did not eat meat or fish and that our food was cooked only in salt and water. She replied that in that case she would not give us meat or fish, but for the rest we would do as the Apostles

[18] After a first short stay in the Valais in the spring of 1796, Madame de Condé arrived in Vienna during the summer and stayed at the Visitation monastery until she obtained from her director, Father de Bouzonville, authorization to enter La Trappe. She left Vienna about the middle of 1797 and entered Sembrancher on 26 September.

[19] Letter of 25 July 1798.

did, eat whatever was served us. So all the time we stayed there we did not fare as Trappists, because our portions were made only with butter and milk, and twice a week we had pastries.[20]

After 6 June Madame Louise gave her father other details of the hospitality at the Visitation:

The convent of the Visitation gave us lodging but outside; we say some of our Office in the part of the Church open for the people, and an incredibly large crowd appeared. The people seemed to view us favorably enough. The courtyards we have to cross are full and the Church is packed, so much so that last Sunday (3 June) they were obliged to have guards. Believe me that this reminded me of the feasts at Versailles, except that instead of being Madame the Princess de Condé, I am behind Sister Dorothée in rank, and instead of being aware of signs and glances of approval that someone might give to my youth and finery, I notice an air of respect for my new state, for my habit. Finally instead of that sort of embarrassment and timidity which was natural to me in public, I feel proud to show myself clothed in the livery of Jesus Christ, or rather it gives me so much happiness that if it were allowed, I would like to cry out in a loud voice: "If only you knew the gift of God".[21]

Royal Encounters

In the same letter, Sister Marie-Joseph recounted with her customary spontaneity an occurrence that happened to her that day:

This morning I made the acquaintance of the Empress in unbelievable circumstances.[22] You have to be a Trappist

[20] *Relation* S. M., p. 12.

[21] Letter of 6 July 1798.

[22] The Empress, wife of Francis II.

> for that. She had heard our Mass inside the convent, and I did not know it. As we were going through the courtyards through the crowds to get to our lodgings, the Reverend Father stopped me under an arcade where from under my veil (which was lowered) I had only noticed some people standing against the walls to watch us pass. He said to me: "Look, there is the Empress coming out of the convent and she would like very much to see you. Stop and speak to her." I looked up and saw coming towards me a young lady who was only three steps from us. I must say I was extremely astonished at this sort of presentation, the opposite to what I would have had take place. Actually, she seemed very pleased with what I said, and was herself very talkative and obliging on what concerned us. She did not refer to my healthy appearance, in spite of our way of life (for all who see me it is the same), treating me much more as a princess and highness than as Sister Marie-Joseph.[23]

A similiar encounter deeply affected the heart of Sister Maur. This was a meeting with Princess Marie-Thérèse, daughter of Louis XVI, a young orphan who was a prisoner in the Temple after her father's execution on 21 January 1793 and that of her mother, Marie-Antoinette, in October. The princess had been exchanged in 1796 for some Republican prisoners and returned to her Austrian mother's family.

'We were notified', recounts Sister Maur, 'that we were going to see Madame Première, daughter of Louis XVI. Actually she came to visit Madame the Princess de Condé and she wished to see the entire community. Joy and sorrow were in my heart at seeing again this princess. Thinking of her misfortunes and those of France, I could not believe that she had escaped the impious hands that had shed the blood of her august father, her mother, and her aunt (Madame Elisabeth)'.[24]

[23] Letter of 6 June 1798.

[24] *Relation* S. M., p. 11.

The stop at Vienna which was supposed to have lasted only for a few days was drawn out. What happened?

Only thirty monks and nuns were authorized to enter Russia. Dom Augustin stepped up his efforts to assure a home, at least provisionally, for the still quite numerous monks and nuns who had to stay on the Austrian border. He counted on the benevolence of Francis II, which was evident from the beginning, but the Emperor was not master in his own domains. As Sister Marie-Joseph said to Father de Bouzonville on 26 July:

> The reception of our Reverend Father by their Imperial Majesties [of Austria] and their kind dispositions, gave us hopes of an establishment, but the Ministers were only disposed to allow us a simple refuge in Bohemia. The Revered Father paid a short visit [and had been enchanted, as you can well believe] with our good archduchess Marie-Anne who supports us with all her heart.

As early as the sixth of June the activities of the Father Abbot created a presentiment that the departure for Russia would be delayed. Sister Marie-Joseph said as much to her father:

> I am just writing to the Empress of Russia to inform her of the reasons for our delay in arriving in her territories, which may surprise her after all the goodwill she has given to this business. When our affairs here are settled to our advantage, as I hope, and you will be informed, I would like (if you have kept in touch with the Emperor)[25] that you write a word of appreciation.

[25] The Prince de Condé, who had fought on the side of Austria against the revolutionary armies, had been requested by the Tsar to come back to Russia as early as January 1797. As early as 1793, Catherine II had offered Condé a command in her army or an establishment in the Crimea. Her son followed this movement of resistance and opened up a harbor for the army of Condé in Volhynie. (cf. *Vie de la princesse Louise de Condé* by Rabory, p. 232).

ON THE WAY TO RUSSIA

Departure

On 25 July, two days before the departure for Orsha, Dom Augustin reserved to himself the task of guiding the double colony as far as the place that had been offered them, with the hope of going on to Saint Petersburg to obtain other houses from the Tsar, since all hopes of founding monasteries in Austria and Bohemia had fallen through.

The Abbot named as prior of the group of monks a Father Etienne Malmy and put him in charge of watching over the material and spiritual needs of the nuns at Orsha. The nuns had as superior Mother Sainte-Marie Laignier, already mentioned several times. Among the others we are able to identify, in addition to Sister Marie-Joseph and five novices who left their schedules of profession at Orsha: Sister Madeleine Guyot, Sister Benoît Isambert, Sister Marie-Madeleine Zacharie, and Sister Jean-Baptiste Chassaignon, all of whom entered at Sembrancher, and Sister Julie Favot who entered at Augsburg. Two other novices did not stay in the Order: Sister Brigitte de La Rozière and Sister Maur Miel. The first left at Orsha, the second at Danzig.

Thanks to Sister Maur we have some interesting details of the journey to Russia and life at Orsha over about eighteen months. Before they left, the Father Abbot redistributed the group lodged at the Visitation, and Sister Maur found herself separated from Sister Thérèse Janis, the companion who had been with her until then. The fifteen nuns destined to go to Russia left behind them in Vienna about ten sisters who formed a fourth community. Of the two other groups, one was in Bavaria at Dürnast and the other in Bohemia at Busterhad. Sister Maur had the good fortune to be destined for Russia with Madame Louise. The departure took place on 27 July:

> Our group travelled to Russia sometimes by water, sometimes by road, stopping at all the towns along the way.

Every time we disembarked from the river, a huge crowd gathered on the banks to watch us, following us everywhere we went, because we had on our religious habits, an altogether strange sight for these people. It was only in convents, [when we could find them] that we were left undisturbed . . .

Finally, we arrived in Poland and stopped at Cracow, the capital of the whole Kingdom. As it was morning, we went to hear holy Mass in the church of the Dominicans in this city. Although it was so big, the church was immediately filled with countless people who, having learned of our arrival and our misfortunes, came bringing us alms as to the poor, which we truly were, including Madame the Princess who was not recognized. She was so overjoyed at receiving alms that she could not keep silent! Next we went on to Warsaw, where a Polish Princess instantly implored our Princess to stay several days with her and her companions.[26]

A Stopover in Warsaw

A letter of Sister Marie-Joseph to her father, the Prince de Condé, written on 21 August 1798 (Tuesday), describes some incidents of this stay in Warsaw. She had to give this letter to a woman whose name she did not know, but who had been sent to her by her father. This lady was to take her letter along with some other news. The Princess spoke of 'her wandering life, so little to my taste and so oddly in harmony with my ideals. I think that never has anyone seen so much tribulation and been obliged to make so many journeys to become a religious. I assure you, a counter-revolution would not cause as much trouble. May God grant that Orsha will be the place where I can finally achieve my constant aspirations, but I do not presume to delude myself too much again. Tell me then, where on this earth is there

[26] *Relation* S. M., p. 14–15.

a place where a monastery is tolerated; no matter where it is, I will go, because the difficulties do not discourage me anymore than they do you'.

Many of her companions shared this inflexible determination to find a place where they could be permanently dedicated to God. We see here the secret of an existence sustained by the grace of the call that nothing could extinguish. This is clearly proved by the way in which most of these courageous women ended their lives.

Let us return to Warsaw, where the travellers arrived on Saturday, 18 August. Sister Marie-Joseph continues her letter:

> We have been here since Saturday. We were only going to stay two or three days, but when we arrived, the Reverend Father, who had quite carefully made all the arrangements for his monks and nuns in the Tsar's States [unfortunately not as the personal goodwill of this sovereign had at first given us to hope for], the Reverend Father, as I said, found here some letters which told him about endeavors and intrigues of persons of ill-will trying to destroy everything that had been arranged. As he was very zealous, he did not hesitate to leave immediately for Vienna, so we are waiting here for him. He is travelling day and night and hopes to be back within two weeks. Our small community is lodged in an apartment of the Princess Schannvland [I think] or perhaps it is some other name, who is the sister or sister-in-law or maybe a cousin [this is all I know] of the king of Poland, who is perhaps living or perhaps dead [I know nothing more]. In any case for all these sorts of questions, it is really comic to talk about these things when one is a mother of La Trappe. I can see you laughing at this word 'comic', which you can hardly imagine goes with my way of life, and that travelling does not make it in any respect any less austere, as they say in the world. I assure you that I do not find the life sad, and in spite of everything it pleases me and makes me happier than I can say, to the point that without saying it, I am often merrier than I should be.

And, as if she wanted to give her father some evidence of this, she added these light-hearted lines:

> This lady whom you know and I do not, will be able to tell you that she found me old and ugly, but certainly not appearing in bad health. Also she will be able to add that she has seen me eating my beans cooked in water with more relish than you have seen me eat the brains of pheasant from the plains of Vaillant that M. Sabatier serves you on your little plates. But what a lot of rubbish I am talking! Please do forgive me. Having had this letter one or two days in some corner of your room, taking everything into account, please have the goodness to send me a reply . . . .

ARRIVAL IN WHITE RUSSIA

Meanwhile after leaving Warsaw on an unknown date, Sister Maur will be our guide along the road.

> From there we took the road through Lithuania to make our way into Russia, where we were eager to arrive. After walking many days we finally arrived in this huge Empire where we found an archdeacon sent by the Emperor waiting for us . . . but we still had a hundred and twenty leagues to go before arriving at our destination. After staying some days with the Augustinian Recollects, we started off again, accompanied by the archdeacon who took charge of everything. A courier was sent on ahead to have our meal and beds prepared in all the places we had to pass through. And all our expenses were paid for the rest of the journey. Successively we stopped in a Benedictine convent and another of the Carthusians; they had both received orders from the Emperor to welcome us, and we were well accommodated. The first village I saw in Russia did not impress me much, as in all the frontier towns there were a lot of soldiers; but on going

further into the country, we found a lot of destitution and brutality.[27]

After a long dissertation on the houses, way of life, and food in the villages they passed through, and the miserable condition of the serfs and slaves, Sister Maur continues:

> We went through a forest of eighty leagues in which we found no town or village, but only some houses where they had some post horses and slaves to take care of them and harness them to the coaches. But they did it so badly that after we had gone a few paces everything came undone, and then the slaves were beaten with sticks which made them cry out in a dreadful way. All this was new to us and all the more distressing. After walking several days in this forest, we finally arrived at the place of our destination at eight in the evening, about the 8 of September according to the calendar in this country. Their calendar is 12 days behind ours, and we had already begun the fasts from the Exaltation of the Cross [14 September]. So we did not keep the fast for eight days as the Father wanted us to conform on this point to the custom of the country.[28]

The arrival in Orsha was somewhat distressing. The newcomers were to occupy a house of Trinitarians whose numbers were so low they had been asked to go elsewhere by order of the Tsar. The evicted tenants had taken everything they could remove and their convent awaited the travellers quite empty. Sister Maur, even after thirty years, never forgot those dramatic hours.

> When we arrived and the archdeacon had the coaches brought into the courtyard, he went in and made a dreadful scene with these poor Fathers, because they were still there. But it was much worse when he saw that they had left almost nothing. He shouted so loudly that we could

[27] *Ibid.*, p. 15

[28] *Ibid.*, p. 17–18.

> hear him inside our coaches, where we had stayed, very upset at such an encounter. Finally, he put them out, but he wanted them to prepare a meal for us before they left. So it was almost ten in the evening before they left. When they had gone, the archdeacon gave Madame the Princess possession of all the house, and though it was not large, it was quite a palace compared with our previous houses.[29]

These final impressions of the day did not disturb the travellers' sleep. Our narrator adds:

> Of our trappist Fathers I have not yet said anything. When they arrived they were shown to an old abandoned convent which was falling into ruins situated on a hill not far from us. They put it into order as best they could and we ourselves were considerably reassured.

And so the regular and peaceful life to which all the nuns aspired was at last going to be organized in this monastic setting, where space and resources would be adequate, without luxury or shortage. This experience was to last eighteen months.

[29] *Ibid.*, p. 18.

CHAPTER THREE

THE MONASTERY AT ORSHA

AFTER EIGHT TO TEN MONTHS of negotiations and wanderings, a first community of fifteen nuns seemed at last to have some hope of some stability; even if the future was not very certain. According to the Tsar's terms, Orsha was only a refuge, not, strictly speaking, a foundation able to receive new members. Moreover, Dom Augustin could not be satisfied until he had some hope of finding other asylums for his 'flocks' still in Austria, Bavaria, and Bohemia. The respective governments had received them only for a limited time.

Through Sister Marie-Joseph he informed the Tsar Paul of the arrival of the monks and nuns at Orsha, and that he hoped shortly to have an audience with the emperor of all Russia at Saint Petersburg. On the 20 September, the Empress replied to her cousin and friend:

> My dear friend, I have learned with the utmost pleasure of your happy arrival in our country and I congratulate you with all my heart. I hope that when you are well settled in with us, you will be henceforth sheltered from all worries and troubles . . . I will speak with enormous interest with the Father Abbot of my dear beloved friend; but I must admit that I am going to have the eternal regret of having no hope of seeing you here. I will be only too pleased if the emperor, when making the rounds of his provinces, would deign one day to allow me to accompany him. May I have that pleasure of seeing you and embracing you.[1]

[1] *Lettres de piété, correspondance intime*, p. 217.

The emperor had himself, six days earlier, written to Madame Louise that 'all those who are able to come, of her whom he had known at Chantilly, will be dear to him'. This raised Dom Augustin's hope of a warm welcome, 'the depository of all which fills my heart'.[2]

The welcome was in fact all that the abbot could desire. The emperor promised him some monasteries in the provinces of old Poland reunited to his Empire and restored to the Austrian States, such as the Palatinate of Brzesc (which was part of Lithuania), Volhynie, and Podolie . . . Moreover, Paul I, always full of goodwill, granted pensions for fifty persons . . . Dom Augustin, on his return to Saint Petersburg, hastened to make his arrangements with the [Catholic] Metropolitan of Mohilev.[3]

Once he had concluded all this business, Dom de Lestrange made no delay in organizing the departure of the various groups of monks and nuns still in central Europe, who had already been asked to leave by the authorities in these places of refuge. Before following the different colonies of nuns on their journeys converging towards Lithuania, however, let us return to Orsha where little by little the first community was settling in.

THE MEMBERS OF THE COMMUNITY

The sisters numbered fifteen, not counting the children. We have already met some of the sisters. Dom Augustin put the

[2] J. Rabory, *La vie de Louise de Bourbon*, p. 276.

[3] *Ibid.*, pp. 270–271. From this meeting problems of authority soon arose between the Father Abbot and the Metropolitan. It was an opposition which was not to be without influence on the inclinations and plans of Dom Augustin. The cistercian abbot claimed that the monks and nuns were exempt from all secular and diocesan authority. The Metropolitan argued that exemption had disappeared with the destruction of Cîteaux. From then on Dom Augustin thought of leaving Russia for America, something about which he had already been speculating.

monastery under the patronage of Saint-Coeur de Marie, and appointed as superior Mother Sainte-Marie Laignier, whom we have already met. As an assistant—under the title Sub-prioress and novice Mistress—he gave her Sister Brigitte de la Rozière, a former Benedictine from the abbey of Saint Paul de Beauvais, who had entered the monastery of La Sainte-Volonté-de-Dieu in August 1797, at thirty-three years of age. She herself was still a novice, having not yet completed her canonical year of novititate; but the Father Abbot had confidence in her previous experience of monastic life.

Among her novices were Sister Marie-Joseph de Condé and Sister Maur Miel and some others who were to make their profession the following year. The Register and professsion schedules done at Orsha give us their names. Let us look at who they were, according to the dates of their entrance at Sembrancher.

The eldest was Sister Madeleine Guyot, a thirty-eight year old widow, one of the first to introduce herself to the Father Abbot in Switzerland. She came from Paris. Her father was a master harness-maker, and her husband had been a copperplate engraver.

The second, Sister Benoît Isambert, was the daughter of a laborer at Chartres. She was twenty-nine when she entered Sembrancher in June 1797. She did not hesitate to leave for the East or to make her profession, and then come back with the community. She died when she was only thirty-three, soon after arriving in Germany.

Sister Jean-Baptiste Chassaignon, a sister of the Annunciation from Lyon, was the daughter of a wholesale merchant in that town. She arrived at Sembrancher at the same time as Madame Louise, and had a similiar fate as Sister Benoît Isambert. She died at Paderborn on 12 February 1802, being then forty-six years old.

Sister Marie-Madeleine Zacharie was a Poor Clare from Auxonne, the daughter of a *bourgeois* from Lyon. She had followed her aunt, Sister Donat Donis, to Sembrancher in

October 1797. She was then thirty years old. She made her profession in the community of Trappistines at Orsha, came back to the West, stayed at Hamm and Paderborn, and then returned to Switzerland, where she died at thirty-seven, after seven years of an eventful monastic life always on the move.

The fifth novice who made her profession at Orsha was Sister Julie Favot, who entered in Bavaria in 1798. She was already a religious, but we do not know what Order or Congregation she belonged to. Neither do we know her place of birth or the name of her parents. She is not on the list of sisters who 'entered during the journeys', in the register of La Sainte Volonté-de-Dieu, but we do have her schedule of profession, signed on 29 October 1799, at the monastery of Saint-Coeur-de-Marie. We will meet her again later among the foundresses of the monastery in England.[4]

DAILY LIFE AT ORSHA

The nuns followed the same horarium and regulations as they had at Sembrancher. There were, however, some very interesting details of the life of this community, which two months' journey as a small group living a very communal existence must have knit closely together. They are provided by the indefatigable Sister Maur. We always follow anything she had to say with a great deal of sympathy. Her succinct description of the place and circumstances gives us a good picture of the location where over eighteen months this austere Cistercian-Trappist life unfolded:

[4] Recently communicated by M. Francey, an article of Grégor Muller, 'Die Trappisten in Orsza', in *Cistercienser Chronik Mehrerau*, 24 (1912) n° 275- 286, confirming the presence at Orsha of the sisters indicated here (the spelling of the surnames has been distorted) and adding three more names: Sister Arsène Mouillard, Sister Maria Brun, and Madeleine Martin, a five-year old!

> The house was well built in brick, with all the places and offices necessary to a religious house. There was also a very nice garden, and a field big enough for four cows, some barns and everything that was required for a farmyard. In addition there was a beautiful well. We had almost no difficulty in settling in . . . At the end of the garden there was a small paddock where our Fathers sowed some wheat, but as soon as it ripened the birds ate it.[5]

We glean in passing a little incident where the Father Abbot behaved like a real desert father to test the obedience of 'his daughters':

> The Trinitarian Fathers had sown some hemp in the garden. When it was ready to root up, the Father Abbot told us to do it, but after we had worked one hour, he came back and said that we were in too much of a hurry and that we must replant it shoot by shoot. Obviously it was essential that we say nothing about his decision, and that it was our duty to obey, but it was in vain, because it was impossible to replant them as they had been beforehand. After spending more than a hour at this work, he came back and told us to stop. But alas! I think that our simplicity was far from being that of the first Fathers of the Desert.[6]

We find a little remark on Sister Marie-Joseph, whom Sister Maur still looked on with great compassion, always calling her Madame Louise:

> Madame Louise was always the first at the most laborious work, because she said she was the strongest; but she was not the most expert at laundry work, since there were only thick woollen articles to wash. Often she was well-scolded as she had not easily understood how to do it, but

[5] *Relation des voyages*, p. 19.
[6] *Ibid.*, p. 20.

she received the correction with admirable humility, and always accused herself first.[7]

Soon after their arrival, the garden no longer produced enough to keep the community, who were obliged to stay within the enclosure. The trappist fathers, who lived not far from the nuns' convent, watched over the material needs of the sisters. The Emperor Paul I, full of sollicitude for the well-being of Princess Louise and her companions, had allotted a considerable sum of money to her on their arrival. Sister Maur tells us:

> We bought three cows to have some dairy products when there was no fast, and also for the children and the sisters of the Third Order who are in charge of their education and care. They only have to say the little Office of Providence and are not obliged to keep the austerities of the Order. They wear linen, sleep on a straw mattress, can have four meals, and keep only the fasts of the Church and abstinence from meat. Our Fathers provided us with all that we needed. In the first place they bought a great quantity of wheat. When they said it was for the princess, they could have all they wanted; otherwise nobody would give them anything.[8]

The admirable Sister Maur was very happy in this little corner of paradise at Orsha, as she said and often repeated; all the same she added this negative note:

> However each night someone came in and took something away, always something that had belonged to the Trinitarian Fathers (the poor Trinitarians were roaming about town). We ourselves only noticed the theft because things we needed went missing from one day to the next, but we never discovered the thieves.[9]

[7] *Ibid.*
[8] *Ibid.*, p. 21.
[9] *Ibid.*, pp. 21–22.

Winter was approaching, and the cold was particularly intense that year, 1798–1799. In Bylorus, called White Russia because of the heavy snowfalls, the thermometer can drop to 30 degrees below zero centigrade. Sister Maur wrote:

> The first winter we were there was very severe; the local people said that they had never known it so bad for sixty years. We suffered a great deal from the cold. The Regulations laid down that there was to be no fire for the community except in one place and that one could stay only for fifteen minutes; but as it was so cold, this point could not be followed. The Father Abbot gave permission for the entire community to stay in one large room where a big stove kept going day and night, and where we could go after Matins, because in La Trappe you did not go to bed again after the Office. He even ordered that we all sleep in this room because of the extreme cold. Nevertheless this did us a great deal of harm, because the heat from the stove made us sweat and we had to go like that to Matins, where we spent two or three hours, and this gave us the most dreadful colds. We preferred to make our dormitory in a big room where the walls (as in all the house) were just ice so that, in spite of the severe frost, we would not have such heavy colds. Father Abbot gave each one of us a present of two fox furs, because the furs in this country are a lot thicker than in ours. One of the skins covered our feet and the other our hands, so we were able to sleep. The second winter [1799–1800] the Fathers nailed together some planks and a piece of cloth in the wooden framework of the beds that the Trinitarians had left behind; this was not so cold as sleeping flat on the floor.[10]

The winter and the hardships it brought did not last. Spring arrived, and life again took on its normal round. This created an atmosphere of relaxation which is perceptible in the recital of Sister Maur:

[10] *Ibid.*, pp. 22–23.

> After Easter, when the snows and frosts had melted, we followed the Regulations for the summer. At five in the morning we went to work in the garden until ten, when we returned to hear holy Mass and to say Terce and Sext if it was not a fast. Then we had dinner at midday. We were given eight ounces of bread and a very generous portion of food. At five in the evening, we had supper, four ounces of bread with some dairy products or a vegetable salad. When it was a fast of the rule, we had dinner at two in the afternoon. Then we were given a pound of bread and some soup. In Lent, we had dinner at four fifteen. The first three Fridays we were given a pound and a half of bread and some soup. The last three Fridays, two pounds of bread only. Ash Wednesday we recited the psalter barefoot and Good Friday we were barefoot all the time until the Office of Matins.[11]

We left Dom Augustin busy organizing the transfers of the communities of monks and nuns still in central Europe to places in Russia promised by the Tsar. Dom Augustin set off from Orsha quite soon, probably in October, leaving the care of the nuns to Father Etienne Malmy, the prior of the monastery of monks. He proved to be a very devoted father because 'in spite of the short distance between the two monasteries, the snow was sometimes nine feet high and seemed to be an insurmountable barrier for all commuication. But the indefatigable Superior managed to clear a pathway through all these obstacles, and made several visits each week to his daughters'.[12]

It must have been this same Father Etienne who obtained the fox furs for the nuns, since Dom Augustin did not appear in Orsha for ten months, nor did he reply to any letters written to him. This absence weighed heavily on the exiled community, cut off from all regular communication with the outside world.

[11] *Ibid.*, p. 23.

[12] Gaillardin, *Histoire de La Trappe* (Paris, 1844) 2:212.

THE UNCERTAINTIES OF SISTER MARIE-JOSEPH

In the letter collection of Madame de Condé published in the nineteenth century, only two letters are dated from Orsha and both are addressed to the Prince de Condé, her father. They are dated 8 October and 2 November 1798, so both come from the beginnings at Orsha when the Princes de Condé were still in Russia and in favor with the Emperor. Sister Marie-Joseph complained in both letters of having received no paternal reply to her letters. In the second letter, from November, she still hopes that the community can be permanently established in Russia, attributing to her father, moreover, the goodwill shown by the Tsar. But she also expresses some beginnings of disillusionment.

> I am writing to you still as a novice, although my year of probation has ended [she had taken the habit on 1 October the previous year], but circumstances have held up my profession, which my heart has never stopped desiring with the same constancy, the same strength, and the same ardor. There will hardly be any question of profession until the return of the Father Abbot, who believed it his duty to leave as soon as possible to gather together and bring back all the members of the Order dispersed at present in Germany.[13]

Dom Augustin it seems, still believed in the possibility of settling in Russia and, after a year at Orsha, visualized some professions for the monastery of Saint-Coeur-de-Marie. Nevertheless, during his long absence he looked for other possible places for foundations for the nuns, Westphalia and England, where there were already two foundations of monks. But even more he was dreaming of America.

All this filtered into community talks and disturbed Sister Marie-Joseph, who had for some time been anxious about

[13] *Correspondance*, p. 205.

the instability of the direction given by Dom Augustin to his Order. She was also troubled at having the accent put principally on penance, when she herself was attracted to putting the accent on love. Being aware that penance was a part of the religious state, she put it like this: 'I cannot find it [penance] in the *happiness* and *delights* of passing the days and part of the nights singing the praises of my God; to observe silence with all creatures which easily promotes communication with the Creator'.[14]

In a very long letter written on 7 August 1797, just before she entered La Sainte-Volonté-de-Dieu, Madame Louise de Condé had opened her heart to the abbot of La Valsainte, and already explained her thoughts on this point:

> Since it has pleased my God to draw me to Him a little more closely, retirement from an easy life is strengthened and it is even joined with an attraction for a life entirely to the contrary . . . Nevertheless this attraction does not go so far as to include works of penance which really make nature suffer. I do feel in myself a readiness to deny it enjoyments on a continuing basis, but not at all to inflict passing pain on it. In all this, the only thing I feel to be of consequence is the merit of obedience . . . it has been impossible for me, until now, to feel that it would be able to be of any use as an expiation for my sins. It appears to me as nothing compared with the crushed and torn sentiments in my heart that it has pleased my God to let me experience sometimes on hearing these two words: *Peccavimus, Domine* [We have sinned, O Lord]. Ah! this is where I sense the penance and expiation; I see it solely in the adorable blood of Jesus Christ . . . As to the refusal of all the pleasures of nature, they have the effect in my heart of so many acts of love, and that is why they are delightful to Him.[15]

[14] Quoted by J. Rabory, *Vie de Louise de Condé*; the quotation is taken from her 'Mémoires spirituels', p. 5.

[15] *Lettres de piété, correspondance intime*, 2:152.

Much later she was still showing these sentiments to the Father Abbot with the same rectitude. She declared later in a letter to the Prince de Condé that she had 'presented these reflexions without any success to the Abbot'. Certainly it was very difficult for Dom Augustin to listen to these counsels of wisdom, given the situation he was in and the course of events that rendered it unworkable in his eyes. The abbot of La Trappe was not, moreover, a man to let himself be deflected from a decision once taken, even though it was clearly imprudent or hazardous. We will see this plainly in what follows.

Sister Marie-Joseph thought about all this deeply, seeking the will of God and consulting Father de Bouzonville and Father Etienne. On the twentieth of April she decided to write to the Emperor; but he misunderstood what was in her mind and replied to her on 7 May:

> Madame, my cousin,
>
> I have received the letter of your Highness dated 20 April, and I have at once given the following orders to the Metropolitan Archbishop Sestrertshewitsk, head of the Roman Catholic Church in my States, to appoint your Highness, as soon as she has pronounced her vows, Abbess of the religious of La Trappe; [and] that the convent of the Basilians at Orsha be put at her disposition. In giving these orders with the best intentions in my heart, I believe that I have fulfilled all your wishes.[16]

All this only confused the situation. Sister Maur from her observation post had seen things differently:

> The Father Abbot had decided that Madame the Princess would not pronounce her vows until she had passed a year in our new monastery;[17] but when the time came

[16] *Ibid*., Letter of the Emperor Paul, p. 221.

[17] This decision applied to all the novices who came to Orsha. The first and last ceremony of profession took place 29 October 1799: the year of the novitiate had then been prolonged some weeks.

> the Emperor wrote to the Father that his will was that as soon as Madame de Condé had pronounced her vows she was to be appointed abbess and be totally independent of the Trappist Fathers. Nothing could have ruined more the good relations which had until then prevailed between the monks and nuns of La Trappe. Also Madame Louise, to whom the Father communicated this news, would never wish to consent to it. She wrote to his Majesty that she could not fulfil his wishes, and if there was no other means of appeal, she would much prefer to withdraw. But she implored him [she was withdrawing only with regret and on principle of conscience] to retain his good favors towards the monks and nuns that she had brought into his States. The Emperor promised this to her; but he did not keep his word for long.[18]

In her distress, Sister Marie-Joseph decided to explain everything to the priest who knew her best and had followed her all along in her religious vocation. We do not have this letter, but we do have a copy of the reply, very clear and firm, from Father Bouzonville. It begins like this: 'As soon as I had read your letter, which reached me on 16 July, I gave myself to prayer'. Then he reflected, enunciated principles for the discernment of spirits, and applied them to the information provided in her letter by his spiritual daughter. After having spoken of her recourse to God, he underlines the questions troubling the mind of Sister Marie-Joseph. Let us listen to his own words expressing her perplexities:

> You have consulted yourself, and you still continue to consult yourself; but if the result of this enquiry, which you have been engaged in for a considerable time, is that according to your knowledge and experience this establishment of women-trappists is only a collection of individuals made without choice, and that it goes beyond the reform of the venerable Abbot de Rancé only through very serious drawbacks coming from excessive austerities and

[18] *Relation des voyages*, p. 24.

> the harshness of the conduct of the superiors; if the result is that the Regulations taken literally are impracticable, that the spirit of the regime is only in your eyes one of harshness of life for both soul and body, then you cannot believe that you are called to consecrate yourself there.[19]

This much is clear, and the conclusion is as obvious as the firm counsel given at the end of the letter.

> You have consulted the minister of God, and you have consulted him again; you have shown yourself to him with sincerity and good faith. He knows the inside of your soul, the details of your whole life, your tendencies at their source, and the constant character of your heart. He knows your accustomed views, your thoughts, your good and bad dispositions, your doubts, your inclinations and your aversions; so he can give you some salutary advice . . . *You are not called to bind yourself by vows to the Order of Trappists*, and you must not make your profession there . . . You must look on the days spent in the solitude of La Trappe, far from the perils and pitfalls of the world, far from the vicissitudes and inconstancy of the things of men, as so many days when it has pleased the Lord to try your faith and to form you to the silence of a life hidden and buried with Jesus Christ.

After having recommended a great deal of discretion to his penitent because of the effect that her departure could have within the community, as well as outside it, the result of which could be injurious to the house and to the superiors who had received her, he concludes by saying:

> There is only one other thing that I would like to add on the course of action that you must take when you leave La Trappe. I think that you must choose a dwelling dependent on a religious house of your sex in some town. If possible, associate with one or two women recommended

[19] Copy in the Archives T., ref. 55, 24/2.

> for their piety and virtues, and live there together a retired life. I think that you should see yourself as a *precious stone* held in God's hands awaiting his time. He will explain himself. Who knows if you are not destined one day to give to our unfortunate country the greatest examples of all the virtues? The moment of God will come for you. A soul always ready and always persevering is fitting for his designs. Await them with patience. There is more than one way to celebrate the marriage of the faithful bride and that of the divine Bridegroom.[20]

The Departure

Thus assured and enlightened, Sister Marie-Joseph was not slow in deciding to depart. She must have spoken of it to her novice mistress, Sister Brigitte de La Rozière, who was still also a novice in the Order. She too, no doubt, had recourse to prayer and resolved to follow the princess. We have nothing at all in writing about how this double decision was communicated to the mother prioress. We can suppose that there were several interviews between the superior and the two sisters, and that it was not without sorrow that she saw them leave. There is just a note in the Register of La Sainte Volonté-de-Dieu:

> Louise-Adélaide de Bourbon, daughter of Louis-Joseph de Condé, the Princess de Condé, Prince of the Blood of France, and of Charlotte Gottfride de Rohan-Soubise;

[20] We can consider the end of this letter as a prophecy. Madame de Condé, at the moment of the Restoration, was to be the foundress of the Benedictines du Temple in Paris, re-united in the very place which had been the royal family's prison in 1792. When the Government of the Second Republic decreed that this place, too heavy with historical associations, should be pulled down, the community transferred to the rue Monsieur. A hundred years later, because of urbanization, they had to move again. The Benedictines du Temple are now today at Limon (Essonne).

> entered our monastery 26 September 1797, aged forty years old, received our holy habit on 1 October the same year under the name of Sister Marie-Joseph. *She left at the monastery of the Sacré Coeur-de-Marie at Orsha in White Russia on 14 August 1799.*

The entry on Sister Brigitte says only: 'She left with the Princess from the monastery of the Sacré-Coeur-de-Marie at Orsha in White Russia 14 August 1799'.

The two novices took with them the young Erminie de Rougé, entrusted to the Princess' care by her mother. Following the advice of Father de Bouzonville, they found shelter at a convent of Benedictines at Nieswicz in Lithuania. In a letter of 18 November 1799, written from Nieswicz, she explains to the Prince de Condé, her father, the reasons for her departure from Orsha. She does so with great serenity:

> A word now about me. I have no doubt that you have not learned publicly what I have not been able to tell you myself, not having any news of you or knowing where to write to you. I wanted to tell you of my leaving the Trappists after about two years of novitiate passed in the same firm desires and sentiments. The very recent institution of nuns of this Order did not appear to me to have the necessary solidity, and I did not think it wise to decide on final profession. My own experience convinced me that the zeal of the one who wanted to create it was far too excessive and, far from providing solid foundations, had in fact left not a few gaps in this regard. After having presented my reflexions [Dom Augustin] without any success—reflexions made before God and in the sight of God—I have followed, as on all other occasions and without any human respect, the impulses of my conscience and sound reason, always in harmony with religion. In consequence, I have left Orsha, and have retired to a benedictine convent at Nieswicz, where I pay board and lodging and live privately, having without ceasing offered to the Lord the sacrifice of a vocation as ardent as it is

> constant, but one which, until this day, He has not deigned to grant any attainment of this desire.[21]

Her spirit has been enlightened, and she took the courageous path that her conscience dictated in fidelity to God. The letter continues:

> His great goodness has given me as a companion in my retreat the novice mistress whom I had, whose virtues, qualities and amiability are well suited to alleviate my position . . . It is with her that I left Orsha. That moment was rather distressing. I had nothing, not even any chemises, and I was obliged to borrow some money while waiting for a reply from the Emperor, which fortunately was favorable . . . However, for the future nothing is certain . . . The first night of my journey, I had the misfortune to catch a complaint which caused me no little expense. At the moment I am better, even healed, of this I am assured. But I still feel some small effects of this illness, which by and large does not prevent me from going about, but has caused me considerable sufferings.[22]

It is with a certain regret that we see Madame de Condé leaving La Trappe, and if we have quoted at some length of this departure, it is because the documents allow us some glimpses into the causes of this separation. The two years Sister Marie-Joseph stayed in the community of Sembrancher were very fruitful for those who lived this adventure with her. First, of course, because of the serviceable support of her relatives, but also and above all because of her good sense, her lively spirit, her faith, her humility and her simplicity. Her strong personality, so totally submitted to the will of God, whatever it must have cost her, was also a stimulant for those weaker than herself.

[21] *Correspondance*, p. 207.

[22] *Ibid.*, p. 208. This may have been erysipelas (*Lettre de piété* 72, p. 242).

We do not know directly the reactions of the community at the time of this triple departure, other than the respectful silence of the register, which gives no inkling as to the reasons behind this decision. Sister Maur notes that 'the nuns of La Trappe were very distressed to have lost so virtuous a Princess'.

PROFESSIONS AT ORSHA

Let us go back now to Dom Augustin. During the months when the abbot did not appear in Orsha, he was actively engaged in the business of transferring into Russia the groups of monks and nuns still staying in Bavaria, Bohemia, and Austria. Some Italian monks of Monte Bracco in the Piedmont, fleeing before the revolutionary armies, had joined up with the monks in Austria. We shall see in the next chapter how they all reached the Russian frontier under Dom Augustin's leadership.

Installing the monks at various places, and assembling all the nuns together in one place, was concluded by about the month of September 1799. Dom Augustin, who had not been unaware of the departure of the Princess and her companions, made no delay in going back to Orsha, both to reassure the community and to prepare a profession ceremony, since almost a year had passed since their arrival in Orsha. Sister Maur's account can be used as a trustworthy report on events in this period:

> For some months we were quite at peace, and the Father Abbot was busy preparing those who were to be professed and I was among them. I was very much reassured by the promises of the Emperor that he would support us in our house. I hoped to make my vows with all my heart, believing that God had called me to this Order. I was very happy and hoped that the Lord would give me the grace to persevere until death.

Some days before we started our profession retreat, the Father gave us a touching exhortation on love for the predilection that God had shown us by calling us to such a holy Order. He stopped a minute, then continued: 'God calls souls either for life or only for a certain time, but it is always a great grace, etc'. But alas! what trouble and distress these words caused me; God either calls for always or for some time! If God calls me for always, I said to myself, I have nothing to fear; he will give me the grace to persevere. But if he does not call me, he is not obliged to give me this grace, and what will become of me if he does not powerfully help me in a way of life so hard for nature? Day and night these tormenting thoughts beset me, so I told the Mother Prioress, who said that it was a temptation I must disregard. So I did all I could to get rid of these thoughts, but in vain; they had made too strong an impression on me. In the meantime, the Father Abbot told us to start our retreat for profession. I did not want to say anything, so I started the retreat with the others, but the more it advanced the more tormented and undecided I was. I do not know if Mother Prioress told Father that I was wavering, but he came the evening of the fourth day of the retreat to tell us that we would make our profession the next day. This did not suit me at all, and I was hardly disposed for it, but I did not wish to say anything. However after Matins each one wrote out her schedule. They made me a sign to do likewise, but instead of writing my vows I wrote this note to the Father Abbot:

> My Reverend Father, I am not sufficiently sure of my vocation to make my profession today. That is why I beg you for a delay, so that I may have more time to be sure of the will of God. The troubles in my conscience that I have suffered these last few days have obliged me to beseech you to accord me this grace.

Immediately on reading my letter, he asked to have me to come to the parlor, asked me a lot of questions, and finally granted what I had asked, adding: "In six weeks time I have to bring here several sisters who are still at

> the frontiers, to make their profession here, I will not be sorry if you are among them".
>
> My companions pronounced their vows that same day; there were nine [of them][23]

At the beginning of the chapter we mentioned five of the sisters for whom we have profession schedules made at Orsha on 29 October 1799. We will find the other four in later documents where they are identified as professed. Among them were two Sisters of the Annunciation from Sens, who arrived together at Dürnast on 20 October 1798: Sister Marie de la Résurrection de Montron, who was to be appointed prioress of the community reunited at Hamm in October 1800, and Sister Gabrielle Lucottée. Both died at Darfeld. Orsha is the only place where any professions took place during their travels, and the only place where they stayed for over a year.

Sister Euphrosine Mairesse, professed Cistercian of the abbey of Notre-Dame-des-Prés, joined the itinerant community 4 May 1798 in Bavaria. She travelled all over Russia and went into Switzerland with the community of Paderborn in 1803.

The last, Sister Séraphique Van den Kerchove, professed at the Carmel at Valenciennes, became a Trappistine at Vienna in July 1798. She was still there in October in very poor health. Courageously she ended her course as one of the three professed foundresses of Darfeld, where she died at thirty-nine in December 1802.[24]

Soon after the professions were over, Dom Augustin left Orsha. Sister Maur continues her recital:

> He left immediately to go and fetch his children who were waiting for him at the frontiers. As for me, I did not cease entreating the Lord to make known to me his holy will,

[23] *Relation des voyages*, pp. 25–26.

[24] It is not certain that these four professed ever reached Orsha. See Part IV, Chapter Three, n.4.

> and to make it known by some definite sign. He did not delay in fulfilling my request.
>
> The six weeks passed and the Father Abbot did not arrive with the others, because everything was covered with snow and he could only travel by sledge. As for us, we were quite undisturbed all the winter.[25]

In this way the community of Saint-Coeur-de-Marie lived for another six months, striken by the climate and the departure of two of its members, but comforted by the professions of nine of its members: a pledge of stability—if not of place, at least in the Order of Cistercian-Trappists.

[25] *Relation*, p. 27.

CHAPTER FOUR

REGROUPING IN LITHUANIA

WHILE THE COMMUNITY at Orsha lived through its joys and sorrows, three other communities of nuns at Dürnast in Bavaria, at Buštěrhad in Bohemia, and at Vienna in Austria, respectively knew that they were in lands of refuge only for a limited time. They hoped to reach, without too much delay, a permanent place where, reunited at last, they could lead the monastic life they longed for in peace and with the hope of handing it on to new members.

We have seen that Dom Augustin obtained from Tsar Paul, after October 1798, the authorization to establish several monasteries in his states. Leaving in haste to go back to the West to organize the departures, he had to secure passports for each of the groups, the monks and the nuns, and find some means of transport for the persons and their baggage, carriages, carts, horses, and sometimes river boats, according to the route they followed. There were still about two-hundred persons to transfer to other places. This vast operation required a great deal of time and money.

The Father Abbot then had the idea of utilizing the wishes of the imperial government to have the immigrants depart as soon as possible. He applied for some *corvées* (a sort of tax still used at that time in the Austrian Empire and in Russia). The peasants, in exchange for certain advantages, were required, according to circumstances, to work one or two days extra each week or month, with their own tools and horses, for the expenses of the state. These *corvées* were used especially for the transport of merchandise and sometimes people. So it was that the emigrants' trips came to be organized by the commissars of the government and consequently paid for by the state.

In this narrative we are concerned only with the nuns, then divided into three groups: one group at the château of Buštěrhad in Bohemia, not far from Prague; a second group which had stayed in Vienna after fifteen of the nuns left for White Russia; and a third group received by the principality of Freising in Bavaria.

FROM BUŠTĚRHAD TO LEMBERG

The first group to leave was the one in Bohemia, which had as its superior Mother Sainte-Marie Bigaux. The nuns had been living peacefully for five months under the kind auspices of the Archduchess Marie-Anne. About the middle of October they received the order to leave for the Austrian-Russian frontier and go to the town of Léopal, formerly called this in Polish, but under Austrian protection called Lemberg.[1]

In this town there was a community of Benedictines of the Blessed Sacrament founded by the monastery at Rouen, and Dom Augustin had made arrangements for the Trappistines to stay there for the winter. Their chaplain was not a monk, but a secular priest of great intellectual and spiritual worth, Father Jean-Joseph Fayt, who enjoyed the entire confidence of the Father Abbot. He was entirely devoted to his duties for the sisters under his charge. In particular, he kept the Registers of admissions, professions and deaths with great care.

Sister Stanislaus Michel, who was among this group, tells us what happened to them. She says specifically: 'We were

[1] In 1946 this town was allocated to the Soviet Union, becoming part of the Ukraine, and since then has been known as Lvov.

about fourteen or fifteen'. The narrative of this part of the journey is given in detail and particularly poignant. 'In the month of October' [1798], wrote Sister Stanislaus,

> we received from the Reverend Father, the order to go into Poland. This was a long and arduous journey. Poland is a country where the cold is very severe. We walked, nearly always in snow and ice. We could find nowhere to lodge along the way because there were few hostelries in this country and the few we found were kept by Jews. So we suffered a great deal from cold and hunger. Sometimes it was evening before we could find some bread and cheese of poor quality, and a stable to rest the horses and put in the wagons which had brought us, and where we were obliged to stay for the night, in spite of the confined space and most unpleasant place.
>
> We were on the road until 7 December, the Eve of the Conception of the Blessed Virgin, when we arrived in the town of Léopal, which was our destination. We learned with joy and gladness that the benedictine nuns of Perpetual Adoration of the Blessed Sacrament willingly welcomed us to stay in their monastery until we could go into Russia.[2]

After arriving in December 1798, the small community of Mother Sainte-Marie Bigaux stayed in this hospitable house until the following July. During all this time the charity of the Benedictines was unstinting in spite of tribulations at the beginning, related to us by Sister Stanislaus:

> We were conducted and received into this community the same day with a great deal of charity. The superior of this house was a French religious who took a great interest in all of us.[3] Her community also followed her sentiments,

[2] *Relation,* pp. 204–205.

[3] This superior was 'Anne-Catherine Beagle, called of Saint-André, Victime de Jésus. Born in Lille 25 April 1750, she received the habit with the Benedictines of Caen on 3 January 1773. She went on the second

> and all the time we stayed there, we felt the effects of their charity, above all, during the first days of our arrival. The sufferings and fatigues of a long journey,[4] the poor food we had along the way, plus the change of climate, made us all very ill. Hardly had three weeks after our arrival passed when we were all stricken with a very violent sickness; fourteen of us had a high fever. In this situation we had the misfortune of losing our Reverend Mother and one of our sisters already ill on the journey.[5]

The Register of professions kept during the journey allows us to identify this sister. She was Scholastique Baron, the daughter of a master saddler from Besançon, and formerly a Poor Clare of Poligny in France-Comté. She was sixty-one years old, and thirty six years professed when she entered Sembrancher on 23 August 1797. She received the habit the following 8 September. She made her profession 'on ashes and straw' on 20 December 1798, at Lemberg in Poland. Her profession was received by Father Fayt, priest and director of the nuns of La Trappe and delegated to this office by Reverend Father Colomban, prior of the monks and nuns of this Order.[6] She died six days later on 26 December, at sixty-two years of age. On 12 January, Mother Sainte-Marie Bigaux, the prioress in charge, in her turn died. She was not quite thirty-six years old, a nun of great worth. 'Several others were in extremity', adds Sister Stanislaus.

> Our worthy confessor [Father Fayt] who had accompanied us on our journey and shared our fatigues, was also

---

foundation at Lvov on 12 February 1786, then to the first monastery of Lvov on 13 August 1791. She was prioress from 1797 until her death on 9 February 1799.' See also Catherine de Bar, Mother Mechtilde du Saint-Sacrement, *En Pologne avec les Bénédictines de France*. Original documents assembled and presented by the Benedictines of the Blessed Sacrament at Rouen (Paris, 1984) p. 442.

[4] The distance from Prague to Lvov is about 850 km (530 miles); it was covered in about six weeks.

[5] 'Relation de la Fondation', *Cîteaux* (1984) pp. 205–206.

[6] Register of professions and deaths during travels.

> struck down with the same sickness. He was taken to the hospital where he received the last sacraments, but God granted us the grace of his recovery.
>
> But the worst blow that touched us most deeply was that the superior of the house, who came frequently to see us and helped us in the sad situation in which we found ourselves, was a victim of her charity. She also caught our sickness and in a few days was taken out of this world. [It was 9 February 1799]. I leave you to imagine what a dreadful calamity this was for our hearts, so full of gratitude for all the kindnesses that this worthy religious never failed to bestow on us. But we have to adore and submit to the designs of God.[7]

So passed the very harsh winter of 1798–1799, which the sisters at Orsha had also endured with ill effects.

FROM VIENNA TO BRZESC

In July 1798, twelve nuns and two young girls were still at the monastery of the Visitation in Vienna, waiting for orders to leave for Russia. There were some monks waiting as well. In November they received the word to go to Cracow and there spend the winter. Some documents recently called to my attention by a kind Austrian Benedictine, have permitted me to reconstruct the names.[8]

The community was made up of three professed Cistercian-Trappistines and nine novices. Of these novices four were not entered in the Register of Admissions, but we know that three of them persevered in the Order as we have their death notices. The fourth, who entered just at the beginning of the journey, is not otherwise known to us.

[7] *Relation*, p. 206.

[8] This is taken from lists obligingly communicated by Father Dr Ildefons Fux, osb of the Abbey of Göttweig (Austria) along with many other documents quoted further on.

Their names and characteristics are recorded on two lists drawn up by Father Colomban Moroge, then prior. To him the abbot of Valsainte, always on the move, had delegated full powers of administration. One of the lists was destined for the Imperial Police and is preserved in the state archives. The other list was for the local administration. A second hand has added to this last list some information on the state of the health of five of the sisters:

> Sister Thaïs is weakened by an illness to which she is subject; Sister Séraphique is at this moment attacked by a serious illness; Sister Bernard, who is in very poor health, is now ill; Sister Joséphine finds herself very disabled; Sister Lutgarde is in a state of infirmity leading to consumption.

The superior was Mother Marie-Michel Ducourand, aged forty six, a former Capuchine of Armentières who had made her profession at La Sainte-Volonté-de-Dieu on 24 October 1797, after a year's novitiate. The two other professed were Sister Rose Sergent (thirty-seven years old), a Poor Clare from Besançon, who had made her profession the same day; and Sister M.-Thaïs Bassignot (twenty-six years old), professed eight days later on 1 November. Two of the novices were professed religious in their own Institutes: Sister Bernard Lezille de Montarles, a Benedictine of the Blessed Sacrament at Charenton near Paris, who came from Noyon; and Sister Séraphique Van den Kerkhove, born in Brussels and a Carmelite from Valenciennes, who was not entered in the Register, but joined the community in July 1798, according to the list of Father Colomban. We have the notice of her death at Darfeld in December 1802.

Of the seven other novices, four entered at La Sainte Volonté: Sister Anne Parain, Sister Lutgarde Lessus, Sister Dorothée Coët, and Sister Joséphine Fouillé. The other three entered at the time of the departure from Sembrancher or just afterwards, in January or February 1798, and were not recorded in the first Registers. They were

Sister M.-Rose Methains, fifty-four, already a religious and indeed Superior General of the Soeurs de la Providence at Portieux, and Sister M. du Sacré-Coeur Marchand.

Five or six months of community life had already welded the members of this community together, even though they had come from such diverse backgrounds, but they were also well supported by the professed and novices who had entered at La Sainte-Volonté-de-Dieu. Of this community of twelve members, ten died in the Order. One left during the return journey, and what happened to the other, the last, we do not know. Also staying at the Visitation was a group of monks, with twenty young boys of the Third Order. Dom Augustin had obtained authorization for their entry into Russia.

This was the sum total of the two groups who were told to leave in November for Cracow, where they were to spend the winter. The monks and nuns had to stay six months at the hospitable monastery of the Visitation. Brothers and sisters, children and mistresses, were surrounded with every care and attention by the religious and the boarders.

Father Colomban and seven of the monks, in the name of everyone, signed a memorial of this heart-warming stay with the daughters of Saint Francis de Sales. They asked that their testimony 'be attached to this place where our community has resided for the longest period of time'. The card is worded as follows:

> Vive Jésus! To God be all the glory. In the year 1798, the very honorable Mother Marie-Julienne de Trauttmansdorff, the Superior of the Dames de la Visitation de Ste-Marie of the monastery at Vienna in Austria, by the workings of a charity without parallel, has exercised since the twenty-eighth day of May until the twenty-fourth day of November, a hospitality most attentive towards the more than fifty-three persons [and even during the first months, there were no less than a hundred persons] composing a part of the body of the community of the Reform of Notre-Dame-de-la-Trappe, Order of Cîteaux, exiled from

the monastery of La Val-Sainte in Switzerland, to protect them from the misfortunes which menace religion, and to "preserve their *saint état*".

May the Lord be their recompense forever.[9]

Of the fifty-three travellers, eight were monks, twelve nuns, and twenty-two children, among whom were two thirteen year-old girls according to the official lists of the police and civil administration. The eleven other travellers remain unknown.[10]

From this 'testimonial' we know that the departure took place 24 November. The season was hardly favorable, but the order had been given and it was pointless to hesitate. Winter was coming on and their stay at Vienna had already been overlong, even if the charity of the Visitandines had never wavered.

Among the monks staying in Vienna was Father François de Paule Dargnies, whom we have already met on more than one occasion. Again he tells us about the journey, and particularly about conditions along the way, on which the group was led under the direction of a government Commissar.

In his letter (N°21) he wrote:

> From Vienna to Cracow we had a hundred leagues to cover, which was not too difficult because the Commissar who accompanied us attended to the post horses and paid for everything. We had only the bills at the inns to pay, because only rarely could we lodge in the large abbeys as we usually did. However the weather was very severe for most of the way. The wind and the snow blizzards forced us to stay closely packed together in our carriages, which

[9] Ildefons Fux, OSB, published an extract from the 'Annales du monastère de la Visitation Sainte-Marie de Vienne en Autriche' in *Cistercienser Chronick* 46 (1934) p. 388.

[10] Österreichisches Staatsarchiv. Ava Polizeihofstelle ad Nr 899/1798 et Niederösterreicharchives, Landesarchiv, Regierungsarchiv, cultus 6, Nr 4723 ad Nr 1545/1798.

> prevented me from satisfying my curiosity as I would have wished. We did not have any adventures on this journey, other than some overturned carriages, which happened quite often because we were travelling in public carriages which were in a very bad state of repair. What was more annoying was that these accidents usually happened to the carriages of the nuns rather than ours. Happily nobody was hurt, but I was called each time to go and help them with anything they needed, which to me was very troublesome because of the bad weather. Mostly it was only fright, or sometimes a little sprain or scratch. I made them take a drop of brandy to help them get over the shock, then went back to my carriage, leaving them to recover from their distresses as best they could.[11]

Our narrator does not seem to have been very courteous, and even appears in a bad humor, but this evaporated in the presence of the sick sisters he is called on to take care of in various places. He could show great compassion too, by pleading with the Father Abbot to mitigate the Regulations when they applied to the nuns.

His 'Memoirs' provide us with a small detail about the arrival and stay at Cracow:

> On arriving in Cracow, which happened during the first days of December [1798] the Commissar assigned us our lodgings in various religious communities. We were divided into three equal groups, composed of monks, lay brothers, and children . . . . The nuns were not separated, but lived together all the time in the same community house.[12]

[11] Mémoires, letter 21e, p.117.

[12] The welcoming community was that of the Norbertines of Zwierzyniec, which was then outside the walls of Cracow. See the article of K. Kramarska-Anysz on the History of the monastery of Norbertines of Cracow in *Nasza Przeszlosé*, 47 (1977): 'In gratitude they (the Trappists) planted a vine and built a greenhouse', information fraternally communicated by Sister Marguerite Borkowska, OSB, of Zarnoviec (Poland).

By the end of April 1799, winter had passed and the emigrants could continue their journey. This time they took a river route. They left on several boats, following the course of the Vistula until Deblin, the place on the river nearest the Russian frontier. At their embarkation, notes Dargnies, the nuns arrived in two big coaches, and the Father Abbot was there, hurrying to get the nuns into the boats 'to shield them from the curiosity of the crowd'.

On the Vistula, which did not have the same steady flow as the Danube, the boats easily ran aground. The boatmen were obliged to wade into the water up to their waists to get the boats afloat again. Moreover, the villages were far from the banks, and it was difficult to land, which made getting provisions troublesome. This journey took three weeks. At the end of it the travellers were given for a lodging, as Father François de Paule tells us,

> an immense barn, well built, which could have contained an entire regiment. We stayed there at least six days. It was the feast of the Blessed Sacrament (*Corpus Christi*) [23 May 1799]. We went to the Church and took part in the procession . . . We had plenty of time to get tired of doing nothing at this dwelling place, while the Father Abbot worked hard to get us some transport, because we had to go the rest of the way by road, and we had neither horses nor carriages. As we were always accompanied by the government Commissar, the abbot used this means to procure us some coaches by *corvées*. In this country all the common people are [treated] like slaves.[13]

The departure was delayed yet more by having to cross the Vistula by ferries, which transported the coaches (about fifty for people and baggage) at a pace so slow that the whole operation took nearly all day. This last stage of the journey to Terespol-Brzesc (Brest-Litovsk), was the hardest. It was made by coach and horse-drawn sleighs.

[13] Mémoires, letter 21e, p. 132.

On their arrival the nuns were conducted to a community of Brigittines. It was June 1799. There they waited for the two other groups, those who had wintered at Lemberg and those who had stayed in Bavaria.

FROM DÜRNAST TO BREST

The reader will not have forgotten that in Chapter Two of this third Part, we left a group of nuns at the castle of Dürnast in Bavaria. Under the direction of Mother Augustin de Chabannes they had welcomed some new recruits. This hospitable group had in its turn received the order to take the road for Russia and did so during the first days of April 1799. The winter was now over, those in weak health had regained their strength, and the final two clothings took place on the 5th of April.

In an article published in 1984, Ildefons Fux, a Benedictine of the abbey of Göttweig in Lower Austria, included two extremely interesting pages about the short stay in his abbey of a group of Trappists who were welcomed fraternally by the community. He very carefully reports of the Austrian police and the archives in his monastery. He notes the arrival in 1799 of eleven Trappist monks from Italy (Monte Bracco), who wanted to stop at Linz in Austria until the arrival of their Superior General with whom they were to go into Russia. But as regards the monks, trust was not of the order of the day! The Burgomeister received 'a warning to watch them closely to make sure they did not try any clandestine proselytism, or perform any monastic activities of a public character which would cause a useless sensation or to begin any hot-headed guidance'. Perhaps we have here some hint that the procession in which they walked two by two through the streets of Vienna the previous year, had ill-disposed the philosopher - ministers towards them.

Father Ildefons continues:

> At the beginning of April the Abbot General Augustin de Lestrange (1754–1827), entered the town of Linz with forty-nine members of his Order. They soon continued their journey by going down the Danube in boats. They came alongside the quay at Stein at ten in the morning. Apprehensive of his previous experience, hardly friendly, with the authorities in Vienna in 1798, Lestrange decided to enter Russia from Krems [without going through Vienna] by taking the way which passes through Znaim, Brunn and Krakau. Before undertaking the journey, however, they needed a few days rest. So they asked for hospitality of the monastery of Göttweig not far away. The prior, Wolfgang Schlichtinger, immediately paid for their transport and announced their arrival and installation in Chapter that evening. This was in the absence of the Reverend Father Abbot Leonhard Grindberger [1799–1812] who resided in Vienna. The next day Father Wolfgang hastened to inform his abbot of the news: 'We have here some guests'—they were in all sixty persons, among whom were twenty-nine nuns and a young girl—and to prevent any possible remonstrations, he added; "They eat very little and cause us hardly any trouble".[14]

On his side, Dom Augustin wrote to the abbot on 11 April to express 'his gratitude and his total admiration on seeing such goodness . . .' This handwritten letter is still preserved in the abbey at Göttweig.

Father Ildefons' article goes on to underline the admiration and astonishment kindled in the community at the great fidelity of the Trappists to fasting, watching, and abstinence, and the silence practised by these itinerants.

> Very early in the morning and at midday they performed their choral prayer in the Community church, monks and nuns singing in alternate choirs. Many priests celebrated Mass, the lay brothers and nuns communicated twice

[14] *Französische Geistliche in Göttweig in Hippolytus*, NF 6 (Polten, 1984) pp. 64ff.

> during their stay at the hands of their abbot. All this was so impressive that the prior of Göttweig, visibly moved, could verify: "One could see in them nothing, but a great devotion and a very strict way of life".

On the eighteenth of April, early in the morning, they left in the direction of Morava. Lestrange was supplied by the Chancellor of State with a passport which contained no indication of the number of persons with him on the journey, and used some carts to take with him twenty-eight nuns, six priests and two domestics. They arrived at Brünn on 22 April . . . A second group led by the prior, Jean de la Croix [Bodé], took to the road on foot . . . He arrived at Brünn on 25 April. They all lodged with the Frères de la Miséricorde.

After having recalled their meticulous fidelity to the Observances, 'conduct which is perhaps difficult to accept today', Dom Ildefons concludes: 'One must surely say: this lofty measure of observance and discipline has assured the survival of the Order'.

No details on the rest of the journey of this large group have come down to us. Probably they took the same route as the preceding group without the long stop at Cracow. They all arrived in Brest without doubt towards the end of June, because in the month of July, Mother Augustin was sent by Dom Augustin to Lemberg to fetch the group which had wintered with the Benedictines of the Blessed Sacrament and bring them to Brest. The nun charged with this mission carried with her the necessary passport to enter the states of the Tsar. Lemberg was in Austrian Poland and Brest in Russian Poland.

FROM LEMBERG TO BREST

The short account of Sister Stanislaus on the new transfer is clear and specific:

> The Reverend Father having obtained permission for the enitre Order to go into Russia, Mother Augustin [de Chabannes] was sent to fetch us [and bring the passports necessary to cross the Austrian-Russia border]. Our hike was not very long, the nearness of the country and the beautiful weather made it less arduous. We made our way to the convent of the Brigittine nuns at Brest in Russia. Several of our sisters who had come from Bavaria were waiting there for us.[15]

This was the second group. The first, arriving from Cracow, was also in a convent of Brigittines, as the manuscript of Dargnies clarifies: 'The nuns were all settled at Brest in two communities of women, under the direction of Father Fayt who had brought from Leopol the group which had been entrusted to his care, to join up with the others and share their lot'.[16]

The stay at Brest-Litovsk lasted three or four months, according to the dates of the groups' arrivals. During this time the father infirmarian, who lived in the cistercian abbey of Wistycze not far from Brest, came to visit the sisters 'among whom there were many very ill. One of them was so seriously ill that she died on 14 September in the Brigittine convent. This was Françoise Jacoulet, nineteen years old, a novice since 24 March 1798. She was buried in the vault of the Brigittine sisters, and the Register kept during their journeys tells us that the Father Abbot in person presided at her burial. The notice is signed by Dom Augustin and Sister Rosalie Augustin, prioress.[17] Another novice, Sister Lucie Mivelaz made her profession on 'straw and ashes' about the same time. In Sister Stanislaus' account we read that:

> We passed some time in this house [of Brigittines] and in the month of October 1799, we all left, following the

[15] *Relation*, p. 206.

[16] Mémoires, letter 24e.

[17] Register of deaths during travels.

> Reverend Father who walked first, ahead of us, to the castle of Berzoviene[18] in the diocese of Vilna, which was not very far away. It was in this place that all the groups were reunited, except that of Mother Sainte-Marie [Laignier] which was in the monastery at Orsha in White Russia.[19]

THE COMMUNITY AT BEREZOVKA

Three of the four groups were reunited at Berzoviene, the exact name of which was unknown for a long time. There must have been about fifty persons: twelve from Vienna, twenty-eight (?) from Bavaria, eleven or twelve from the group that passed through Bohemia and Lemberg.

Since 14 September, as we saw above, the community had already lost one of its members. Her companion, who had made profession at Brest, died on 26 November at the castle and was buried in the village cemetery. Marie-Anne Mivelaz, Sister Lucie, from Fribourg in Switzerland, had entered La Sainte-Volonté-de-Dieu on 19 August 1797, when she was twenty years old. Another novice, Sister Anne Parain, from Sempsal in the canton of Fribourg, followed her

[18] Lengthy researches have at last enabled us to identify this 'château', the spelling of which varies from one document to another, and there are even three variant spellings in the Register of deaths. Here is read: Bezerisex, Bresouviex, Bersoviex, Bersoviene; and elsewhere, Bersovie. Sister Marguerite Borkowska, OSB has consulted a very detailed map at Cracow, and has written to me as follows: 'The name of the "château" could not be more common: *bereza* means birch tree, and in this part of the world there are so many of them that innumerable localities are named after them. But about five or six km northeast of Brest there is a place called Berzovka. The map, which dates from the beginning of the twentieth century, calls it a small farm and not a village; a geographical dictionary of the same period does not mention any manor house there. But it seems very likely that quite a large country house, built by the Lord of the place for his own convenience, probably in wood, was called a château by the sisters, for want of a better name. Since it has been destroyed, it no longer figures in dictionaries'.

[19] *Relation*, p. 206.

to the grave on 31 December 1799, according to the Register of deaths during the travels. She was forty-six years old.

Two other deaths occurred at the beginning of 1800. Sister Lutgarde Lessus, daughter of a laborer from Bonnétage in Franche-Comté, had entered Sembrancher on the 8 July 1797, when she was twenty-three. After she had taken the novice's habit, on 26 January 1798 she transferred, from the 'First Order' to the Third Order. Doubtless they needed her to take care of the small girls who left for the East with the nuns, and perhaps too, her health was not good and this was the reason for the change. She died on 11 February 1800, aged twenty-five.

At the beginning of April a fifth death occurred, that of Sister Marie-Rose Sergent. Daughter of a school master at Besançon, she had been a Poor Clare for eighteen years when she entered the monastery of La Sainte-Volonté-de-Dieu on 12 October 1796. The following year she made her profession on 24 October, when she was thirty-six years old. She was buried in the cemetery at Brzesc on 6 April.[20]

Less than two weeks after this, on 15 April, they all had to take to the road again, this time in the reverse direction. There could no longer be any question of remaining in Russian territory, on which all their hopes had been fixed for two whole years as towards a haven of peace and stability. The long march which had left many dead along the way, would be drawn out again, and would last months and years, along roads, on rivers, and over the seas.

[20] Register of deaths during travels.

CHAPTER FIVE

THE RETURN WEST (1800)

IN THEIR SOLITUDE at Orsha the Trappistines were scarcely aware of political events. Believing themselves safe, far from revolutionary France, they counted on the kindness of the Emperor Paul I, who had renewed his promises to Madame de Condé when she left the community at Orsha. At the end of March 1800, however, the tsar notified the Order and all french immigrants, particularly the Trappists, that they must leave his states within fifteen days. They were obliged to leave around Easter, which fell that year on 13 April.

What had happened?

Like his mother, Catherine II, Paul I detested the French Revolution. After Campo Formio, he had taken Condé's army into his pay, and authorized Louis XVIII to reside within his territory at Mitau. But the tsar had an unstable character, and his policies showed its effects. Disappointed by the defeat of the Russian army at Zurich in September 1799 and by British *manoeuvres* in the Mediterranean, and dazzled by Bonaparte's success in Egypt and the Brumaire *coup d'état*, he made attempts at *rapprochement* with the conqueror who only wanted Russia as an ally against the English.

There being no possibility that the Trappists might stay permanently in Russia, they had to pack their bags and take to the road again, heading West. Dom Augustin dreamed more than ever of America, land of liberty, where monastic life could thrive and develop. Would not this be the best means to *conserver ce saint état*?

We have two accounts of this hasty departure from Russia: one by Sister Stanislaus Michel of the community at Berezovka in Lithuania, and one by Sister Maur in the community at Orsha. The two accounts are different, and complement each other. The community at Orsha had much further to go to arrive at Brest, and reached the frontier only fifteen days after the first group. I will give the accounts separately, beginning with that of Sister Stanislaus.

FROM BEREZOVKA TO DANZIG

> We had thought at the time that we would be able to remain in this country and establish ourselves in a monastery in accordance with the hopes that had been raised in us. But the hope one puts in men is vain and deceptive. The very people who had allowed us to come soon forced us to flee. And so, having travelled such great distances with so much weariness and at such a cost, having passed the winter in a country where the cold is so severe and having lost there several of our sisters, we found ourselves obliged to leave in April 1800.[1]

The disappointment was cruel. The negative balance of two years of exodus would have come close to engendering deep bitterness, had the hope of continuing their longed-for cenobitic life not burned in the depths of their hearts.

> After our departure we stopped for some days at Terespol,[2] in a hospice belonging to some Dominican friars who

[1] '*Relation* of Sister Stanislaus', *Cîteaux* 35 (1984) 207.

[2] The frontier town on the Bug, opposite Brest, belonged to Russian Poland, but Terespol was in Austrian Poland. Sister Stanislaus is mistaken; they could not have crossed the border between Russia and Austria without passports. This should read Brest.

welcomed us warmly, as they had had the charity to do on our first visit, but we were soon obliged to leave the country, even though we still had no passports. One must surrender to violence. But God—who never abandons those who are his own and has given us so many signs of his special protection in all we had gone through—made it possible in this predicament for a charitable man to make us a loan of a vessel of which he was the master, so that we could shelter in it until we had obtained passports to continue our journey.

And so, with this help furnished by divine Providence, we embarked on a river whose name I do not know, but I do know that we remained in the same place for at least fifteen days on an island, without being able to obtain passports.[3]

This strange situation came about because the residential permits in Russia had been cancelled, but the Prussian government had not yet opened its frontiers to the French who were driven out by the tsar. The river Bug was a natural frontier, and not far from the bridge there was an island which belonged neither to Russia nor to Prussia nor to Austria, which again had refused to receive the exiles. This 'no man's land' became the enclosure of a double monastery. Sister Stanislaus describes it for us:

We were there in peace on our boats just as in the monastery. We made a fire on the island to do our cooking and washing. All the regular exercises were followed. Holy Mass was said, and the sacraments administered, because our Fathers had their side of the boat and gave us assistance. Silence was observed on our journeys as in our houses and our boats; when we travelled by water or by carriage, or along the roads, these became our travelling monasteries where all our rules and regulations were

[3] *Relation*, p. 207.

observed, the hours of the holy Office, the silence, the fasts, and even the Chapter of Faults.

So you see that if in such stormy times and amidst such hard circumstances *the love of our holy way of life* made us keep all its observances, what should we not do now that we are in peace and have all the means of maintaining all our observances and making of our houses sanctuaries where God is pleased to dwell?[4]

They were then at Terespol, the frontier town on the Bug, linked naturally to Warsaw by a navigable river. Actually the Bug flows into the Vistula some 30 km north of Warsaw, and the Vistula joins the sea not far from Danzig. The narrator continues her recital of the journey as far as the Baltic Sea.

Finally, after fifteen days had passed like this, we started off, still on the water. For about two months we were on the river. In the evenings we stopped on the banks and our fathers got out of their boat, landed, and put up some tents on the sand or grass to sleep there for the night. Those who were ill, and there was a great number of them, stayed in the boat. During this time one of our lay sisters died and was buried at the place of the Capuchin Fathers in the suburb of Torne.[5] Also one of our pupils died the day before we arrived in Danzig, and was taken in a carriage to be buried at the convent of the Brigittine nuns in this town, where we were all lodged. The same night of our arrival in this convent another of our sisters who was ill died. God thus afflicted us in many ways.

We stayed in this house about a month. During this time, the group of our sisters who were at Orsha in Russia, and who had been obliged to leave like us, arrived and found us there.[6]

[4] *Ibid*., pp. 207–208.

[5] Thorn or Torun, a town situated on the Vistula.

[6] *Ibid*., p. 208.

FROM ORSHA TO DANZIG

Sister Maur in her lively way recounts the departure from Orsha. She believed that it was the manipulations of the Trinitarian Fathers, expelled eighteen months earlier, which had moved the powers to evict the nuns after the departure of the princess. 'They succeeded so well', she says, 'that on Easter Tuesday it was announced in His Majesty's name that all of us, men and women, had to evacuate the house within eight days and the Empire within fifteen days . . . . We had to sell or give away our provisions without knowing where we would be able to settle. We were only told that the Father Abbot wanted everyone to go to America.'[7]

This last piece of news was the final blow to the vocation of this trappistine novice. She went and explained everything to the Prioress, declaring that she could not go on like this. She pleaded, however, to be able to remain with the group until they reached the frontier, and there she would try to join the Benedictines in Poland.

> The night before we left, they came and took away all the wooden cups and spoons that the Trappist Fathers had made us, and at five in the morning the Trinitarians came to turn us out. This meant into the courtyard, where we stayed while our baggage was loaded into about a dozen carriages, and so they did to us exactly what we had done to them on our arrival. Finally we arrived at the Russian frontier where there was a very big river which separated this empire from the other kingdoms in Europe. There was there a fine bridge and a small island quite high surrounded with bushes. When we arrived on the bridge it was the eve of the Ascension [21 May) in the evening. It was too late to cross over, and the guards on the other side would not let us through either, so our drivers stopped on the bridge and began to unload our baggage, making signs to us to get down. But we

[7] *Relation* of Sister Maur, p. 28.

could understand nothing in this language, we were so convinced that nothing could oppose our departure. In the end they made us understand and put us down on the bridge, leaving us in the most extraordinary situation of all.[8]

This again was the bridge over the Bug near the village of Terespol. The communities coming from Orsha found themselves in the same situation as the brothers and sisters who had come from Brest several days earlier, with the variants pointed out in Sister Maur's account.

A great crowd of people who seemed to be sympathetic surrounded us, but we could make out nothing of what they said. Nobody dared to offer us shelter, even for passing the night. In the crowd there happened to be a Frenchman who was moved to pity for us and said with tears in his eyes: "Ladies, what is going to become of you? It is late, where will you sleep?" In the end, a French general who was in the service of the Emperor was notified. He had a regiment camped nearby. In our acute distress at such an embarassing plight, he came quickly to our aid. He tried first of all, but in vain, to make the guards on the bridge give way, but they replied that they had been expressly forbidden to let anyone pass under pain of death. He on his part had the same orders forbidding us to re-enter the town. However he thought up a remarkable expedient which was actually the only solution possible for us. He ordered a large boat to come alongside and put us on board. The Fathers he put on the island which I have already mentioned, and gave them some tents so they could have some shelter. We stayed in the boat which was moored alongside the island. He then brought a long ladder to make it possible to descend from the bridge to our boat, so that all that was necessary could be brought to us, and we paid all that they asked. But we had to pass between two rows of soldiers whom the same General had

[8] *Ibid.*, pp. 29–30.

> ordered to come, to get to the river bank. This was purely formal and for our security rather than distrust, because without doubt none of us had any desire to escape. We stayed in our floating monastery like that for twelve days.[9]

Having arrived on the eve of the Ascension, the travellers found themselves still on the island on the eve of Pentecost, deprived of Mass. But the Fathers were resolved to sing the Mass for Pentecost 'after having spread the sails of the boat', adds Sister Maur. They were able to leave the following Tuesday for Danzig.

Here our narrator inserts another recollection that leaves us somewhat perplexed: 'We were obliged to stay two days in the town [Terespol?] because two of our sisters were dying and we lodged with the Dominicans.' What had happened? Were the two sisters dying or dead when this occurred, causing the community to stay two days in the town? The Registers make no mention of two sisters dying at Terespol. It is possible that the memory of Sister Maur, who was thirty years older when she wrote these things down, has somewhat confused the places, dates and events.

Leaving Orsha on Easter Tuesday, the monks and nuns followed the course of the river Bug, which flows into the Vistula north of Warsaw. Our narrator thought they travelled without stopping. On the other hand, she remembers very well a short stop at Thorn (Torun) with some religious, the same ones who had received the first group fifteen days earlier. She tells us that these first sisters had left behind three who were ill. This is confirmed by the account of Sister Stanislaus.

This stop with the Benedictines provided Sister Maur with an unhoped for opportunity to see if she could find a place of refuge which permitted her to *conserver son saint état* as a Benedictine without having to trek all the way to America. She herself describes this discovery:

[9] *Ibid.*, p. 31. The name of this french general was de Longeron.

First of all we went into their Church, which rescued us from the crowd who had followed us since we got off the boat. They let us into a chapel which had a grille and was not very noticeable, where they went to receive Holy Communion. There, Holy Mass was said. During it I had more than one distraction, and it seemed so long, because I had looked at the three altars that were there and I saw two pictures, one of Saint Benedict and Saint Scholastica, and, on the other altars, Saint Maur and Saint Placid. Going out after the Mass I asked our Mother Prioress [Mother Sainte-Marie Laignier] if we were in a benedictine house [as I did not know] and I hastily added that if they would be willing to receive me, I would like to stay. She replied that it would be quite difficult to make them understand such a proposition, as we knew hardly any of their language. We talked about it together, however, and she spoke to the Father Visitor who accompanied us to see if he would speak to the chaplain about this in Latin and then the Chaplain could speak to the Mother Abbess. Before going as far as that, however, I wanted to consult the Father Visitor myself, to be assured in conscience that I could be in a mitigated house. [The sisters had been robbed of everything by the Prussian government, and had been obliged in their extreme poverty to accept pensions from their families, which were not put to the common use]. He replied that I would have a safer conscience in following their good way of life than by staying in the world. From then on, I thought of nothing other than being able to stay there. During this time dinner was served. After the meal, the kind religious took me all over their house, showing me the beautiful books for the choir and making signs that they would like me to stay with them. Once the chaplain had informed the abbess of my wish, she agreed with great pleasure and received me very kindly, above all when she learned that I was a Benedictine. But while we were congratulating each other, an exceedingly tiresome hindrance occurred. The commandant of the town, who was a Lutheran and happened to be there, seeing that I wanted to stay, said immediately to the abbess that she could not keep me, at least not until I had the permission

> of the king of Prussia, and that I must go personally to Danzig to get this permission. So I had then to re-embark with the Trappists.[10]

This disappointment did not discourage Sister Maur, who wanted more then ever to leave the Trappist community in spite of all the obstacles she was going to encounter. We continue the journey with her as far as Danzig.

> So I had to re-embark with the Trappists and do sixty leagues on the Vistula with a contrary wind. We took almost fifteen days to arrive at the town where we stopped to sleep. In this town there were some Lazarist Fathers and a hospice served by the Sisters of Charity, who received us most warmly, and we stayed in their hospice. The next day, the good Lazarist Fathers sent us enough provisions to last us three months. We went on again for four leagues on the river, and were warned to have enough fresh water, as the river would become saltier nearer to Danzig where we were going.[11]

The narrator does not seem to have realized that the Vistula pours into the sea a little east of Danzig, and that the last part of the voyage was accomplished on the sea along the coast. She continues:

> As we approached this town we found many boats on the water, which were being tested as we were near a dockyard.[12] The unchanging courses they kept to made us think our poor little boat would be shattered; we cried out for mercy . . . but we escaped with nothing more than fright. Arriving in Danzig we were taken to some Brigittine nuns, where there was already a good number of Trappists who had preceded us and were waiting for us.[13]

[10] *Ibid.*, pp. 33–35.

[11] *Ibid.*, p. 35.

[12] The dockyards of present day Gdansk.

[13] P. 36.

THE STAY IN DANZIG

For the first time since their departure from Bavaria, Dom Augustin had everyone assembled together—at least those who had escaped death or had not withdrawn during the two and a half year pilgrimage. He also saw the most courageous professed in the Order and aspirants who had entered along the way. Dom Augustin had been so unsparing of himself during this eventful time that he felt his strength exhausted. He was run down with fever and dysentery, which had spread among the two groups of monks and nuns lodged respectively with the Brigittine Brothers and Brigittine nuns in Danzig. Their welcome was full of charity in spite of the difficulties of language. The language of the heart to which the habitual silence of the Trappists is particularly sensitive is understood by each and everyone.

After a period of rest, but with his strength hardly recovered, the Father Abbot busied himself about the transport of his flock, not indeed by direct route to America, but to places which would allow them to go on there later on. Dom Augustin made Hamburg his goal. All of them could reach it by way of Lübeck. Boats, not too big, would have to be found, so that the voyage could be made in three groups: the monks and lay brothers; the Third Order and the children; and the nuns. Once again Providence came to the aid of the exiles in the most unexpected way.

A Lutheran ship owner came to see Dom Augustin on a day rife with uncertainty, and offered to take all the Trappists as far as Lübeck. He himself would meet all the expenses of the ships, and he proposed to the emigrants three boats of medium tonnage, with the necessary provisions and food for all the journey.[14] Everything was quickly made ready. The only thing lacking was a favorable wind, and for

[14] Cf. Gaillardin, 2:225; *Odyssée monastique*, p. 187; *Vie de Dom Urbain Guillet*, p. 117.

eight days the monks and children waited on shore, camping in tents. The nuns had already boarded their boat—compulsory enclosure! They were accompanied by Father Etienne Malmy, their faithful 'director' at Orsha.

The Perplexities of Sister Maur

In the midst of all these preparations, Sister Maur did not lose sight of her project of joining the Benedictines at Torun. For this she needed the permission of the king of Prussia to stay in his states. She was not to get it without a great deal of trouble. The prioress of the nuns all re-united together was no longer Mother Sainte-Marie Laignier, but Mother Augustin de Chabannes, who had arrived from Berezovka with the first, and the largest group. Sister Maur had to explain the problem to her:

> I asked the Mother Prioress to get the Father Abbot to find me someone in the town who spoke French, so that I could obtain the permission I had come for, but either he forgot, or he did not want it. I was there three weeks without seeing anyone to speak to. I started getting very annoyed at not being able to return to Thorn. Suddenly I decided to go myself, I went and gave notice to the Mother Prioress of my resolution to leave La Trappe that very day to arrange myself the necessary business, to obtain the permission required, because nobody else was going to do it. They could not give me my old clothes back or other things I had brought because of the confusion of travelling. So I left La Trappe with the habit I had on, a small packet which I had been able to keep in a workbag and without a *sou*! I thought the Brigittines would stall me when I went to open the door, but they let me pass without any difficulty. When I was on the street I went along with no idea of where I was going, hoping to find someone who spoke French, but it was useless.[15]

[15] *Relation* of Sister Maur, p. 36–37.

She went into a small shop, hoping to find a French interpreter, but the shopkeeper took her for a beggar. She received a few coins and then, went into a bakery, suddenly feeling hungry. This gave her the idea of returning to Thorn by foot, begging bread along the way. Just then she was seen in the street by the director of the hospice, a good Catholic who took pity on her and gave her a substantial meal. As he knew no French, he took her to a Protestant minister who understood the language. This minister undertook to procure the necessary authorization from the king of Prussia. While waiting, Sister Maur found lodging with some friends of the director of the hospice, but the abbess of the Brigittines, informed of her situation, offered her hospitality. Sister Maur accepted with a grateful heart, very happy to return to the cloister. Here a very touching act took place which showed the generous spirit of Sister Maur. As we listen to her tell what happened, we hear her for the last time.

> The Trappists embarked soon after on the sea to go to Hamburg, but several sisters who were too ill had stayed behind, and Mother Sub-Prioress who knew German,[16] stayed to care for them, but she herself was suffering badly from a chest complaint. I went to see her and offered myself to stay with the sick for the night. I said I would watch until Matins, and she would stay with them for the rest of the night. Moreover, she had nothing to fear, since I knew the silence of La Trappe, which did not permit any speaking to the sick except for a dire necessity. She accepted my offer with great pleasure and thus we passed

[16] It is very likely that the sub-prioress was Mother Edmond-Paul de Barth, a Cistercian of the Abbey of Koenigsbruck near Haguenau in Alsace. We will soon meet her again as superior of the first foundation made from the mother community, which founded Notre-Dame-de-l'Eternité at Darfeld (Westphalia), which later—in 1804—was to become Notre-Dame-de-la-Miséricorde.

> fifteen days and nights. The sick sisters being recovered, left to join their sisters in Hamburg.[17]

If I have paused for some time over the departure of this Trappistine novice on the return trip, it is because a certain number of her companions also withdrew, discouraged, along the way, even though the circumstances were very different. These departures, however, were all part of the history of this community on its journey, and it seemed to me good to describe a typical case. The circumstances were not at all easy in such withdrawals, either for those leaving, or for the community, which hardly possessed the material means of helping them. In this regard, the nuns were very dependent on the monks. Only with difficulty could they take initiatives which in similiar circumstances during times of peace would have been normal.

ON THE BALTIC

We left the two communities of monks and nuns on the shores of the Baltic waiting for a favorable wind. This arrived on 26 July and they weighed anchor without delay. The first few hours at sea were excellent, but as they sailed out of the bay at Danzig, they ran into a storm. Sister Stanislaus has left us an account of this. The sea voyage left her with a disagreeable souvenir.

> We all embarked on the sea, with the exception of four of our sick sisters, who stayed on for some time in this convent [that of the Brigittines], because they were in no

[17] *Relation* of Sister Maur, p. 45. We will not be following Sister Maur again on her numerous adventures before she was finally able to return to her monastery in Paris about 1807. Passing over the Rhine again at Strasbourg, she said herself: 'It is ten years since I crossed over this same bridge'.

> state to survive the voyage. One of them actually died a few days after we had left.[18]

This death took place on 26 July, the day they sailed, but we must not forget that the nuns had been in their boat for eight days by then. This nun was Sister Donat Donis, a Poor Clare of Auxonne in Burgundy who entered La Sainte-Volonté-de-Dieu on 12 October 1797, at the age of seventy one. Her niece also entered there the same day, a Poor Clare from the same monastery. She made her profession at Orsha on 28 October 1799. We do not know if Sister Donat was a professed of La Trappe, but one thing we can be sure of is that for the love of her *saint état*, in spite of her age, she had undertaken this really extraordinary exodus, and she died faithful to her Lord and her promises.

Sister Stanislaus continues:

> As for those of us at sea, we certainly had to suffer, not only from the dangers we ran into and the terror inspired by the fury of the elements, but also from the discomforts of each of us. Only two of our sisters were not sea sick and did not suffer from vomiting and troubles caused by the rolling sea. But we endured this trial like all the others, with the grace of the Lord. Our voyage ended, we reached Hamburg during the month of August. Here we stayed some time.[19]

The historian of La Trappe, Gaillardin, says of this sea voyage from Danzig to Lübeck:

> A violent storm arose, and furiously attacked the monastic fleet. The sailors furled the sails, but despairing of calming the anger of the waves by themselves, they began praying. The three ships were soon separated and blown far apart. In this extremity each one suffered from his own

[18] *Relation* of Sister Stanislaus, p. 208.

[19] *Ibid.*, p. 209. It was not at Hamburg they embarked, but at Lübeck.

> ailments and even more from the sickness of the others. Above all they suffered from the danger to their brothers, whom the sea carried off and might never bring back . . . . The peril was so great that everyone prepared for death.[20]

This trip along the Baltic usually took two or three days; but for our travellers is lasted twelve days. The storm having passed, the three boats could draw near together and reached the port at Lübeck on 7 August. None of the passengers were reported missing. After some rest at Lübeck, all the survivors started off for Hamburg on foot. In some villages quite near, (today absorbed by the town) two large houses had been rented, one at Altona in the suburbs west of the river Elbe for the monks and the Third Order; the other at Hamm in the suburbs, for the nuns. Most of the sisters, but not all, had to stay here from August 1800 until April 1801.

AN ASSESSEMENT OF THE COMMUNITY

Before continuing the recital of events, it seems to me to be a good thing to do a kind of assessement of the evolution of the nun's community since the departure from Sembrancher. The Registers enable us to do this with a fair degree of accuracy. We saw that at the beginning of the exodus towards the East, there were forty-two who volunteered to go. All through these last chapters I have noted some deaths, some departures and also some admissions.

These changes of personnel during different stages can be recapitulated in order of time. Among those who had entered at Sembrancher there were eleven deaths to lament. Four of these sisters had made their profession at La Sainte-Volonté-de-Dieu, the seven others were still novices, but some made their profession 'on straw and ashes' before they died.

[20] Gaillardin, 2:227.

Here are the names of these women ‘fallen on the field of honor’ if I can say that.

The Professed:

- 11 July 1798: Sister Marie-Thérèse Tinturier (28 years) at Dürnast (Bavaria).
- 12 January 1799: Sister Sainte-Marie Bigaux (37 years) at Lvov (Austrian Poland).
- 6 April 1800: Sister M.-Rose Sergent (39 years) at Berezovka (Lithuania).
- 14 June 1800: Sister Lutgarde de Brémon (25 years) buried with the Capuchins at Torun (Prussian Poland).

The Novices:

- 10 August 1798: Sister Anne Petit (28 years) at Bustehrad (Bohemia), professed on her death bed.
- 26 December 1798: Sister Scholastique Baron (62 years) at Lvov (Prussian Poland), professed on her death bed.
- 14 September 1799: Sister Françoise Jacoulet (19 years) at Brest (Lithuania).
- 2 November 1799: Sister Lucie Mivelaz (22 years) at Berezovka (Lithuania).
- 11 February 1800: Sister Lutgarde Lessus (26 years) at Berezovka (Lithuania).
- ? May or June 1800: Sister Catherine Gard (33 years) at Torun (Prussian Poland).
- 26 July 1800: Sister Donat Donis (74 years) at Danzig (Prussian Poland).

During all the course of this period there were also the departures for different reasons. Four novices left the community staying in Bavaria, another on the way to Austria in 1798, two others at Orsha in 1799, and three during the return to the West. Two left at Terespol and one at Danzig. With the result that on arriving in Hamm the community of Sembrancher only counted half of its members, that is 21 sisters; since 11 had died and 10 had left.

However 36 women had entered during the journeys, mostly at Dürnast in Bavaria. Three of them were not listed in the first Registers, but the fact that we find them present at the time of the foundations made soon afterwards - and one or two already professed - makes it certain that they entered during the period of the travels.

Of these 36 admissions, 9 left at Dürnast before the community departed for Russia towards Berezovka. Two sisters died on the return journey: in May 1800, Sister Walburge de Lanselles (28 years) left ill at Torun (Prussian Poland): and 1 August 1800, Sister Arseline Ferre-Mallion (37 years) at Torun or Danzig.

Five other novices left the community. Two at Terespol, two at Torun and one at Danzig. That makes 16 sisters who entered during the journeys who did not reach Hamm.

All this allows us to suppose that the community which arrived in Hamm was composed of 39 members, most of whom were novices.

The Superior was Mother Augustin de Chabannes, who had directed the community all along the way of return. She was then thirty one years of age.

The Father Abbot who had other plans for her, thought it best to relieve her of the charge and put in her place Mother Marie de la Résurrection de Montron. This religious entered at Dürnast on 20 October 1798. She came from Sens where she had been a sister of the Annunciation, and had made her profession at Orsha. Her sister, a former Carmelite from Dole had preceded her by two years at La Sainte-Volonté-de-Dieu. We will meet the two sisters again in the following chapters.

It was under the direction of Father Etienne Malmy[21] already mentioned at Orsha, that the community at Hamm lived a time of relative calm. We shall see later how this was a time of active rest.

[21] This Father Étienne Malmy has a *curriculum vitae* somewhat out of the ordinary. Born in 1744, a non-juring priest in the diocese of Reims, he took refuge in Belgium. He entered the then recent foundation of Westmalle, which soon afterwards he had to flee into Germany; then settled at Darfeld, where Father Étienne cultivated the land with the community. In 1798 Dom Augustin called him to Constance. He was prior at Orsha; then on returning to Saint- Liboire in Westphalia, was in charge of the nuns at Paderborn in 1801. Prior of La Valsainte in 1803, chaplain at La Riedera from 1804 to 1805, then again prior at La Valsainte until 1815, from where he had to go to Aiguebelle as Prior. In 1834, Aiguebelle became once again an abbey, and the elected abbot was Father Étienne. He was ninety years of age. He resigned in 1837 and died in 1840 at the age of ninety-six!

PART FOUR

The New Foundations

DOM AUGUSTIN DID NOT CROSS the sea with his 'flocks', most of whom set sail 26 July. His health was too impaired for so long a journey. He did not delay long, however, but left Danzig accompanied by thc four nuns who were too weak to face the sea voyage. They travelled by mail coach rapidly enough to give the Father Abbot time to entrust his invalids into the care of the abbess of the Benedictine monastery at Winnenberg near Münster. He then departed in haste towards Lübeck to await the arrival of the ships and conduct thc cntire group of Trappists—monks and nuns—to houses rented in the vicinity of Hamburg.

These houses were intended as provisional shelters until March 1801. The Father Abbot busied himself dividing his people into groups at different localities, so they could more easily obtain the necessary provisions without being a burden on the neighborhood. We will concern oursclvcs here only with the group of nuns and the consequences their reception entailed for the monks.

Before following them into the areas where they were sent, let us have a look at the members of the community in August 1800, when almost all the sisters were together at Hamm. This six or eight month stay at Hamm was a crucial time for the long term future of the women's community. During this period they were separated into two groups: one destined for Westphalia; the other for England. This time the separation was to be final.

The community was composed at the time of thirty-eight members, without counting children for whom we have no surviving statistics. There were fourteen professed and seventeen novices of the First Order, six religious of the Third Order and one *soeur donnée*, a sort of extern sister.

Here are the names of nuns we will meet again during the following chapters:

THE PROFESSED

Mother Augustin de Chabannnes, prioress in charge
Mother Edmond-Paul de Barth, sub-prioress, in charge of the group at Winnenberg
Mother Sainte-Marie Laignier
Thérèse Corcelle
Sister M.-Joseph de Montron
Sister Benoît Isambert
Sister M.-Madeleine Zacharie
Sister Séraphique Van den Kerkhove
Sister Madeleine Guyot
Sister M.-Michel Ducourand
Sister M.-Thaïs Bassignot
Sister Jean-Baptiste Chassaignon
Sister Julie Favot
Sister M. de la Résurrection de Montron

THE NOVICES

Sister Dorothée Coët
Sister Colette Jacquaud
Sister Pélagie du Voeux
Sister Joséphine Fouillé
Sister Stanislaus Michel
Sister Thérèse de la Miséricorde Lamb
Sister Thérèse Pichon
Gertrude Lacmand
Sister Scholastique
Sister M. du Saint-Esprit Allard

Sister Hedwige Guillemin
Sister Elisabeth Dedyn
Sister Arsène Mouillard
Sister Thérèse Müller
Sister Placide Parache
Sister Franche Lanfrey
Sister Véronique Sergeant

SISTERS OF THE THIRD ORDER, who took charge of the young girls, some of whom later joined the First Order;

Sister M.de la Croix de Lestrange
Sister Thaïs Gulenberg
Sister Albéric de Saint-Riquier
Sister Euphrosine Mairesse
Sister Gabrielle Lucottée
Sister Madeleine Gleblin

The *soeur donnée*, Pélagie Breton, a kind of extern sister before there were such things, took care of contacts with persons outside the enclosure.

During the stay at Hamm there were two deaths, both novices. Sister Placide Parache, a professed Carmelite from Amiens, who entered at Dürnast 12 November 1798, dying at forty-four years of age on 24 October 1800: and Sister Colette Jacquaud from Lyon, who entered at Sembrancher the 2 August 1797 and made her profession on her death bed. She died four days later, also at the age of forty-four.

Two French women entered Hamm, one in December 1800, the other in March 1801. Neither stayed in the Order. A novice also left the community, Sister Arsène Mouillard, in December 1800. Had she perhaps found a Carmel that would receive her? She was actually a professed Carmelite of Caen.

There were thirty-six members in the community when Dom Augustin sent in October 1800 a first group of nuns to join those who were convalescing at Winnenberg, to form a community destined to join with the monks at Darfeld in Westphalia. A little later a second group embarked for England. After these divisions were made, the mother community counted about twenty members, who stayed at Paderborn for two years before going back to Switzerland.

In 1808, the Father Abbot adopted a foundation made spontaneously in Paris in 1798. This first adoption was to be followed by others during the next century.

CHAPTER ONE

THE FOUNDATION IN WESTPHALIA

NOTRE-DAME-DE-LA-MISÉRICORDE

IN THE FIRST CHAPTER of the second part of this book, I noted briefly the foundation of a monastery of monks in Belgium. We will come across this monastery again in Westphalia some seven years later, as it was to give welcoming support to the first foundation of nuns who had been separated permanently from the community reunited at Hamm.

THE MONASTERY OF MONKS

On 28 August 1793, three monks had left La Valsainte with orders to make their way to Canada. They were provided with a letter from the bishop of Lausanne and a small sum of money to pay for their passage to America. Leaving on foot, they had to beg food and shelter all along the road. They arrived in Amsterdam, having exhausted their resources, and found the port closed because of the war.[1] The bishop of Antwerp offered the monks the monastery of Korsendonk, which had been abandoned by the Augustinians. On the 22

[1] At the beginning of 1793, all of Europe was united against Revolutionary France, under the initiative of William Pitt. The Netherlands, a dependency of the Austrian Empire, was at the heart of the conflict. The colonial war was at its height on the sea.

April 1794, a second group left La Valsainte with orders from the superior to join the first three monks and reorganize the groups so that only a few stayed at Westmalle, and all the others went on to Canada. The first group had at their head a Father Arsène Durand, and the second , Father Jean-Baptiste Noyers.

On 6 June 1794, the group directed by Father Arsène took possession of the former convent of Augustinians which then became their official property. Twenty days later they had to flee before the revolutionary armies victorious at Fleurus. They emigrated to Westphalia in the region of Münster, and found shelter with the Cistercians at Marienfeld, hoping immediately to be able to go back to Belgium. As the delay was prolonged, they took the necessary steps to stay definitely in the state of Münster. In March 1795, the superior was a Father Eugène Bonhomme de Laprade. After a number of projects and set backs, he finally obtained in October of the same year, from the family of Droste zu Wischering, on the lands of Rosenthal, to the west of the castle of Darfeld, a wood that they had to clear before building. In the spring of 1796, they built first of all their church, and then the other conventual buildings. Everything was constructed of compressed earth and clay, and then they gave the monastery the name *Notre-Dame-de-l'Eternité*!

THE NUNS' ARRIVAL

An undated letter from Dom Eugène de Laprade to 'His Serene Highness Monseigneur the Archbishop and Elector of Cologne, Bishop and Prince of Münster, Prince Royal of Bohemia and Hungary', informs us of the prepartion made by the monks of Notre-Dame-de-l'Eternité to welcome their sisters who had come back from the East.

> I have the honor of informing Your Highness very respectfully that those of our sisters coming from Russia who are

> too infirm to cross the sea to America are looking in these civilized countries for a kind and charitable person who will deign to take an interest in their misfortunes. Worn out with exhaustion after so many difficult journeys, they finally arrived in the country of Münster where a pious and respectable abbess, touched with compassion did not wish to send them away. She is the Abbess of Winnenberg who has in all respects expended on them a most cordial charity. However, she can only let them stay a short time and these poor women see themselves exposed on the brink of winter without any shelter, which would be abhorrent to all humane feelings. Our brothers have built, in a corner of their woods, a small house surrounded by walls and ditches, where they will be received as guests in the same way as they were received at Winnenberg, and without acting contrary to any orders of Your Highness. There our brothers will themselves provide the means of subsistence for their sisters without being in any way a burden on the populace, but in the same way that they provide for themselves and their pupils, either by their toil or work, as well as by the money that we procure from France and elsewhere.[2]

During this whole time Dom Augustin realized that a small group of debilitated, sick sisters, could not survive without the support of stronger members to see to all the necessary daily tasks. Once Dom Eugène had given his assent to receiving the nuns, Dom Augustin sent from Hamm, on 28 October 1800, four other sisters to join those who had arrived first directly from Danzig at the Benedictine abbey of Winnenberg. They reached this monastery about November Sixth. Meanwhile their house was being hastily constructed, as the prior of Darfeld explained in his letter to the archbishop. The sisters enjoyed the generous hospitality of the Benedictines for some six or seven weeks, and on 28 December 1800, the eight foundresses arrived at Darfeld.

[2] Archives of the State of Münster, dossier Fürstentum Münster. Kabinett Registratur, N°1126, pp. 88–89 and 91–92.

During this time they received two postulants, one on 24 November, the other the 28 December. When they reached Darfeld there were ten of them and soon after other aspirants sought admittance.

The Members of the Community

The prioress of the group was Mother Edmond-Paul de Barth, a Cistercian from the abbey of Koenigsbruck—Pont-du-Roi, not far from Haguenau (Alsace), the town where she was born 27 May 1754. Her father was a royal bailiff for the prefecture of Haguenau. Her mother's name was Marie-Thérèse Rhoux. Mother Edmond-Paul entered La Sainte-Volonté-de-Dieu on 30 September 1797. She made her stability there the following 20 December. Her mature mind and great regularity had gained the complete trust of Dom Augustin. A remarkable energy of spirit enabled her to dominate her frail health. Two professed, five novices and two postulants accompanied her on her arrival at Darfeld.

Sister Thérèse Corcelle, from Franche-Comté, born 17 February 1760, entered Sembrancher four days after the foundation of La Sainte-Volonté-de-Dieu. She was professed 28 October 1797. Sister Séraphique Van den Kerkhove, already mentioned as among the sisters who stayed in Vienna in 1798, was born 10 July 1763. She died two years after the nuns' arrival at Darfeld, on 12 December 1802.

Of the five novices, three had entered at Sembrancher. Sister M. du Saint-Esprit Allard, Sister Dorothée Coët, and Sister Joséphine Fouillé. The last was forty years of age when she entered on 15 September 1797, having followed the community as it travelled about Europe. She must have been one of the sick sisters brought from Danzig, because she died scarcely five months after arriving at Darfeld, on 21 May 1801. She made her profession on her deathbed.

Two other novices entered during the journey. Sister Scholastique, Rose Methains, who had been superior general of the Sisters of Providence at Portieux when her congregation was dissolved by the revolutionary laws. She managed to join the colony sheltering at Augsburg with M. Bacciochi, on 7 February 1798. On 29 March she received the habit of the Third Order, but on 28 July 1799, she was given the habit of the First Order as a lay sister. She made her profession at Notre-Dame-de-l'Eternité on 21 February 1801.

Sister Thérèse Müller, the last novice, was born at Olmutz. She was twenty-eight when she joined the colony at Dürnast on 14 August 1798. She received the habit eight days later and made her profession, with some of her companions on 20 August 1798.

The two postulants were Sister Humbeline Barier, twenty-seven, a former Sister of Charity in Paris, who came from Fenain (Nord); and Sister Lutgarde Klein, from Belgium, thirty-five. They made their profession together on 18 April 1802.

Accommodations

These ten religious arrived at Darfeld to live in a building newly constructed of beaten earth, adjoining the monk's monastery, but separated by a cloister wall and a ditch. They were obviously very cramped for room in the corner allotted to them. According to Dom Éugene's letter, it will be remembered, they were received there for only a short time. In fact, the nuns lived there for almost twenty-five years. Postulants arrived in great numbers, about fifteen of them sent from Hamm, and others left for Paderborn when the mother community was transferred there. Others entered for Darfeld or came back from Paderborn. At this period the communities were not yet autonomous and changes of residence were frequent. Dom Augustin presided over the exchange of personnel according to the needs of each house.

How many were lodging at Darfeld during the first year in the life of the young community is very difficult to determine. From the month of March 1801, moreover, we see Dom Éugene getting anxious. The Father Abbot's project of sending monks and nuns to Canada had come to a standstill—or was going to be suspended—and the Father Prior was asking himself how he was going to find room for the new arrivals. Father Jérôme du Halgouët wrote on this subject:

> From 14 August 1800, he [Dom Augustin] asked of Mgr de la Marche [the bishop of Saint-Pol, living in London] to intervene on his behalf at the court of Saint James, with a view to transferring to Canada his communities who had come back from Russia. The reply of the Home Department was a refusal to [let them] go to Canada, but permission to reside in England.[3]

Meanwhile, the temporary reception of the nuns at Darfeld threatened to be drawn out, creating a crisis of accomodation, which began to be felt at Notre-Dame-de-l'Eternité. The prior, in view of the limited plot of land (the wood of Rosenthal) granted them by the Prince-Bishop when they first came to Westphalia, had rented at the other end of the parish of Darfeld a farm belonging to the priory at Klein Burlo. He then sent some brothers to go to live there. At the beginning of March 1801, Dom Éugene wrote again to the Archbishop of Münster to seek permission to lease some part of the conventual buildings of Klein Burlo. This small cistercian priory, a dependency of the large abbey of Kamp, had been uninhabited for many years and the various buildings were in a bad state of repair. The prior emphasized that the Father Abbot would make all the necessary repairs at his own expense. This affair dragged on until 1804, and it was only after the repairs and installations

[3] Jérôme du Halgouet. 'Pierres d'attente pour une histoire de l'Ordre' in *Cîteaux* 17 (1966) 104.

had been made, that the community of Notre-Dame-de-l'Eternité could move there in June 1806. Not until this year therefore were the nuns free to occupy the whole cluster of cottages made of beaten earth on the property at Rosenthal. Thereafter the monastery was called *Notre-Dame-de-la-Miséricorde*.

The First Ten Years of the Community

Little by little, under the firm guidance of Mother Edmond-Paul, the community of nuns became organized and better established. A few rare documents from this period inform us of certain aspects of life at Rosenthal.

We do not have the first Register of Admissions and know of some incomplete records of the professed only through a list preserved at Altbronn. In particular the date of entry is missing. A Register of Deaths from 1801 to 1810 was deposited at the Town Hall of Darfeld by Dom Éugene on 2 April 1811. It gives complementary details and makes up for some of the missing items on the list at Altbronn. Also very precious is an *État nominatif* (list of names) of the religious in the community dated 19 August 1809.

This *État* is preceded by the curious title 'Note on the religious of La Trappe called Trappists', followed by a list of monks and nuns. Some young girls, boarders, are also listed on this *État*.[4] It is worth glancing at this document dating from the early years:

> The Trappists are well known in France. His Majesty the Emperor Napoleon has taken them under his special protection.[5] These are the various establishments of their Order existing today in the French Empire, authorized

[4] *Note sur les Religieux de La Trappistes*, Episcopal Archives, Münster: GV MS Pfarrei, Darfeld, 1809.

[5] We shall see what became of this in July 1811.

> by the government, many of which have been founded by His Majesty the Emperor himself. As also the diverse favors that His Majesty has deigned to accord the different houses of this Order, among others: the Safe-Guard and exemption from all Military Service, that has been granted to the Trappists in the country of Münster, His Excellency M. le Maréchal Berthier, Prince of Neufchâtel, Minister of War, by order of His Majesty the Emperor Napoleon.

This solemn preamble contrasts strangely with what follows:

> Their Rule consists in living a retired life, hardworking and as frugal as possible; they only eat vegetables, principally the produce they grow themselves. They only eat once a day during the greater part of the year and sleep on the bare ground, sleeping little, etc.

The description continues like this for a further fifty lines and ends with these three lines, which seem to me the most interesting of all:

> The persons of the feminine sex who wish to be admitted among the religious must have a pension, either secured or brought upon entering, a sum sufficient for them to live on with the help of their work.

This brings us to a brief comment on the evolution of the community.

1) From 1801 on, a great number of postulants entered, as is proved by the many professions between 1802 and 1803. Did all of them fulfill the conditions noted in the text of 1809? We can doubt it, for a good number of those admitted were French or Belgium emigrants, and many came from as far away as Prussia.

2) Among the professed nuns we find religious from very different regions: eleven Cistercians or Bernardines, almost all from Belgium, and two Trappistines from Paris-Valenton, a monastery founded *extempore* under the Directoire. (We will be seeing more about the history of this

house in the next chapter.) Other religious were also professed for the trappist way of life at Darfeld: three sisters of the Annunciation, two Poor Clares, two Ursulines, two Capuchines, and one member each from the following religious Orders: Augustinians, Benedictines, Dominicans, Franciscans, Daughters of Charity and Visitandines. In all, twenty-eight religious from other Orders were among the seventy-five professions made at Darfeld between 1801 and 1810.

3) Even though professions were numerous, so also were deaths. No year passed without deaths. In 1803 and 1804 there were respectively ten and eleven deaths. Many causes combined to provoke these deaths: the results of travelling across Europe, the unhealthy dwellings newly built of beaten earth, the poor diet imposed by the Regulations, overcrowding in badly aired buildings and insufficient heating. From 1806 on, when the sisters possessed the entire plot of land put at their disposition by the monks, the deaths were notably reduced.

It is worth tracing the evolution of the community during its first ten years on a chart. We can only work it out by the number of professed and of deaths. The variable number of the novices is known only from the official list drawn up in 1809. A preliminary remark: there were three professed when the foundation was made on 28 December 1800. In the following April another professed, Mother Marie de la Résurrection de Montron, who had stayed at Hamm as prioress, was sent to Darfeld to help Mother Edmond-Paul with the formation of the novices. She died the following year at thirty-seven. The reader may perhaps remember that she had been an Annunciation sister from Sens when she entered at Dürnast in October 1798, and had made her profession in the monastery of Saint-Coeur-de-Marie at Orsha in 1799 (see the following table).

The official list of 1809 provides the names of seventeen choir professed and thirteen professed lay sisters. There were also twelve novices, four of whom made profession

Years	*1800*	*1801*	*1802*	*1803*	*1804*	*1805*	*1806*	*1807*	*1808*	*1809*	*1810*	*Total*
Professions		2 +1	20	21	0	2	8	4	3	10	5	80 professed
Deaths		1	4	10	11	6	4	3	2	3	1	45
Number of professed in the community	3	5	21	32	21	17	21	22	23	30	34	+8 novices

the following year. Also to be noted is the large number of professions in 1802 and 1803. Some of thesewere deathbed professions, particularly in 1803. The eleven deaths occurred in 1804, without any professions that year, brings the number of professed down from thirty-seven to seventeen between 1803 and 1805.

On 20 August 1802, sixteen novices made their profession; among them were three sisters who had undergone the 'Russian Campaign', and waited all this time to forge their contract in the Cistercian Order. Two others had preceded them; Sister Scholastique Methains, aged fifty-four, was professed as early as 21 February 1801, and Sister Joséphine Fouillé pronounced her vows on her deathbed on 21 May. She died that day at forty-four and had been a Trappistine for three and a half years.

DAILY LIFE AT DARFELD

Some minute details of the daily life during these first years were written down much later in a rather curious document preserved in the archives at Altbronn. This diptych describing how the first two prioresses governed the community between 1800 and 1826, is a sort of portrait contrasting Mother Edmond-Paul de Barth and Mother Hélène Van den Broeck. The one was a former Cistercian of Haguenau, extremely faithful to an austere rule; the other, a former Capuchine from Brussels, who said 'If I must burn in purgatory, I would much prefer that it was for being too merciful rather than too severe'. We will come back to this.

In these portraits a note draws attention to a small incident in which both superiors are represented according to their temperament, and shows quite well the atmosphere of those days. It happened during the novitiate of Mother Hélène, when she was afflicted with some physical pains that we shall meet again about the same time (1806) when the mother community went back to Switzerland. I will let the narrator speak for herself:

> In their extreme poverty and among all the privations with which they were burdened was added that of the vermin, but it seemed rather that the good nuns encouraged by their superior [M. Edmond-Paul] were happy to suffer this new kind of penance.[6] However it was during the novitiate of the following Superior [M. Hélène] who, unable to tolerate this inconvenience, was tempted to leave, that the Reverend Mother took measures to destroy the pests.

For those who had been through the 'Monastic Odyssey' this inconvenience seems to have been a minor detail and an object of asceticism, but the newcomers could not tolerate the consequences of squalor.

Another vivid little note tells us that:

> A sister to whom she [Mother Edmond-Paul] was very attached because of her admirable regularity, at one time had kissed her hand on impulse (!), and was punished in Chapter as if this was a great fault, perhaps in order to lessen the desire in the others to do the same thing.

And again:

> Reverend Father Éugene used to give to the sisters a little wine he received from time to time from charitable

[6] We may correctly suppose that this was nothing new, but had raged all during the long travels in Europe under precarious conditions of elementary hygiene when it must have developed.

> friends; this is how the Reverend Mother could sometimes allow the sisters who were weak or ill a little glass of wine. She gave it secretly and made the sisters recite the Our Father and a Hail Mary each time, so that, she said, the Lord will prevent this comfort from becoming an abuse. She did the same for meat when it was necessary.[7]

If we can believe the photocopy of the *Regulations for meals at the Community* of which the original is in the Office of the Cellarer of the Monastery of N.-D. de-la-Trappe at Darfeld, it was obviously sometimes necessary to sustain the weakest constitutions with meat and wine. The weekly menu was fixed, once and for all:

Sunday	barley gruel
Monday	potatoes
Tuesday	beans and carrots
Wednesday	barley gruel
Thursday	peas
Friday	potatoes with carrots or turnips
Saturday	peas

Two and a half pages of explanations follow, from which I quote the beginning:

> The soup is normally made with the leftovers of bread and vegetables from the evening before, to which is added about eight or nine ounces of ordinary bread for each sister. If there was nothing left over, the soup will be made with buckwheat flour or something similiar, and the quantity of bread will be reduced.
>
> In Lent or Advent, if there are some cabbages or lentils, these can be given on Sundays in place of the gruel. When there are some large beans these can be given on Tuesdays instead of the peas.

The Cellarer could change the menu a little if necessary, with the permission of the superior, in such a way 'that the

[7] Archives of Altbronn, A4d.

total expense of this table never exceeds the price of a good ten and a half pfennigs every day for each sister'.[8]

We can suppose that these Regulations for the monks had the approval of the nuns, who depended entirely on the monks for their provisions. It is no wonder that on such a diet those with poor health were prematurely cut down. During the first ten years at Notre-Dame-de-la-Misericorde there were forty-five deaths. The average age at entrance was thirty-six and a half. The average length of time these forty-five nuns were in the Order was three and a half years, and the average life expectancy was forty-one and a half years.[9]

By August 1809 at Darfeld, there were no survivors from Sembrancher.

The Two Pillars of Darfeld

Before leaving Notre-Dame-de-la-Miséricorde, let us take another look at some characteristics of the diptych setting the first two Prioresses side by side:

> One was filled with the spirit of penance, and the fervor with which she abandoned herself totally to it made it seem that she only wished to live according to the maxim, 'to suffer or to die'. She had the very special grace of

[8] The pfennig was 1/100 of a mark. What could one buy for 10½ pf in 1806? Did the poor peasants need more to survive? According to a balance sheet drawn up for the daily cost of living of a worker in Berlin round about 1800, a pound (four hundred seventy grams) of home-made bread, came to seven pf; vegetables, salt and groceries twelve pf, 1 quart of beer twelve pf, one hundred twenty gr of meat 5½ pf. That comes to 36½ pf for the daily ration. But as the monks and nuns drank only water and did not eat meat, for them 19½ pf would have done. (I am grateful to M. Büchner of the Social Institute of the University of Heidelberg for this calculation, and to a Lutheran friend of mine of the Ordo Pacis, who asked him to undertake it.)

[9] The Appendix at the end of this Chapter gives a list of names and a summary of the statistics.

> inspiring others to this love of suffering, so that the sisters in distress or bodily sufferings who had recourse to her, went away saying, 'The good God will look after me; I don't yet suffer enough.
>
> The other was gifted with a spirit of tenderness and compassion and exceptional piety. For her sisters she had a love like a most affectionate mother. She rejoiced with those who were joyful and grieved with those in distress. The poverty of the community did not permit her to alleviate her sick sisters as her kind heart would have wished; she said in tears, 'If I had no other assistance, I would sell the sacred vessels rather than let them want for anything'.
>
> [The first being,] of an even temper received without emotion all the troubles and adversities which happened to her, saying 'The Holy Will of God'. She was moved only by infractions against the Rule, and she never left them unpunished.
>
> [The second was:] humble and simple. The authority with which she was invested was to her a heavy burden and she often repeated; 'If I had known that they would make me a superior at La Trappe, I would never have come.' She delighted in mingling with the lay sisters and taking part in their work.
>
> [Mother Edmond-Paul:] was very careful to hide her infirmities to prevent indulgences and remedies. She never accepted any service that she could do for herself, and even went so far as to punish the little signs of affection the sisters wanted to show her.
>
> Having no pity on herself, she nevertheless knew how to discover the real needs of her sisters and succour them according to the Rule. After long suffering, she succumbed to a cancer that had eaten away her left side. The hope of uniting herself to her God in heaven radiated her last moments with an inexpressible joy that was even communicated to those who surrounded her.

This occurred on 29 August 1808. She was fifty-four years old, and had lived the monastic life of La Trappe for eleven years.

> [Mother Hélène:] Of weak health, received with gratitude the cares and attentions that the sisters loved to show her . . . She took particular care to instruct her daughters on the practices of the interior life. Her frailty did not allow her any great austerities; she tried to make up for this by a tender piety which animated everything she did.

Having entered Darfeld on 11 September 1806, she made her profession the following year and was named prioress one year later. 'She died of dropsy after having suffered for long years', at Oelenberg on 12 May 1826. She was fifty-nine years old, and had lived almost twenty years of trappist life.

These two remarkable women, each in her own way, were models of their community, bringing a cohesion of complementary qualities, expressing an identical love for their *saint état* and showing an exemplary fidelity in their profession. We will meet Mother Hélène again during the storms which shook the Order, and with her the community during the next twenty years. Solidly built on these two pillars, the community of Notre-Dame-de-la-Miséricorde in the nineteenth century became Our Lady of Altbronn, and continues to this day.

Etat nominatif des Religieuses de la Trappe, du Departement de l'Ems, Grand Duché de Berg.

Noms de Religion	Noms de Famille	Âge	Lieu de Naissance	Profession précedente	Epoque de l'Entrée
La R. M. Helene Superieure	Van den Broeck	42. ans.	Bruxelles	Religieuse de l'ordre de St. [illegible]	11. 7bre 1806.
S. Therese	Müller	38. ans. 5 mois	Allmutz	Gouvernante d'Enfans	14. Aoust 1798.
S. Benoit	Heijmann	44. ans	Lambeck	Religieuse	28. mars 1801.
S. Victoire	Chuffard	43. ans. 3. mois	Templeuve	Religieuse celestine	21. mai 1801.
S. Jean Baptiste	Piton	39. ans. 5. mois	Tournai	Religieuse de St. augustin	15. 7bre 1801
S. Marie Bernard	Van Derschmissen	31. ans.	Liege	Gouvernante d'Enfans	14. mai 1805.
S. Anne Marie	van Derschmissen	28. ans. 7. mois	Liege	Gouvernante d'Enfans	14. mai 1805.
S. Joseph Therese	Hermans	43. ans	Thurnout	Couturiere	18. mai 1805
S. Stanislas	Scheij	29. ans	Reinsberg	Institutrice de Demoiselles	6. Jet 1805.
S. Elisabeth	Piette	23. ans. 4. mois	Liege	Sans profession particuliere	2 7bre 1806.
S. Marie Sophie	Folting	26. ans.	Hassenwinkel	Couturiere	5. Aoust 1806.
S. Catherine	van Derstrappen	30. ans. 2. mois	Weerdt	Gouvernante	10. aoust 1807.
S. Seraphine	Gavet	25. ans. 10. mois	Mericourt	Sans profession particuliere	11. avril 1808.
S. Antoinette	Daume	57. ans 7. mois	Anspelu	Religieuse de l'ordre de St. [illegible]	16 Juillet 1808
S. Angélique	Cools	29. ans.	Casterle	Gouvernante d'Enfans	16 Juillet 1808.
S. Agnes Edmond	Thulliez	41. ans 6. mois	Garberet	Religieuse de l'Ordre	13. 9bre 1808.
S. Jean Baptiste	De Furneron	28. ans.	Paris	Religieuse de l'ordre, professe de la maison de la Trappe à Yerres près Paris.	10. Aoust 1809.
	Soeurs Converses.				
S. Marie Humbeline	Barriere	36. ans.	Janceaux	Soeur de la Charité de Paris.	24. 9bre 1800.
S. Lutgarde	Klein	43. ans 10 mois	Schijck	Sans profession particuliere	28. Decbre 1800.
S. Bernardine	van Drelst Van der Elst	45. ans	Heerenbodegem	Religieuse	21. mai 1801.

Figures 5a, 5b, 5c

The State Register of the community at Darfeld 1806–1809

Suite de l'État nominatif des Religieuses de la Trappe.

Noms de Religion	Noms de Famille	Âge	Lieu de Naissance	Profession précédente	Époque de l'Entrée
S. Madeleine	Konnink	30 ans	Schovenberg	Servante	25 Août 1801
S. Collette	van Thel	53 ans 5 m	Groewendonck	Religieuse Ursuline	13 Avril 1804
S. Gertrude	Schey	34 ans 8 m	Heinsberg	Gouvernante d'Enfans	22 7bre 1804
S. Jeanne	Beelens	23 ans	Hamme	Sans profession particulière	22 7bre 1804
S. Elisabeth	Wessels	38 ans 6 m	Hasselt	Ménagère	14 May 1805
S. Benoît Joseph	De Schrijvers	43 ans	Zietenvelde	Gouvernante	26 may 1805
S. Marie Barbe	Boonen	43 ans 2 m	Popering	Sans profession particulière	18 Août 1805
S. Agathe	Candeloos	27 ans 6 m	Capenhoud	Servante	11 7bre 1806
S. Marie Anne	De Kinder	34 ans 6 m	Overmeer	Sans profession particulière	22 fbre 1807
S. Cunegonde	Verdels	30 ans	Duren	Couturière	30 Avril 1808

Novices.

Noms de Religion	Noms de Famille	Âge	Lieu de Naissance	Profession précédente	Époque de l'Entrée
Catherine	Horeman	34 ans 6 m	Watersloh	Sans profession particulière	11 Juin 1809
Bernardine Joseph	Buttgens	40 ans	Düren	Maîtresse d'École	3 Septembre 1808
Constance	Cool	33 ans 10 m	Gorkom	Gouvernante d'Enfans	13 Octobre 1808
Marie Claire	Foucart	35 ans	Mainvault	Sans profession particulière	25 Septembre 1808
Françoise	Rijps	36 ans	Hasselt	Sans profession particulière	12 May 1809
Marie Joseph	Casters	48 ans 7 m	Racourt	Fermière	7 Mars 1809
Marie Lucie	Köppen	53 ans 5 m	Wart	Sans profession particulière	13 Avril 1809
Marie Madeleine	Antoinet	35 ans 6 m	Namur	Demoiselle de Compagnie	9 Juillet 1809

Tiers Ordre des Religieuses de la Trappe.

Prenoms	Noms	Âge	Lieu de Naissance	Profession précédente	Epoque de l'Entrée
Marie Elisabeth	Spaun	57 ans 5 m.	Arlon	M.tresse d'Ecole	4 Juillet 1806.
Anne marie	Kickenkamp	50 ans	Durle	Servante	11 Juillet 1806.
Anne Catharine	Schmitz	29 ans	Aix la Chapelle	Sans profession particuliere.	13 Octob. 1808.
Helene Dimphne	Gistermans	41 ans 6 m.	Bracht	Journaliere	13. octob. 1808

Enfants

Remarque: On apprend à ces Enfants, à coudre, à tricoter, à filer, à broder, à lire, à écrire, on leur donne quelques principes du dessein. Ils ne sont aucunement tenus à embrasser la profession religieuse.

Prenoms	Noms	Âge	Lieu de Naissance	Observations
Catherine	Caton	11. ans.	La Fere	Son père mort. reçue en 1802. à la recommandation de M. son oncle Capitaine demeurant à la Fere.
Elisabeth	Bonsak	20. ans.	Amsterdam	à ses Père et mère reçue en 1804.
Francoise	Piton	15. ans.	Tournai	Sa mère morte, Confiée en 1804 par M. son Père, Employé à Tournai.
Marie Claire Helene	Cramer	17. ans	Amsterdam	Soeurs. Leur Mère est morte, leur père Religieux Trappiste. Confiées par M. leur Grand oncle Cramer, Aumonier de sa majesté le Roi d'Hollande et Doyen des Curés d'Amsterdam. en 1805.
Marie Anne Elisabeth	Cramer	13. ans	Amsterdam	

Certiffié veritable à Burlok: le 19 Aoust 1809.

Fr. Eugene de la Prade Abbé de la Trappe.

Pour copie conforme à l'original

Schücking

APPENDIX II
The Deaths at Darfeld (1801–1810)

Year and date	*Names of the dead*	*Age at entry*	*Age at death*	*Years of Trappist life*
1801 21– 5	S. Joséphine Fouillé	40	44	4
1802 19– 2	S. Marie-Jeanne Molet	?	38	?
23– 2	S. Angélique Früyt	64	65	1
24– 3	S. M. de la Résurrection de Montron	33	37	4
12–12	S. Séraphique Van den Kerckove	35	39	4
1803 19– 3	S. Cunégonde Conne	24	25	1
18– 4	S. Benoit-Joseph Clouet	24	26	2
23– 5	S. Marie-Thérèse Vaultier	28	30	2
20– 6	S. Marthe Centerijck	31	33	2
2– 7	S. Dorothée Coët	48	54	6
13– 7	S. Elisabeth Schebers	27	29	2
29– 7	S. Barbe Ginroms	35	37	2
17– 8	S. Angélique Binard	33	36	3
20–11	S. Robert Poulman	38	40	2
31–12	S. Julienne Duroque	?	34	?
1804 31– 1	S. Pélagie Braeckman	24	26	2
17– 2	S. M-Claire Looters	23	26	3
8– 4	S. Gertrude Hulsman	22	25	3
14– 4	S. Pétronille Van Yvo	36	38	2
30– 4	S. Albéric Cousine	38	40	2
2– 6	S. M.-Joseph Bresschiel	52	55	3
4– 7	S. M.-Catherine d'Erbaix	40	43	3
14– 7	S. Agnès Paelinck	39	41	2
22– 8	S. Ida Janssens	35	38	3
10–12	S. du Sacré-Coeur Willart	59	62	3
28–12	S. Pauline de Brye	57	60	3
1805 2– 2	S. Pétronille Van Spuyenbrock	41	45	4
7– 2	S. Antoinette Van Boxtel	36	39	3
13– 4	S. Joseph-Thérèse Gillain	29	32	3
21– 5	S. M.-Bernard Van Hems	47	50	3
4– 7	S. Michel Vermeire	41	45	4

APPENDIX II (continued)

Year and date	*Names of the dead*	*Age at entry*	*Age at death*	*Years of Trappist life*
8–10	S. M.-Anne du S.-C. Boele	45	50	5
1806 4– 3	S. M.-Sophie Lucotté	31	39	8
25– 5	S. M.-Augustin Desjardins	47	49	2
2– 6	S. M.-Etienne Verkanteren	34	38	4
5– 6	S. M. de la Providence Heckers	?	58	?
1807 3– 2	S. M.-Albéric de Saint Riquier	39	48	9
22– 3	S. Louis de Gonzague de Francquen	?	43	?
5–10	S. Catherine de Sienne Klits	21	26	5
1808 3– 5	S. M.-Françoise Van Langendonck	23	26	3
29– 8	M. Edmond-Paul de Barth	43	54	11
1809 9– 1	S. Marie-Rosalie Wieger	26	29	3
7– 7	S. Thérèse de la Croix Corcelle	36	49	13
12– 7	S. Scholastique Methains	51	62	11
1810 23– 6	S. Jeanne Baetens	?	43	?

N.B. - The ? indicates that the sisters have not been mentioned on the record at Altbronn, but only on the obituary notice.

CHAPTER TWO

THE FOUNDATION IN ENGLAND

THE GROUP OF SISTERS sent into Westphalia had hardly settled down under the courteous and kindly help of the prior of Darfeld when Dom Augustin had the idea of making yet another division. He took advantage of a necessary trip to England to sound out the attitude of the English government and of the monks, already established for four years in the country, as to the possibility of a foundation of nuns not far from the monks.

THE MONASTERY AT LULWORTH

Readers will remember that this foundation, made by the monks of La Valsainte, had originally been destined for Canada. They had left Switzerland in April 1794 and, according to the instructions of the Father Abbot had joined the brothers delayed at Westmalle. After some exchanges between the two groups, Father Jean-Baptiste Noyers had set sail from Rotterdam for London with four companions. They had arrived without hindrance in England, where there were already many French refugees, particularly clergy, loosely gathered under the authority of Mgr. de La Marche, bishop of Saint-Pol-de-Léon, who acted as an intermediary with the English government.

Some of the English Catholic families took an interest in the plight of the emigrants, particularly the priests and religious. Four of these families offered the new arrivals the means of staying in England. When Dom Augustin was consulted he gave his consent to their remaining.

> Finally it was a Mr Weld, a Catholic with a great heart, and a real saint, who provisionally received the small group of monks in a lodge in his park at Lulworth Castle,[1] while he had built at some little distance an attractive monastery by the sea. The monks were installed there at Easter 1796, and at the same time they were provided with a well furnished chapel and some land to cultivate. 'I would sooner lose three-quarters of my goods than my good Trappist Fathers', said Mr Weld.[2]

These first impressions lasted some years. But with time and the initiatives of an over-zealous superior difficulties arose. The Father Abbot was warned as early as 1799 by Mgr de La Marche (although the letter travelled all over Europe) of the differences that had arisen between Dom Jean-Baptiste and the good Mr Weld.[3] Father Jérôme Halgouët says of this:

> On 2 February 1801 Dom Augustin arrived without warning at the house of Dr Milner [parish priest at Winchester], who was a friend and confidant of both Mr Weld and Dom Jean-Baptiste. The worthy priest of Winchester assured Mgr Sharrock [the Vicar Apostolic of Plymouth, to whom Lulworth was subject] that he would do all he could to bring about a complete agreement on all points between Mr Weld and the Father Prior. But, he added, clearly impressed, 'My influence is nothing in comparison with the talents and authority of the 'General', who appears

[1] In Dorsetshire, not far from Weymouth. Cf. J. du Halgouet, 'Le fondateur disparu. J.-B. Desnoyers,' *Cîteaux*, 17 (1966) 89–118.

[2] *Ibid.*, 94.

[3] It was a matter of the monks or the superior himself going to the market to sell the monastery's produce and causing regrettable incidents which public rumours exaggerated. The superior would not admit that he had injured British sensibilities, and this was the reason for Mr Weld's uneasiness.

> to have come here principally for another project' . . . Dom Augustin was considering the establishment near Lulworth of some of his nuns with Madame de Chabannes as Superior.[4]

THE NUNS' FOUNDATION

Although nothing specific seems to have been decided, the 'General' returned to the continent and immediately gave orders for a second group of nuns to depart. He had been planning this foundation of nuns since October 1800. He had released Mother de Chabannes from the care of the community still at Hamm, and replaced her with Mother Marie de la Résurrection de Montron, to make sure that during the months of waiting she would be able to govern the mother community. He had already chosen Mother Augustin to direct the small group going to England, as he considered this only as a stage on the way to Canada. He had seen the strength of character of the young superior, her aptitudes for government, her great openness of heart and spirit of fidelity amid all the trials. These qualities had very quickly caused her to be called 'the eldest daughter' of the Father Abbot, not because of her date of entry at La Sainte-Volonté-de-Dieu (she was the twenty-fourth postulant) but because of the spirit which animated her. Later in this chapter we will have occasion to speak of this again.

In March 1801, there were four nuns ready to embark on the sea again for an unknown land. A place for their foundation had not yet been found. Appointed by the Father Abbot, who decided everything, the community included, in addition to Mother Augustin de Chabannes, Sister Marie-Joséphine de Montron, the sub-prioress, and Sister Julie Joséphine Favot, all three of them professed; with them

[4] Episcopal Archives of the Western District, letter of 2 February 1801, quoted by Halgouet, pp. 103–104.

was Sister Thérèse de la Miséricorde Lamb, a novice who entered at Dürnast and a Scot. She was to be of great assistance in initiating the French sisters into a new culture milieu and in the reception of young English recruits.

Leaving Hamburg by boat about the middle of March, they disembarked at Saint Catherine's Docks in London sometime before the end of the month. The exact date has not been recorded. 'There', says the monastery chronicle,

> they were met by a Mr Wright, a Catholic banker, who devoted himself generously to the relief of the French émigres and especially the religious. He drove the four Cistercians to his own house, where they received every kindness and attention until the house which had been rented for them could be made ready. This was Blyth House, Brook Green, Hammersmith, very near London. They remained ten months at Blyth House, and received three postulants, only one of whom persevered.[5]

During this time Dom Jean-Baptiste, the prior of Lulworth, interested Mr Weld in this foundation project. His zeal found an excellent outlet in these activities. About twenty miles from Lulworth in a hamlet called Steephill[6] he found a small property belonging to the estates of Lord Arundell of Wardour, another of the noble Catholics who showed such generous kindness to the French refugees. The two families, the Welds of Lulworth and the Arundells of Wardour, were connected by marriage, and under the evident influence of Mr Weld, Lord Arundell offered this property for the purpose of establishing a community of Cistercian nuns.

This same house had sheltered Jesuits for many years during the penal times when they lived under the constant threat of persecution. But since 1773 the Society of Jesus

[5] *La Trappe in England*, p. 83.

[6] The more descriptive name Steephill can be found in old maps and the first records of the abbey of Stapehill. See *La Trappe in England,* p. 85.

had been suppressed by the Church, and the last Jesuit 'missionary' still at Stapehill, Father John Couche, moved with two children to an old cottage known as the 'Pilgrimage', where he continued to live for some time.

To adapt the house for the purpose of a Cistercian monastery, required some additions as well as alterations to the existing buildings and these were carried out under the directions of Dom Jean-Baptiste, who put his whole heart into the work. When he was replaced as prior of Lulworth on 27 May 1802 by Father Bernard Benoît, sent from Darfeld by Dom Augustin, he was free to give all his time to the alterations at Stapehill.

In January 1802, through the generosity of Lady Mannock, a great benefactress of the French refugees, the foundresses had moved from Hammersmith to be closer to Stapehill. They were welcomed at Burton House, near Christchurch, about ten miles from Stapehill, and stayed there during the alterations to their monastery until October 1802. A French emigré priest, Father Gilles Viel, acted as their chaplain. Four postulants joined them during this period at Burton House, which lasted until 21 October 1802.

The Monastery of the Holy Cross

The account of this even at the beginning of the earliest Register at Stapehill written in the handwriting of Madame de Chabannes, is clear and brief as a bugle call.

> They entered their monastery of the Holy Cross of Our Lady of La Trappe, founded by R. P. Jean-Baptiste, on October 21, 1802, and celebrated their entrance on November 13 of the same year. They then numbered nine: three professed religious, one received to profession, and five novices.

It is interesting to know something about each one of them. We already know Mother Augustin, whom we have met many times during the course of this history. I am leaving to the end of this chapter some unique characteristics of this remarkable woman, who through untold trials directed the foundation in England over forty-three years. She was to be the last survivor of the de Lestrange adventures and an indisputable sign of fidelity to her *saint état*. She lived to be seventy-five years old, sixty of them spent in the cistercian way of life.

She was especially supported in the first years of the foundation by Mother Marie-Joséphine (Pierrette de Montron), daughter of Antoine de Montron, master shoemaker of Dôle, and of Thérèse Michel. She was the elder sister of Mother Marie de la Résurrection whom we met at Hamm and again at Darfeld. Born in Dôle, in Franche-Comté, on 7 September 1763, she had been a professed Carmelite for sixteen years when she entered La Sainte-Volonté-de-Dieu on 10 October 1796. Here she made her profession on 1 November 1797. Given the opportunity of returning to her former Order of Carmel, she declined to do so, declaring that 'although she had been very happy as a Carmelite, she had found in the austere life of the Trappist reform a contentment she had never before experienced'. During all their wanderings she had been a devoted infirmarian to the sick who were never lacking. She continued this office of charity at Stapehill and also filled the offices of sub-prioress and chantress. She died on the Feast of Saint Benedict, 21 March 1814, at fifty-one years of age.

The third professed, Sister Julie Joséphine Favot, entered at Augsburg in March 1798. There is no trace of her in the Register preserved at Rivet. The Register at Stapehill is not much more informative. It tells us nothing of the place or date of her birth, nor of her parents. It says only 'Has made profession at the Monastery du Saint-Coeur-de-Marie at Horchat [*sic*] in White Russia. She died 13 October 1803, and was buried the next day at our Monastery of the Holy Cross'. The author of *La Trappe in England* adds that she had been a professed religious (of what Order we do not know), that she was forty-six when she died and that she was the first nun to be buried in the cemetery of the community.[7] This cemetery had been blessed by Dom Augustin when he came to visit his daughters on 16 March 1803.

At the same time he received the profession of Sister Thérèse de la Miséricorde Lamb. Mary Emily Lamb had been born in Edinburgh on 1 May 1769 (so she was almost a twin with Mother Augustin, born on 19 May). Her parents Robert Lamb, a ship's captain, and Anne Masterton were both Protestants. Mary must have converted to Catholicism at a very early age, as she was already a professed nun of the Annonciades Célestes at Sens by the time she was eighteen. She joined the exiled Trappistines at Dürnast in Bavaria, where Mother Augustin was prioress. She came from the same convent as Mother Marie de la Résurrection de Montron and Sister Gabrielle Lucottée. All three arrived together 20 October 1798 and received the cistercian habit on 1 November, but circumstances then separated them. Sister Thérèse had waited a long time to make her perpetual profession in the Order. Hers was a solid vocation. Mother de Chabannes, who had received her in Bavaria, knew her well and immediately appointed her mistress of novices, an office she kept until her death on 6 August 1831. She was then in her sixty-second year.

Some explicit notes embellish the administrative indications in the Register. Written in Mother Augustin's hand, they emphasize the practical spirit of the prioress, who sought to discover the best ways of developing the talents of her sisters for the common good. Near to the name of Sister Marie-Joséphine we read: 'She knew the art of drawing, all kinds of fancy work, and was very caring for the sick'. And of Sister Thérèse de la Miséricorde 'she knew embroidery and linen work'.

[7] P. 94.

The Novitiate

The five novices mentioned above were in reality two novices and three postulants who received the habit on 13 November, the official day of the foundation. The three week delay was necessary for the nuns to become accustomed to the place and arrange the house in working order.

One of the novices, the only one of the three postulants who entered at Hammersmith to stay, was Sister Marie Bernard, forty, a doctor's daughter from Yorkshire. She entered on 8 August 1801 and received the habit at Burton House on 15 January 1802. Her health was not as strong as her vocation, and she could not endure the austerities of La Trappe. Even so, she remained as a choir oblate and received the black veil in February 1803. A little note adds: 'She is musical, can draw and make quite nice molds for statuettes'. She died at forty-nine on 15 October 1811.

On 4 January 1802 a Carmelite from Huy in the diocese of Liège entered at Burton House, Marguerite-Marie-Justine de Femeron de Verriers, born at Versailles on 1 August 1774. She received the Cistercian habit on 15 January. She was the daughter of a Master of the Petitions of His Majesty at Paris; her mother was from a noble family of Nantes, Claude Prévot d'Artencourt. She had been baptised in the parish of Saint Sulpice. 'She knows a little about drawing, music, and does all kinds of fancy work and reliquary ornamentation. She knows how to work with wool and can perhaps be a very good wardrobe keeper', [i.e. in charge of the sewing room]. Sister Jean-Baptiste was to disappoint Mother Augustin, however as she left Stapehill on 3 May 1805 'for reasons of health', says the Register. We will find her again elsewhere two chapters later.

On 26 August 1802 three promising recruits from Cambrai entered together, and received the habit on 13 November, the Feast of All Saints of the Order. The first of these was Catherine-Jeanne Wastrenez, who became Sister Scholastique. She was born on 26 September 1758 to Jacques

Wastrenez, a wheelwright at Vielly, and Marie-Antoinette Sorriou. 'She knows how to embroidery and is well fitted for the work of housekeeeper', says the Register. The second was Anne-Elisabeth Quatrelivres, who became Sister Madeleine. She was sixty-four when she arrived at Stapehill and had been a Canoness of Saint Augustine at Cambrai. The daughter of a farmer from Neuville Bougonval (diocese of Cambrai) she was, notes the Register, 'very suited in the kitchen because of her exquisite cleanliness and economy'. We will see, too, also that despite her age the hardest field work did not discourage her. The third was Sister Humbeline Le Fèvre, thirty-five years old, also a farmer's daughter from Florenville (Cambrai). She had been a Religious Hospitalière de Saint-Augustin at Cambrai. In the Register, the prioress noted, 'She can embroidery, and understands dairy work, baking and field work'. These three companions in exile made their profession together on 24 May 1804 and were a real treasure in the material and spiritual development of the young foundation.

The Solemn Inauguration

We quote here the account as it was written by the foundresses themselves:

> After having been turned out of our holy retreats and obliged to abandon our country, to traverse many strange lands in order to find a refuge where we could freely carry out the duties of our holy state, and unable to remain anywhere, we have at last been sent by our Reverend Father Abbot, Dom Augustin, to England, where Divine Providence has willed to prepare the retreat for which we have been longing, in this Protestant country, once the Isle of Saints.[8]

[8] *La Trappe in England*, p. 96.

After recalling some benefactors, the text continues:

> Having arrived in this little sanctuary, so ardently desired, penetrated with gratitude, and after making a three days' retreat in preparation, we have celebrated our taking possession of the house with great solemnity, for the first time, on November 13, Feast of Our Holy Fathers, and have undertaken for ourselves and for all who come after us, to renew the memory of it on the same day . . . . Dom Jean-Baptiste said Mass, and immediately before the communion came to the grille holding the ciborium in his hands. The community knelt down, and Madame de Chabannes recited in the name of all a solemn act of thanksgiving and renewal of vows. After Mass, the *Te Deum* was sung, the antiphon *Inviolata* in honour of Our Lady, and another in honour of the Holy Cross.[9]

The Stapehill Property

The sisters had to set to work to get the best out of the land placed at their disposal. Poverty and hard work were the order of the day, especially during their early years, for the nuns had no other resources than their own courage. They were, however, helped a little by pensions granted to French refugees by the British Government; one pound per person per day.

The site was perfectly adapted for the kind of the monastic life that they envisaged. It was southeastern Dorsetshire and at the very center of a spacious, bare stretch of moorland covered only with heather and gorse and crossed by the valley of the river Stour. About ten miles to the southeast only a deserted line of sand banks marked the site where, in the second half of the nineteenth century, the great holiday resort of Bournemouth would spring up.

[9] *Ibid.*, p. 97.

Holy Cross was ideally sited, although the soil was very poor and mostly uncultivated. Yet there was a farm which had been enlarged by various buildings erected according to need and following no particular plan. The author of *La Trappe in England* says that the monastery presents more the appearance of a small village than a monastery. The rest of the original buildings, which had only mud walls and were roofed with thatch, (somewhat similiar to the beaten earth at Darfeld) have long since disappeared.

The intrepid nuns attacked the moors which surrounded the house on three sides and themselves dug ditches and drained the low lying meadows in the valley of the Stour. Sister Humbeline in particular undertook extraordinary labors clearing the uncultivated land, with only one sister of seventy, Sister Madeleine, to help her. Madame de Chabannes herself would fill carts with manure between four and five in the morning after Vigils, so that they would be ready for the hired man when he came at six to collect it for spreading on the cultivated patches of ground.

The monks of Lulworth showed themselves true fathers and brothers to the little community, helping them both spiritually and temporally. Father Antoine was appointed confessor to the nuns, and came over on horseback every Saturday. In the early days he was always accompanied by a lay brother bearing a barrel of milk. This continued until the nuns received the welcome gift of a cow. The brothers made the nuns' shoes, and the nuns in return washed the monks altar linen and mended their clothing.

In spite of the nuns' efforts, the difficulties of English farming evidently proved too great for them. They knew absolutely nothing of local agricultural methods and by reason of strict enclosure could not work all the land at the little farm or be helped by neigbours. The only remedy was to engage a local farmer, who proved to be a faithful servant to the community and gradually the farm became a small source of income. Some time later, about 1808, a brother came from Lulworth, Brother Patrick, an Irishman, took over the direction of the farm and stayed until his death in 1823.

The Growth of the Community

This came about very gradually. The original community was composed of former religious, except perhaps Sister Scholastique from Cambrai and the Oblate Sister Marie-Bernard from Yorkshire. In October 1804, a young girl of nineteen arrived, Mary Slade, daughter of a carpenter at Lulworth. She waited until February 1807 to receive the habit of a choir novice under the name Sister Juliana. She made her profession in October 1809, and died at age thirty-two on 7 May 1817.

Local recruitment was tenuous and sporadic. More emigrée religious came to augment the community: a Religieuse Hospitalière of Saint-Nicolas from Vrons, a Benedictine of Forest in Brabant, a Carmelite from Antwerp, a Colettine of Cîteaux who had come from Spain, and a Visitation sister. Nevertheless during the first sixteen years there was an almost steady growth of new members at Holy Cross Monastery. The chart and the diagram on page 263 follows the Register of Admissions, Clothings and Professions and summarizes these statistics.

Note that among the postulants who entered during the early years there were two children, admitted in accordance with the suggestions of Dom Augustin when he created the Third Order. They were not received at Stapehill until 1807.

Between 1807 and 1815, eleven children were admitted, the youngest five years old and the eldest sixteen and a half. Several of them came from Protestant families, received conditional baptism in the sacristy of the church adjoining the monastery, and then were confirmed and made their First Communion. Later, eight of them took the cistercian habit, and six died before they were twenty-five years old. The fate of the other two has not been recorded.

GENERAL TABLE

31 December	*1801*	*1802*	*1803*	*1804*	*1805*	*1806*	*1807*	*1808*	*1809*	*1810*	*1811*	*1812*	*1813*	*1814*	*1815*	*1816*		
Admissions	4+3	4	0	2	0	1	4	3	3	2	2	10	4	2	3	2	51	Admissions
Novices	2	5		1			3		2	3	1	6	4		3	1	31	Clothings
Professions			2	3			3		4	2	2	2	3	3	1	2	27	Professsions
Deaths			1						1		3		1	1			7	Deaths
Departures	1	1		2	2		1	1			2		1	2	1		14	Departures
Number in the community	6	9	8	8	6	7	10	12	14	16	13	23	25	24	26	28	28	Members

[10] There are some uncertainties in this Table because of missing details in the Register on the destiny of about a dozen subjects, owing to a missing date, either for their death or departure

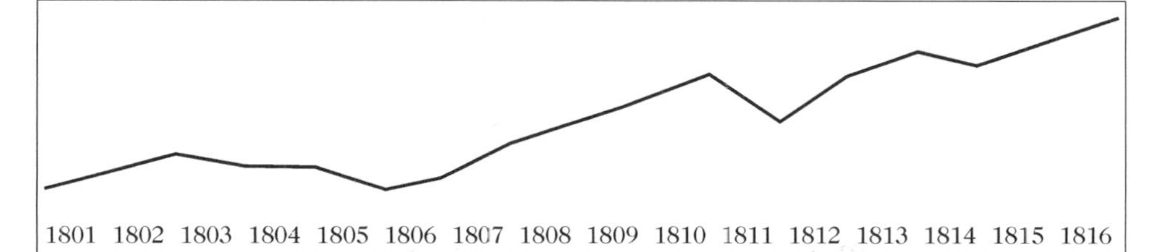

On his return from America in 1815, Dom Augustin brought with him several Americans. He entrusted two to the community at Stapehill. Johanna Scherrick, born at Belmont in April 1785, had already received the habit of a novice under the name Sister Thaïs. She made her profession on 6 January 1817 and died on 21 October 1819, being then thirty-four years old. The second, Catherine Dillaway, was born in Baltimore on 15 January 1800. After spending some time with the children, she received the habit the next year and made her profession on 21 March 1822, taking the name Sister Benedict. The Register has noted in another hand: 'She was sent to America and died on the voyage'.

The Adjoining Mission

The property of the house at Stapehill had been put at the disposition of the nuns only under certain conditions. The most burdensome was the juxtaposition of a 'Catholic Mission', a sort of associated parish which used the nun's chapel. The nuns were also required to lodge and keep the parish priest. The priests who succeeded one another during the first years were a considerable source of anxiety for the Mother Prioress, and this resulted in many exchanges of letters with the Vicar Apostolic, Mgr Sharrock, a man of rather narrow and rigid mind. This trait was manifest when it came to the subject of the confessors and the powers granted to them. Many letters dealt with this, but behind all of them lay the question of the jurisdiction of Dom Augustin over the nuns, always a burning issue in relations with the local Ordinary.

Furthermore, the mission church was also the nuns' church, and while this assured them of daily Mass it raised difficulties for two separate congregations. The building, which had been the chapel of the former Jesuit residents, was far too small for the parish and the community, especially as the number of nuns increased and zealous priests built up the mission flock. It was not until between 1847 and 1851 that the existing church could be built. This was a double church with parallel naves, the two sanctuaries divided by a wooden screen. [The present wrought iron grill was designed by one of the sisters in the 1960s, replacing the original rather drab partition—trans.] The old chapel then became the nuns refectory.

A Corner Stone

Before leaving Stapehill, let us pause to look at the personality of the first superior of the foundation, whom we have always called Madame de Chabannes. Her real identity is noted in the parish register of Langogne in Gévaudan (Lozère):

> Rosalie-Marie, legitimate daughter of the noble Antoine de Vergezes du Mazel and of Dame Marianne Clavel de Chaudeyrac, married in the town of Langogne, was born on the nineteenth of May in the year 1769 and the same day was solemnly baptised. Her godfather was Pierre Clavel du Monteil, her first cousin, and her godmother Marie de Vergezes du Mazel, her sister.

She was the twelfth and last child of the family. At the age of five she was sent as a boarder to the abbey of Sainte Antoine-des-Champs-lez-Paris, where her eldest sister Marie, then aged twenty-three, was the mistress of the boarders. She herself recounted this incident to the sisters at Stapehill, and it has been preserved in the chronicle, where one can already see in the child a woman of strength of character.

> When the abbess led her to her sister and told her that the latter would be her mistress, the child drew back in the most determined manner and declared, 'Mama says that one sister cannot exercise authority over another' greatly to the amusement of the abbess and all present.

Marie-Rosalie knew what she was doing, as she had six sisters older than herself.

When she left boarding school at fifteen, she entered the novitiate at Saint-Antoine and took the name of Sister Augustin. Three years later she made her profession, on 3 June 1787. She left the abbey when the community was dispersed, at the latest in September 1792, and was able to find cistercian life again at Sembrancher on 21 June 1797. Here she made her new stability on 29 October 1797, before leaving to make her way through Europe. We have followed her during the years of peregrination in which she perfected her experience of governing, and became ever more anchored in the desire of preserving her *saint état*. She remained well aware of this as she faced the thousand and one trials which shook the community through all the years she was prioress. Some are noted briefly in the archives. The grinding poverty, harassing anxiety, the long silences of Dom Augustin, from whom she awaited directives and encouragements, the difficulties caused in community by two or three sisters whose vocation had not been well tested, the uncertainties over twenty years of the intentions of Lord Arundell and his family, a serious fire which could have reduced the house to cinders, the projects of a transfer and foundation in Ireland which came to nothing, the departure of the monks from Lulworth who returned to France, and on it went. Besides all this she had a very delicate constitution which she surmounted with fierce energy. She was the last survivor from the monastery of La-Sainte-Volonté-de-Dieu and of the emigration in Russia.

The supreme trial of all for her, however was juridical separation from the Order in 1824, which was arranged without her knowledge by the Vicar Apostolic, Mgr Collingridge, who had succeeded Mgr Sharrock. He had become alarmed at seeing the community gradually diminish, because so many of the young nuns were dying under the strict Regulations of La Valsainte. Mother Augustin did all she could with her usual strength of purpose to keep a close relationship with the monasteries of the Order. She procured cistercian monks as chaplains to keep the spiritual tie with the cistercian life she had so courageously maintained. This desire stayed alive in the community after her death, but it was not until 1915 that the monastery was again restored to the jurisdiction of the Order.

What was the secret of her strength of soul? We quote here from what has been said by her daughters in the chapter of *La Trappe in England* devoted to her spirit.

> A truly Cistercian silence surrounds, in death as in life, this great and saintly religious. Nothing of her inner life has been left on record; like the Psalmist, she 'kept all her strength for God'. It was in silence that she found this strength to endure to the end amid the many and heavy trials that beset her path . . . the whole course of her life was nothing but a progressive series of detachments, the outward indication of the purifying action of God within her soul. To her natural energy of character was added a high degree of the gift of fortitude, enabling her to undertake great things for God, and to endure all contradictions in carrying them out. This fortitude, combined with an intense spirit of faith and an unbounded confidence in God, made her, indeed, the 'valiant woman' of Holy Scripture able to lead others and inspire them with her own courage and confidence.[10]

Even though all her personal writings have not been preserved, some notes of her Conferences taken down by

[10] *La Trappe in England*, p. 72. Marie-Rosalie, in addition to her eldest sister had four other sisters in religion: Marie-Anne, a Cistercian at Mercoire; Adélaide, a Benedictine at Yerres; Marie-Marguerite and Catherine-Justine, Cistercians at the abbey of Saint-Antoine. Only her sister Agathe, ten months older than herself, married. She also had a brother who was a priest, Charles de Vergèzes, parish priest of Blavignac in Lozère. Only one brother, Michel, married. Pierre-Charles died at five; of Pierre-François and Alban we know nothing. (Information taken from notes given to me by M. Grenié of Paris, the great-grand nephew of Marie-Rosalie de Vergèses du Mazel, called Madame de Chabannes).

the sisters enable us to glimpse something of the spirit which animated her. It was a spirituality of the cross. Had she not named the foundation Monastère de La Sainte-Croix, which became Holy Cross Abbey. This was no lip service. She insisted on a demanding realistic view:

> Do not forget that true devotion to the Cross consists in bearing generously the crosses God sends us. To content ourselves with adoring and venerating this precious Cross, and yet to shun the occasions of bearing it, would be an illusion.
>
> You have come here to seek the Cross [the monastery possesses a relic of the true Cross], and you must not rest content with finding it before your eyes to adore and venerate, but it must be in your heart and mind, and in all the members of your body by mortification. This prospect would terrify cowardly souls, but those who take Jesus Crucified for their Spouse should count those days the happiest on which they have most to endure, for those are the days which unite them more closely to Him whom alone they should love.[11]

This strong language did not prevent her from being lenient towards some weaknesses: she was very attentive to each of her daughters, taking their part, seeking their good so that no one became discouraged. Her letters to Dom Augustin show her attentive solicitude for all the nuns. And they all loved her deeply—too much, sometimes, to her way of thinking. She was afraid of being an obstacle between them and God.

More than once she asked her superiors to allow her to resign, but this favor was never granted, in spite of her growing infirmities. On 19 May 1844 she turned seventy-five, and breathed her last on 13 June. No details of these last days have come down to us. In accord with cistercian ritual, her body, clothed in the white cowl, was buried without a

[11] *La-Trappe in England*, p. 136.

coffin in the cemetery blessed forty years earlier by Dom Augustin de Lestrange himself.

A reputation of holiness spread rapidly in the neighborhood, and six months later her body was exhumed in the presence of many witnesses, and particularly of a Protestant physician, Doctor Stewart. The body was intact, no mark of corruption was to be seen as the infirmarian wiped the damp earth from her face and clothes. But no one thought to draw up a legal testimony, duly signed and witnessed. The body was placed in a coffin and re-interred in a vault specially prepared in the middle of the cemetery and surmounted by a graceful stone cross, some twelve feet high, supported on a base of three steps. The inscription on the steps runs as follows in Latin:

> IHS. This cross has been erected to the memory of our Reverend Mother Rosalie Augustin de Chabanne, foundress and superior of this monastery over forty-two years. Here her remains lie in peace, awaiting the glorious and immutable resurrection through Jesus Christ our Saviour. She died on 13 June, fortified by the sacraments of the Church, in the year of Our Lord 1844. She was professed fifty-seven years and was seventy-five years old. *Out of the depths I cry to thee, O Lord*. R.I.P.[12]

[12] *Ibid*., p. 137.

Translator's note. The nuns left Stapehill in November 1989, and spent a year at Boxmoor, Hemel Hempstead, just north of London, in a convent belonging to the anglican Sisters of the Love of God. A search for a permanent home, after many hopes and disappointments, led them to a property near Whitland in South Wales. The new Holy Cross Abbey is only a few miles from the ruins of Whitland Abbey, the first cistercian house in Wales, founded from Clairvaux in 1141, while Saint Bernard was abbot. The sisters moved to Whitland at the end of 1990. Stapehill itself is now open to the public, and the buildings have been preserved intact. (For this information I am indebted to Dom John Moakler, abbot of Mount Saint Bernard Abbey in Leicestershire—trans.).

CHAPTER THREE

THE RETURN TO SWITZERLAND

THE COMMUNITY which had stayed on at Hamm after the departure of the groups to Westphalia and England also had to think about transferring. The houses rented near Hamburg were available only until mid-March 1801.

After his return from England in February, the Father Abbot had to organize lodgings for the monks and nuns who had come back from Russia. With this end in view he had recourse to the prince of Paderborn. A letter of Dom Éugene de Laprade to the Prince of Münster mentions this request:

> In this critical circumstance the Reverend Father Abbot of La Trappe has appealed to the kindness of the Prince of Paderborn who very willingly granted him and his own, asylum and protection in his States.[1]

This princely protection allowed the nuns to be welcomed at Paderborn itself, in a former convent of Capuchins near the Cathedral. As a sign of continuity with the monastery at Orsha in White Russia, they called it Saint-Coeur-de-Marie.

The mother community had to make several more moves, however, before it finally found a place to settle down. In this chapter we will accompany them to four successive residences between the years 1801 and 1805.

[1] Undated letter of Dom Eugène de Laprade to the Prince Bishop of Münster, Staatsarchiven Münster, file Fürstentum-Münster, Kabinettsregistratur, n°1126, pp. 105–106.

After settling in Paderborn, a scouting group went into Switzerland in October 1802, staying at Villarvolard in the canton of Fribourg. The rest of the community joined them in June 1803. The whole community then transferred to La Grande Riedera in August 1804. A final transfer to La Petite Riedera took place in November 1805 and the monastery then took the name Notre Dame-de-la-Sainte-Trinité.

PADERBORN: APRIL 1801 – MAY 1803

We come back again to our faithful chronicler, Sister Stanislaus Michel. After having emphasized the sufferings of separation exacted by the Westphalian and English foundations, she continues:

> In the month of April 1801, we also made our way into Westphalia to the town of Paderborn, in the hope of being able to establish a monastery in that country. But God did not wish this. He has willed that Switzerland, the place of our birth, was also to be that of our growth. Some days after our arrival in Paderborn, our Superior, Mother de la Résurrection [de Montron], was sent to Darfeld, and Reverend Mother Sainte-Marie [Laignier] again took her place [as Superior], which [position] she fulfilled until her holy death.[2]

The Members of the Community

The community which arrived in Paderborn counted seven professed nuns; three of them had made their profession in the Order at Sembrancher, the other four travelled eastward before the end of their novitiate, and made their vows at Orsha. Twelve novices also went with them. Four of them

[2] 'Relation,' *Cîteaux*, 35 (1984) p. 210.

left the next year, and the other eight died professed in the Order.

Besides these nineteen professed and novices, there were three sisters of the Third Order and a sister *donnée*, who looked after contacts outside the monastery. In all, there were twenty-three women, without counting the pupils of whom we have no statistics.

A rather curious profession schedule was drawn up, and seems to have been pronounced at Paderborn. It is not dated, but is the schedule of profession of our guide, Sister Stanislaus Michel. She never speaks of any sojurn at Darfeld, yet her schedule mentions this fact. The text reads:

> I, Marie-Stanislaus, Jeanne-Thérèse Michel, promise stability and conversion of manners and obedience according to the Rule of Saint Benedict, Abbot, before God and of all the saints whose relics are here in this place called Notre Dame-de-la-Miséricorde of the Order of Cîteaux, constructed in honor of the Blessed Mary Mother of God, situated at Darfeld in the country of Münster, into the hands of the Reverend Father Augustin, Abbot of La Valsainte and of Reverend Mother Marie du Saint-Esprit, residing in the place of Villarvolard in Switzerland.[3]

It can be supposed that Dom Augustin had destined Sister Stanisalus for the community at Villarvolard, then being planned, and had taken the opportunity of a visit by Mother Marie du Saint-Esprit to Paderborn to allow Sister Stanislaus to make her profession, which she had so long looked forward to. Actually it was simply a new stability: from being a Cistercian of Avignon, she became officially a Trappistine.[4]

[3] From a packet of schedules preserved at Maubec, which transferred to Blauvec in November 1991.

[4] The exceptional circumstances of the times may to some extent justify the procedure employed by Dom Augustin on several occasions in regard to the monks (Dom Gérard Guérout). Father du Halgouët speaks

Growth of the Community

The admission of aspirants was in general reserved to the Father Abbot, who had the last word on their admission and destination. He distributed persons as he pleased. It appears that during the uncertain period at Hamm while the mother community was waiting to transfer to a more permanent house, Dom Augustine sent postulants first of all to Darfeld. But once the house at Paderborn was established after the end of May, fifteen postulants arrived successively from Notre-Dame-de-la-Miséricorde: four together on 30 May, two others on 4 June, another four again on 1 August, and yet five more during the following weeks. All received the habit at Paderborn in 1801.

The following year, 1802, fifteen new aspirants entered directly at Paderborn, while at Darfeld recruitment continued as usual. Of these thirty new recruits in less than two years, twenty-one left and only nine made their profession.

Life at Paderborn

We have very few details of events in the life of the community during the two years they stayed at Paderborn. One

of a request made on 19 June 1800 by the abbot of La Valsainte to the former nuncio in Switzerland, for the annulment of a profession made at Orsha by a sister, when the community had already left Orsha two months earlier.

'It is the request for an annulment which puzzles the consulters . . . . What intrinsic force had the Regulations published at Fribourg in 1794? Were they approved at any time by apostolic authority? . . . Documentation would be needed on the communities of women belonging to the Institute in question, which they created on their own authority . . . . especially since we are in total ignorance . . . we do not even know whether any women's communities existed before this under the rule of La Trappe . . . .' (Vatican archives, SS. Svizerra, Add.VIII, f°s 74–76), *Cîteaux* (1977) 81. Father Jérôme adds: 'The fundamental problems remain open. But Dom Augustin does not think about them any more' (*ibid*). Furthermore, no direct reply was made to Dom Augustin, and the novices continued to make profession in the Lestrange reform.

thing stands out in October 1802, the visit of Mother Marie du Saint Esprit. It was the signal of the hope to return to Switzerland. In fact, Dom Augustin had come to fetch a party of monks for La Valsainte and was looking for a means of also transferring the nuns at Paderborn.

But before we leave Paderborn it would be good to stop and see something of the sisters who finished their earthly life there. There were six.

The first died on 1 September 1801. Sister Benoît Isambert, who came from Annay in the diocese of Chartres, entered Sembrancher when she was twenty-nine on 20 July 1797. Professed at Orsha, she travelled almost 6000 km, but by the time she was thirty-three she was totally exhausted.

The second is known to me only by a death notice registered in the cathedral:[5] Jeanne-Catherine Defrevrimont, also thirty-three, who died 18 January 1802. Was she a postulant or a novice? The death Register says only, 'Sister of the Order of Trappistines'.

Three weeks later, on 9 February, another death followed, that of Sister Jean-Baptiste Chassaignon, a former Annunciade Céleste from Lyon. Entering Sembrancher on 26 September 1797, when she was forty-one years old, she made her profession at Orsha on 28 October 1799. She was, like the Princess de Condé, a spiritual daughter of Father de Bouzonville. On 25 July 1798, Sister Marie-Joseph wrote to him from Vienna, 'Sister Jean-Baptiste asked me, through our Reverend Mother, to send word to you that, in spite of the travelling, she is happier every day in her *état*.[6]

Sister Geneviève Belhomme, from the parish of Saint-Nicholas-des-Champs in Paris, joined the community at Dürnast on 30 March 1799, just as they were getting ready to

[5] The archives of Lyon-Vaise preserved at Maubec [Blauvac] possess three death notices. Some photocopies from Paderborn confirm these three deaths and indicate three others that our Register has noted. (Dompfarrei Paderborn Kirchenbuch, Band 3).

[6] *Lettres de piété*, or intimate correspondence of the Princess Louise-Adelaïde de Bourbon-Condé (Paris, 1843) p. 216.

leave for Lithuania. She was then twenty-six years old. She followed the community through its various stages and was nominated for Paderborn when she was still a novice. She finally made her profession on her deathbed on 19 March 1803. Two days later, on the Feast of Saint Benedict, she died after four years of Trappist life.

Hardly a month had passed when, in her turn, Sister Françoise de Langhe also died on 5 April. Daughter of a middle class citizen of Gand, she had arrived at Darfeld on 30 April 1801. Sent a month later to Paderborn, she,like Sister Geneviève made her profession on her deathbed, and ended her life after less than two years of Trappist life. She was forty-three years old.

In the same year, 1803, a third death caused great sorrow in the community. Mother Sainte-Marie Laignier, the prioress, died at age fifty-three. It will be remembered that she was the first superior of the community at Sembrancher. Foundress and co-foundress with Dom Augustin de Lestrange, she was considered 'The Mother of Our Reform', as the first Trappistines loved to say. In a report written some thirty years later by a sister of the Third Order, who had been a pupil in the first years at Villarvolard, we read that: 'They were staying at Paderborn where the Reverend Mother Sainte-Marie died in the odor of sanctity. I heard a lot spoken of her eminent virtues, above all her obedience'.[7]

To this we can add her modesty and self-effacement. Nothing concerning her personally has come down to us. I would have liked to say more, but not a single trait has pierced the silence which envelops her life. She gave herself to others with no thought for her own interests and let herself be changed over and over by the Father Abbot, who with unbelievable ease alternated the periods when he appointed her superior, and then withdrew the care of

[7] Archives de la Trappe, cote 217, pièce 16.

the community from her. She went to God on 27 April 1803. This death finally resolved the closing of the house at Paderborn.

VILLARVOLARD: OCTOBER 1802 – AUGUST 1804)

The Journey of the Pioneer Group

Mother Stanislaus recorded what happened:

> In the year 1802, the French having left Switzerland[8] the country was again enjoying peace, so our Reverend Father tried to see if he could return there with his monks. God blessed this enterprise and the monastery of La Valsainte was given back to him and the monks returned again to live there. This happy outcome gave him hope that the community of nuns could also return to Switzerland. He chose as superior of this community our Reverend Mother Marie du Saint-Esprit, who was then at Darfeld and the person the most capable of filling this post.[9]

Mother Marie du Saint-Esprit had made her profession at Darfeld on 20 August, and come under the orders of the Father Abbot to Paderborn, and 'took with her five of our sisters whom the Reverend Father had chosen to accompany her'.[10]

They set out on 4 October, but after the retreat of imperial troops, outbreaks of civil war were rife in Switzerland, because not all the population accepted *l'acte de la Malmaison*. The mediation of Bonaparte was sought and Marshal Ney entered Switzerland on 30 September. Not

[8] Cf. Georges Lefebvre, *Napoléon*, pp. 115–117: 'Following the *Acte de la Malmaison* accepted by the Swiss Confederation on 29 March 1802, Bonaparte gave the order to evacuate Switzerland in July 1802; also he accorded the Independence promised by the Treaty of Lunéville.'

[9] 'Relation,' *Cîteaux* 35 (1984) 210.

[10] *Ibid.*

until 19 February 1803 was civil peace restored by *l'Acte de Médiation* accepted by both parties.[11]

An echo of the repercussions this event had on the journey the sisters undertook at the beginning of October can be seen in the account of Mother Stanislaus:

> During our travels towards Switzerland, some new disturbances arose at Fribourg. It was feared that if we went near the town our way would be barred on that side. But this daughter of obedience [Mother Marie du Saint-Esprit] was by no means frightened of any warning of danger. Nothing could stop her from obeying, and under the protection of her God, she arrived with her small flock without difficulty at her intended place in the month of October 1802. Because our monastery of Valais had been sold along with that of the Fathers by the Superior, to prevent the malicious action of some ill-willed persons who threatened to burn them, it was at Villarvolard in the canton of Fribourg where this community was established and was very soon increased with several new members.[12]

The dwelling they arrived at was a rather large country house built at the beginning of the seventeenth century by the Repond family, merchants from Fribourg whose descendants still own the property. It is situated above the village to the northwest, and seems to defy the winds and time. Thanks to the courteous co-operation of Madame Denis de Rougemont, *née Repond*, whom we found there the day we arrived (18 August 1987) we were able to visit both inside and out, not without deep emotion on my part. Some of the rooms still contained tapestries from the 18th century; but most impressive was the kitchen, still just as it had been two centuries ago,[13] the floor paved with huge uneven stones. A

[11] Cf. G. Lefebvre, (n.8) same pages.

[12] 'Relation', pp. 210–211.

[13] Madame de Rougemont explained to us that the house had remained in the joint ownership of the descendants of the Repond family and had had very few additions or restorations since that date.

fireplace in the middle of the room was formed by a thick flagstone edged on each side by a stone of the same width and fifty cm high. The pot hanger, still there, supported a huge cauldron covered with soot. I could visualize the sisters bustling about, preparing the meagre allowance of food for the community. The magnificent view framed in the window would make up for all the discomforts.

A little further downhill at the entrance to the village is the house where the Fathers lived who served the sisters' material and spiritual needs. Between the two houses is the village church, surrounded by a cemetery where three sisters were buried during the twenty-two months the community stayed at Villarvolard.

The First Months at Villarvolard

The prioress, as we have seen, was Mother Marie du Saint-Esprit Allard, whom we have already met several times. Daughter of Jacques Allard, *bourgeois* of Lyon, and of Catherine Rubic, she was a Capuchine from a convent in Paris when she asked to enter Sembrancher on 14 July 1797. She was then forty-two years old. She received the habit the same year on 10 August. Seriously ill at Lemberg (Lvov) in January 1799, she made her profession *in articulo mortis*, but recovered enough to travel with her companions to Lithuania the following July. Sent to Darfeld, she made her final profession on 20 August 1802.

Of the five novices who accompanied her from Paderborn to Switzerland, two had entered at Dürnast, one on 30 March and the other 2 April 1799, just before the departure for Lithuania. The three others who had entered Darfeld as postulants received the habit at Paderborn. All five made their profession in the Order. The first, Sister Véronique Sergeant, was professed on 29 April 1803. We have a charming eye-witness account of this nun who was the thirty-seven year old daughter of a middle class family at Gisors, bequeathed to us by Catherine Bussard, then a pupil of the Third Order at Villarvolard.

> The holy mothers had suffered so much on so many journeys that they were almost all infirm and could walk only with the help of sticks or crutches, which did not prevent them from singing in choir like angels. I saw in the house two who had to be carried to choir: Mother Véronique, a choir nun, and Sister Lutgarde [Zurkinden], a novice. She shuffled along, and many times I helped her. I used to give her both my hands, pulling her and walking backwards. I can still see Mother Véronique who was always laughing. I was so happy when I could help carry her or prepare a place for her to sit down. She always welcomed me so kindly that I was enchanted . . . She was buried in the cemetery of the parish at Villarvolard. Many of the young girls came to the door of the house to fetch her body.[14]

The other novices were Sister Gertrude Lacmand of the Paris suburb of Saint-Antoine; Sister Antoinette Valin, Sister Lutgarde Zurkinden, daughter of a notary in Fribourg, who was a Cistercian at Feldbach in Switzerland;[15] and Sister

[14] Archives de la Trappe, cote 217, pièce 16. Catherine Bussard, who came from Gruyère (Switzerland), was fourteen years old when she was entrusted to the care of the sisters of the Third Order by her father. Her mother had recently died. She received her entire education at the convent and entered as a sister of the Third Order when she was nineteen. She followed the nuns into France in 1816. Her father re-married. She came to Forges, near Soligny in 1816, and from there in 1818 went to Gardes, where she made her profession in the Third Order on 18 May 1822. By order of the Father Abbot she left for Mondaye the next year; from there she went to Louvigné du Désert, where she kept school until 1839. Once the Third Order was suppressed we lose all trace of her.

[15] On a small piece of paper written in German, Sister Lutgarde has left a very brief *curriculum vitae* in these terms: 'I entered La Maison de Dieu at Feldbach (a Cistercian abbey on the southwest shore of Lake Constance). On 3 May 1798, I came back to the house. On 23 June 1801, I again departed on a journey to go to Westphalia [Darfeld, 16 July, then Paderborn, 1 August]. On 26 October 1802, I came back to

Albéric Vialet, who went from Reims to Darfeld and then Paderborn.

Very soon other postulants arrived: twenty-one between October 1802 and June 1803. But only eight later made their profession at La Riedera, when the whole community was re-united and its legal status assured.

Relocation of the Community

Let us return to the narrative of Mother Stanislaus, whose precise notations mark out the route:

> In the month of April the following year [1803] after the death of Reverend Mother Saint-Marie at Paderborn, the Reverend Father Abbot gave us the order to leave so we could all be re-united, with the exception of five of our sisters who were not able to undertake so long a journey, because of sickness, so they were taken to the house at Darfeld. Thus it is that charity, which is the bond of our union, helps us to support one another's burdens and infirmities . . . This order was received with joy as at last we were all going to be re-united. This was what we had yearned for. The journey was very long[16] and we did not arrive at Villarvolard until the sixth day of the month of June. We were twelve in number . . . We stayed fourteen months from our arrival in this house. Only very few postulants were received as the premises were too small.

This last assertion surprises us, because if we look at the Register, we see that sixteen postulants entered between

---

my own country [Switzerland].' Born on 26 January 1773, she made her profession at Notre-Dame-de-la-Trinité on 21 January 1810, and died when she was forty-one years old on 30 January 1814, after thirteen years of monastic life.

16 'Relation', p. 211. They had to travel seven or eight hundred kilometres. The name of these five sisters is known to us by the Registers: Sister Gabrielle Lucottée, Sister Albéric de Saint-Riquier, Sister Pauline de Brye, Sister Victoire Chuffaut, Sister Marie-Thérèse Vaultier.

8 June 1803 and 5 August 1804. It is true that only five persevered in the Order, and the fate of three of these is not certain. But it is possible that a good number of the postulants who later entered at La Grande-Riedera had already expressed a wish to join the community at Villarvolard.

Before we leave Villarvolard we must say something about one postulant whose name was forgotten in the Register, but who was to become famous in the religious world, as much through her holiness as the admirable work she was to later do. Anne-Marie Javouhey, under the name Sister Justine, stayed hardly three months at La Trappe—perhaps two, from the end of July to the beginning of October 1803. This was the decisive moment in her life. She was seeking God's will for her future when she left Chamblanc in Burgandy with her brother Pierre, who was marked for conscription and like so many others was fleeing to La Trappe at Valsainte.[17] There she met the abbot, Dom Augustin, who directed her to his community of nuns to have the time to discern her vocation, because Marie-Anne felt herself called to found a religious institute for the education of the young. With open frankness, she confided everything to the abbot, who had become her spiritual father. He saw in her an intelligent woman transformed by the Holy Spirit, a cornerstone for his teaching Third Order. On the morning of taking the habit, after a retreat entirely orientated to the first steps of entry into the Order, the Father Abbot again saw the postulant. 'Have you really decided to take the habit

[17] By a letter of 9 November 1803, the *Landammann* (Federal Governor) of Switzerland brought the attention of the Petit Conseil of Fribourg to the case of Pierre Gavouhey (Javouhey), sought by the Imperial police. The Petit Conseil had to ask the abbot of La Valsainte to give an account of his conduct in regard to this 'fugitive'. The superior replied that he had refused to admit him at La Valsainte, and he had left without giving any address (Archives d'Etat de Fribourg, 11 December 1803). See also the archives of the Sisters of Saint Joseph of Cluny, a letter of the abbot of La Valsainte to M. Javouhey (the father), dated 12 August 1803, in which he replied in a manner identical to what he would say four months later to the Petit Conseil.

my daughter?' he asked. 'I think so', said Sister Justine. 'The will of God has shown me this through you and I am ready.' 'Well no, you will not take it, you can go and simply attend the Mass. Afterwards you are free to follow the attraction of God and you will go and found your Congregation.' This took place perhaps the 26 September 1803. In the following years, the Congregation [of Saint Joseph de Cluny] was born and rapidly developed under the patronage of Saint Joseph, with its first novitiate at Cluny. 'La Sainte-Volonté-de-Dieu' is still the motto of the Institute.[18]

Legal Recognition

The first six nuns entered Switzerland at a moment when the country was struggling with civil unrest. This small group of ordinary family size attracted much less attention than a large group would have done, especially as they hardly ever went out. Even so, some postulants asked to be admitted. When the political unrest had calmed down the group from Paderborn arrived.

Dom Augustin thought the moment had come to apply for authorization to acquire for the nuns one or another of the *châteaux*, which had been put up for sale by the Senate at Fribourg to pay its debts. The *château* of Corbières was refused him in May 1803 and that of Vaulruz on 16 August the same year. These repeated applications raised the question of whether these religious were authorized? The attorney of the Petit Conseil of Fribourg wrote on 16 August 1803 to the Department of the Interior: 'Above all it is important to examine if this Order of Trappistines-femelles [*sic*] which is established in the canton without authorization of the government, can be tolerated. Would

[18] Archives de Saint-Joseph de Cluny, letters of Dom Augustin to Anne-Marie Javouhey (1807), and a very interesting file which reveals a much less well known aspect, of the abbot in his role as a spiritual father.

you kindly consider this question and let us have your opinion?'[19]

An official requisition was made the same day, 16 August, to Dom Augustin de Lestrange 'whether he has the approbation of ecclesiastical superiors or of the government?' They received a dilatory and rather vague reply on 12 October 1803. On 14th October the Department of the Interior noted that the reply of the Father Abbot was not explicit, and invited him to explain himself in a more positive fashion.

At a meeting on 24 October 1803, the Petit Conseil recommended tolerance to the Grand Conseil, but at the same time certain restrictions against 'too great a freedom to acquire real estate, both as regards the nuns and the monks'.

The bishop of Lausanne, Mgr Guisolan who lived in Fribourg, wrote a letter on 25 November 1803 to the Petit Conseil, fervently recommending that the Trappistines be permitted to stay in the canton. Finally, on 19 January 1804, the attorney of the Grand Conseil gave authorization to the establishment of the Trappist nuns on these terms:

> Having taken into consideration the usefulness of the establishment of the Trappist nuns which is presented under diverse forms, principally that of public education, it has, on the proposal of the Petit Conseil, permission to continue this establishment under the following conditions:
>
> 1. The number of choir nuns must never exceed twelve.
> 2. The number of teaching sisters, who form the most essential and most useful part of this house, will not be

[19] Arch. EF man. 1803, pp. 46, 320, 471. On 5 November 1803, Canon Fontaine of Fribourg wrote to the Vicar General of the bishop of Constance: 'You have asked me if it is with permission of the government that all these establishments of the Trappists have been made. Undoubtedly no, not even the one in the capital. It is one of the principal methods of Père Augustin. He starts by doing it, and from after that there is no way of refusing to comply with him, *propter populum*.' (AEF Fonds Raemy d'Agy). Quoted by Tobie de Raemy, in *L'émigration française au canton de Fribourg* (Fribourg, 1935) p. 338.

limited. This number must normally be proportioned to the services they will be called upon to give in different localities of the canton, which will judge where and how they will be needed.

3. The sisters *données* destined for the domestic services of the house can never exceed twelve.
4. The trappist nuns can have only one house in the canton.
5. The house is permitted to acquire some real estate for twenty four thousand francs.
6. They cannot receive any dowry from the girls of the canton who wish to follow this way of life.

7 – 8 and 10 – 11 Concern the schools.

9. No involvement with the above-mentioned house will enable the removal of the school mistresses from the authority of ecclesiastical superiors in what concerns religious discipline or from the supervision of the Council for public instruction in what concerns their functions as school mistresses.[20]

As can be seen, their reception was somewhat restricted and limited to the services which the Third Order could give in education. The rest was only a slender edict of tolerance. The abbot of La Valsainte had the wisdom to content himself with this.

LA RIEDERA: AUGUST 1804 – NOVEMBER 1805

Purchasing the Property

After that, it was easier for Dom Augustin to acquire land where the nuns could settle permanently. The house at Villarvolard, too small and unsuitable for a monastery, was in any case not for sale. And as the two *châteaux* he had hoped for had been refused him, Dom Augustin began hunting for

[20]*Bulletin des lois*, 1:263.

a place long dreamed of and now at last accessible. Mother Stanislaus wrote:

> In this year [1804], our Reverend Father, in his great concern having obtained permission for us to stay in the country, acquired for us a property called La Petite-Riedera, about two leagues from Fribourg, in order to build a monastery for us. In the month of August 1804, he had us leave Villarvolard to come and take possession of the property. We lodged in the *château* of La Grande-Riedera, not far from the monastery that the monks of La Valsainte were building for us our of their generosity . . . . We stayed at La Grande-Riedera fifteen months. God afflicted us with the death of six of our sisters and one of our pupils. Their bodies were carried to and buried in our cemetery by our Fathers.[21]

The contract of the purchase was signed on 28 July 1804 by the former owner, M. Tobie de Gottrau de Billens and Dom Augustin. The sale included:

> generally all the property that M. de Gottrau possesses in the parish of Praroman, in the place called La Petite-Riedera, consisting of a large house with a chapel and a small courtyard surrounded by walls. A garden adjoining the said house, also surrounded by walls, a house for a farmer, two granges separated from each other, a furnace, some fountains for the use of the buildings, about forty-five poses of meadows [a little more than forty-five hectares], three poses of grazing land on which a small chalet still exists . . . also a farmhouse on about seventeen poses of land . . . .
>
> The sale price was ten thousand and one *écus*, for the goods of the owner, and thirty new *louis d'or* for lawyer's fees, making altogether the sum of twenty five thousand and four hundred eighty-two francs and five Swiss baches.[22]

[21] *Relation*, pp. 211–212.

[22] AEF Reg. not., n°1055, quoted by Tobie de Raemy, p. 340.

As we can see the property was quite large and had existing buildings, which still stand today. But it was necessary to adapt the place and to build a church and some premises for the Third Order. A team of monks: chaplain, cellarer and lay brothers for the development of the property—found lodging in the farm buildings. During the fifteen months the work lasted, the nuns lodged in nearby La Grande-Riedera, the summer residence of the family of François Philippe-Joseph-Louis de Gottrau. His wife, Marie-Emmanuelle de Montenach, appears to have been a benefactress of the Trappists, says T. de Raemy. It seems that Dom Augustin had obtained her agreement that the nuns would not have to pay rent during their stay, but other documents speak of a tenancy.

Settlement in the Area

During this time, the Fathers and Brothers, helped by 'twenty-two masons and twenty-two carpenters without counting casual labor', worked at the constructions and installations needed. One of the brothers, not named, has left us an account on a loose sheet of paper, now preserved in the archives at La Trappe. He says that all these workers had to

> maintain two water saws. They had one, but had to construct another to saw planks to make an enclosure for the nuns and give them a garden and some pasture land so they could go out for a walk, because they were so shut in [at La Grande-Riedera] that many died. The pine wood was easily available and they bought a corner of the forest.[23]

In spite of the limitations imposed on the buying of property (set by the Grand Conseil at twenty four thousand

[23] Arch. La Trappe, cote 217, pièce 44.

francs), Dom Augustin increased the value of the property even more by new acquisitions: woods, a mill, the construction of a sawmill. This expansion, coupled with the free and easy manner shown by the masters and children of the Third Order, led to complaints by the inhabitants of the commune of Montévraz, to which La Riedera belonged. A 'letter addressed to the attorney and counsellors of the Petit Conseil at Fribourg' expresses opposition to these strange beings in the form of an indictment:

> These monks or postulants to be, big and little, pay no attention whether or not they trample on someone else's property, whether or not they leave gates open or shut, and whether or not it happens by their negligence that damage is done to the property of others. They seem to consider themselves exempt from all responsibility and all supervision, except in reference to the one who has brought them to acknowledge himself as their one and only superior.[24]

The diatribe against the intruders continues like this for five large pages. The Petit Conseil investigated and made inquiries, then replied calmly that there was no question of an an unlawful establishment, as the population of Montévraz suspected, but that it had been made legally with the express authorization of the Grand Conseil.

In their seclusion, the nuns were totally unaware of this ill-natured gossip. Faithful to their enclosure, they had not provoked it. The difficulties of daily life they had to face, the health worries, receiving new recruits, the work of the house, and above all the Divine Praises, were enough

[24] Documents very kindly communicated by M. Francey ('Lettre adressée par la Commune de Montévraz à l'Avoyer et aux Conseillers du Petit Conseil de Fribourg', 17 September 1804), Archives Canton de Fribourg.

to fill their days and the silence was a guarantee of their solitude.

The Stay at La Grande-Riedera

All this coincided with the work of settling at La Petite-Riedera. The sisters had moved from Villarvolard during the first two weeks of August 1804. In the parish cemetery, they left in addition to Sister Véronique, Sister Marie-Madeleine Zacharie, the daughter of a citizen of Lyon, who entered Sembrancher on 12 October 1797. She had been a Poor Clare in a monastery at Auxonne, where her aunt was the novice mistress. She was chosen to go to the monastery at Orsha, where she made her profession on 29 October 1799. She was thirty-seven when she died on 14 March 1804, and had lived the monastic life for seven years. A third sister, Sister Pierre Rouph, a former Carthusian from Savoy, died as a novice at Villarvolard. Seventeen sisters entered as postulants during the first weeks at La Grande-Riedera. Eleven of them left quite soon, as did three more later. Five made their profession. During the same period, six nuns died and one of the pupils. At least this is what is written by our chronicler. The Register of Admissions is silent, and we cannot even identify the sisters who died. The Register of Deaths in the parish of Praroman is missing for this period, and so does not allow us to be sure of the names of the survivors. A rough approximation can, however, be made beginning from the deaths registered after 1805 and the names of the sisters still present in 1816 after the return to France.

La Grande-Riedera was only a temporary home and La Petite was looked upon as a permanent monastery, so it was there they buried the sisters who died in the *château*: 'they were buried in our cemetery by our Fathers'. The list of deaths of La Petite-Riedera has recently been found in the bishop's house at Fribourg, and this fills in some of the gaps in our Registers for the following period.

NOTRE-DAME-DE-LA-SAINTE-TRINITé

The entire community at La Grande-Riedera was waiting impatiently for the moment to leave. The lack of an outdoor enclosure prevented the sisters from going out. Furthermore, for the same reason, the windows remained shut. All this did not improve their health and made life in confined seclusion very difficult. So we can understand the joyful exclamations which runs through the recital of Mother Stanislaus as she relates the happy transfer.

18 November 1805 was a date of profound joy:

> At last the end of our exile arrived, our church and our choir were built and finished; our Reverend Father came and told us the happy news that we were soon going to enter and be enclosed in this sanctuary so long awaited and desired.
>
> He fixed the day of our entry, or rather of our triumph in this holy place, for the 18th of November 1805. At four in the morning of the said day, with our Reverend Mother at our head and all of us following, we went to the side of our church where the Reverend Father Abbot was waiting for us, and let us in by the door of the sacristy which led into our choir. There he gave us his blessing and exhorted us to keep the Rule in all its severity in acknowledgement of our gratitude.[25]

There follows an exhortation at great length on the attitudes and virtues required of a true nun. She continues:

> Let us come back to that memorable day and tell of the events. The same day of the entry into our monastery, Mgr

[25] 'Relation', p. 212.

> Maxime Guisolan, bishop of Lausanne, took the trouble to come to our Church to bless our two bells and then give the sacrament of Confirmation to some of our sisters and pupils at the grille of our choir.
>
> The next day, the 19th of the same month, he came back, accompanied by his chaplains and some other priests, for the solemn ceremony of the Dedication of our Church. This impressive ceremony is very beautiful and very long, it took five hours. The community attended in choir. The bishop entered in procession to take the relics, exposed on a table, that were then deposited on the high altar.
>
> Our Church was consecrated and dedicated in honor of the Mother of God under the name Notre-Dame-de-la-Sainte-Trinité. This ceremony filled us with consolation and feelings of gratitude . . . .
>
> Thanksgiving a thousand times over a thousand be rendered to you, O Lord, in time and eternity, for all the souls who will have the happiness of dwelling in this holy house.[26]

The Members of the Community

After this outburst of enthusiasm, Mother Stanislaus, who always kept her feet well on the ground, informed her sisters with exactitude about the members of the community after their entry into Notre-Dame-de-la-Trinité:

> The community was not very large when we entered into our monastery; God had called to himself several of our sisters, and the place where we lived was too small to receive many subjects.
>
> We were ten professed, three novices, and one postulant for the choir. One professed, six novices, and one postulant for the lay sisters, and two sisters of the Third Order, thirteen pupils and four sisters *données*.

[26] *Ibid.*, 212–213.

> We hope that God who has led us here, will sustain us and will see fit to send us some good subjects to maintain the regularity of this house. This is the object of our all our desires.[27]

We have been able, with good probability, to draw up a list of names of the community as they arrived at La Petite-Riedera, with the help of the Register of Admissions, the list of subsequent deaths, and some notes in the short account of Catherine Bussard.

The prioress was still Mother Marie du Saint-Esprit Allard, the sub-prioress Mother Stanislaus Michel. The eight other professed choir nuns were: Sister Magdeleine Guyot, Sister M.-Michel Ducourand, Sister Thaïs Bassignot, Sister Hedwige Guillemin (who all entered at Sembrancher), Sister Euphrosine Mairesse and Sister Gertrude Lacmand (who both entered in Bavaria); and Sister Marie-Toussaint Deschamps and Sister Félicité Domino (both from Darfeld). The three novices were: Sister Lutgarde Zurkinden (who did not make her profession until 1810), Sister M.-Madeleine Garot-Maupoux, a widow, and Sister Robert Baumgartner. The postulant, Sister Marie-Bernard Dufour passed to the Third Order.

The lay sisters counted one professed, Sister Euphrasie Mivelaz, and six novices. Sister Antoinette Valin, Sister M.-Joseph Pernet, Sister Louise Mercier, Sister Thérèse Dehoux, Sister M.-Thérèse Caître, Sister Pierre Michaud; and a postulant, Sister Pélagie Lanviron, who took the name of Gertrude when she received the habit. In the Third Order: Sister Louise de Lestrange, Sister M.-Joseph Lagrange.

The four sisters *données* were Sister Julienne Breton (who entered at Sembrancher), Sister Albéric Vialet, Sister Claudine Repond, Sister Elisabeth Collin.

A good number of these sisters ended their days at Notre-Dame-de-la-Trinité according to the list of deaths found in the Appendix to this Chapter.

[27] *Ibid.*, 214.

Variations in the Size of the Community

We have, over ten consecutive years, a numerical census of the community at La Petite-Riedera sent to the Petit Conseil at Fribourg about the middle of the year. We give it in the form of a Table. The Petit Conseil at Fribourg was then able to verify that the conditions laid down in the authorization for remaining in the canton were respected. After comparing this Table with the entries in the Register, as far as it is possible to evaluate this, given the uncertainties hidden in the available data, I can state that the figures as a whole correspond to reality.

Year	*June 1806*	*June 1807*	*May 1808*	*May 1809*	*May 1810*
Choir professed		9	8	7	
Choir novices	} 11	4	4	5	} 11
Lay professed		4	4	7	7
Lay novices	} 10	6	7	1	1
Postulants	3	1	1	2	2
Sisters données	3	5		5	7
Familiars (tourières)			} 7	1	1
Mistresses of the Third Order	4	3	4	4	5
Pupils	16	13	11	13	13
Total	47	45	46	45	47

Year	*May 1811*	*May 1812*	*May 1813*	*May 1814*	*May 1815*
Choir professed	13	11	10	8	7
Choir novices	1				
Lay professed	5	5	5	4	4
Lay novices	2	1	1		
Postulants	2	1			2
Sisters données	6	5	3	5	5
Familiars (tourières)	1	1	1	2	2
Mistresses of the Third Order	7	5	4	4	5
Pupils	12	9	13	14	12
Total	49	38	37	37	37

Material and Economic Aspects of the Life

The nuns, at least at the beginning, do not seem to have enjoyed much autonomy in these areas. The Trappists of La Valsainte, like their sisters, were obliged to submit an account of expenses and income to the Petit Conseil each year. The archives of the canton contain some large sheets of these accounts. Other than the title, there are receipts, with inevitable debts and declarations of stock. A second page shows the expenses and what remained in cash at the end of the year. For the first two years, 1805 and 1806, there is a joint account for La Valsainte and La Riedera. But from 1807–1808 the accounts are separate. This was because the monks paid off the debt of the building works carried out in 1804 and 1805 for the monastery of the nuns over the first two years. From 1 September 1805 to 14 June 1806, the account shows 45,546 Swiss *francs* and nine *sols*. From 14 June 1806 to 8 June 1807, the expenses had gone up to 77,950 *livres tournois*, sixteen *sols*, six *deniers*. The next year the expenses are only for the nuns at 6,836 *francs*, twelve *sols*, six *deniers*. The accounts are signed by the superior of the house. We give here in a Table the calculations for the years which preceded a serious crisis in 1811, which we will explain further on.

Years	*1807–* 1808	*1808–* 1809	*1809–* 1810	*1810–* 1811	*1811–* 1812
Fund	Nil	984,8,6	724,9	803,73	870,6,8
Receipts in cash	6 621,1,6	8 306,2	5 510,8	6 659,11	7 406,6,6
Returns from the property	1 200	1 200	1 200	1 200	1 200
Expenses	6 836,12,6	9 706,9,6	6 691,1,3	7 792,12	8 921,15[28]

[28] Archives of the canton of Fribourg, unclassified, under the title: 'Compte de l'Abbaye de La Valsainte N.D.-de-la-Trappe et du monastère de La Riedera, rendu au Dépt. des finances du Canton de Fribourg'.

One question can be asked: where did the money come from? Certainly not from paid work; such a thing was unheard of at the time. Perhaps the sawmill or sales of farm stock brought in some income, but the most likely source was probably pensions granted by the sisters' families (we will see an instance further on) or pensions from England; alms, and perhaps some renumeration given voluntarily to the sisters of the Third Order. In any case their poverty was very real, but the needs of the sisters were reduced to the minimum, both by the austerity of the Regulations and by the scarcity of resources.

The Health of the Nuns

All this had a bearing on the health of the sisters, especially in the climate at the altitude of 880 metres. Catherine Bussard tells how during a very severe winter when the sisters and children slept under the rafters, all they had for bedding was some *lodiers* (cloth bags filled with dry moss). Several lost their teeth, one lost an eye, a young girl of fifteen died of pleurisy, and others of pulmonary 'inflammation'.

The brother who left an account of the building construction at La Riedera visited the place again some two years later in February 1806 and stated: ' . . . of our sisters who have been in their new monastery for six months, and eighteen months at La Riedera, we saw in the cemetery that twelve had died.[29] There are still fifty persons including the children . . . .' The Report submitted to the Petit Conseil lists forty-seven persons on 14 June 1806. One sister *donnée* had died between the two dates. What he had seen was accurate.

The Father Infirmarian whom we have met several times in these pages, Father François de Paule, in his *Mémoires*

[29] Arch. La Trappe, cote 217, pièce 44.

sous forme de lettres made some shrewd reflections on the health of the nuns.

> I forgot to tell you about the nuns of whom there are at the moment three communities: one in England about which I have no news; one at Darfeld, where the poor women are shut up in unsatisfactory buildings, overwhelmed by infirmities, and living wretchedly on the help they receive from the charity of the faithful and some religious at Bourlo. A third community is at La Riedera, where, as I had the honor to tell you, they are at their wits' end as to how they can survive as they fight unceasingly against the illnesses waging a constant war on them. When I was at La Valsainte [he became the parish priest of Charmey, not far away, in 1808], I did all I could to persuade the Reverend Father Abbot to mitigate some of the austerities for the nuns. I even presented him with a memorandum to this effect, since I regard it as a barbarity that women should be compelled to follow the same rules and the same austerities as men. I received no reply, and nothing of all I said produced any alleviation.
>
> Nevertheless, I spoke knowing what I was talking about, since I had been their doctor on a thousand occasions. You will find at the end of these memoranda details of what I presented to him on the subject. I earnestly desired that the government [at Fribourg] would have opened its eyes to what was going on. I cannot conceive that they could have authorized the establishment of these women in the canton without first being assured that the Rule was not beyond the capacity of their weakness. Eventually, there was only one sister left who was capable of singing in choir, all the rest were *hors de combat*![30]

Perhaps the writer was carried away by his personal tendency to take great care of his own health; however the facts are there to justify what he says. These thoughts seem

[30] P. 253 of a text preserved at Timadeuc.

to have been constantly in his mind, because he came back to the same subject a little further on.

> These generous women, despite the weaknesses of their sex, are compelled to follow all the observances of the reform without any exception. It can be said that they do this with a zeal and heroic generosity that is well able to leave us dumbfounded. But how do they do it? . . . For the most part they drag out a miserable and sickly life. After following the life of the reform for only a few months, nature rebels and entirely loses all its resources; they then succumb to some infirmity which in its turn is the source of many others; to this already a great number of sisters have fallen victim. But while we grant that the reform of La Trappe does not require any mitigation for the monks, does sound reason not demand that austerities be moderated for the weaker sex, who in the ardor of their devotion are too carried away and stray from the rules of prudence?[31]

Vermin, another affliction already met with at Darfeld, tormented the sisters continually. It would take several years before they completely got rid of this consequence of the lack of hygiene and habits contracted during their travels.

In the midst of so many sufferings of all descriptions, the sisters possessed a serenity that was the admiration of the young Catherine Bussard, then fifteen years old. She gives a glimpse of the spirit which animated these 'holy mothers' as she sketched the character of the sub-prioress, Mother Stanislaus Michel:

> Mother Sub-Prioress, a former religious from Avignon, was a model of all the virtues, very feeble in health, but so mortified that she was hardly ever in the infirmary. As she had a life pension of eighteen hundred *francs*, she

[31] *Ibid.*, p. 276.

> always feared that they procured remedies for her out of this consideration. She was born of a very distinguished family and was always thought to be too delicate. She was so mortified in everything that she did not care for her nails, except when she was commanded to do so. She admitted to me several times that having her nails and hands dirty was a great penance for her.[32]

This was an age when contempt for the body went to extremes, and delicate natures were deeply affected. In their generosity they found a means of self-denial which we today find astonishing. The accent on corporal penance had already disconcerted the Princess de Condé. All the positive aspects of the contemplative life—the profound attraction to praise and serve God who is Love in a delicate mutual awareness, the one commandment of love in its two expressions—were obscured by the heavy emphasis on penance—obscured in the official language of the Regulations, but alive in the depths of their hearts. The essentials remained as a fire under the ashes and communicated themselves in the form of a peaceful expectation of eternal life.

An Abortive Foundation

Regardless of the poor health of the nuns at La Riedera, Dom Augustine decided in the spring of 1811 to associate the nuns with his new attempt at a foundation in America. He chose four sisters: Sister M.-Magdeleine Guyot, Sister Thérèse Malatesta, Sister François-Xavier Faucheux, and the fourth whom the Registers do not mention by name, either as a postulant or novice.

They left La Riedera on the 7 May 1811 to join the Father Abbot who was going to embark at Bordeaux, with two other

[32] The account of Catherine Bussard, Arch. La Trappe, cote 217, pièce 13, p.5.

priests or brothers. We will see in the following chapters that the Father Abbot was not able to go. The first three sisters had to return to La Riedera for some reason we do not know. Only the sister not listed in the Register left with the two monks. She had come from a community which has yet to be identified. Traces of the existence of a community more or less Trappist can be found in a Report of a General Chapter in 1883.[33]

The three sisters who returned to La Riedera on 27 August 1811 were still there in 1816 when the house was closed. We will see each of them at the head of three groups which little by little came together again in France.[34]

[33] Acts of the General Chapters (Vincent Hermans), p. 489.

[34] Research by Father Felix Donahue, formerly archivist of the Abbey of Gethsemani (USA), has brought to light the identification of the sister of the Third Order who left for America with the monks. She was a young English (or Welsh) girl, Marie-Joseph Llewellyn. They embarked on 15 June 1811, and arrived at Boston the following August sixth. Sister Marie-Joseph, after several unsuccessful attempts to make a trappist foundation, joined the Sisters of Charity, newly founded by Elizabeth Ann Seton, and died there on 25 March 1816.

APPENDIX
DEATHS IN THE FOUNDING COMMUNITY

	Names	*Status*	*Date*	*Age*	*Time in the religious life*
PADERBORN (April 1801-August 1803) :					
1801	S. Benoit Isambert *	Professed	1- 9-01	33 years	4 years
1802	S. Jeanne-Catherine Defrevrimont	Postulant	18- 1-02	33 ——	?
	S. Jean-Baptiste Chassaignon *	Professed	9- 2-02	46 ——	5 ——
1803	S. Geneviève Belhomme **	Professed	21- 3-03	30 ——	4 ——
	S. Françoise de Langhe **	Professed	5- 4-03	43 ——	2 ——
	M. Sainte-Marie Laignier *	Prioress	27- 4-03	53 ——	7 ——
VILLARVOLARD (October 1802–August 1804)					
1803	S. Véronique Sergeant **	Professed	1- 5-03	37 years	4 years
1804	S. M.-Madeleine Zacharie *	Professed	14- 3-04	37 ——	7 ——
1804	S. Pierre Rouph	Novice	17-07-04	42 ——	1 ——

LA GRANDE-RIEDERA (August 1804–November 1805) :

There were six sisters and one pupil who died during this period, according to the account of Mother Stanislas Michel, and buried at La Petite -Riedera. Their names were not inscribed in the Register, nor on the list preserved at Bishop's house in Fribourg, which only records the deaths at La Petite-Riedera.

LA PETITE-RIEDERA (November 1805–October 1816) :

1805	Anne Brezet (S. Stanislas)	Pupil Third order	2- 7-05	15 years	?
	S. M.-Michel Ducourand *	Professed	11-12-05	53 ——	9 years
	S. Félicité Domino	Professed	29-12-05	37 ——	4 ——
1806	S. Louise Mercier	Professed	6- 1-06	24 ——	3 ——
	S. Scholastique Martin	Professed	8- 2-06	25 ——	2 ——
	S. Gertrude Lacmand **	Professed	12- 2-06	49 ——	7 ——
	S. Albéric Vialet **	Donnée	25- 4-06	31 ——	5 ——
	S. Louis de Gonzague Mondu	Postulant	27- 9-06	29 ——	1 ——
	S. M.-Magdeleine Garot-Maupoux	Third Order	11-11-06	37 ——	2 ——
1807	Claudine Lamy (S. M. des Anges)	Pupil Third Order	26- 3-07	5 ——	?
	S. Hedwige Guillemin *	Professed	26- 5-07	35 ——	10 ——
	S. M.-Thérèse Dufour	Third Order	20- 6-07	?	?
	S. Hélène de la Croix Vuillin	Novice	11- 9-07	24 ——	1 ——
	S. Albéric Giray	Professed	13-11-07	28 ——	1 ——
1808	S. M.-Bernard Dufour	Third Order	24- 1-08	?	?
	S. Antoinette Valin	Professed	2- 5-08	46 ——	7 ——
	S. Louis de Gonzague Chonet	Professed	26- 7-08	58 ——	1 ½ –
	Félicité Tonnard (S.Dorothée)	Pupil Third Order	25-12-08	16 ——	?
	S. M.-Magdeleine Morel	Professed	27-12-08	28 ——	2 ——
1809	S. M.-Toussaint Deschamps	Professed	8- 3-09	47 years	6 years
	Marie Martin (S. Marthe)	Pupil Third Order	26- 7-09	16 ——	?
1810	S. Scholastique Mivelaz	Professed	2- 3-10	28 ——	8 ——
	S. Catherine Kerrel	Third Order	23- 5-10	28 ——	1 ——
	S. Félicité Drezet	Professed	18-10-10	32 ——	?
	S. Françoise Litts ou Lotte	Professed	16-12-10	39 ——	4 ——
	S. Augustine-Jeanne Rousseau	Third Order	22-12-10	?	?

APPENDIX (continued)

Names		Status	Date	Age	Time in the religious life
1811	S. M.-Claudine Repond	Donnée	14- 1-11	30 ——	8 ——
	S. M. Christine Bapst	Professed	10- 8-11	37 ——	5 ——
	S. Robert de La Poype	Third Order	18- 8-11	29 ——	1 ——
	S. Etienne Rigaud	Professed	8-12-11	49 ——	5 ——
1812	S. Euphrosine Mairesse **	Professed	2- 1-12	59 ——	14 ——
	S. Bernard Guérin	Professed	20- 7-12	56 ——	6 ——
1813	S. Elisabeth-Adélaïde Collin	Donnée	21- 1-13	33 ——	10 ——
	S. M.-Stanislas Michel *	Professed	5- 9-13	57 ——	16 ——
	S. Pierre Michaud	Professed	12-11-13	32 ——	8 ——
1814	S. Lutgarde Zurkinden	Professed	30- 1-14	40 ——	13 ——
	S. Gertrude Lanviron	Novice	3- 1-14	41 ——	8 ——
	S. Catherine de la Providence Cusance	Donnée	2- 9-14	51 ——	8 ——
	S. Pélagie Marsault	Professed	19-10-14	45 ——	12 ——
	S. Julienne Breton *	Donnée	10-12-14	46 ——	17 ——
1816	S. Placide Noël	Professed	24- 6-16	45 ——	9 ——

* Entered at La Sainte-Volonté-de-Dieu.

** Entered during the travels at Dürnast.

? Not entered in the Register of Admissions.

The question marks indicate that the sisters have not been noted in the Register of Admissions.

But their names appear on the necrology list of Bishop's House at Fribourg.

Between 1 September 1801 and 24 June 1816, that is 15 years, there were 56 deaths :

– 51 adults, of which 30 Professed (plus 7 of unknown status), 2 novices, 2 postulants, 5 données, 5 Third Order – Plus 5 pupils of the Third Order.

CHAPTER FOUR

SPONTANEOUS GENERATION

A VERY TURBULENT history is connected with a trappist foundation which appeared in Paris itself under the Directoire in July 1798, at the moment when the two swiss communities of Dom Augustin were already sheltering in the heart of Austria.

THE BEGINNINGS

Three women met on 2 July in the Ursuline convent in the faubourg Saint-Jacques.[1] One was a professed Benedictine of the Blessed Sacrament; her two companions were young 'workers', says the Register, both aged twenty-three. On 8 July a widow of fifty-two joined them, then a 'cook' of fifty-three, and a 'school mistress' of forty-three; then on 2 September, a 'worker'of sixteen camc. It seems obvious that labelling each one was a cover in case a police raid

[1] Two police notices preserved in the National Archives, kindly communicated by M. M. Guillot, show the presence of Trappists of both sexes, the first on 6 *floréal* year IX (26 April 1801) 'to the formerly noble Ursulines, rue du fauxbourg Saint-Jacques' (F7 3829), and the second of 21 *brumaire* year XI (12 November 1802) 'Rue des Anglaises, fauxbourg Saint-Marceau' (F7 3831). It can legitimately be supposed that between these two denunciations the communities were warned, and that they moved. The second document adds: 'It has been said that the women were going to retire to a house six or seven leagues from Paris, north of Choisy' (Soisy-sous-Etiolles).

discovered the hideout of this 'trappist sect', as it was called by Father François de Paule Dargnies.

Soon afterwards, a former novice of La Trappe, Xavier Miquel, from Agen, in his turn brought together some other monks or lay men, young and not so young, all desirous of leading a life in common. After a narrow escape from the massacres of Carmelites on 2 September 1792, Xavier Miquel, a deacon, sought refuge in Fribourg, where he was ordained priest on 25 November 1792. He visited La Valsainte and made contact with Dom Augustin, but did not appreciate his new observances. At Paris-Sénart he followed the Regulations of de Rancé which he had followed at La Trappe.

When and how did the group of nuns and the group of monks meet in Paris? No documents provide details. It must have been quite early for the nuns' Register notes that on 15 March 1799 a sister who had entered in August 1798 'departed, lacking courage, against the advice of the Father Superior'. Was this Dom Xavier Miquel? It seems so, because no mention is made of the bishop of Paris, and for good reason. Refractory and non-juring priests had to undergo at that time almost the same sentence—the pontoons—for their resistance to the ten-day cult [a 10 day Revolutionary week] and theophilanthropy.

The two trappist groups were still in Paris at the beginning of 1800. But shortly afterwards the community of nuns was at Soisy-sous-Etoilles on the right bank of the Seine, on the southern edge of the forest of Sénart. The monks were in a former hermitage in the forest. Nothing definite is known about this period, except that the Register continues to record admissions, departures and deaths . . . and professions with an astonishing regularity. It records that in 1798 there were eight admissions, in 1799 seven and in 1800 ten. Of these twenty-five admissions, ten left during the same period and others later; but ten died quite soon after their profession, and only one lived until 1810.

We will speak again later of the general view provided by these figures from 1798–1811.

A TURNING POINT

The reader will remember that in the chapter on the foundation in England, we mentioned a certain Father Jean-Baptiste Noyers, superior of the foundation of monks at Lulworth. He was relieved of this function in May 1802 by his immediate superior, the abbot of La Valsainte. He is next found exercising his zeal at the recent foundation of nuns at Stapehill. In June 1804, Dom Augustin decided to recall him to La Valsainte. His obedience is somewhat open to doubt, but in fact he did leave, and then stopped along the way. A letter of Mother de Chabannes to Mgr Sharrock (25 July 1806, two years later) explains what happened:

> Father Jean-Baptiste left England with the intention of returning to La Valsainte with Dom Augustin. He stopped in Paris for some weeks owing to ill health . . . He was lodging in a house of the Order near Paris, where most of the community were former monks of La Trappe. They chose him unanimously as superior and his nomination was approved by the diocesan bishop [of Versailles]. Soon afterwards the Sovereign Pontiff [Pius VII] came to Paris. Father Jean-Baptiste had the good luck to have three audiences with His Holiness, in which he explained the reasons that your Lordship knows perfectly well. He was invested by His Holiness with all the powers of superior over the two houses, because there was also one of nuns which had been founded first and was much larger than that of the monks.[2]

[2] Archives of the Western District, 25 July 1806. Cf. Jérôme du Halgouet, *Cîteaux* 17 (1966) 106. 'What Father Jean-Baptiste actually asked for was secularization, that Dom Augustin himself dates from the first visit of Pius VII to Paris (1804) for the consecration of the Emperor'.

Father Xavier Miquel, trying to come to grips with a thousand difficulties of all kinds, particularly financial, had in 1801 asked Father Coudrin, founder of the Congregation of Picpus, to be incorporated into his Institute: he only asked to be relieved of the office of superior. This union never took place. The arrival of Father Jean-Baptiste was his salvation. In a letter preserved in the Archives of the Seine-et-Oise the new Superior explains what happened:

> Arriving from abroad in August 1804, I was most earnestly entreated by M. Miquel, who was then superior of the Society of Trappist for ladies and gentlemen [*Messieurs et dames trappistes*] to take his place, for he did not wish to remain there, above all after the countless disagreements he had suffered and continued to suffer. After taking sufficient time to reflect, I finally agreed to take charge of this Society . . . . I had hardly got to know about the state of affairs, when I was appalled by the extreme poverty. I did all I could to remedy this situation . . . . The two communites were separated, men and women in two houses. To simplify things I have united the two houses in the same place.[3]

According to a Report of the *Ministre des Cultes*, Bigot de Préameneu, it was a spinster from Reversaux who 'bought the common house for them', a former convent of Camaldolese. There the monks lived under a superior, the women under a female superior, and they adopted as general superior, a certain Mr. Desnoyers'. An earlier report of Portalis [the *Director des Cultes*] describes this double community as the New Trappists 'who are not affiliated to the Old, which are those of Dom Augustine de Lestrange'. For these in the Paris region 'the Bishop of Versailles is their Superior, and his delegate in the place is called Desnoyers'.[4]

[3] Archives de Seine-et-Oise, V, 570; quoted by J. du Halgouet, *ibid.*, p. 108.

[4] Archives Nationaux F 19 586 and 6283, (*ibid.*, p. 108).

For the third time therefore the community of nuns had to move house. From south of the forest of Sénart they went north to the former Camaldolese convent in a place called Grosbois, in the commune of Yerres on the Seine-et-Oise. They lived there from 1804 to 1808 in somewhat unusual conditions that Dargnies describes in a spirited fashion:

> When the Reign of Terror was over, the business of the Church could be put in order, and the individuals of this trappist sect acquired the house at Sénart. I do not know how they managed to live there—the men in one wing, the women in the other—but they did, and practised all the exercises of the Reform of La Trappe unostentationsly; yet it was well known. Someone who had actually asked to be admitted there assured me that the men and women sang the Office together in the same church day and night, and that this community was especially under the protection of Mgr the Bishop of Versailles. Without doubt all this will seem unbelievable to posterity, given that this was at a time when no community gathering was tolerated under any pretext whatever. One could see at the gates of Paris, living peacefully, a type of community that until then had been unheard of in France. However that may be, they existed quite a long time. But deprived of a superior capable of directing them, this community necessarily went astray. They adjusted the Regulations of La Valsainte to suit themselves. The total lack of financial management opened them to the failure of their project.[5]

Adoption

The administration of Father Jean-Baptiste only aggravated the material situation, and in addition 'the two communities in the same buildings could only cause gossip', said Father Jérôme du Halgouët. He continues:

[5] Cf. Dargnies, *Mémoire en forme de lettres*, pp. 251–252 of a manuscript at Timadeuc (typed copy).

> The bishop of Versailles had recourse to Dom Augustin as Visitor in December 1807, imploring the Father Abbot of La Trappe (who was then in Paris on business) to take charge of the house and put it in order . . . But the debts were too enormous and had to be paid without delay. Also the Father Abbot had too many other commitments at hand to take on the responsibility of paying them off himself. So he resolved to abandon this house to destruction even though it caused him great pain; it was an evil he could not prevent.[6]

Nevertheless Dom Augustin had second thoughts, and on 16 March 1808 his 'opinion is that once the debts were paid, it would be very easy to run the house, even with economy and the blessings of heaven to make it prosper. To get Dom Jean-Baptiste out of the way, they took advantage of a business trip he had to make to Burgandy for three weeks. When he came back, he found that the bishop of Versailles had appointed Dom Augustin superior of the house, and he had installed Father Jean de la Croix Bodé called de Gênes. Dom Jean-Baptiste, not at all pleased, saw himself refused so much as entry into the house, and he complained to the Mayor of Yerres. However he was obliged to agree to sign the Sale of the Camaldolese on 24 April 1808 for forty thousand *francs* (its debt was fifty-five thousand)'.[7]

It was with the help of such charitable persons as the Duchess of Sully 'the last of this illustrious family', says Dargnies, and also Napoléon himself, who was in negotiation with Dom Augustin for the establishment of a trappist monastery at Mont-Genèvre, that the financial situation was completely reorganized.

Once the debts were paid off, the Father Abbot had hastily to find another lodging for the nuns. In December

[6] Art. quoted, pp. 109–110. The quotation included: Archives Nationaux F 19.

[7] *Ibid.*, p. 110. Archives of Seine-et-Oise, V, 570, letter of 22 April 1808.

1808, the community left Grosbois-Camaldolese for Valenton, nearer to Paris. An interesting document, a kind of report of an official declaration by which the sisters informed the Mayor of Yerres of their departure for Valenton, ends with a short couplet of goodwill, and is addressed to the mayor of Valenton. The mayor of Yerres, Antoine Martin, said:

> We must also commend to the kindness of the Mayor of Valenton the worthy group that his commune has the happiness of welcoming, and which we cannot see leave us without deep regret. The care that these pious persons have given to the education of the children of the poor, the care that their admirable charity knows how to lavish in the midst of the unfortunate, and their holy example was for our administration what it will be for the people of Valenton, a valued source of gratitude and veneration.[8]

This was the fifth move in less than ten years since the foundation. We will come back to this Report, which is not dated, but appears to come from the beginning of 1809.

THE EVOLUTION OF THE COMMUNITY

We can follow the development of the community by means of the Register and the schedules of profession, most of which are preserved in the archives at Maubec [today Blauvac]. We will see in the sixth part of this book how this community had to undergo even more trials in the course of its history. They were badly shaken by external events, and also by their generally poor state of health, which put their very existence in peril.

The various troubles at the beginning did not noticeably affect recruitment, even though the pioneer of this foundation, Magdeleine-Julie Didier—in religion Mother Saint

[8] Paris, Archives Nationales, dossier of the general police F 19 6325, n°16.

Louis de Gonzague—after her profession in Paris on 16 August 1800, had asked for 'the liberty to retire from the house, which the superior had very willingly granted her'. This must have taken place between 25 March and 8 September 1802, because a Sister Aimée de Jésus La Ronde made her profession under Mother Saint Louis 25 March, and on 8 September this same sister (as superior) received the profession of two other sisters: Sister Pétronille Verg, who entered 17 June 1800, and Sister Mélanie Sevestre, a Cistercian from the abbey of Bival, who entered on 24 April 1801. [On 12 April 1803] the same superior also received the vows of Sister Saint-Joseph Le Clercq, who came from Liège and had entered on 29 August 1801, at twenty-two. The Register points out that Mother Aimée de Jésus retired eighteen months or two years after her own profession; that was about the middle of 1804. This coincides with the departure of Dom Xavier Miquel and the arrival of Dom Jean-Baptiste from Lulworth. After this date there is a gap which leaves uncertain the name of the superior who succeeded Mother Aimée de Jésus.

In February 1805, a former Benedictine from the abbey of Notre-Dame-de-la-Victoire at Saint-Malo entered, Marie-Anne Chateaubriand. She was a first cousin of the writer. She received the cistercian habit the following month and made her profession on 6 April 1806. Her schedule makes no mention of the superior's name, but on the following 19 July and 13 September, she herself figures as the superior on the schedules of three professions. During the time the community was 'double'. Was this the reason why Mother Aimée de Jésus departed? Had Dom Jean-Baptiste himself taken on a plurality of offices to 'simplify' the functions of the superior of the monks and the superior of the nuns during these eighteen months? And had he then named Marie-Anne de Chateaubriand (Mother M. des Séraphins) prioress of the nun's community? There are many questions to which the documents give us no reply; but knowing the character of Dom Jean-Baptiste it can well be suggested that the answer in each case must be 'Yes'.

Whatever the reasons behind these frequent changes of direction, the community continued to grow in the regular manner. The following Table gives an overall view of the movement of personnel during the first thirteen years of trappist life lived in the various places where it developed.

Years	*1798*	*1799*	*1800*	*1801*	*1802*	*1803*	*1804*	*1805*	*1806*	*1807*	*1808*	*1809*	*1810*	*1811*	*Totals*
Admissions	8	7	10	12	10	11	16	13	6	11	1	9	6	1	121
Professions			4	4	8	2	3	4	12	8	1	1	3	3	53
Deaths			1	3	1	4	2	3	3	3	1	2	2	1	26
Departures		3	2	12	5	4	8	4	4	5	8	1	1	9	66

Out of the fifty-three professed who pronounced their vows, five left the community during this period. Some of them certainly left because of the ups-and-downs experienced during the constant changes of direction brought by the successive male superiors. Their vows of obedience did not prevent them from seeing what was going on, or from resolving by departure the problems of conscience raised by directives contrary to the ideals they held to. But the great majority of the professed, with consciences more or less clear, stayed on in the hope of a better future.

Under the governance of Dom Augustin sometime about the middle of 1808, we do not know exactly when, there was another change of superior. Mother M. des Séraphins was replaced by Mother Saint-Joseph Le Clercq, who on 7 November 1808 received the profession of Sister Félicité Marlot. This fact is confirmed by two civil documents of 1807 and 1809 in which Marie-Anne Le Clercq is at the head of a list of names of community members; but in 1811 we again find Mother Marie des Séraphins de Chateaubriand, who from this date on remained superior of the community until her death in 1832.[9]

Was it the departure of five professed sisters which gave Dom Jean Baptiste the idea of officially renewing the professions of those who had made their profession when living at Grosbois-Camaldolese under his government? The Register shows that seven of them renewed their vows on 11 April 1805. One of the still extant schedules, that of Sister Saint-Joseph (Marie-Anne Le Clercq), mentions: 'in the presence of Dom Jean-Baptiste Superior, and of his legitimate successors' (these last few words have been crossed out, which is only right for the reality of the phrase: the legitimate successors were not 'present').

One last remark concerns the sociological nature of the recruitment of the community. Out of the total of one hundred twenty-one entries, thirty-three came from various religious communities which had been dissolved. All did not become Trappists: two Benedictines out of fourteen left, two Cistercians out of five, one Carmelite, two Poor Clares, three Daughters of Charity, one Fontevriste, one Ursuline, one Sister of l'Ave Maria and one religious from an unknown community. The other nineteen all died professed in the Order, including two Visitation Sisters.

Of the eighty-eight lay women who entered, fifty-one departed, including five widows out of six. Thirty-seven made their profession and were faithful until death.

The Situation of the Community in 1809

To my knowledge there is no document in any private archives on the life of the community after it had been put in order by Dom Augustin. The two documents preserved in the National Archives of which I have already spoken bring in some new elements. The first is headed: State of

[9] *Ibid.*, F 19 6325, n°16, and F 19 474.

the community of nuns of La Trappe situated at Valenton and follows the format:

I. Personnel
Baptismal Names Family Names Names in Religion Age

There follow two pages in four columns. Here we find the same names as in our Register. Nineteen nuns are also inscribed, to which is added a list of six lay sisters and, a little further down, young pupils; they are three sisters, Marie-Thérèse, Marie-Jeanne, and Marceline Minet.

II. Material

1. Residence at Valenton, private property.
2. Income. Produce from their garden, small pensions from the government, reduced by a third for those who were former religious. Goods from their family if the Revolution had left them anything. Finally the work of their hands.
3. Debts. None. As that of the monks.
4. Expenses. About four hundred *francs* per head.
5. The Rule. As that of the monks.
6. Occupations. Divine Office, manual work, care of ladies who wish to come and spend some days in retreat. Instruction, whether on the one hand for the poor, or on the other for the rich, according to the expression of the Holy Rule.

Education is also proper to their Institute, just as it is for the Dames of Saint Benedict in the rue du Regard, at the head of which is Madame du Chaulnois. They both follow the Rule of Saint Benedict, but those of La Trappe keep it more strictly to the letter. We can be assured of this by the copy of a testimony from the Commune where they were before, which we believe it is our duty to add here.[10]

This point follows the deposition given by the Mayor of Yerres that we have cited above.

[10] *Ibid.*, F 19 5325, n°16.

This 'State of the community' is in a style easily recognizable as that of Dom Augustin himself, who after having written the report in a very regular and elegant hand, signed it with a very thick pen.

The second document is of quite another composition: it is a letter written by the Prefect of Seine-et-Oise, 'Chevalier of the Legion of Honor, Count of the Empire, Chamberlain to His Majesty the Emperor' [the Count de Gavre], addressed 'To his Excellency the Minister of the Interior, Count of the Empire', on July 1811.

> My Lord,
>
> By the letter that you have done me the honor of addressing to me on 30 June last, you inform me that reports have reached you regarding the Trappist Dames of Valenton which would tend to prove that the rule and the extremely severe practises which the Dames observe greatly harms their health and that they succumb after a few years. You also invite me to give you accurate information to put you in a position to understand this institution in some depth.
>
> On 25 April last, the Minister of the Police commissioned me to gather details on the administration of the house called Camaldolese of the Order of La Trappe, and to send them to him along with a list of the number of persons and the spirit in which they are directed and conducted. He did not ask for any details on the Dames at Valenton, but there is no doubt that, with a few exceptions they observe the same Rule as the men, since they live under the same Institution, bear the title of Religious of La Trappe, and according to the accounts that have been submitted to me, they are likened in all things to the male religious with whom they formed only one community until they were separated by ecclesiastical authority.
>
> Taking these facts into account, my Lord, I think you need only to know the spirit and regime of the one to be able to form an opinion about the other. Consequently I have the honor of sending you a copy of the report

addressed to me by the mayor of Yerres which will inform you of the internal regime of the house of Trappist men. I add to it a list of the names of the monks and those of the Dames of Valenton.

As regards my own personal opinion, I have already made it known to his Excellency the Minister of the Police. I do not regard these groups of individuals as dangerous to the State, since the members are subject to an obedience of the most passive and absolute kind, and they are condemned by their own will to privations, work and macerations that reason itself seems to repel. But in the social order I consider them useless. If it has been the policy of the state to suppress for all time all the religious bodies, even if many have rendered great services in the distant past, why conserve associations which cannot be of any help to society? They only exist and work in some way for themselves alone.

On the other hand, no association or religious congregation can remain in the Empire if they are not authorized by decree and if their statutes have not been approved by His Majesty. It has not come to my knowledge that either the Trappists of Camaldolese or the Dames of Valenton have been authorized to exist in community.

Therefore, My Lord, I think that these two establishments must be suppressed or obtain a legal status . . . [11]

There follows the list 'by names, first names, and ages of persons living in community at Valenton and known under the name of the religious Dames of the Order of La Trappe'.

There are twenty-eight names of religious and eight names of boarders aged eight to eighteen. At the end of the list is added the name of the chaplain, Fleury Jean-Louis, thirty-nine years old, and a lay brother Halie Louis-Charles, aged fifty-eight, a former architect. The three lists

[11] Paris, Nat. Arch., F 19 474. The day of the month is blurred in the photocopy I have at hand. However that may be, on the 28 of July 1811, the Emperor signed a decree ordering all the trappist monasteries, of men and women, in the Empire to be closed down. We will see why in the fifth Part of this book.

are certified by the Mayor of the commune at Valenton, Boullenoir, and the private secretary, G. Macau.

Health and Deaths

We are not very surprised to learn that the Minister of the Interior worried about the number of deaths registered by the Commune at Valenton among the ranks of the *Dames Trappistes*, who 'succumbed within a few years'. We have seen this phenomenon in all the foundations of Dom Augustin which followed the Regulations of La Valsainte. In this adopted community this was aggravated by the fact that since about the beginning of 1802, the sisters had inserted in their profession schedule a victim offering. Here is the example of Sister Sainte-Pétronille, the 8 September 1802:

> I, Sister Sainte-Pétronille, offer myself as a sacrifice to God, as a victim for my sins and those of all men. I unite my sacrifice to that of Jesus Christ my Saviour in reparation and honorable amendment for the outrages done to his Sacred Heart. In this spirit I promise perpetual stability in this Society, conversion of my manners, and obedience according to the Rule of Saint Benedict and constitutions of victims of the very holy will of God, the Order of Cîteaux of the Strict Observance, in the presence of God, of the Holy Mother of God, whom we take very specially as our Mother, of the saints whose relics are here present, and between the hands of our very Reverend Father Xavier our Father Superior, and of Reverend Mother Marie-Aimée de Jésus, our Mother Superior . . . [12]

By a similiar formula Sister Saint-Joseph Le Clercq committed herself on 12 April 1803. After that, we see the word

[12] Taken from a collection of schedules of various provenances (Stapehill, Maubec, Chamborand) now in Arch. G.

'victim' disappear from the schedules, but some wrote it on the reverse side of their profession schedule which was worded in the conventional style. A certain impetus had been given in this direction, and it made an impact on their extremely austere life. We will have occcasion to notice this in what follows.

If we look at the Register, we can see that the first six sisters who died had not reached the age of thirty, and had hardly lived two, three or four years in the community. Sometimes alongside their death notice in the Register there is a brief 'funeral oration'. One example is that of Sister Saint-François-Xavier Véron, one of the first three foundresses, who entered at twenty-two years on 2 July 1798: 'who died in a most edifying way after having received the last sacraments of the Church, on 13 August 1801'. The Register also notes that her life had not been without difficulties: she 'was almost sent away, put last among the novices for her lack of docility and respect for her superiors, then having gone out by her own will, she came back the next day full of regrets for her fault, and was then faithful to her vocation'. She died in her twenty-sixth year, after three years of religious life.

Sister Mechtilde du Saint-Sacrement Gaumont, who also entered on 2 July 1798, survived only one more year. She died on 30 August 1802 'with great courage and humility'. 'She was a model of regularity and fulfilled well the employments which were entrusted to her'.

From 1800 to 1811 there were twenty-six deaths. All those who died were not as young as these two. Many among them, former religious, were older when they entered and in general, found themselves out of breath less quickly. Among them, Sister Marie des Anges Frère, who entered at forty-eight on 9 July 1800, lived until 24 May 1810. Ten years of so austere a life appears to be a record. Other sisters who entered during the first years continued their religious life for sixteen, twenty-two and twenty-seven years.

Clouds on the Horizon

The final part of the letter from the Prefect of Seine-et-Oise to the Minister of the Interior, while showing every appearance of reasonableness, allows us to see that a storm was brewing. These slightly mad people, socially useless in spite of their educational activities in the opinion of the State in 1809, deserved to be suppressed for their autism: 'they exist and function only for themselves alone'.

We can therefore inquire about their legal status: were they, monks and nuns, authorized? Had their Statutes been approved? The Prefect had no knowledge of this. What followed? The answer is clear—it was only reasonable to suppress these houses. Even if the Count de Gavre seems to conclude with a query, the suggestion is obvious.

In the event, the Minister of the Interior did not have to convince the Emperor to suppress these useless communities. In this same month, July 1811, Napoleon was already persuaded by the facts that these useless people were dangerous to the Empire, and on the 28 July he decreed the closure of all trappist monasteries in the territories he ruled, after putting a price on the head of the abbot of La Valsainte. The causes and the consequences of this decree will be sketched out in more detail in the following chapters.

PART FIVE

Storms

AFTER RETURNING FROM RUSSIA, the monks and nuns of the reform of La Trappe were able to enjoy several years of relative peace and acquire a certain stability. Their one hope, to preserve *leur saint état* seemed on the way to fulfillment.

It might easily be thought that the nightmare of continual migration and painful separations was at last ended. The life was, of course, still very austere, but it generally brought with it peace of heart for the fervent, and leisure to devote to the divine praises and to fraternal charity. In the monasteries of Westphalia and England the Trappists made every effort to cure the physical afflictions of the brothers and sisters who had exhausted their strength on the roadways of Europe.

Once the last of those withdrawing from Russia had returned to Switzerland, La Valsainte was again inhabited by monks; and the nuns were given a house not far away which had been built for them in a magnificent setting. The man whom Providence had provided to direct all these religious with dexterity and devotion, and with an undeniably upright intention, was, however, carried away with a zeal that knew no bounds. He seemed possessed by a fever to make foundations, and in all good will and honesty, he thought it his duty to continue limitless expansion. The brothers themselves began to lose patience and 'cracks in the edifice' appeared somewhat surreptitiously. Even the success of the survival of the reform of La Trappe was like a blindfold over Father Abbot's eyes.

In 1802, he returned to his obsession with a foundation in America. In November, Father Urbain Guillet suggested leaving on orders from Dom Augustin with a lay brother and a child of the Third Order. Eleven months later they reached Baltimore. Another monk, Father François de Sales Burdel, with some Italian refugees from earlier foundations, took over again the old monastery of La Cervara, in the Gulf of Rapallo in the Republic of Genoa, then in the imperial domain. We will see further on how this monastery provided the occasion for a foundation proposal made to Dom Augustin by the Emperor himself.

With such a favorable wind it was not easy to foresee the storm, or to calculate its consequences. This was particularly true for the abbot of La Valsainte. His best lieutenants tried every means to make him see reason, but as one of them was later to say: 'when Father Abbot gets an idea into his head, he never lets it go'. [1]

> Dom Augustin had an ardent and burning spirit. When a pious (or another) thought came to him, he proceeded to its immediate execution with all the fire of which he was capable, as if everyone else had reached the same degree of incandescence as himself. [2]

The 'Savior of La Trappe', demonstrated in the two storms that the following chapters describe, that he very nearly became the destroyer of his reform. And in fact it did not survive in the form he cherished as the apple of his eye.

Everything had to give way before the authority of the remarkable strategist who had directed the monastic Odyssey.

[1] Dom Antoine, abbot of Lulworth (quoted by J. du Halgouet, *Cîteaux* 19 [1968] 275).

[2] The opinion of Dom Antoine, quoted by a chronicle in manuscript at Bellefontaine Abbey (Halgouet, *Cîteaux* 20 [1969] 44).

In the two events described later, this authority—which had become dictatorial, underwent two frustrating, bitter disappointments. Even though the first event did not directly concern the history of the nuns, it had repercussions on their unity with the feminine branch of the reform. The second made them completely one with the monks.

The documentation of the following chapters is owed, for the most part, to two articles of Jérôme Halgouet, who has closely examined all the archives which could furnish information on this question, including the National Archives [of France] and the Vatican Archives.

CHAPTER ONE

THE INTERNAL STORM

THE BREACH BETWEEN DARFELD AND LA VALSAINTE

THE COMMUNITY OF MONKS founded at Darfeld by La Valsainte between 1794–1796 had lived for ten years in relative autonomy under the direction of Dom Eugène de Laprade, its prior, who had been nominated by the abbot of La Valsainte. They did not have to go into exile to Russia, for Westphalia was not threatened by revolutionary soldiers. The community had received new members and through the careful management of the property left at their disposition by the Baron Droste Zu Wichering, had reached economic stability.

The First Difficulties

Contrary to the custom of the Order Dom Augustin arrogated to himself universal authority over all the houses of his reform, both of monks and nuns. He even signed his letters, 'Abbot, however unworthy, of the monks and nuns of La Trappe'. His authority—absolute, and sometimes arbitrary—was exercised in a variety of ways both over the individuals he moved about and over their goods which he disposed of as he wished. On the return from Russia the malaise grew. The community at Darfeld was subject to his whims: both the best monks whom he removed elsewhere, and the numerous children he imposed on them to educate free of charge.

Already in 1798, Dom Augustin nominated Father Étienne Malmy for the exodus being prepared, so that he could entrust to him the direction of a group of nuns. In 1802, a monk from Darfeld, Dom Bernard, who was sent to England to replace the founder of Lulworth, Dom Jean-Baptiste. On returning to Switzerland, Dom Augustin took Father Amand Levêque, a professed monk of Darfeld, as Prior for a foundation at Géronde. Faced with the removal of these valuable men whose loss he felt keenly, Dom Eugène could say nothing, as his assent had not been asked and, according to the Father Abbot, did not need to be asked.

In addition, Dom Augustine accepted all proposals for foundations, which required men and money. For funds Dom Augustin had been granted pensions by the English government, for the monks and nuns returning from Russia. He added to the list the names of the monks in Westphalia and some children in their care. But the subsidies which should have gone to Darfeld were used in other ways. This is plainly shown by a letter of the abbot of La Valsainte to a former monk of Morimond justifying his actions. In it the abbot openly admitted that he was in no hurry to send money to Darfeld and 'that the monastery he had founded for the nuns in Switzerland was again the cause of his delay'.[1]

In all good faith Dom Augustin believed that he had the sole authority to manage the goods of all the monasteries under his jurisdiction. Many felt this was an irregularity, as it was—in fact, quite contrary to the Charter of Charity which since the twelfth century had governed the Cistercian monasteries.

Clearly black clouds were gathering over the reform of La Valsainte. The nearest and darkest of these lowered over Darfeld. It would not be long before the storm broke.

[1] Archives of Sept-Fons, cote A 26.

Crisis and Conflict

One day in the spring of 1806, Dom Eugène, the prior of Darfeld, decided to go to London to clarify the business of pensions granted by the English government. To go on this journey he did not think it necessary to ask permission of his Father Immediate, the abbot of La Valsainte. The abbot hearing of such independance and 'believing it his duty, descended on Darfeld and made known in no uncertain terms his displeasure with the heavy hand of a master. The second superior who was in charge during the absence of Dom Eugène de Laprade, was not the man to be intimidated by this. Dom Augustin considered, or convinced himself, that the superior showed a spirit of dissent, and that this Father Germain Gillon inveighed against the authority of the reigning Pope.' [2]

This 'accusation' was to be the leading edge of Dom Augustin's defence before the roman authorites. In fact it seems not to have lasted long. Jérôme du Halgouet makes the following reflection:

> Was there anyone in the world of the émigrés which formed the Trappist ambience who was not disappointed by Pius VII? Had he not given the crown of Saint Louis to this insignificant Jacobin general, Bonaparte? And on the contrary, Dom Augustin, who was a curious mixture of extreme inflexibility and strange pliability, had just converted to Bonaparte! At this moment all his thoughts were on the Emperor, on the monastic-military hospice to be built on the road to Italy, and on the establishments that could perhaps be opened near Paris. [3]

His visit to Darfeld did not have the hoped-for success. Father Abbot left the matter 'open', promising to send his decision in writing. In fact, he sent someone in person. At

[2] *Cîteaux* 28/4 [1977] 307ff.
[3] *Ibid.*

the beginning of May (the visit was dated end of April), Father Amand Levêque presented himself at Burlo as emissary of the abbot of La Valsainte to be the new prior of the house.[4] But despite being a professed monk of Darfeld, he was not welcomed by the sub prior and the community as Dom Eugène's replacement.

The New Superior

Forty years after the events, he described his adventures:

> In 1806, I was in the monastery of La Valsainte when Dom Augustin, after having made a visit to the monastery at Darfeld, came and gave me the order by word of mouth and in writing to pack and go to Darfeld to fulfill the office of superior in the place of Dom Eugène who was then in England. He did not make known to me any reason for this replacement, except that he was very displeased with Father Germain the sub prior at Darfeld, but he did not give me any further explanations. When I arrived at the place, Father Germain did not wish to receive me in my new capacity. Once all the brethren had assembled in Chapter, I said to them that according to the rules we had always been taught they could not refuse to receive me, since Dom Eugène—being only a prior—could be changed. It would not be the same if he were abbot. 'Very well', replied Dom Germain, 'we will elect him as Abbot.' Seeing that I was a source of discord, I withdrew to Münster and wrote to Dom Augustin about my heated reception and handed him my resignation. I consulted with the Vicar General of Arras, who honored me with his friendship and who was very attached to Darfeld. He wrote immediately to Darfeld. This letter impressed Father Germain, who sent a carriage to fetch me . . . .[5]

[4] It will be remembered that the monks, leaving their house to the nuns, had moved a short distance away to a priory called Burlo (Klein Burlo).

[5] Declaration of Dom Amand Levêque, Arch. PS.

Father Amand added a postscript:

> I can also certify that the election of Dom Eugène took place on the day of my arrival (6 May 1806), or the day after that . . . . As for me, I went [to Münster] on the day after my arrival at Darfeld; I stayed the entire time at the house of the Princess Gallitzin, where all the monks of Darfeld stayed when they came to Münster, and it was there that I was honored by the visit of the Vicar General of Arras.[6]

While the community was electing its Abbot, the superior had to give up his business in London by the express order of his Father Immediate, without moreover receiving any authorization to return to Darfeld. He had to wait for an explicit order before doing so. Where did he go? To Lulworth or Stapehill? At Lulworth there is no trace of his having been there in the meantime. The account book of Stapehill shows that on 16 May they gave him ten pounds. This was only fair after all Dom Eugène had done for the nuns at Darfeld.

Disputes

On 6 June 1806 the monks of the community at Darfeld-Burlo, having expressed their wish to see their prior become abbot, put themselves under the protection of the Vicar General of Fürstenberg, who acted as the ordinary of Münster as well as Paderborn.

Dom Augustin appealed to the papal nuncio, while Darfeld presented all the requisite explanations to representatives of the Holy See. After waiting five months, Dom Eugène, still having received no orders from Dom Augustin, decided that he should return to his monastery. This was about 15 October. At the same time, Dom Augustin sent a report from Fribourg to the nuncio in Switzerland for the

[6] *Ibid.*

pope, concerning the crisis now become acute through the authorized election and the resistance of the community.

Letters crisscrossed between the protagonists and representatives of the Holy See without ever receiving genune replies. The Father Immediate fulminated excommunications against the monks who had dared to revolt and elect an abbot without any reference to his own authority. He hoped that the person elected would put his sons back on the straight and narrow road—but he did nothing of the kind.

Dom Eugène in his turn took up his pen to explain to the Father Abbot of La Valsainte in a very long letter, the reasons which had driven his community in desperation to take such a solution. There are twenty-five pages, followed by a post-scriptum of eight pages; all written and dated 13 December 1806. But the letter did not reach Dom Augustin at La Valsainte; he was already on the road to Darfeld by way of Paris. From there, he wrote to his nuncio on the 3 January, and then left for Darfeld. There, on the sixth or eighth of January a stormy Chapter was held under Dom Augustin's presidency. His secretary had brought the lengthy letter, and found himself obliged to read it out before the assembled community. As each of the arguments for the defence appeared he was required to refute them one by one. The uproar is not hard to imagine. Wounds on both sides went even deeper.

The Roman Verdict

I will not give here all the details of the bargaining the two camps did with Rome. The roman court took its time reflecting. It invited each side to send representatives, and carefully considered the rights and the wrongs. Three quarters of the year 1807 were passed in anguished waiting by both parties. On Darfeld's side as on Dom Augustin's, there were flagrant legal irregularities. On 3 October, a decree of the Congregation of Bishops and Regulars suspended the jurisdiction of the abbot of La Valsainte over the house at Darfeld, which was to pass— 'provisionally', says the decree—to the jurisdiction of the Ordinary of Münster. By this means studying the case could become less stormy. The monk-secretary left at Darfeld the previous January by Dom Augustin was able to return to Paris at the beginning of 1808; his mission had come to an end with the suspension of Lestrange's jurisdiction.[7]

Nine months after this change, a Roman Decree erecting the Darfeld community into an abbey at last arrived, on 21 June 1808. In the meantime, warnings had been given to the two protagonists: Darfeld was not to pretend prematurely that it was an abbey, and Abbot de Lestrange was not to exercise any jurisdiction over the nuns at Darfeld.

The matter thus settled by the sacred congregations in Rome and confirmed by the pope, caused a rupture which was to remain as an open wound in the Reform in both its branches. Repercussions on the feminine branch resulted in a division. Relations between Notre-Dame-de-la-Miséricorde in Westphalia and Notre-Dame-de-la-Sainte-Trinité in Switzerland were also broken. Each monastery of nuns must be under the abbot appointed as father immediate according to the proximity of the monastery.

We saw in Chapter Four of Part Four that Dom Augustin, when he had been asked to take responsibility for the Trappistines of Grosbois, had at first refused. Now, in 1808, having a presentiment that rupture with Darfeld was all but inevitable, the Father Abbot thought better of it and accepted the proposition made to him. In this way he made up for the loss of the two communities in Westphalia by

[7] On all this see Jérôme du Halgouet, in *Cîteaux* 28/4 (1977) 307–326. The author consulted principally the Vatican archives, those of the Cistercian Order—*Miscellanea*, III, f.322–341, La Trappe, Port-du-Salut—and the historian Gallardin. I mention this breach, in which the nuns had no part at all, because of its consequences on the feminine branch. That is why it seemed to me I could well abridge the circumstances of this conflict.

adopting two Parisian communities. He imposed on them the Regulations of La Valsainte to the letter, as a condition *sine qua non* of liquidating their debts.

Returning to the Regulations of de Rancé

The rupture provoked by his 'unauthorized' election compelled the new abbot, Dom Eugène de Laprade, to reflect at length on the legitimacy of the Regulations of La Valsainte and on their excesses, which had disastrous effects on the health of members of the communities, especially the nuns. His contacts with Pius VII, a prisoner at Fontainebleau, and with his entourage, had brought to light the mistrust the Holy See had for the Regulations, which had never been approved.

A second storm broke out in 1811, interrupting these reflections with urgent matters requiring attention. The suppression of all trappist monasteries located in the Empire obliged the communities to disperse yet again. Members of the community at Darfeld reassembled in small groups, creating small monastic islands in Belgium and various other places.

From Belgium Dom Eugène, in 1814, after the abdication of Napoleon, sent the monks and nuns under his obedience a circular letter entitled *Exhortation to the Monks and Nuns of the Reform of La Trappe in Westphalia, at the time of their deliverance after the arrival of the Allied Troops in 1814*.[8] On the title page, the second abbot of Port-du-Salut, Dom François d'Assise, wrote:

> This exhortation, composed and written in the hand of R. P. D. Eugène de La Prade, Abbot of Darfeld and abbot-appointee of Port-Reingeard [a monastery he never directed as death overtook him], has as its purpose, the

[8] Arch. PS, no reference.

> justification by sound reasons of his intention of transferring his monks and nuns who follow the Reform of Dom Augustin, in which they made their profession, to that of M. de Rancé.

The text begins:

> La Sainte-Volonté-de-Dieu
>
> My Brothers and Sisters,
>
> Blessed be the Lord, the God of all consolation who by his great mercy has consoled us, and has delivered us from the rage of these howling wolves who attacked the sheepfold and scattered the sheep . . . How can we give thanks? . . . by adding on more penances? . . . No, my brothers, no, my sisters, no. God does not ask that of you.

The abbot then went on, with a certain note of respect for the generosity of the first monks of La Valsainte, to explain at length the atmosphere of fervor in which the Regulations had been drafted. He then added that the experience of twenty years had shown that not only do they exceed the strength of many people, but they also go beyond the discretion required by Saint Benedict and the first Regulations of Cîteaux. This was why the Church had never approved them and was troubled by the prolonged use of these Regulations. It seemed better then to follow the Regulations of Rancé, which had been approved and praised by Benedict XIV on 10 March 1732 by a papal brief addressed to Dom Malachie, then abbot of La Trappe. Dom Eugène concludes: 'So we will conform to the Regulations of M. de Rancé, as they were practised at La Trappe before the Revolution, and we will observe them in entire submission to the Church in any way in which it will please her to ordain that we add to or change them.'

This moderate and wise exhortation, given at the very hour when trappist monasteries could again settle in France, was well received among the dispersed groups who had remained under the obedience to Dom de Laprade. This proposal did not, however, extend to those under obedience to Dom de Lestrange. Nor did it receive a great deal of publicity, for at the time all efforts were concentrated on finding suitable places to re-establish monasteries in France. It passed almost unnoticed amidst the more pressing concerns occupying the monks at this exciting time of restoration.

But twenty years later, after Dom Augustin's death, when the Holy See wanted to bring together the two Lestrange reform groups, separated by the rupture of 1808, the question of observances—those of de Rancé or those of Lestrange—became a bone of contention which persisted obstinately throughout the nineteenth century. (Remember that in 1808 the Roman Brief foresaw only a 'provisional' removal from the jurisdiction of the abbot of La Valsainte). We will have more to say later about this 'war of observances', which happily came to an end in 1892.

CHAPTER TWO

THE NAPOLEONIC STORM

CLOSURE OF THE TRAPPIST MONASTERIES IN THE EMPIRE (1811)

REVERSAL OF ALLIANCES was common in Napoleon's strategy, in dealings with both nations and individuals. When someone at a personal or a national level fell in with his own plans at a personal or national level (ultimately aimed at his own prestige or glory) or when they opposed him more or less openly, then favors or proscriptions succeeded one another at a brisk rate. The history of the Empire abounds in these reversals. Dom Augustin de Lestrange, who at one moment enjoyed imperial benevolence, was about to experience in his turn, to his own misfortune and the misfortune of his communities, just how far the wrath of the despot could go when he had been offended.

THE ERA OF FAVORS (1805–1807)

On 18 May 1805, Napoleon had himself crowned King of Italy at Milan; the Ligurian Republic (Genoa) spontaneously submitted to the Conqueror of Europe to prevent worse things happening. The superior of the Trappists of La Cervara, Father François de Sales Burdel, knew that french conquest was usually followed by the suppression of monasteries. He addressed a petition in latin verse to the Emperor, on the road to Genoa, asking for the preservation of his monastery, situated on the Gulf of Rapallo:

> Glorious Monarch, what a difference there is in our destinies. I possess nothing at all on this earth and everything is obedient to your authority. Yet I do not envy you, because if you have the best part, know well that mine is even better. *Nam tibi si bona pars, optima, scito, mihi.* All that I ask of you, generous Prince, is that it may not be taken away from me, so that as nothing is lacking in your domain, nothing may be lacking in mine.[1]

The monarch, very flattered, made inquiries about the Trappists to find out whether they could be used to staff a hospice in the Alps for troops passing from France to Italy. Receiving a positive response, Napoleon had a letter sent to Dom Augustin by his Minister Portalis; not only would he safeguard the monastery of La Cervara, but he wanted to found a hospice at Mont-Genèvre, one league from Briançon on the road to Italy.

The abbot of La Valsainte accepted the overtures of the Emperor, and set to work immediately organizing the establishment of Mont-Genèvre. In June 1806, he himself went with six monks to prepare the work and design a plan for the hospice to submit to the Emperor. While waiting for construction to begin, the small community settled in the former Abbey of Oulx, and then withdrew to a small isolated cottage. The Emperor preferred the plan drawn up by the monks to that of the civil engineer and work was begun.

A little later, Dom Augustin purchased property at Mont Valérian, at the gates of Paris, with the intention of establishing a house of the Third Order. Never forget that this was an era when recognition by the government depended on the criterion of public usefulness. A hospice or a school gave value to the trappist institution, and Dom Augustin entered

[1] Quoted by Gaillardin, *Histoire de la Trappe*, 2:255.

fully into the game to hold on to his Reform and to promote his Third Order.

THE WIND CHANGES (1809–1810)

Yet all was not going well in France for the 'master of the moment'.

> What alarmed the nation were the politics of Napoleon himself. His triumphs never restored confidence, because everything always had to be begun over and over again . . . . 'France is sick with worry', wrote Fiévée to the Emperor . . . Decrès, in private, spoke more bluntly: 'The Emperor is mad, absolutely insane; he will destroy himself and we will all be ruined with him'.[2]

Wars followed one after another: Spain 1806, Russia 1807, Austria 1809.

> In the midst of danger the Emperor remained imperturbable; he even went ahead with a venture which was the most likely to sow disaffection among his own subjects. On 17 May (1809) he decided to annex Rome. When he received the news that Pius VII was about to excommunicate him, he gave the order to abduct and deport him. On 6 July, the day of the battle of Wagram, the pope was led away by the *gendarmerie*, and on 17 February 1810, a decree of the Senate regularized the annexation. The ordering of such an act at the very height of the crisis gives us a true picture of the man. With an unruffled countenance he played double or nothing. Once again, he forced destiny.[3]

What historian Georges Lefebvre here briefly summarizes requires the more precise detail. They are given by André Latreille:

[2] G. Lefebvre, *Napoléon*, 6th edn. (Paris, 1969) 303.
[3] *Ibid.*, pp. 309–310.

> On 17 May 1809 he [Napoleon] signed the famous Decree by which, invoking the peace of *his* people and *the dangers brought about by the mixing of spiritual and temporal authority*, he pronounced the permanent reunion of the Pontifical States with the Empire . . . On 10 June, to the accompaniment of artillery salutes, the Decree was read publicly throughout the city . . . During the night the Bull *Quem memoranda* appeared, pasted to the walls of churches and replaced whenever it was torn down; it pronounced major excommunication against *all those* who were guilty of the sacrilegious violation of the patrimony of Saint Peter . . . At the publication of the excommunication, Napoleon on 20 June wrote [to Miollis] *ab irato* speaking of Pius VII: 'He is a madman who must be locked up. Arrest Pacca and the other adherents of the Pope . . .'.[4]

André Latreille tells us of the arrest:

> During the night of 6 July 1809, the general of the *gendarmerie*, Radet, under the orders of Miollis, broke into the Quirinal by smashing the doors with hatchets. Penetrating into the pope's personal apartment, where Pius VII, standing and holding a crucifix in his hand, awaited him, he informed the Secretary of State and the pope that he had orders to take them with him. At dawn, the people of Rome, aghast at so sacrilegious an abduction, of which they had had no suspicion, learned that they no longer had a shepherd and that from now on they belonged to Caesar.[5]

The bitter conflict between the pope and the emperor did not stem from a difference along spiritual lines or call into question the authority of the Sovereign Pontiff over the christian people as a whole. Instead, it concerned the

[4] A. Latreille, *L'Eglise catholique et la Révolution française, 2:1800–1815*, p. 164.

[5] *Ibid.*, p.164.

temporal power of the pope over territories coveted by the Emperor. Even so, the conduct of Napoleon towards Pius VII aroused serious misgivings among many Christians, and the violence of it was certainly regarded as sacrilege. Yet the fear the despot inspired caused a cloak of silence to fall over the Church in France, a silence which covered an underground effort to publish far and wide the very document which Napoleon wanted to keep hidden at any price: the Bull of Excommunication.

Dom Augustine de Lestrange had been one of the first to concern himself with the fate of the pope, who had not only been abducted from the Quirinal, but had been taken to Florence, then to Alessandria not far from Genoa, then to Grenoble, and finally to Savona. The abbot of La Valsainte went to see him without delay. Napoleon heard of this, and began to harbor suspicions about the abbot of the Trappists, who now had no doubts about how he needed to act toward the sovereign from whose hand he had accepted many benefits.

THE OATH (1810–1811)

At the end of 1810 an oath of fidelity to the Constitution of the Empire was imposed on the Italian clergy. The Prefect of the Appenines, to whom La Cervara was subject, arrived at the monastery to exact the oath from the monks. The prior consulted several serious-minded persons, who told him that the pope allowed the oath. In good faith, he and his community took the oath demanded by the zealous Prefect who had pressed him to take this step.

Dom Augustin had not been consulted. In his eyes, to swear an oath to the Constitution of the Empire was to approve the confiscation of the Pontifical States, and subsequently to acknowledge all the acts which could assail the rights and liberty of the Church, the laws the emperor might succeed in extracting from a pope in captivity, or decrees of a national council. All that was distasteful to the conscience of the Father Abbot. So he expressed his disapproval to the monks at La Cervara and after Easter 1811 sent the prior of Mont-Genèvre to them in his stead, to receive their retraction. This took place on 4 May.

During this same time the abbot of La Valsainte was preparing to go to America with some monks and sisters of the Third Order to prepare for permanent foundations on the new continent. He was at Bordeaux, ready to embark, when the Prefect received the order to arrest him and put him in prison without any reason. The order was carried out, and from his prison Dom Augustin wrote a very long letter to La Cervara, inviting the community to make a public retraction.

While the Father Abbot, through the intermediary of powerful friends, found himself released, his sons of La Cervara did not hesitate to obey his injunctions and made their public retraction on 16 July, before a large group of people who had come for the Sunday Mass. The bells were rung in full peal. Dom François de Sales, in the name of his brothers, read from the pulpit the text of retraction of 4 May. The monks were under no illusions about the consequences of their act on the community and each one of them; The reality was to surpass their expectations.

The Wrath of a Great Man

The 'master of the moment' soon learned what had happened in the region of the Appennines, and how a handful of men had dared to oppose the victor of Austerlitz and Wagram. The penalty was not long in coming, and it arrived under the form of a decree written from Saint-Cloud on 25 July 1811. It was peremptory, dry and stinging, like a discharge of grape-shot, and it mobilized all the ministers to ensure its execution. The text is given by Gaillardin in his history of La Trappe:

Napoleon, Emperor of France, King of Italy, etc., We have decreed and we do decree that which follows:

Art.1. The convents of La Trappe are to be suppressed throughout the entire Empire, even that at Mont-Genèvre. A sequestration will be appended on the furnishings and real estate.

Art.II. The monks of the Trappist convent of Cervara will be arrested and indicted in the citadels.

Art.III. The superior of the convent of Cervara who has made a public show of rebellion will be prosecuted before a military commission, to be judged and sentenced as such. General Porzon will go to Cervara with a mobile column and will appoint the said commission.

Art.IV. All concessions which we made to the Trappists in property, lands, or any other exemptions will be revoked.

Our Ministers of Worship, Police, Finances, the Interior and War are responsible, each in his own sphere, for the execution of the present decree.

Signed: Napoleon

The Minister, Secretary of State, Count Daru.
Certified true copy, the Minister of Finances, The Duke of Gaëte.[6]

The day after the Decree for the suppression of the Trappists, 29 July, Napoleon dictated a violent letter to his Minister of Police, which was much altered and even incorrect in places: . . . If M. Lestrange is not arrested before his arrival in Switzerland, write to my Minister to have him arrested at Fribourg and at the same time to take possession of his papers. You have received my decree to have the superior of the convent of La Cervara court-martialled and shot, and the monks arrested . . . I suppose that the military commission will do justice to this superior who has dared to preach a sedition in this way . . . .[7]

[6] P. 309.

[7] Archives Nationaux A I-IV, 392, f°369, quoted by J. du Halgouet, in 'Pierres d'attente', *Cîteaux* (1967) 68.

Locked up, intimidated, and ill-treated, the monks of La Cervara were not freed until the Empire fell in 1814.[8]

The Flight of the 'Prime Culprit'

Dom Augustin had already arrived in Switzerland, in fact, and knew he was being hunted down. On 14 August he assembled his monks at La Valsainte and gave them instructions in writing, to act with great steadfastness in the face of the impending persecution. He then left for La Riedera where at midnight, before the assembled nuns he celebrated the Mass of the Assumption, and left with only one companion, his brother, the Chevalier de Lagrange.[9]

The swiftness of his horse enabled him to reach Germany. The next day the Petit Conseil of Fribourg sent a contingent of police to arrest the abbot on the orders of the Emperor. Not finding the 'culprit', they took only a letter in which the abbot spoke of his health and his need for the waters of Plombières! . . . It was so convincing that the imperial police took the hunt into the Vosges. But in vain. So as not to appear ineffectual they had it noised about that the 'culprit' had been arrested at Hamburg, disguised as a policeman, and shot on the spot. This news filtered as far as England. Father Halgouet comments:

> Several texts in French, Latin, English and Italian allude to this tragic death: 'The unhappiness of our Reform cannot be in any doubt. We have a genuine confirmation: our Father Immediate and La Valsainte we looked up to no longer exist . . .' The chronicle of our sisters at Stapehill, written some ten or twenty years later, includes the following note: 'In the year one thousand eight hundred and *eleven* [scratched out] after having *believed* for so long

[8] Halgouet, 'Pierres d'attente', 68.

[9] A novice at La Valsainte and a former soldier in the army of de Condé.

> that our Reverend Father Dom Augustin had been shot by the order of Bonaparte, we had all the services for the dead and said all the prayers we are obliged to say for him in case the news was true; we then had the happiness of seeing him again and he made the Regular Visitation here on 4 January in the year one thousand eight hundred and twelve.'[10]

What had happened to the two fugitives, Dom Augustine and his brother, the Chevalier de Lagrange, between August 1811—when they left La Valsainte—and 1812—at end of which they reappeared in England? They had ridden and lodged for various lengths of time in Germany, Poland, and Lithuania, and then reached Riga (Latvian). There after traversing all the scandinavian countries, they took a boat for England. This long clandestine detour across Europe, with the constant fear of arrest as they thwarted frontier patrols, and the gruelling sea voyage, all sapped the strength of the Father Abbot. When he landed in England, he was obliged to stay for six weeks in hospital in an English port. He caused a dramatic sensation when he arrived, unexpected, at Lulworth about December 1812. Four months later he embarked for America by way of the West Indies with a few monks and did not reappear in England until the end of 1814. As a result, he was not present when his monasteries were dispersed.

DISSOLUTION ON THE CONTINENT

On the continent the Trappist Order within the territory of the Empire consisted of four houses of monks and two of nuns.[11] They were all affected by the Decree of 28 July 1811, dissolving the monasteries.

[10] See J. du Halgouet, *Cîteaux* 17/1 (1967) 71. The chronicle made an error for the year: read 1812 and 4 January 1813.

[11] Monks: Darfeld, Westmalle, La Cervara, Le Mont Genèvre. Nuns: Darfeld, Valenton. Two monasteries of monks remained outside the Em-

Two monasteries of monks were the first to feel the blow. On 2 August three commissionaries from the government arrived at Westmalle. There they made an inventory and demanded that the novices be sent away. The Prefect of Antwerp however, was kind enough to allow the professed monks time to put their things in order. When he was censured for this, he immediately put the Decree into execution, and on 3 October the house was left empty. Each monk had to find his own means of subsistence and lodging.

The closing of La Cervara on 5 August was much more brutal. The superior had an especially cruel fate. Transported to Corsica and prosecuted on orders of the emperor before a military commission, he was condemned to death. His friends managed to obtain a commutation of his sentence to twelve years of imprisonment. The other twenty-six monks were kept in prison on the Island of Capraia for a long time, and were later transferred to Corsica, where they stayed until the fall of the Empire.

At Mont-Genèvre the expulsion was also brutal. The monks who were working outside when the police arrived were not allowed even to go back into the house. They were taken to their respective family parishes and assigned a residence under police supervision.

The monastery of Mont Valérien was placed under sequestration.

In Westphalia the Prefect of Münster presided over the removal of the monks from Darfeld, where it was hoped that a few monks who were too ill to move, could stay until they died or recovered and could leave.

La Valsainte remained to be liquidated. On 11 October 1811, the ambassador of France in Switzerland received the order to suppress the abbey. The Petit Conseil of Fribourg tried to resist, but the decision went beyond the limits of

---

pire: Sainte-Suzanne, which took refuge in the Balearic Islands during the Peninsular War; Lulworth (monks) and Stapehill (nuns) in England. La Valsainte and La Riedera both suffered the consequences of these events.

its jurisdiction. The ambassador insisted, calling on the higher authority of the Grand Conseil. The papal *nuncio* at Lucerne advised the monks to submit, because resisting the emperor could have dire repercussions on the country that had befriended them. The decree of suppression was finally carried throughout by the Grand Conseil on 30 November and conveyed to the monks on 7 December. The Grand Conseil granted a delay of five months, until 1 May, however in evacuating the monastery. This occurred during the month of April. On 1 May, Father Étienne Malmy, accompanied by two lay brothers, assumed the dress of secular clergy, with permission to stay there as chaplain of the church.

THE FATE OF THE NUNS

Valenton

The first nuns affected by the Decree were those nearest the capital. The suppression of their monastery was carried out at the same time as that of Mont Valérien. The Register of Admissions (page 81), briefly notes the event: 'The community left the house of Valenton 12 August 1811. They left Paris 19 February 1812. Arriving at Tréguier the 4th or 6th of March of the same year; and stayed there 1812–1813-1814. After which they went to Bayeux in Normandy.' The superior at that time was Mother des Séraphins de Chateaubriand. A friend and protector found lodgings for her community in a building at the end of a courtyard in Paris itself. They stayed there eight months, following their Rule and discharging their obligation to singing the Office and Solemn Mass daily. They were offered a house at Tréguier in Brittany. They accepted, as they were not without some fear of being discovered by the police in Paris and so running the risk of being a liability to their benefactor. They made their way to Tréguier by various routes at set intervals so as not to attract attention, and all managed to arrive at their destination.

They took up the regular life of their *saint état* again under the kind auspices of their Breton neighbors. Here they lived in peace until the Emperor's abdication.

Darfeld-Rosenthal

As we have seen, the Prefect of Münster arranged the expulsion of the monks at Darfeld and Burlo. He affixed official seals on the furnishings. Divided into groups, the monks made their way to asylums in Belgium and Germany which had been prepared by friends or by Dom Eugène, who had left at the beginning of the crisis. The nuns were driven in groups to Cologne, Liège, and Ghent. The community was then composed of forty sisters, three oblates and seven postulants. 'The first superior, Mother Hélène Van den Broeck, was sent by the Reverend Father Abbot to Cologne with most of the Flemish and German sisters, to the house of a very pious widow who received them with open arms.'

This widow, Madame Hirn, managed a factory where she engaged the nuns as workers. Some sisters stayed on at Darfeld, too ill to be moved, along with a few others who looked after them. Mother Agnès-Edmond Thuilliez, a cistercian religious then forty-three years old, who had made her stability at Darfeld on 12 April 1809, directed them. There were seven sisters. Except for the last sister, who entered after 1809, we find the others on the official list drawn up in 1809: Sister Thérèse Müller, Sister Victoire Chuffaut, Sister Jean-Baptiste Piton, Sister Lutgarde Klein, Sister Colette Van Fiele, Sister Anne Hilaire.[12]

It seems odd that in this group there were no deaths, but at Cologne the Register notes the return to God of four sisters. On December 8 and 9 respectively, Sister Madeleine Antoinet, aged thirty-nine, after three years of monastic life,

[12] Arch. alt., Mémoire des religieuses d'Altbronn, printed at Mont des Olives (1909).

and Sister Gertrude Schey, aged thirty-eight, after eleven years in the community, died. Sister Stanislaus Bouchez followed on 31 May 1813, at twenty-five, Sister M. Antoinette Daume died on Christmas Day of the same year; she was a former Capuchine of sixty-two, who had lived five years at La Trappe.

The group of ten sisters who went to Belgium found asylum in a *château* in the region of Liège at Borsut. Four of these sisters were among the foundresses of Sainte-Catherine at Laval in 1816: Mother Elisabeth Piette, Sister Séraphine Gavot, Sister Marie-Claire Foucart, and Sister M.-Joseph Casters.[13]

La Riedera

The officials at Fribourg were in no hurry to execute the orders of the Emperor, as we saw above. Their benevolence towards the nuns was even more generous. In the archives of La Trappe is a notebook which tells the story of the nuns at La Riedera on two pages. This text, written by a lay brother in a quite fantastic style and spelling, states bluntly: 'As for the nuns, Bonaparte had said nothing; the Government of Fribourg said, we will say nothing either! So the nuns were left in peace'.[14]

Another account left by a pupil of the Third Order, Catherine Bussard, adds a note of piquancy:

> They came to search our monastery looking for him (Dom Augustin). When they came to the Third Order they made me open an old cupboard shut only with a turnbuckle. There was nothing inside other than instruments of penance; haircloth, hairshirts, and iron disciplines.

[13] Arch. alt., Catalogue of various Registers noting the departure of the professed for Borsut.

[14] Arch. Tr., ref. 56, piece 44.

> When the gentlemen saw all that, they were dumbfounded . . . And then they went to our chaplain's house where Father Jérôme (Roger) and our dear Father Augustin (Pignard) lived. They made them open two trunks that belonged to Father Dom Augustin. In one they found a roasting-spit and a fan. They hooted with laughter and said that it was a good contrast to the instruments of penance they had found at our place. With the roasting-spit they found a letter which proved where these objects had come from. Madame la Comtesse de La Tour had given them to him to make up for her lack of money and she had made an estimate of their value.
>
> Before leaving, these gentlemen came to assure us that we could stay in our monastery, that they would take us under their protection, and that if the emperor said anything about us, they would have some idea of what to tell him.[15]

This recital is only anecdotal. It shows how the plight of the monastery was seen from the outside. In reality, the nuns of La Riedera experienced the same threat of dissolution that had struck La Valsainte. They were advised to petition for their own dissolution, so that it could then be arranged on the best possible terms. This request was granted by the Grand Conseil and the notice given in the Decree of 15 May 1812. Article 3 of the Decree stipulates 'that it will be permitted to the Trappistine dames to stay in their convent and to keep their present chaplain (Father Augustin Pignard) until all their goods are sold and their business is concluded.[16]

In fact nothing was concluded before January 1816, when the sisters themselves arranged for a first group to return to France. But during the last five years in Switzerland, their life was very precarious; they were worried and

[15] *Ibid.*, ref.217, piece 16.

[16] Cf. Tobie de Raemy, *L'émigration française dans le canton de Fribourg* (Fribourg, 1935) 352 (n.1, Archives d'Etat de Fribourg, manuel du Grand Conseil, p. 299).

somewhat disorganized as is shown in their Register. In 1811, there were nine admissions, but eleven departures, and only one profession before the despotic Napoleonic Decree; there were no more professions at all after that.

In the crucible of this suffering a future was being prepared for the three houses of nuns which we shall watch progressively come to light in the sixth part of this book.

PART SIX

New Beginnings

BETWEEN AUGUST 1811 and May 1814 passed nearly three years of anxious and uncertain waiting for some turn of events, favorable or unfavorable, to the despot who had put an end to the hard but peaceful existence of the trappist communities.

Even though news circulated more slowly than it does today, sooner or later it reached those who were waiting (together with sometimes contradictory comments), and each person reacted with hope or despair according to his expectations. Everyone was well aware, with varying degrees of insight, that the Emperor was multiplying diplomatic and military errors, and they saw his genius turning hysterical in the face of opposition and setbacks. His impulsive boldness did not help revive confidence in the future among the most perceptive of his friends, nor among the population subject to his authority.

The disastrous campaign in Russia in 1812; the Concordat of Fontainbleau extorted from Pius VII in January 1813, promulgated as a law of the state in February and then, retracted two months later by the imprisoned Pope; the stalled battles of Lützen and Bautzen; the allies ranged along the Rhine by the end of 1813; the seventh coalition; and the liberation of the pope in January 1814, all spelled a decline from which there was no escape. No one dared to rejoice, but many looked upon this event as the dawn of liberation.

In fact, the allies entered Paris on 31 March:

> They declared that they would not negotiate with Napoleon and demanded that the Senate set up a temporary government. The Municipal Council and the official bodies acted immediately to reinstate the Bourbons. On 2 April, the Senate decided that the Emperor had forfeited all right to authority. This was proclaimed on 3 April, with the agreement of the legislative body . . . . Then on 6 April they recalled Louis XVIII to the throne. During this time at Fontainbleau the marshals refused to go along with their commander and pressed him to abdicate in favor of his son. Napoleon gave way on 4 April . . . . His fate was settled on 11 April by the Treaty of Fontainbleau; for himself he obtained the island of Elba with an annual allowance; for Marie-Louise and her son Parma, and for his relations some pensions. On the 20 April he bade goodbye to the troops whom he had treated with so little consideration, but who had remained faithful to him until the end.[1]

As soon as the news became known, exiles and those dispersed abroad, cistercian–trappist monks and nuns in particular, began setting about finding their monasteries, if they still existed, or some other place in France where they could again lead the common life according to their *saint état*. Some of them had no sympathy for the man they called in their letters 'the tyrant'. Soon the news reached America, where Dom Augustin de Lestrange was still to be found. Leaving these first attempts to make a foundation, which were not going well, the monks divided into two groups and sailed for France.

On the european side of the Atlantic, projects were sketched out in the general euphoria and Dom Eugene de Laprade was not slow to make his way to Paris to sound out the intentions, presumably favorable, of the new government.

[1] G. Lefebvre, *Napoléon,* pp. 565–566.

However, 'incapable of being resigned to his fate, and fearing that they could make it worse, he [Napoleon] tried his luck for the last time',[2] in the words of the historian Georges Lefebvre. 'It had been foreseen that the solitary reigning on a tiny island would have time to dream of new strategies on a grander scale. He had no lack of these!'.

On 26 February 1815 Napoleon embarked for France, reaching the Gulf of Genoa on 1 March. From there he moved quickly to Grenoble and then to Lyon, where he received a triumphal welcome and rallied La Bedoyere and Ney to his cause. On 20 March he entered the Tuileries, from which Louis XVIII had taken flight the previous night. Public opinion is fickle. On 6 June Napoleon, having hastily re-assembled some troops, sent them to battle against the allies. Some quick local victories were swallowed up in the defeat at Waterloo by English troops under the Duke of Wellington. Defeated Napoleon returned to Paris on 21 June, and finally left La Malmaison on the 29th. The surrender of Paris was signed 3 July. On 8 July, Louis XVIII returned and gave orders that his rival should be handed over to the English. But by 3 July Napoleon had taken the road to Rochfort. Six days later he was negotiating with the English for his transfer to America or England. Confident of their good faith, and relying also on his own, he embarked on 15 July on the English ship the Bellerophon. It anchored in Plymouth Sound, but Bonaparte was forbidden to put foot on English soil. The order was given to take the prisoner to Saint Helena. On 4 August Napoleon wrote:

> I appeal to history: it will say that an enemy who for twenty years was at war with the people of England went freely, in his misfortune, to seek asylum under her laws—and what more striking proof could he give of his esteem and trust? But how does England respond to such magnanimity? She pretends to offer this enemy the hand of

[2] *Ibid.*, p. 567.

> hospitality, and when he gives himself up in good faith, she sacrifices him.[3]

Recalling these events allows a better understanding of the difficulties and uncertainties experienced during the years 1814–1816 by trappist monks and nuns anxious about returning to their mother country.

[3] Quoted in and assembled by J. Burnat, G.-H. Dumont, E. Wanty, *Le dossier Napoléon* (Paris, 1962).

CHAPTER ONE

FROM COLOGNE TO ALSACE AND FROM BELGIUM TO FRANCE

FROM DARFELD TO ALTBRONN

Return to Darfeld

When Dom Eugene de Laprade heard of the arrival of the Bourbons, he hurried to return, at least provisionally, to Darfeld where, it will be recalled a group of seven nuns had been authorized to remain. From 26 May 1814, their sisters, sheltering at Cologne under the direction of the prioress of the house, Mother Hélène Van den Broeck, were able to go back to their monastery of Notre-Dame-de-la-Miséricorde, resuming their habit and religious life in its entirety. Under the directives of Dom Eugene, however, they adopted the Regulations of de Rancé.

At the time of their dispersal the community had forty members. Seven stayed at Darfeld, ten left for Belgium and four died at Cologne. There were twenty-four left, then; two are missing from the list: Mother Agnès Thuilliez, who was the superior of the small group which had stayed behind, and Sister Thérèse Müller, her companion.

In the Register preserved at Altbronn, which is a summary, we read that Mother Agnès left for Borsut (near Liège), where she would have rejoined the French or Belgian sisters who had arrived in Belgium in 1811. The other sister can be found on the list, where her death is noted at Darfeld on 11 November 1821. This sister, born on 6 May 1770, came from Olmütz in Germany and entered at Dürnast on 14

August 1798. She took the habit as a lay sister the following 20 August. In 1800, on 28 July, she took the habit of the Third Order, then on 20 August 1802 made her profession at Darfeld as a choir nun. She was fifty-one when she died and had lived the monastic life for twenty-three years.

Difficulties With the Ordinary of Münster

A rather curious letter written by Dom Eugene de Laprade from Paris on 16 August 1814 arrived at Münster on the twenty-second. It explains perhaps why Sister Agnès Thuilliez left Darfeld for Borsut. To 'Monsieur le Baron de Drost zu Wichering', the abbot wrote:

> My brothers have brought to my notice a letter that M. Greves, your business manager, has communicated to us as coming from you, by which we must move out of Darfeld, monks and nuns alike, leave there only five or six infirm who remained here last year and Sister Agnès to whom you have entrusted the house with all its outbuildings, the administration of its goods, and also the disposition of the harvest.
>
> All this was excellent during the time of persecution by the Tyrant and under a government which used trickery and deceit. But now that, thanks be to God, we are delivered from this state of oppression and terror, the truth can be brought into the open.
>
> You have too much piety, religion, and instruction for it to be necessary for me to tell you that our beloved Sister Agnes and any other religious who have made a vow of obedience between our hands and a vow of poverty at the foot of the altar do not have at their disposition anything in the world, not even the disposition of their own persons. They cannot accept any employment or administration, or own anything personally, without the consent of their superior and of us, or still less anything which would prejudice the authority of their superior or our own authority, without contravening those sacred

> engagements which not even the power of Bonaparte was able to undo.
>
> I know that M. the Vicar General thinks that in his quality as superior he is free to make all the changes he judges fit . . . .

There follows a long 'canonical' dissertation on the powers of the said superior and of those which belonged to the local superior. It concludes with this peremptory reason: 'Darfeld is well and truly the dwelling of monks, this is my title as Abbot! Your declaration on this subject has been sent to Rome and deposited in the archives of the Holy See'.[1]

We see here another side of the 'gentle Dom Eugene', one we hardly recognize! But this long quotation has as its chief object a suggestion that the disappearance of Sister Agnès from the community reunited at Darfeld must have its cause in details made known about her in this letter. She had directed the small group of infirm religious over the course of three years. She came from Gosbeque (France), says the Register, and was born on 16 February 1767. Already a Cistercian before the Revolution, she entered at Darfeld on 13 September 1808, and had made her stability there in April 1809. Two years later the community was dispersed. No doubt she had shown a natural capacity for the administration of the small community which had stayed behind. This could have created difficulties between her and Mother Hélène during the three months when the communities were again reunited. Likely this was the reason Sister Agnès left Darfeld. Did she really go to Borsut? It is as difficult to be sure as to deny it, because at this point we lose all trace of her, and Borsut has no extant archives, like so many other communities during these years of insecurity.

In the same letter, Dom de Laprade alludes to a foundation that never matured for nuns at Zawendberg in the

[1] Archives of the Drost Wischering family, Darfeld/Westphalia, file: Rentee Darfeld, Hasselkampsbusch/Trappisten (shared with me by M. W. Knoll de Rosendalh).

suburbs of Aix-la-Chapelle. Speaking of Darfeld and the monastery of monks he adds:

> The nuns are only there provisionally, not to stay permanently. Actually, they will leave Darfeld as soon as the monastery, which is being built for them at Aix-la-Chapelle, is ready for occupation, and I trust that until this is ready you will be pleased to allow that we give them hospitality.[2]

This permission was certainly granted as all the nuns were still there in August 1825, in spite of the small foundation at Aix-la-Chapelle.

Departure From Darfeld

The Congress at Vienna in 1815 accorded Westphalia to Prussia, and a troublesome police force contrived to make life impossible for both the monks and the nuns. They were forbidden to receive novices. The superior of the German monks who had stayed at Darfeld until 1825, Dom Pierre Klausener, looked for a refuge in France. With the help and through the kindness of the bishop of Strasbourg, he found a former monastery of Canons Regular of Saint Augustine not far from Mulhouse in Alsace. The place was called Oelenberg or Mont des Olives. The monks arrived there on 29 September 1825. The nuns were supposed to follow them, but their superior, Mother Hélène, wanted to go first and see the small group in the foundation of Aix-la-Chapelle.

Before leaving, Mother Hélène wrote to the Baron de Drost on 4 June 1825. She took into account the regrets expressed by the Baron at seeing the religious move away from Darfeld, but there were also allusions to difficulties arising between the community and the 'very honorable Founder'.

[2] *Ibid*. This foundation was called Notre-Dame-du-Mont-Sion, and was located at Zawendberg, a suburb of Aix-la-Chapelle (Aachen).

While expressing her gratitude for the benevolences of His Excellency, and recalling the weekly offering of a Mass for the intentions of His Excellency and his family, the Mother Prioress spoke of an earlier letter concerning the dissolution of the contract between the Baron and the community. It involved some land put at the disposition of the monks twenty five years beforehand, and on which had been built the monastery of beaten earth and clay. The Mother Prioress was of the opinion that the 'buildings constructed by alms and our own work, in the eyes of God, should be shared'. She said also:

> I find that I must make the journey to Aix-la Chapelle to visit our sisters who live there in a small convent. I have to leave on Monday and this does not give me time to conclude with Monsieur, your bailiff, the arrangements that Your Excellency has communicated to him; otherwise I would not have been so bold as to raise with him the objections I took the liberty of addressing recently to you. They are a matter of conscience. Without doubt according to the laws of men our pretensions are unjust, but in the Tribunal of God everything is judged differently; there the intentions of our acts are considered, and those of our benefactors in this circumstance have been in our favor. This is how our late Reverend Father Abbot interpreted it and how it is still interpreted by all those who have the advantage of knowing the religion of Your Excellency. After this last observation, Monsieur le Baron, we ourselves are totally abandoned to your wishes.[3]

Some weeks later, on 2 August 1825, the cellarer, Sister M. Stanislaus, wrote in the name of the Prioress who was absent. She asked the Baron what to do about 'some grain, fruit and garden produce, the cultivation of which Your Excellency has deigned to confer on us until this present time, not being able to use this produce without being informed

[3] Archives Drost Wischering, f° 153.

of the dispositions that M. le Baron wishes to make. I make so bold as to ask you to have the goodness to inform us of your pious intentions on this subject; we await your orders so that we may carry out your wishes'.[4]

The reply soon arrived, on 5 August:

> Madame, It is with great pleasure, Madame, that I pray you to use in the way you find most fitting, the grains and fruit that you harvest on my land this very year.[5]

This reply, written by the Baron's secretary was recopied by himself, and another hand has noted in the margin:

> I feel deeply the irreplaceable loss of your departure, and humbly recommend myself and all my family to your very devout prayers.[6]

By then Mother Hélène had left for Aix-la-Chapelle. The journey had a somewhat dramatic outcome, as we hear from the historian of La Trappe, Gaillardin:

> A woman travelling accompanied only by one other woman made the Prussian Government uneasy. A commissary was sent in haste to overtake her and discover by a formal declaration exactly what her intentions were. What had she come to do? When would she return? As she fell ill, she was not able to leave at the appointed time, so a doctor was immediately dispatched to find out the real state of her health. But she believed it unfitting for her to receive him. This refusal appeared to be defiance worthy of immediate banishment. She was ordered to leave with her companion within twenty-four hours, under penalty of being put into the hands of the armed forces. To this they added at the same time, that the religious she had come to see must also leave. A delay of six days was all

[4] *Ibid.*, f°156.
[5] *Ibid.*, f°157.
[6] *Ibid.*

they were allowed. They were obliged to leave Germany in the month of January 1826, during a very severe spell of cold weather. The superior, who was ill, suffered intensely and her death which occurred in May that year, was the consequence of such a hasty journey.[7]

The Nuns at Oelenberg Transfer to Altbronn

Harassments and frequent investigations by the Prussian administration notwithstanding, the community of nuns at Darfeld, Notre-Dame-de-la-Miséricorde, had continued to receive new recruits. In 1824 they had eight who received the habit and one profession, with the result that when they arrived at Oelenberg in 1826 the community counted twelve professed, five novices, and two postulants for the choir, and fourteen professed lay sisters and five novices. In all, thirty-eight members.

Even before the death of the prioress by May, there were several new professions in the early months of 1826. Postulants were very numerous, as they were everywhere else in the communities who had returned to France in 1816.

When they arrived at Oelenberg, the monks put at the nuns' disposal a section of their huge monastery, but totally separated from the monks' quarters. The enclosure was very clearly marked and very strictly observed. To distinguish the two communities, the name Mont des Olives was assigned to the monks, and Oelenberg reserved for the nuns, who wished to keep their original patronage under Notre-Dame-de-la-Miséricorde.

After 1814 both the monks and the nuns had returned to the Regulations of de Rancé. In 1833, they both petitioned the Holy See to be raised to an abbey: this was granted both communities.

[7] Gaillardin, 2:418–419.

The two communities stayed together until 1895. In that year the nuns were transferred to Notre-Dame d'Altbronn, on the outskirts of the village of Ergersheim in the southern part of Alsace, which later became the Bas-Rhin in the diocese of Strasbourg. These two abbeys still continue today.

FROM BORSUT TO LAVAL

Difficulties and Hesitations

After three years of separation the Trappistines sheltering in Borsut near Liège seem to have had no thought of rejoining the community from Cologne at Darfeld to which they seem to have had returned at the end of May in 1814.

An undated letter of a Flemish Father Maur Mori, a professed monk of Westmalle who later went to the west of France, explains to his correspondent the perplexities of Dom Eugene over the nuns remaining in Belgium, and the plans of the monks at Westmalle for the sisters in England. The unpolished style of the document does not prevent it from casting a small ray of light, the only one we have on this period and this place.

> It has been said that the transactions of Father Eugene were not going very well. He is at the moment near Darveld [*sic*] in a small *château* with some brothers, but they were waiting for him at Darveld to come from Louvain. During these days he returned to France, looking for somewhere to make a foundation. Some of our sisters were at Darveld and some were near Liège, on a hill badly situated and very poor. They had no wish to stay there, the place being very inconvenient. There are still two who live in Flanders in a village [*would this be Sister Agnès Thuilliez and Sister Thérèse Müller?*].
>
> We would like to know if the plans for our sisters at Stapehill has had any success here, that is, of joining them to those whom the Reverend Mother has brought

> here, and I do think that this would have worked out well, at least for some of them. It has been said that Brother Bernard, the lay brother from Brussels and Father Eugene's alms collector and recruiter in our country and in France, has obtained from a lady in France a property for these poor Trappistines.[8] [*written in poor French that is impossible to convey in translation.* —trans.]

Here the fragmentary letter ends. Another document, this time in Latin, a letter from the Vicar Apostolic of Malines, named Forgeur, to a Father Alexis, superior of Westmalle, is quite clear on the nature of the difficulties Dom Eugene encountered in making a foundation of nuns in Belgium. It must be remembered that by the Treaty of 1815, Belgium was incorporated into Holland; the two countries were then called the Low Countries, both under one government. Catholic Belgium was ruled by a Protestant Prince, William I, heir of the 'enlightened despots and of the Josephist tradition'.[9] The letter of the Vicar Apostolic is not dated, but is postmarked 15 October 1815. The content of the message drafted in Latin reads:

> I cannot approve of a foundation of nuns in Belgium. *I fear* that this foundation will only cause you many problems, because not only do *I fear* that the Government will forbid it, but I *also* fear that this foundation will be the cause of you yourselves being expelled, because the government is not at all well disposed towards monks. Several times already the Conqueror has written that you have returned to your monastery and resumed the religious habit.[10]

In these few lines the *timeo*, 'I fear', is repeated three times, a sign of the panic which had gripped the Church in

[8] Arch. Tr., ref. 215–216.

[9] See A. Latreille, *L'Église catholique et la Révolution française* (Paris, 1970) 2:273f.

[10] Arch. Tr., ref. 218–1, piece 11.

Belgium. Actually, William I had "already closed the door of the state to the apostolic administrator, Ciamberlani, who had been sent to Malines to sort out an inextricable situation" [*sedevacante*].[11]

DOM EUGENE IN FRANCE

As early as 20 August 1814, Dom Eugene de Laprade had obtained the permission to re-establish his monks in France in an audience granted him by Louis XVIII. He was looking for a place where they could be reunited and had begun negotiations to buy La Trappe, but on rather burdensome terms. His faithful friends proposed to help him by starting a fund. Then on 19 November 1814, Dom Augustin landed at Havre and by 1 December was in Paris. Dom Eugene, upon learning that Dom Augustin was looking for somewhere to settle, anticipated his hopes by proposing to let him have the buildings of La Trappe which he was in the process of purchasing. He put at his disposal not only the place but even the funds that had already been collected. Dom Augustin quite simply accepted everything.

This generous gesture gained for Dom Eugene a providential response. M. Leclerc de La Roussière, a noble émigré who had previously received asylum at Darfeld, during the Empire had bought the former convent of Génovéfains, called Port-Rheingeard, situated near Entrammes in the Mayenne, 10 km from Laval. He offered this place to Dom Eugene at no cost.

Monks under the direction of Father Bernard de Girmont, appointed by Dom Eugene, put the buildings in good order and solemnly installed themselves there on 21 February 1815. The monastery took the name Port-du-Salut.

At the beginning of 1816, Mlle Letourneur-Laborde, a friend of the La Roussière family, made proposals for the

[11] Latreille, p. 374.

foundation of a monastery of cistercian nuns in the old priory of Génovéfains on the edge of the town of Laval. Dom Eugene, who was consulted, approved of the project, which had already been authorized by Mgr de Pidoll, bishop of Mans. Laval had not yet been erected into a diocese. Dom Eugene appointed Mother Elisabeth Piette, a professed of Darfeld, as superior of a small group composed of Sister Séraphine Gavot, a professed choir nun who had entered at Darfeld, Sister Marie-Joseph Casters and Sister Marie-Claire Foucard, both professed lay sisters, and six postulants who had entered at Borsut, five for the choir and one as a lay sister.

The ten religious left in three separate groups on 16 April 1816, Easter Tuesday. They re-assembed at Lille. The sister who wrote down this history much later has noted one practical detail: 'They carried with them all their worldly wealth in the form of *louis d'or* sewn into a belt, which Sister Gertrude had to guard and which she wore day and night'.[12]

At Lille the three groups met M. Jean-Baptiste Schollier, their workman at Borsut, who had been sent in advance by Dom Eugene with a huge covered wagon fitted out with benches and filled with luggage. In this vehicle they continued their journey. All along the road they sang the Divine Office, did their spiritual reading and gave themselves to prayer, taking their meals on their laps. In the evenings the wagon became a dormitory, stopping in the corner of a field when their devoted driver could not find a handy convent to shelter them.

When one of the sisters fell ill, they received hospitality with the Dames du Sacré-Coeur (in Amiens?). At Rouen they stayed with the Sisters of Providence. When they arrived at Alençon for Pentecost, they spent the feast and several days with the religious of the Visitation. Finally,

[12] 'La Fondation du monastère de Laval', an unnumbered typescript which I received through the kindness of the sister in charge of the archives. What follows is taken from the same document.

on Thursday 6 June they arrived at Laval about ten in the morning.

Their benefactress, Mlle Letourneur-Laborde welcomed them at the house of the daughter of M. de La Roussière, a Madame Dubois-Beauregard. As the monastery of Sainte-Catherine which had been set aside for them was not yet ready, they were driven the same day to the country house of M. de La Roussière at Louvigné (Mayenne).

The abbot of Darfeld, Dom Eugene de Laprade, had only a few days to live when the sisters reached Laval. He died on 16 June 1816 at Verlaine (Belgium) in one of the refuges of the monks who had been dispersed in 1811. His last years had been particularly burdened with worries and exhaustion caused by countless business matters. But by means of these he had prepared for the future. He had sent two groups into France, one of monks and one of nuns, and they were destined to give back to the country a well-tested form of monastic life.

THE PRIORY OF SAINTE-CATHERINE

The nuns who had come from Borsut took possession of the former priory of the canons of Sainte-Geneviève on 18 November 1816. They stayed nearly six months in the country house of M. de La Roussière, called La Doyère near Louvigné. On 20 November their enclosure was finally established. The next day, the six postulants who had come from Belgium with the four professed received the religious habit. Some of them had waited a very long time, during years of exile in Belgium. Two other aspirants who had come from Mayenne and Maine-et-Loire also received the habit the same day; perhaps they had rejoined the first group at La Doyère. So it was that the community began to lead the regular monastic life with twelve members. Very soon new postulants would come to join them.

A petition was sent to the Holy See by Mlle Letourneur-Laborde with a view to having the monastery canonically approved. An inquiry into the matter was made to the bishop of Mans by Rome, for information on the living conditions in this new community. The information from the bishop is dated 4 August 1817. A reply from Cardinal Consalvi on 31 July 1818 communicates the approval of the foundation by Pope Pius VII. It was officially registered on 6 December 1818, by the abbot of S. Bernardo alle Terme in Rome, who was at the time appointed by Rome as President General of the Order of Cîteaux. Since 1792, in point of fact, there had been no abbot of Cîteaux to whom anyone could refer, nor had there been any general directives from the abbots of the Order in General Chapter. For the time being, the Roman Curia had to make do in the absence of a supreme authority in the Order.

The trappist branch of the Cistercian Order had to undergo several more setbacks in its structures before being stabilized with a Common General Chapter of the two Observances which had been separated in 1808.

The Members of the Community

From the beginning as we have seen, the community was made up of two professed choir sisters, two professed lay sisters, and six postulants. We know about each of them from the first two Registers, now preserved at the monastery of Laval.

The Superior was Mother Elisabeth Piette. Born in Liège on 28 May 1785 of Servais-Joseph Piette, barrister, and of Marie-Joseph Agathe de Thiermay, she received at baptism the names Amélie-Gertrude. She entered Notre-Dame-de-la-Miséricorde at Darfeld on 2 July 1806, received the habit on 7 July, and made her profession on 18 January 1808.

Sister Séraphine Gavot, baptised Marie-Madeleine, was born on 16 October 1783 at Mirecourt in Lorraine of Nicolas

Gavot, lace merchant, and of Marie-Magdeleine Colin. She entered Notre-Dame-de-la-Miséricorde on 11 April 1806, received the habit on the 16 April, and made her profession on 20 April 1809.

The third, Sister Marie-Joseph Casters, born at Racourt in the diocese of Malines on 17 December 1760, of Jean-Pierre Casters, farmer, and of Catherine Gérard. She entered at Darfeld on 7 May 1809, received the habit of a lay sister on 16 May, and made her profession on 4 September the same year.

The fourth, Sister Marie-Claire (Rose Foucard), born on 15 February 1770 at Mainvault, in the diocese of Cambrai, of Pierre Foucard, linen manufacturer, and of Marie-Joseph Breteur, entered on 3 September 1808, received the habit of a lay sister on 8 September, and made her profession on 4 November 1809.

Of the six postulants who came from Belgium, we do not know when each had rejoined the group at Borsut. Here are their names:

— Sister Marie-Gertrude Piette, born at Liège on 14 May 1792, was the sister of the group's superior.
— Sister Scholastique Delatte, born at Neuville in the diocese of Boulogne on 18 June 1861 of Jean-Baptiste Delattre, brewer, and of Françoise Salambrin, was a former Benedictine.
— Sister Marie-Thérèse Billon had been born at Liège on 16 October 1784 to Lambert Billon, jurist and lawyer, and Anne-Elisabeth Dadseux.
— Sister Louis de Gonzague Dubuisson, born at Wodecq, Belgium, on 29 August 1791 to Benoît-Joseph Dubuisson, farmer, and of Marie-Joseph Dubois.
— Sister Hélène Masson born on 30 April 1790 at Wodecq to Françoise-Philippe Masson and M.-Thérèse Delbouvry.
— Sister Augustin Burette (baptised as Séraphine Angélique) was born at Neuville in the diocese of Boulogne, to Françoise Burette, clog maker, and Séraphine Leblond.

These six novices of 21 November 1816 made their profession all together on 17 December 1818.

Two other postulants joined the community before it was transferred to Saint-Catherine. The date of their entry was not been noted, but they received the habit on 21 November 1816. They were:

— Sister Marie-Bernard Paumard, born at Thouarcé in the diocese of Angers on 15 August 1761 to Mathieu Paumard, iron merchant, and Geneviève Bernier. She was a Bernardine religious and made her stability on the day when the seven others made their profession.
— Sister Thérèse Trouillard, born at Mayenne in the diocese of Mans on 28 December 1789 to Joseph Trouillard, weaver, and Renée-Marie Guillon. She was the first of the Foundresses of Sainte-Catherine to die, on 21 June 1822.

The Regular Life at Sainte-Catherine

In a letter written by Mother Elisabeth Piette to Mother Augustin de Chabannes in England at the end of 1824 or the beginning of 1825, we read:

> We have been here eight years, and we have had twelve deaths among the professed choir nuns, lay sisters, novices and postulants. We have in our house at this moment sixty-four sisters; it seems to me that this is not many deaths among such a great number . . . .[13]

Actually the mortality rate was much higher in the monasteries which had kept the Regulations of La Valsainte. This was the case in England, where the rising death rate caused Mgr Collingridge, the ordinary of Stapehill, to remove Holy Cross Abbey from the jurisdiction of Dom Augustin.

[13] Stapehill Archives.

During the same period (1816–1824) the community at Forges-Les Gardes had to register eighty deaths in eight years, that is, about ten deaths every year. In this community they followed the Regulations of La Valsainte. The mortality rate was nearly seven times greater than among those who followed the Regulations of de Rancé with some mitigations required by the Holy See of the bishop of Mans, as we shall see in what follows.

The same letter I quoted above explains:

> It is with great pleasure that we send you the information you requested. I should add that the Sovereign Pontiff in the Brief of Approbation, having granted the mitigations we asked for, did not think them sufficient. He gives us permission to ask from our bishop, with the consent of our abbot, all the mitigations we consider necessary. Since this clause opens the door to every kind of relaxation, we wish our observances to be fixed invariably, and it is our intention to ask Rome for a Bull giving positive approval for us to follow our actual observances. Yet already Mgr our Bishop as well as our Father Immediate judge it necessary that we ask again for mitigations which they consider indispensable. You will find them enclosed with this letter.[14]

I think this document important enough to be included here in the original, and the photocopy is clear enough to be easily read.

The copy Mother Elisabeth Piette made for Mother Augustin is accompanied by a small commentary on each item made by the superior of Laval. Everything is arranged in two parallel columns.

I will give Mother Elisabeth's text which can be read and compared with the original. This allows us to see how at this period the least detail of the Observances had a special importance and had to be minutely examined. It is quite

[14] *Ibid.*

strange to see a bishop legislating on the details of a life of which he had no personal experience. Probably he had been advised by the abbot of Port-du-Salut who also signed the document. The Abbot had been informed by the Mother Superior of the 'mitigations' desired.

Mother Elisabeth, in her brief commentaries, clarifies or rectifies the different points by referring to the Regulations of the Abbot de Rancé:

> 1° The Regulations of Mr. de Rancé do not at all permit the sick to say their Matins the day before, other than for special reasons, nor should they say it then except by permission of the Reverend Mother. Apart from this, the sick must rise at 3 am and say their Matins at the same time it is said in choir.
>
> 2° The Regulations do not permit the use of sugar, except in remedies which cannot be made without it, nor do they permit wine, except for slight weaknesses to recover one's strength.
>
> 3° Nothing.
>
> 4° According to the Regulations, one must eat at midday on the fast days of the Church.
>
> 5° The Regulations do not at all allow eggs at midday to those who are having an indulgence, but they are given soup and a vegetable seasoned with butter, nothing else; but in the evening they are given four eggs, even on fast days of the Order and of the Rule, but nothing else.
>
> 6° According to the Regulations, see N°15.
>
> 7° The Regulations only allow two ounces of bread on the fast days of the Church, and three ounces on fast days of the Order.
>
> 8° The Regulations allow six ounces to the lay brothers at all times and on this point it has been judged right to deduct one ounce for our lay sisters on fast days of the Church, by reason of the fact that men, being more robust than the women and working harder, should have more to eat.
>
> 9° The Regulations do not allow a walk in the garden, except for the infirm.

10° The Regulations make this distinction for Pascaltide, along with time between Trinity [Sunday] and the Exaltation of the Cross: that cooked portions are not permitted in the evening outside Pascaltide, but if some sorrel cooked in milk is taken, then no cheese is served.

11° According to the Regulations, our lay sisters are to say Prime after the Mass *de Beata* [early morning Mass] and then immediately go to their work. On days of two meals, as on fast days, they are not to have their supper or collation until half an hour after the community [does].

12° According to the Regulations there should be stitched straw mattresses, except in the infirmary.

13° The Regulations say nothing.

14° The Regulations say nothing.

15° According to the Regulations, bread for the sick is made of wheat, and the sixth part of a bushel of rye is added. That of the community is made of half wheat and half rye from which the rough bran has been removed.

16° According to the Regulations the siesta is taken at midday on ordinary [ferial] days; on Sundays and feast-days, after Matins; and on fast days before dinner.

17° According to the Regulations, no milk is taken in Advent and Lent.

PS As to the numbers 16 and 17, we have obtained the superior's permission not to observe them but to follow the Regulations.[15]

The Management of the Community

The official style of this document may surprise us. Its various topics are not classified according to content and are of unequal importance. In reality it is a concrete and practical adaptation of the Regulations of de Rancé for the daily life and physical constitution of nuns. It results from lived experience and we can easily believe that Mother Elisabeth

[15] *Ibid.*

Piette was the instigator in establishing what became their rule of life.

To convince all concerned, she thus clarified all the points of observance which could cause problems in the community. She had at the time the official approbation of those in authority—her Bishop, under whom she and the abbot of Port-du-Salut, had had the wisdom to place themselves from the beginning. Actually, the Order in France had lost its exemption from the bishops' authority with the closing down of Cîteaux and the General Chapters; in any case, this exemption was strongly contested after the Concordat.

Furthermore, these two communities' relationship with Rome were excellent. Port-du-Salut had been erected into an abbey on 10 December 1816, and less than ten years later Sainte-Catherine also became an abbey by an apostolic bull of 14 April 1826. On 27 April of the following year, Mother Elisabeth Piette was elected abbess for life and governed her community for a quarter of a century. She died on 6 September 1852, after having helped the foundation of Mondaye in 1837 and in 1844 founding the monastery of Notre-Dame-de-Saint-Joseph d'Ubexy.

In April 1859, the community transferred to Avesnières, at the gates of the town of Laval, to the new monastery of La Coudre and was placed under the patronage of the Immaculate Conception.

Michel Joseph de Pidoll
par la grace de Dieu et du St. Siège Apostolique
Evêque du Mans, &c. &c.

Sa Sainteté, par son Rescript en date du 31. Juillet 1818, ayant érigé en Monastère de l'ordre de Citeaux réformé de la Trappe, la Maison de Ste. Catherine de Laval; S. S. ayant placé le dit Monastère sous la Direction de l'Abbé du Port du Salut, et ayant confié à notre sollicitude paternelle le soin de faire aux Réglements de l'illustre réformateur de La Trappe, l'Abbé de Rancé, les modifications que comportent les circonstances, et la complexion délicate d'un Sexe dont les forces n'égalèrent jamais le Courage;

De l'Avis et à la Demande du R. P. Abbé de l'Abbaye du Port du Salut, Père immédiat du dit Monastère de Ste. Catherine ordre de Citeaux,

Nous avons arrêté, & nous arrêtons:

1°. Les Malades diront Complies après Vêpres, & Matines après la Collation ou le Souper.

2°. L'usage du Sucre et du Vin sera permis aux Infirmes.

3°. On ne mettra les Agonisantes sur la Cendre que lorsqu'elles le Désireront.

4°. La Communauté dînera une demie heure plutôt que ne le prescrivent les Réglements, aux Jours de Jeûne d'ordre et d'Église.

Figures 6a, 6b, 6c

Letter of the Bishop of Mans.

5°. On donnera des œufs aux Infirmes au réfectoire, même pendant le Carême, excepté les jours où ils sont défendus par l'Eglise.

6. On donnera du pain blanc aux Infirmes.

7. On donnera à la Communauté, aux jours de Jeûne d'Eglise, quatre onces de pain à la Collation, et cinq onces, aux Jeûnes d'ordre.

8. Les Sœurs Converses auront cinq onces de pain à la Collation aux Jeûnes d'Eglise; et six onces, aux jeûnes d'ordre.

9. Les Religieuses pourront se promener en silence dans les Jardins, pendant une demie heure, après les repas.

10. Le Souper consistera en deux portions depuis Pâques jusqu'à l'Exaltation de la Ste Croix; l'une sera une Salade, ou quelques herbes au lait que l'on pourra faire cuire: l'autre Portion consistera en fruits ou fromage.

11. Les Sœurs Converses auront un 1/4 d'heure d'oraison après la Messe de Beatâ, et souperont, & collationneront en même tems que la Communauté.

12. Les Sœurs coucheront sur une Paillasse ordinaire dans un Dortoir commun, mais on pourra donner aux Infirmes des Paillasses de paille hachée.

13. On fera tous les Ans une retraite de dix Jours.

14. On exposera le Très Saint Sacrement à la Grand-Messe, et au Salut, les fêtes de Sermon, les Dimanches, et les fêtes de garde; On donnera la Bénédiction avec le St. Ciboire au Salut seulement.

15°. Le Pain de la Communauté pourra être de pur froment, dont on ôtera le gros Son.

16°. En Été, on ne prendra point de Méridienne après Midi. Cette heure de repos sera ajoutée à celle de la nuit.

17. Les Portions au Carême et en Avent seront apprêtées avec du Lait, mais seulement les Dimanches.

Donné en notre Palais Episcopal ce Vingt-sept Janvier 1819.

+ Mich. Jos. Ev. du Mans.

Par Mandement de Monseigneur

Dubois

Sous-diacre Secrétaire

f. Bernard Abbé quoiqu'indigne

Par Mandement de notre Révérend Père Abbé

f. Joseph P.tre Secr.

CHAPTER TWO

FROM BRITTANY TO NORMANDY

THE COMMUNITY OF VALENTON had taken refuge at Tréguier, where they had resumed conventual life under the abbacy of Mother Marie des Séraphins de Chateaubriand. Having lived among the Bretons in relative tranqullity, after the first abdication of Napoleon, the superior was in no hurry to leave their refuge. She did not start moving until the spring of 1815, about the same time the fallen emperor set out on the way to France.

THE RETURN JOURNEY

The community was so poor, says the chronicle, that they made the journey on foot. A donkey carried their meagre baggage. This is the only detail that has come down to us. It can be supposed that during the three years of exile there had been some deaths in the community. During this time and shortly afterwards, the Register has many gaps which make it difficult to give even a brief account of this period.

The Mother Prioress, Mother Marie des Séraphins, it is said, had the intention of recovering the house of Valenton. But while they were on the way, the nuns were offered the opportunity of buying a former Abbey of Premonstratensians, Mondaye (*Mons Dei*) situated not far from Bayeux, near the village of Juaye. At the Revolution the abbey had become national property, and been sold to a M. de Foustier, who had in turn sold it to a Madame Widmes. It was she who proposed it to the Trappistines.[1] They took possession of the property on 8 May 1815.

The Premonstratensian Abbey in Normandy

The abbey, extremely well built and almost intact, and still standing today, is now once again inhabited by members of the religious family of the builders and first occupants. In their archives the Premonstratensians keep records of the nuns who occupied the abbey from 1815 to 1845.

A plan drawn up for a land survey in 1836—while the nuns were living there—gives a good idea of the setting.

The monastery chapel had become the parish church of Juaye. But it was easy, among the regular places left intact, to find a suitable place for the celebration of the Divine Office and Mass. The practical nature of Mother de Chateaubriand knew how to make do.

Marie-Anne-Renée de Chateaubriand was born at Saint-Malo on 15 June 1761, of Pierre de Chateaubriand and Marie-Thérèse Brignon de Lehen. In 1780 she entered the Benedictines of Notre-Dame-de-la-Victoire, situated opposite the Grand-Bé and from the ramparts, overlooking the small arm of the sea which separates the mainland from the little island where François-René de Chateaubriand, her first cousin, was later to be buried. From her youth Marie-Anne showed herself to be a capable woman, who knew how to cope with the difficulties which fell on her family at the time of the Revolution. With her sisters in religion, she had to leave the monastery in 1792. She was imprisoned, as were her relatives, because her brothers had emigrated with

[1] Cf. Archives of La Trappe, ref. 217, piece 40. This document is undated and does not give details of the sale price, or of who paid for it. The great poverty of the sisters was emphasized. Was it the sale of the house at Valenton which covered the cost? Or was it a third person? I have not been able to find any answer to these questions. The sisters themselves have left nothing in writing on this subject.

other noblemen determined to fight against the Revolution. The family possessions were put under sequestration. Determined to be respected, she stood up for her rights in legal proceedings and even sued the liquidators.

Heedful of her consecration to God, she took the road towards the convents springing up in Paris in 1798, and on 13 February 1805 she entered the community of Grosbois. She made her vows the following year on 7 April (1806). Named superior soon afterwards, she was removed from office by Dom Augustin in 1808. In 1810, he again appointed her superior. She took great care to hold the community together and was unsparing of herself in her sage and prudent undertakings toward this end.

The Members of the Community

The chronicle notes that only seven nuns came to Mondaye. The obituary drawn up at Mondaye in 1935 allows us, by comparing it with the Register which was concluded in 1827, to find the names of some of the survivors of the community of Valenton.[2]

Other than Mother Marie des Séraphins (Marie-Anne de Chateaubriand), the prioress, we recognize:

— Sister Joséphine Bessirard de La Touche. Born on 19 September 1767 at Nogent-le-Rotrou, in the diocese of Chartre, she had been a Benedictine in the monastery of Nazareth in Nogent, and had joined the community at Grosbois-Camoldolese in April 1806. She received the

[2] This necrology, drawn up by a Premonstratensian in 1935, is a kind of early photocopy, *avant la lettre*. Using tracing paper the patient archivist copied out all the acts of Registers: that of 1816 to 1825 in the Register of the Roman Catholic church; that of 1826 to 1845 in the Register of the Civil State of the commune of Juaye-Mondaye. During this double period of thirty years, there were seventy-six deaths in the community. (Archives of the Abbey of Mondaye, serie CM, packet 38).

habit the next month on 14 May and made her stability on 19 July 1806. She died one year after her arrival at Mondaye, on 24 May 1816; she was forty-nine years old.

— Sister Bernard Le Caux. Born on 9 December 1761 at Bonneville (Manche), she was also a former Benedictine. She entered at Valenton in October 1809 and made her profession on 2 February 1811. She lived the monastic life for a longer period and died when she was sixty-six years old, on 19 March 1825.

— Sister Lutgarde Langécourt. Born at Valognes on 1 February 1787, she was twenty-two when she joined the community of Valenton on 14 October 1809; she made her vows on 22 December 1810. She persevered in the monastic life until her death on 19 February 1831; she was then forty-four years old.

— Sister Placide Brunehaut. Born on 20 August 1769 at Ruillé in the Mayenne, she entered at Valenton in May 1810 and made her vows on 21 June 1811, just before the nuns were dispersed. She followed the community to its various asylums and died after fourteen years of trappist life on 13 October 1824 when she was fifty-five years old.

— Sister Saint-Joseph Le Clerc, the oldest of the group. Baptised at Saint-Adalbert-de-Liège, she entered at Paris on 29 August 1801. She was then twenty years old, having been born in April 1781. She received the habit on 15 September 1801 and made her vows on 12 April 1803. She renewed them on 11 April 1805. She was sent to England by Dom Augustin in June 1820. She died at Stapehill on 8 January 1861. She was then eighty-years old, of which sixty of these she had lived in La Trappe: a record for this period.

— Sister Benoît Richeux. Born at Beaumont-le-Roger, in the diocese of Evreux, on 10 January 1760, she was a former Cistercian of the abbey of Bival, near Neuchâtel-en-Bray. She entered Grosbois-Camaldolese on 14 June 1806, and made her stability there on 19 June 1807. Sent by the

Father Abbot to 'another house of the Order' not named in the Register, she died on 26 May 1819, when she was fifty-nine years old.

Very soon postulants began to arrive. The first, Sister Perrine Rossignol, the daughter of Pierre Rossignol and Marie Vautier, was already known to the community. She had entered Valenton in 1811, and received the habit on 21 June, but on 1 August, because of the expulsion, she had had to leave. She managed to rejoin the community at Tréguier on 31 March 1815 'in the emigration' says the Register. She recommenced the novitiate so abruptly cut short and on 22 June 1816, she was admitted to make her profession 'on straw and ashes' on her death bed. She died three days later. Sister Perrine was the second of the seventy-four Trappistines to be buried in the cemetery of the norman abbey.

In 1816 four women entered; in the following year; nine and in the next, four. Recruitment proceeded regularly until 1827, when the last entry was made in the Register. All the sisters who entered during this period made their professions, but they often died very soon afterwards, especially the younger ones. We may wonder whether the Register, which was kept by a different secretary than the one who kept the first part, only recorded sisters after they had made their profession.

The Table on page 384 summarizes the information entered in the Register. The first two lines are identical, because they correspond to the same persons who entered and were professed at various dates. Some doubtful figures are noted by a question mark. The number of deaths is that of the current year.

Daily Life at Mondaye

The fervor was intense, as though redoubled by the exile outside the regular places. There was a constant concern

Years	*1815*	*1816*	*1817*	*1818*	*1819*	*1820*	*1821*	*1822*	*1823*	*1824*	*1825*	*1826*	*1827*	*Total*
Admissions	1	4	9	4	8	4	4	9	1 or 2	2	4	2 ?	3 ?	56
Professions	1	4	9	4	7 or 8	4	4	9	1 or 2	2	4	2 ?	3 ?	56
Deaths		2				2	4	6	7	2	4	1	4	30

for fidelity to the Will of God which invited the survivors to an obedience that was prompt and entire. So much so, says the chronicle, that the superior had to be on guard lest her words be taken literally and lead to inappropriate actions.

It was the most characteristic note of this community, the extreme poverty of their daily life, that aroused the admiration of Dom Augustin. He expressed this in an official document which followed the Visitation he made to this community. In this 'Visitation Card', he says what he found there. The document is not dated, but it is worth quoting in full:

> We the undersigned, Brother Augustin, abbot of the former house of La Trappe in Perche and Father Immediate of all the other communities of men as well of women in the same Reform, declare and certify that having made the Visitation in the community of Madame (de) Chateaubriand, established for the moment in the Abbey of Mondaix in the diocese of Bayeux have found the said community in a situation of penury and destitution so great that we ourselves have trembled, even accustomed as we are to living in a state of poverty for a very long time. Theirs is so great that they do not have a fire, even in the infirmary for the sick. No oil to put on their salad, no second habit to change into to wash the other, and certainly they do not have sufficient coverings on their beds to keep them warm at night. But we must add for the glory of God and to God alone, that in spite of all this, we have found them in such great peace and so great a state of contentment, that we can only let ourselves admire the power of grace.

In witness thereof we have signed with our own hand and caused our secretary to countersign the present declaration.

Fr. Augustin, Abbot of La Trappe[3]

It seems evident that the Father Abbot himself admired a life obviously marked by grace and inspired by himself. For us, however, this angelism is profoundly shocking, and at the time it shocked monks who witnessed these excesses while having no means to remedy them.

It was only after the death of Dom Augustin in 1828, that the Abbot of Melleray, Dom Antoine Saulnier de Beauregard, who had been named by the Holy See, as Apostolic Visitor of all the houses of the Reform, was able to intervene to remedy this poverty. It had become real deprivation, which had been maintained by the spirit of 'victimhood' infused into this community from its inception, even though this was not expressed in their vows.

These measures arrived much too late however, and the exhausted community saw its members dwindle little by little. Certainly the entries diminished, and from 1827 we have no Register of Admissions to give us any information. Only the necrology shows that there were more deaths, not compensated by the arrival of new members.

The Dissolution of the Community

Mother Marie des Séraphins de Chateaubriand died on 18 March 1832. She was seventy-one years old and had lived this austere life for twenty seven-years. She had led and upheld her sisters by her example and exhortations. Perhaps she had done this with an ardor that surpassed the strength and capabilities of the greater number not endowed with an equally strong physical constitution.

[3] Archives of La Trappe, ref. 55–71.

At the death of the prioress, the sub-prioress was provisionally in charge of the community. She was Mother Marie des Sacrés-Coeurs-de-Malles-de-Graville, born in Caen on 7 October 1782 and baptized in the Church of Saint-Sauveur. She had joined the community at Mondaye on 2 October 1817, she was then thirty seven years old, and made her profession on 9 January 1817.

On 1 August 1832, Dom Antoine Saulnier de Beauregard, named Superior General of the monasteries of La Trappe in France by the Holy See, wrote to her from Melleray:

> I have learned, my dear daughter with much sorrow of the death of your worthy and dear superior . . . I name you provisionally superior of your community, and command you to continue as usual until other arrangements are made for your monastery.
>
> I also agree with the plans and projects of Father Joseph-Marie [Hercelin], superior of La Trappe, to transfer the community to another house on the outskirts of Mortagne. But I still do not wish to conceal all the difficulties that such an establishment will cause in the present circumstances . . . I am convinced nevertheless that your community, after the loss of your superior, will have a great deal of trouble to stay on at Mondaye, and I do want to retain the community; therefore I comply with all that you have asked . . . .[4]

The survival of the community was already a problem by this time, as much because of the irremediable poverty, as because of the small number of the religious, many of whom were elderly and infirm—a double handicap which had hindered recruitment. Consequently a powerless Mother Marie des Sacrés-Coeurs took part in the decline of the community. Between 1833 and 1836, nineteen deaths weakened

[4] Archives of La Trappe, ref. 152, piece 1.

the community still more. The sisters who remained were at the end of their strength.

We have an echo of this distress in a brief paragraph from the Acts of the General Chapter of 1836 (1–18 August), the second since the Union of the two Observances by the Holy See, in conforming to the Decree of 3 October 1834.

> The proposition of a foundation has been presented to the Reverend Trappist Fathers by the nuns near Laval of Saint-Catherine and rejected unanimously, or rather we have proposed another project: that they come to the aid of the community of nuns of "Mons Dei" (Mondaye) where the weakened sisters are inflicted with frequent infirmities.[5]

In a letter of 3 September 1835, the abbess of Laval, Mother Elisabeth Piette, wrote to Dom Joseph-Marie Hercelin, now become abbot of La Grande Trappe and then Vicar General of the Congregation of the reunited Trappists. She explained her plans to make a foundation at Baugé (Maine-et-Loire), in a former convent of Capuchines. The community of Sainte-Catherine now numbered seventy-nine persons; the regular places were too small; only two places were available in the dormitory and six postulants were waiting to enter.[6]

On 31 October 1836, Mgr Robin, newly named Bishop of Bayeux, wrote to Dom Hercelin:

> Your letter concerning the saintly religious of Mondaye has deeply troubled me. Indeed is it not painful for a bishop to learn suddenly, and without having been in any way prepared, that a community so edifying on all points and so long established, to find that they must leave his diocese at the very time when he is daily acquiring

[5] Vincent Hermans, *Actes des chapitres généraux des Congrégations trappistes au XIXe siècle*, p. 29.

[6] Archives of La Trappe, ref. 172, piece 1.

information about it. And in addition to this unforeseen distress there is the personal embarrassment of replying to you.

How can I sanction or postpone the departure of these poor daughters, if I do not know either the extent of the difficulties, or the causes that have brought this about, or the remedies that could be applied? Such is my position. I have been at Bayeux only two months; I have never been to the house at Mondaye or even had any dealings with it. I cannot find in the bishop's house any documents on this place . . . Please be good enough to furnish me with some information which will help me to make a decision with full knowledge of the facts.[7]

Extracts from other letters permit us to follow events concerning the dissolution of the community. On 10 November 1836, from bishop's house in Bayeux, a priest with an illegible signature wrote to the Abbot of La Trappe:

My Lord Bishop, full of concern for the the community of Mondaye and desiring to preserve it, today wished to make a visit there and asked me to accompany him. He told the religious all the distress it would cause him if they were to leave, and he also made them realise that they could not do so without his permission, promising to do all he could to help and support them . . . .

His Lordship fears that it may already be too late, for he has learned of the arrival of a superior from the region of Marseille to arrange for the transfer of the community[8] . . . The matter is neither clear nor comforting, and you, Reverend Father, must know more about it than anyone else . . . The bishop intends to send me to you to discuss ways and means for reviving this most worthy

[7] *Ibid.*, ref.146, piece 2.

[8] This was the prioress of Maubec, near Montélimar, to which the community of Lyon-Vaise had been transferred by her. We will see more about this in the next chapter.

> house which you yourself cannot see disappearing without many regrets . . . .[9]

In a later letter, written by the bishop himself to the prior of La Grande Trappe, Father Benard Dugué, he expressed his reservations in agreeing to give financial aid before the religious left 'for the new establishment' on the assurance that there would be future benefactors . . . 'I would be imprudent if I guaranteed a determined sum before the foundation . . .'

'The matter is neither clear nor comforting', said the bishop's secretary. We can now see that this was no longer a matter of a community dying out. It was a substitution which necessitated the dissolution of the existing community, so new arrivals could have a clear field.

We may be allowed to think that the community of Mondaye, which originated somewhat differently from the other Trappist foundations, and therefore had its own traditions, might perhaps have accepted help from the religious of Sainte-Catherine on the condition that they could keep their own superior, Mother Marie des Sacrés-Coeurs.

On the other hand, the mother abbess of Laval, thwarted in her designs for a foundation in Maine-et-Loire, was able to insist that the new superior be a nun of Laval. Furthermore, Dom Hercelin, as the Father Immediate, held absolutely that La Grande Trappe should keep this daughter house, and he used his authority as Vicar General to dissolve the community and leave the field open for the newcomers, imposing on them in return the Regulations of La Trappe. The matter was regulated juridically at the end of January 1837.

THE FOUNDATION OF MONDAYE II

On 11 January 1837, the abbess of Sainte-Catherine of Laval wrote to the prior of La Trappe:

[9] Archives of La Trappe, ref. 146, piece 4.

> I have communicated your last letter to our worthy Reverend Father Abbot [of Port-du-Salut]. He respects the intentions and wishes of our most Reverend Vicar General. In consequence, he does not raise any difficulty. On our side we are well disposed to agree with the views of our very good and most worthy Vicar General [Rissime], but we hope that he will have the goodness to show us his wishes and at the same time authorize us in this foundation; this could be done by two lines of writing . . . [10]

The reply of Dom Hercelin, written in his own hand, is dated 27 January 1837:

> My very dear daughter,
>
> You know that I have always wanted to keep the community at Mondaye and that the General Chapter of 1836 shared this wish. It even approved the sending of some of your own daughters to help this distressed community. But now that our former sisters of Mondaye have fallen too low in numbers and have withdrawn, I give my willing consent for you to make a new foundation in the place they left.
>
> I pray that God will continue to lavish his graces and blessings [on you], so that the group you send will preserve the spirit which has reigned for twenty years in that house and that it will recall all the virtues which were practised there . . . .
>
> [And in a post-script]. It is understood that the Reverend Mother Abbess of Sainte-Catherine will give an account of the value of their property to the religious who have left Mondaye.[11]

[10] *Ibid.*, ref. 172, piece 8.

[11] *Ibid.*, ref.172, piece 4. All these fragments have been communicated to me by Dom Gérard Guérout, retired abbot of La Trappe. In a covering letter in which he suggested the interpretations proposed in my text, he added: 'I believe (in view of the climate at that time) that Dom Hercelin would have preferred to allow the community at Mondaye to die a natural death, rather than lose the paternity or surrender it to the abbot of Port-du-Salut. If, then, this very worthy community was sacrificed, the

On 18 February 1837, Mother Elisabeth Plet was sent by her abbess, Mother Elisabeth Piette, to Mondaye, where some of the nuns of the dispersed community were preparing to leave. The new superior, born in 1802 at Meslay-du-Maine in the Mayenne, was professed at Sainte-Catherine on 2 July 1825. When the abbess, with nine others arrived on 30 April 1837, to make the foundation, the first occupants were already on the road towards the South of France.

They numbered then twenty-six: ten choir nuns and sixteen lay sisters. They were dispersed into three other communities dependent on La Grande Trappe: Les Gardes, Lyon-Vaise, and Maubec. The superior, Mother Marie des Sacrés-Coeurs-de-Malles-de-Graville, arrived at Les Gardes on 24 May 1837, and made her stability there on 10 August 1838. She was elected superior of the community on 5 July 1845, and died when she was sixty-six years old, five months before the end of her three year period of office, on 31 January 1848.

The other sisters made their way to the Midi under the leadership of the prioress of Maubec who had come to fetch them. Seven stopped at Lyon-Vaise, the others went on to Maubec (Montélimar) where at least some of them made their new stability.

The Destiny of the New Community

The community of Mondaye II, notwithstanding the help in personnel and finance they received from the founding community, also felt the pinch of poverty. They stayed only eight years at Mondaye, despite an abundant recruitment. During this period they had six deaths, and the chronicle says there were still thirty-nine sisters when they were

---

person responsible when all is said and done, was Dom Hercelin, who, as a matter of fact, was not able to give sufficiently clear and satisfactory reasons to the bishop of Bayeux.

transferred to the diocese of Chartres, to La Cour-Pétral in 1845. A very generous benefactress offered them a place to live and the means of a livelihood, not without inextricable difficulties which weighed heavily on the Father Immediate.

In 1905, like so many French communites, they took refuge in the diocese of Bois-le-Duc (Holland) at Boxtel. This was closed in 1920. Then in 1935 the community made yet another transfer, to the belgian Ardennes, to Clairfontaine, where they are to this present day.

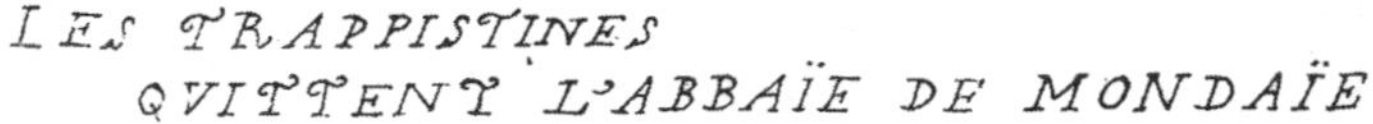

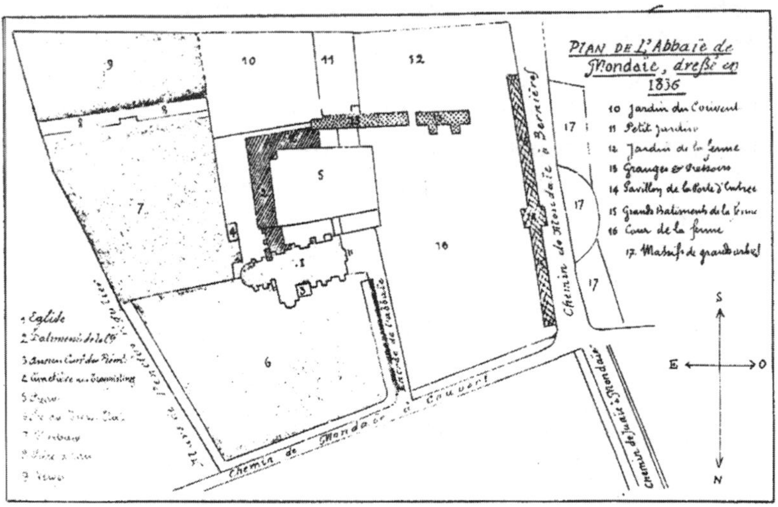

Figure 7

Plan of the Abbey of Mondaye.

CHAPTER THREE

FROM SWITZERLAND TO FRANCE

THE CLOSING OF LA RIEDERA

Preparations

WHEN DOM AUGUSTIN returned from America in 1814, he soon set about summoning monks back to France. We saw that he accepted the generous offer of Dom Eugene de Laprade and had been able to return to the site of La Trappe, its buildings in ruins.

Rebuilding was already underway when he learned of the Emperor's return and his landing at Cannes in March 1815. Dom Augustin left the continent with all speed for England; there he awaited events. After Waterloo, he came back to France and recalled from Switzerland the monks who had rejoined La Valsainte with the authorization of the government of Fribourg. He divided them into two groups: one was to rejoin La Trappe on 16 November 1815, having as its superior Dom Augustin himself; the other group, under Dom Etienne Malmy, the prior, took possession in December of the old cistercian abbey of Aiguebelle in the Drôme. In the west of France, Father Urbain Guillet, who had returned from America with a group of monks, settled at Bellefontaine, a former abbey of the Feuillants near Cholet.

In this way the faithful sons of Dom Augustin were divided into three communities, all continuing under his obedience. Added to these very soon (1817) was the English community of Lulworth 'politely dismissed' by the english government and administered by an abbot, Dom Antoine Saulnier de Beauregard. It was transferred and established at Melleray, a former cistercian abbey near Nantes.

Having arranged all this or seen to it that it would be done, Dom Augustin also wanted the nuns who had stayed in Switzerland at La Riedera to come back to France. To this end, towards the end of 1815, he bought them a property about two or three leagues from La Trappe called 'Les Forges', in the commune of Saint-Ouen-de-Secherouvre.

With the idea of also dividing the community of La Riedera into two, in spite of its reduced numbers (in all twenty-six adults including the sisters of the Third Order), he was looking for yet another place when a house was offered to him at Frenouville near Caen, with the promise of help for the community.

Successive Departures

The community moved in five groups, each with six sisters. On 29 February 1816, two groups left. The first at the head was Mother Thérèse Malatesta. They were destined to go to Forges. We do not know who the five companions of the Prioress were, as their names have faded out in the Register. On the other hand, we know that they were accompanied to Forges by Father Augustin Pignard and Brother Bernard.[1]

The second group left the same day under the direction of a Sister of the Third Order, Sister François-Xavier

[1] Augustin Pignard was born at Cusey-sur Vingeanne (Haute-Marne), near Langres, in 1769. His father was the manager of the salt warehouse in Langres. Maurice-Jean Baptiste was first an officer in the army of the Prince de Condé, then he entered La Valsainte. He was ordained priest at Fribourg on 22 December 1804. He replaced Father Malmy, who was chaplain at La Riedera, as prior of La Valsainte. He dealt with all the business and material affairs of the nuns. We find him again as chaplain at Lyon-Vaise, where he assisted Dom Augustin on his deathbed. He himself died suddenly on 16 January 1832. Brother Bernard was a Brother *donné* of La Valsainte, a man of great piety and simplicity. 'He drove the sisters of La Riedera to the monastery of Forges in a carriage'. He died at La Trappe.

Faucheux. She was accompanied by five pupils, with the intention of founding at Cuignières in the Oise a school dedicated to the Holy Child Jesus. This foundation was dispersed in the spring of 1817. The pupils rejoined Les Forges and Sister Xavier went back to the house at Lyon. The names of three of the pupils can be found on the list of deaths at Forges during the following years. Sister Geneviève Martin, twenty-one years old, died on 10 April 1819, a professed choir nun; Sister Andrée Martin died on 12 July 1818, a professed lay sister; and Sister Lucie Mekay, who came from Baltimore in the United States, died as a novice on 19 March 1821, when she was eighteen years old.

A third group, directed by Mother Thaïs Bassignot, the sub-prioress, left La Riedera on 27 June 1816, and made her way to Les Forges with five sisters:

— Sister Marie-Joseph Perrin, a professed choir nun who fell ill on the way and died at Pontarlier during the journey. She was thirty-seven years old.
— Sister Agnès Le Poué, who came from Malbuisson (Jura), a professed lay sister who had entered La Riedera in 1806 when she was forty-nine years old. She died at Forges on 23 July 1820.
— Sister Claire Girod, a choir novice when she left, was the first to die at Forges, when she was twenty-eight years old, on 8 February 1818.
— Sister Stanislaus Bussard.
— and another Sister of the Third Order whose name has not been noted.

The five religious arrived at their destination on 14 July.

Three months later the two other groups took to the road, this time for Frenouville. On 28 September 1816, Mother Marie du Saint-Esprit Allard, the prioress, took with her:

— Sister Thaïs de Jésus Durdilly, a lay sister and, an ex-tourière of the Ursulines of Saint-Symphorien-le-Château. She came from Châtillon-d'Azergues in the neighborhood of Lyon, and was professed on 20 August 1811.

— Sister Madeleine Grognuz, a lay novice at the time of leaving, was Swiss; the next year she left and went back to her country.

— Sister Thérèse Pechoux, of the Third Order, an ex-religious hospitalière. She entered Villarvolard when she was forty-eight years old, on 28 January 1803, as a lay sister; the following year she passed to the Third Order; she was the infirmarian in the community ('chirurgienne'! says the Register).

— Sister Alberic Ried, a sister *donnée* of very poor health, 'who had been with the pupils' since 22 August 1803.

The travellers arrived at Frenouville on 16 October 1816. They were welcomed by the Father Abbot in person who showed them round the place. For all, this was a great joy and encouragement.

The last group left on 4 October for the same destination. They had at their head Mother Magdeleine Guyot, secretary, one of the first foundresses of 'La Sainte-Volonté-de-Dieu'. She was a widow from Paris. Her father was a Master saddle-maker and her husband had been a copper-plate engraver. She was thirty-six when she entered at Sembrancher and made her profession on 28 October 1799 at Orsha. Aged fifty-six when she left La Riedera, she was an excellent auxiliary for Mother Marie du Saint-Esprit. She died as sub-prioress at Lyon in February 1825. Her travelling companions were:

— Sister Scholastique Sempé, professed choir nun, a former Feuillantine from Toulouse.

— Sister Louise de Lestrange, of the Third Order, who had never been a member of the community under vows. She departed from the community at Lyon about 1820.

— Two professed lay sisters; Sister Thérèse Caître, who entered at Villarvolard on 25 August 1803, came from Auxonne in Burgundy; and Sister M.Bernard Dufour, who came from Clermont sur l'Ariège, was forty-years old when she entered on 4 November 1805.

— Sister Célestine Miserey, a sister *donnée* in delicate health. Having entered in 1813, she had to leave the following year, but they promised to let her come back. She came to rejoin the group on the way to Frenouville on 9 October 1816. She died at Lyon on 12 February 1820 at the age of thirty-four.

Leaving the Property of La Riedera

Unlike the other houses which had sheltered sisters from Sembrancher—such as Darfeld, where no trace of their existence is to be found—the property of La Riedera still stands today. This is what fortunately became of the place.

It remained under the care of Father Augustin Pignard, who was very devoted to this community of nuns of Notre-Dame-de-la-Sainte-Trinité. Then the estate and its buildings were sold to 'a certain Claude Esprit de Rigot, Marquis de Monjoux, former captain of Infantry from Grenoble'.[2] In 1838 the entire property was purchased by the Countess de La Poye, a french émigrée of 1794, along with her mother and sister. Her sister was Pierrette Alexandrine, who entered the monastery of La Sainte-Trinité at the age of twenty-eight on 11 April 1810. Her poor health compelled her to pass to the Third Order on 21 June 1810, where she died on 18 August the following year. Twenty-seven years later, by chance, the countess discovered the place where her sister lay buried; this is what had decided her to buy the house and its surroundings. Later she bequeathed by a testament the whole property to the bishop of Fribourg, Mgr Marilley.

[2] For this information, and for what follows, I am indebted to Madame Anne-Marie Peiry, who now (1987) lives on the ground floor of the house (1987). She takes a great interest in the history of the place and has done some research on it. The property has been leased out since 1859 by successive members of the family Peiry.

She laid down some conditions, two of which were quite burdensome.

1) that on her sisters' grave there be planted a rose bush and that during the summer months the grave be covered with flowers.
2) that the bishop of Fribourg come and celebrate fifty Masses each year in the chapel of the convent. This last clause was difficult to keep, above all during this time, because it meant making such a journey each week, and a Bishop's pastoral duties had priority over all other obligations. Mgr Marilley obtained a special dispensation from the Holy See.

The present bishop of Fribourg, Mgr Mamie, insisted on personally showing me the first floor of the house and the exterior, with the cemetery and the crosses of wrought iron. He keeps a religious vigilance over the place and also over the humble objects used by the nuns: oil lamps, wooden wash bowls, small pieces of furniture etc. A fire destroyed some of the buildings, including the church, which was consecrated in 1805. Since then a chapel has been arranged on the first floor in a large room which contains an altar piece in triptych dated 1586, and several statues with a *Pietà* of the sixteenth century.

We can well imagine that it was a sorrowful day when the sisters had to move from this place which had been such a beneficial halt after their long peregrinations. Once again they had to go into the unknown, and this unknown would require yet more transfers, as we shall see in the following pages. They let themselves be guided by the intrepid monk who had so many times come to their aid.

LES FORGES - LES GARDES

The House

The first group to leave La Riedera to go to Forges arrived at La Trappe and took possession of the building at Forges on 23 May 1816. The estate, thenceforth placed under the patronage of the archangel Raphael, was comprised of a small château which had belonged to the Maréchal de Catinat, one of the great generals of Louis XIV. The Maréchal, who never married, died in 1712; with his heirs were a collateral branch of the family. The family name died out with Madame Levailler de Marsilli *née* Catinat. Her sons and heirs had emigrated and the estate was sold as National Property. 'Sold and re-sold many time', says Gaillardin, 'it had regained its true value' when the abbot of La Trappe bought it. 'Dom Augustin', adds the historian, 'believed it his duty to negotiate with the heirs cheated out of their property beforehand by their mother; and received from them the assurance that they saw with pleasure a religious house on the land which had belonged to their family'.[3]

The various portions of the property bought by Dom Augustin included fifty hectares of arable land, meadows, and woods. Through the sisters' work, helped by the monks of La Trappe, development of the land was able to provide for the needs of the community.

The Community

Very few archives are extant from Forges other than deeds made out by the notary concerning the puchase, then the sale of the property. There is no Register of Admissions, but there is a list of deaths reconstructed by Dom Gérard Guérout, from the Registers of the Civil State preserved in the departmental archives at Orne.

[3] C. Gaillardin, *Histoire de La Trappe*, 2:375. At the time all Christians who bought property, esp. church property, were considered as sacriligious. This was the firm opinion of Dom Antoine de Beauregard, the abbot of Melleray, who openly reproached Dom Augustin for this purchase. Bellefontaine and Les Gardes felt the wrath of Dom Antoine at the time Forges was resold. This was a typical case of the assimilation of royalty with religion: the émigrés goods had the same value and meaning as the goods of the church.

As we will see further on, however, in 1821 all the community at Forges were transferred to Gardes, and the names of the forty-one religious, with their particulars, were noted down so well that we are able to reconstruct the entire community as it was.

The superior was Mother Thérèse Malatesta (Julie Gertrude, Ursule, Marie, Françoise), daughter of Louis Maletesta and of Diamante Politei, born in Assisi in Umbria on 19 December 1779. Her father a merchant, came from Tonelio in the March of Ancona. In 1804, when she was twenty-five, Mother Thérèse accompanied her father to Paris. Did she make this journey with a purpose? Was she seeking her vocation? In any case she heard talk about the Trappistines, who were then at Grosbois-Camaldolese. She was admitted into the community on 1 November 1804, and made her profession on 19 July 1806. Dom Augustin, who had adopted this house in 1808, saw in her a religious of real ability, and sent her in June 1809 to reinforce the community at La Riedera. She made her stability there on 21 January 1810. Eighteen months later she was put at the head of the small group on its way to Bordeaux to make a foundation in America. We saw how this was a failure, three sisters out of the four were not able to embark. Four and a half years later, the Father Abbot assigned Mother Thérèse to become prioress of Les Forges.

As early as 19 May, before they entered the new house, Mother Thérèse welcomed a new arrival. This was a survivor of the community from Valenton who had not joined up with Tréguier or Mondaye. Sister Augustin Chevallier, came from Chaumont in the diocese of Langres and had entered at Sénart before Mother Thérèse. She was fifty seven when she rejoined her, and died after the transfer to Gardes of the age seventy-six. On 15 June Sister Anne Avard came to join them. Born at Bonsmoulins in the Orne, she was a former professed Cistercian from the abbey of Clairets. She also died at Gardes on 24 August 1823, when she was eighty years old.

Between May and December 1816, there were at least sixteen aspirants who entered (I say 'at least' because I do not know the entrance date of those who came to Gardes). Fifteen of them died in the Order. This was very promising for the future of the community. During the following years a great number of postulants also asked to enter; they came from far and wide, from nearby and remote places, from Soligny as also from Carcassonne or from Luxembourg.

Dom Augustin seeing this affluence—in five years there were seventy-four entries, of whom sixty made profession—accepted some invitations to make foundations which were made to him by various persons during his travels.

The Foundations in Anjou

The first of these came from an elderly lady, a neighbour of Bellefontaine. She offered a house and part of her fortune to establish a community of Trappistines within the vicinity of the monks. The Father Abbot immediately sent a small group of three or four sisters, with Mother Thaïs Bassignot at their head. They had a lodging in the borough of Bégrolles-en-Mauges. They stayed there waiting for the old lady to fulfil her promises. But she became senile, and her heirs put obstacles in the way of her proposals. The small group led a very serious life of prayer, silence and work; by this they made the monastic way of life for women known in the neighborhood. In less than ten months, Mother Thaïs received sixteen postulants, seven of whom made their profession in the community at Gardes after the fusing of the group the following year, with the new foundation of Forges.

About twenty km from this place there was a sanctuary dedicated to Notre-Dame-des-Gardes; before the Revolution the hermits of Saint Augustine had the care of this place of pilgrimage. Driven out by the political upheaval, they dispersed and the convent was sold as national property.

The church, abandoned, fell into ruins. One day the inhabitants of the village decided to restore the place and make it a place of pilgrimage again. It seems the bishop of Angers could not spare a chaplain for the place, as priests were then very few in number. One of the leading citizens went to Bellefontaine and asked the monks to revive the piety of the faithful. The Father Abbot, however, proposed instead of the monks, some nuns whose chaplain could at the same time be chaplain to the sanctuary. The prominent citizen, a M. Blanchet, managed to buy what remained of the convent, a condition laid down by Dom Augustin, and six months later, on 7 March 1818, the business was concluded. The following 7 August ten nuns arrived from Forges, with Mother Thérèse Malatesta at their head. On the 14th of the same month Mother Thaïs and her group joined them with some postulants. On the feast of the Assumption there were twenty-two sisters to celebrate the feast of Mary in her ancient sanctuary.

Very soon, in spite of the extreme poverty of the place and of the resources, vocations were abundant. From August 1818 to December 1821 there were one hundred eleven entries, fifty-seven departures and sixteen deaths. During this period the rest of the community at Forges continued to prosper.

Suppression of the Community at Forges and the Transfer to Gardes

Nevertheless black clouds were gathering over La Trappe and Les Forges. A growing dissension between the bishop of Sées and the abbot of La Trappe began to appear. The bishop denied Dom Augustin the title abbot of La Trappe, only recognizing him as abbot of La Valsainte and saying that jurisdiction over the nuns at Les Forges belonged to him alone. The conflict became so bitter that the Father Abbot decided to close the sisters' house on 28 September

1821. He sent them to join the community of Gardes in the first days of October. They then numbered forty-one, under the rule of Mother Hedwige Fabre.

In this way the community at Gardes was doubled within a few days, and numbered about ninety sisters, all of them under the same superior, Mother Thérèse Malatesta. Ever since then, the Cistercian-Trappistines have kept this vantage point on the hill.[4]

FRENOUVILLE - LYON-VAISE - MAUBEC

Welcome at Frenouville

The first group to go to Frenouville left La Riedera on 28 September 1816, and reached their destination on 16 October. Dom Augustin was there, waiting for the travellers. He received them with joy and had them visit the house and the enclosure. Everything was very modest, but some future projects were envisaged and the sisters were reassured by the welcome and confidence they were shown. The Father Abbot then left immediately, leaving the sisters 'some temporary aids and great promises on the part of the local inhabitants', says a chronicle written some twenty years later.

Today there is no clear indication of the whereabouts of the house, nor has any description come down to us. We know only that the furniture and movable objects were very scanty and that the 'temporary aids' were quite rapidly exhausted. However, they had the joy of the arrival of the second group of sisters under Mother Magdeleine Guyot, who had closed La Riedera. The regular life was then begun by the thirteen members who made up the community and the tiny monastery was christened Notre-Dame-de-Toute-Consolation.

[4] For more information, cf. M.de la Trinité Kervingant, *La vie sur la colline. Notre-Dame- des-Gardes* (Cholet, 1983).

The promises of the local inhabitants were not followed with the desired effect, and poverty was not slow to become destitution. The Father Abbot, made aware of the circumstances, hastened to remedy the situation by negotiating with a population less impoverished than the villagers. A town has more resources and he thought of Lyon, the birth place of the prioress, Mother Marie du Saint-Esprit.

The Transfer to Lyon

Lyon had a reputation for generosity. Dom Augustin rented a house in the suburbs of the Croix-Rousse, on the rue de Cuire, and ordered the nuns at Frenouville to take to the road. They arrived in Lyon on 13 May 1817. Again, Dom Augustin was waiting for them. To their chaplain, Father Augustin Pignard, who had concluded the sale of the estate at La Riedera, he entrusted the mission of finding a suitable place in the neighborhood where they could finally establish conventual life.

For the time being, the chaplain turned a downstairs room into an oratory where the nuns could gather to sing the Office and have daily Mass. Some of the people living in Lyon heard of the foundation and came to participate in the liturgy, admiring the courage of these religious, so faithful to their *saint état* through thousands of tribulations. The people set up a Fellowship of Friends for the new community, with the intention of helping them to establish a solid foundation.

Father Pignard, the chaplain was a great source of support in promoting this Fellowship, which was very helpful in helping him in his negotiations to find a suitable place where the foundation could be permanently settled. A place was found on the outskirts of the suburb of Vaise in a district called Gorge-du-Loup, where some buildings, quite large, surrounded by an enclosed garden were located. The selling price was seventy thousand francs. They settled for thirty thousand francs, and the rest came from gifts or from the dowries of postulants from wealthy families. Here, too, postulants very soon flocked to enter.

The first need was to put the whole place in order. This was soon done with the help of the people of Lyon who had now become friends of the community. The nuns entered their monastery on 18 May 1820. A church had been built for the sisters only, but the regular visitors of the house insisted on having an additional church adjoining the choir so they could more easily participate at the Offices. This was completed in 1823.

In this same year, the prioress, Mother Marie du Saint-Esprit, petitioned Dom Augustin to be relieved of her office.[5] Born on 11 February 1755, she was not yet sixty-eight. The difficult and lengthy journeys had had their effect. Her sight was failing daily, making it more difficult for her to fulfil her duties as Superior. However, the Father Abbot did not agree immediately to her request, but waited until the following year; by then the superior had become totally blind,[6] so he sent a young nun from Notre-Dame-des-Gardes (Sister Victime du Coeur de Jésus Olivier) to replace the prioress at Lyon. This sister, born at Celles in the Aube, had entered trappist life when she was twenty-five, on 31 May 1821, and made her profession the following year. She was a little over twenty-eight when she arrived at Lyon-Vaise, without any letter of introduction from the Father Abbot. The chaplain politely showed her the door. This indignity she accepted courageously; the misunderstanding was resolved and fifteen days later she took charge of the community. She remained as superior until her death in 1839.

[5] See a letter of Father Augustin Pignard to Dom Augustin de Lestrange dated 15 January 1823, Archives of La Trappe, ref. 218,10–7.

[6] Copy of a letter of Mother Marie de Jésus (Mère Victime?) dated 7 March 1825, written to Dom Augustin, announcing the death of Mother Magdeleine Guyot, sub-prioress. She mentions the blindness of Mother Marie du Saint-Esprit and of her loss of memory (Arch. Tr. 218,10, piece 2).

It was to be this sister who received the last breath of the venerable mother whom she succeeded on 1 January 1827. The following July, she welcomed the founder of the Reform of La Valsainte for his last day on earth.

The Death of Dom Augustin

A heavy trial was waiting for the abbot of La Trappe in 1825. In the preceding pages, I have already alluded to his misunderstandings with the bishop of Sées and the decision that resulted: the transfer of the community at Forges to Gardes. On all sides trouble was brewing. Letters to the nuncio in Paris or directly to the Roman curia contained accusations against the Father Abbot. Those which concerned his personal conduct were obviously false. Those which concerned his duties as Father Immediate seem more probable. He kept for himself practically all local authority, as Gaillardin explains:

> In his zeal for uniformity, he was afraid to allow someone else the authority to act as he pleased with his own personal ideas; so Dom Augustin reserved for himself the power to regulate everything, even to changing the minor offices in an arbitrary manner that brooked no protest.[7]

In 1825, Dom Augustin received a summons to go Rome and explain his conduct. He left immediately in August, having no doubt of his own rights, so convinced was he of his loyal intentions. But the inquiry was drawn out and the whole business complicated. Almost two years passed in waiting for a decision. The Father Abbot, tired out and worried, decided to leave Rome in June 1827. He made a stop at La Sainte-Baume, where a trappist foundation was painfully developing. There he had an accident, an unfortunate fall which wounded him in the head. Nevertheless, he

[7] Gaillardin, p. 425.

took to the road again immediately, going to Notre-Dame-des-Lumiéres, a house of the Third Order for men near Avignon, and after ten days set out for Lyon. Coming within sight of Vaise, he heard the sound of the convent bells and said to his companion: 'It seems to me that they are tolling for a death!' Was this a simple comment or a premonition?

He thought of staying at Lyon only a short time, but it was here that the Lord was waiting for him. The nuns had never waned in their trust and affection for him, and this was very specially the case with the community at Vaise. He was to have the consolation of being surrounded by their watchful care in his last days, and more directly by that of their chaplain Father Augustin Pignard. Seeing the extreme exhaustion of the Father Abbot, Father Augustin suggested to him that he receive the last sacraments, 'these he received with a faith and a piety worthy of his life', says his biographer. On 16 July, the feast of Saint Stephen Harding, abbot of Cîteaux and author of the Charter of Charity, at the hour when the nuns were singing the *Te Deum* at Vigils, Dom Augustin de Lestrange, abbot of La Trappe, gave his soul up into the hands of God, whose will he had sought and loved without respite.

Thus died the founder of the Reform of La Valsainte, while the living witnesses of his work, his monasteries, continue to live, and little by little to free themselves from an Observance, the inflexibility of which surpassed the limits of human endurance.

> The General Chapter of 1855 expresses the wish that the remains of Dom Augustin de Lestrange, carefully preserved in a vault by the Sisters of La Trappe at Lyon, be transferred to La Grande Trappe, to be deposited in the chapel of Dom Armand de Rancé.[8]

In this way the two Reformers are reunited in common veneration.

[8] V. Hermans, *Actes des chapitres généraux*, p. (272).

Transfer to Maubec and Return to Lyon

Meanwhile, community life went on. With the help of the chaplain the nuns at Vaise found some means of overcoming the problems of the poverty in the house by the installation of a workshop where silk weaving was done under the direction of the religious, who employed young girls from the town.

When there was an insurrection of *Canuts* [workers in silk weaving, so called from the word *cannette*, a bobbin or spool-trans. note] at Lyon in 1831, the sisters' workshops were invaded by demonstrators who ransacked the looms and materials.

This disaster made the prioress seriously deliberate on their position. She was now bereft of her counsellor, as Father Pignard had died on 16 January 1831. After lengthy considerations she finally decided to transfer the community to an area further from a large town. Eventually she found what she was looking for: a large property of more than a one hundred hectares at Maubec, a few kilometers from Montélimar. She received the consent of the bishop of Valence and in 1834 started to transfer in groups the some eighty nuns at Lyon. She left just a few lay sisters in Lyon to look after the house until the place could be sold.

The people of Lyon felt defrauded and protested to the apostolic administrator of the archbishopric of Lyon. They wanted to keep the nuns on whom they had lavished their generosity. After prolonged negotiations, the house of Lyon-Vaise once again in 1837, became the site of conventual life under the direction of Mother Pacifique de Spandl.

In this way, without any preconceived plan, the community of Lyon-Vaise gave rise to a new community of nuns. They had sustained a temporary suspension, only to be reborn and then flourish. For both houses the material situation remained very difficult, however. They had counted on the sale of the Lyon house to be able to buy the land Maubec. Now they owned both.

A final word on the community at Lyon: under the threat of expulsion for unauthorized communities, the nuns took to the road of exile, going to Canada in 1904. There, in Acadia, they became Notre-Dame-de-l'Assomption, at Rogersville, New Brunswick. Lyon-Vaise is no longer a cistercian monastery, but its community lives on.

CHAPTER FOUR

LOOKING BACK

AT THE END OF THIS HISTORY OF TWENTY YEARS OF wandering, it seems essential to take stock of the expansion of communities of Cistercian-Trappistines, all of them stemming from that first community assembled in 1796.

The successive transfers or foundations, provisional or permanent, due to various causes, may tend to obscure the spiritual stability which animated the foundresses and those who joined them. What strikes us, if we look closely, is their constant fidelity to the monastic state, *notre saint état*; this animated these courageous women throughout their travels. Despite deaths and defections at intervals all along the way, they wanted to hand on the life which enabled them to consecrate themselves totally to Christ by sharing his cross.

They followed literally the Lord's injunction to those who wished to follow him, 'If they drive you out of one town, flee to another'.

We have followed them stage by stage through countless vicissitudes. Now it seems a good idea and practically indispensable to recapitulate, by an overall picture, these milestones on the way.

SUCCESSIVE STAGES AND PERMANENT FOUNDATIONS

Chronologically, there appear to be three stages in the life of the first community of nuns after the dispersions which resulted from the French Revolution and its aftermath.

1) 1798–1800: The grouping at Sembrancher, then a life in groups or 'colonies', separated and reunited according to the circumstances.
2) 1800–1808: A double branching off in 1800–1801 which with time became permanent. Hence there were three communities, to which an adopted group was added in 1808.
3) 1812–1816: The division into two of two of these communities.

In 1816 then there were six communities of cistercian nuns, five of which had issued from the original community, as we have recounted in the precedinging pages, and one adopted community.

THE FIRST PERIOD

The Monastery of La Sainte-Volonté
Sembrancher (Switzerland), diocese of Sion

Inaugurated on 14 September 1796, with seven aspirants. Mother Sainte-Marie Laignier, a Benedictine, was appointed Prioress the same day. The monastery was closed and sold in February 1798.

The community of forty-two sisters was broken into three 'colonies' when they left. They travelled from 19 January 1798 until the middle of March of that year, staying at different places in Bavaria, especially the castle of Fürstenried, where Holy Week ceremonies were observed, in the chapel 1–8 April 1798.

At this time the 'colonies' were again reorganized.

The Castle of Dürnast
in the diocese of Freising, near Munich

One colony, led by Mother Augusine de Chabannes, lived here from May 1798 to May 1799. This was the rallying point to which Dom Augustin sent aspirants. There were thirty-six nuns altogether, of whom only fourteen died in the Order.

The Castle of Buštěrhrad
in the diocese of Prague, Bohemia

A second group was detached from the main community between Passau and Linz at the end of May 1798. It was led by Mother Sainte-Marie Bigaux into Bohemia, where they remained from the end of May to the middle of October 1798. They left to go to Lvov-Lemberg (Austrian Poland), where they stayed from December 1798 until July 1799.

Visitation Convent, Vienna
Vienna, Austria

The rest of the mother community, under Mother Sainte-Marie Laignier, went down the Danube as far as Vienna, and found refuge in the Visitation convent there at the beginning of June 1798. On 27 July, fifteen sisters with Mother Sainte-Marie Laignier at their head, set out for Orsha in White Russia. The remaining group, led by Mother M.-Michel Ducourand, left Vienna to go to Poland on 19 November 1798.

Monastery of the Très-Saint-Coeur-de-Marie, Orsha
White Russia, in the diocese of Mohilev

The group which left Vienna on 27 July arrived at Orsha on 19 September 1798. They stayed there until April 1800. On 29 October there were nine professions there.

The Castle of Berezovka near
Brest-Litovsk (Russian Poland), in the diocese of Vilna

The two groups came here from 1) Dürnast, under Mother Augustin de Chabannes, and 2) Vienna-Cracow, under Mother M.-Michel Ducourand. They were reunited in June 1799 at the Brigittine convent at Brest. There they were joined by the group from Buštěhrad which had spent the winter in Lvov. The three groups then formed a single community under the direction of Mother Augustin de Chabannes. In October 1799 they were transferred to the castle of Berezovka.

In April 1800, the two communities of Berezovka and Orsha had to leave Russia in haste. They set out again for the West, first by land and then by river. They were reunited in June 1800 at the house of the

Brigittines in Danzig

The community, once more united, was led by Mother Augustin de Chabannes, whose group had been the first to arrive at Danzig. On 26 July 1800, most of the community, under the same leadership, embarked on the Baltic for Lübeck.

Four sisters who were too ill for the sea voyage left with Mother Edmond-Paul de Barth and Dom Augustin in mail coaches, and were received by the benedictine sisters of Winnenberg.

Hamm
(August 1800-April 1801)

The sisters who disembarked at Lübeck went to Hamburg to

the suburb of Hamm. The superior was then Mother Marie de la Résurrection de Montron.

THE SECOND PERIOD

The Double Foundation

A first group of four nuns left on 28 October 1800 to join four sick sisters who had arrived at Winnenberg from Danzig under the leadership of Mother Edmond-Paul de Barth. There they received two postulants and arrived at Darfeld on 28 December 1800. These ten nuns founded the

Monastery Notre-Dame-de-la-Miséricorde
Darfeld-Rosenthal, diocese of Münster (Westphalia)

The departure of the second group took place in March 1801, led by Mother Augustin de Chabannes. Four sisters embarked for England. They stayed at Hammersmith, near London until January 1802, then at Burton House, near Christchurch, until October 1802, the date on which they took possession of the

Monastery of the Holy Cross
Stapehill, Dorset, Vicariate Apostolic of Plymouth

After these two departures, the mother community now counted only twenty-two members. They then set out for Paderborn, having at their head Mother Sainte-Marie Laignier. The monastery took the name of

Monastery of Saint-Coeur-de-Marie
diocese of Paderborn (near the Cathedral)

In October 1802, five sisters of this community, arriving from Darfeld with Mother Marie du Saint-Esprit Allard at their head, came back to Switzerland to

Villarvolard

near La Valsainte. On 6 June 1803, they were joined by the rest of the community, who came from Paderborn after the death of Mother Saint-Marie Laignier. In August 1804 another transfer took place, to the château de La Grande Riedera, then to La Petite Riedera, which became the

Monastery de la Sainte-Trinité
Canton of Fribourg (Switzerland) diocese of Fribourg

The community then counted twenty-eight sisters.

In 1808 the monastery of Grosbois-Camoldolese joined the Reform of La Valsainte and was transferred to Valenton, under the name

Notre-Dame-du-Sacré-Coeur

The community then counted eighteen sisters.

In 1808, the Reform of La Valsainte possessed four monasteries of nuns:

1. Notre-Dame-de-la-Sainte-Trinité at La Riedera (Switzerland);
2. Notre-Dame-de-la-Miséricorde at Darfeld (Westphalia);
3. Our Lady of the Holy Cross at Stapehill (England);

4. Notre-Dame-du-Sacré-Coeur at Valenton (France, Seine-et-Oise).

THE THIRD PERIOD

The Separations 1811–1812

During the upheavals caused by Napoleon, the monastery of Notre-Dame-de-la-Miséricorde (Darfeld, Westphalia) underwent a temporary dispersion of its members; but they were soon able to come back again together in groups.

A) The German and Dutch–speaking sisters gathered at Cologne (1812–1814).

B) The belgian and french sisters gathered at the château of Bursut, near Liége, and stayed there from 1812 to 1816.

C) The sisters of Notre-Dame-de-la-Sainte-Trinité at La Riedera were not dispersed, but remained through the kindness of the Sénat de Fribourg.

D) The sisters of Notre-Dame-du-Sacré-Coeur at Valenton, after a dispersion in Paris, gradually gathered together at Tréguier (Côtes-du-Nord), under the leadership of Mother de Chateaubriand, their superior.

1814–1816

The fall of Napoleon allowed the communities founded during the emigration to return to France.

1. On 28 May 1814, the community at Cologne came back to Darfeld. On 25 September 1825, they were transferred to Oelenberg, in the diocese of Mulhouse (Haut-Rhin), and became an abbey in 1833. In August 1895 they were once again transferred, this time to:

Notre-Dame-d'Altbronn
Ergersheim, by Molsheim (Bas-Rhin)
diocese of Strasbourg

2. On 6 June 1816, the community of Borsut arrived at Laval. After a six month stay at La Doyère, on 18 November 1816, they took possesion of the

Monastery of Sainte-Catherine
diocèse of Mans (at that time)

This monastery was canonically erected on 21 July 1818 and became an abbey in 1826. On 26 April 1859, the community was transferred to La Coudre (a suburb of Laval) under the name

Abbaye Notre-Dame-de-l'Immaculée-Conception
diocese of Laval (a new diocese erected in 1855)

3. The community of Notre-Dame-du-Sacré-Coeur-de-la-Trappe, which had never left France, but had been compelled to take refuge at Tréguier (Brittany), took the road again for the Ile-de-France in May 1815. On the way, they were offered a home in Normandy in a former abbey of the Premonstratensians.

Notre-Dame-du-Sacré-Coeur-de-la-Trappe
Abbey of Mondaye, diocese of Bayeux

The frail community was dispersed to other houses of the Order and were replaced by a group of ten nuns who had come from Sainte-Catherine at Laval in 1837. They stayed there until 1845 when the community was transferred to La Cour-Pétral, in the diocese of Chartres, and then in 1935 to

Notre-Dame-de-Clairfontaine
diocese of Namur

4. In February 1816, part of the community of Notre-Dame-de-la-Sainte-Trinité at La Riedera (Switzerland) was transferred to the

Monastery of l'Archange-Raphaël
Les Forges, Saint-Oeun-de-Sècherouvre (Orne)
diocese of Sées

On 7 August 1818, ten sisters were sent to the

Monastery of Notre-Dame-des-Gardes
diocese of Angers

They were joined by the rest of the community of Forges in October 1821.

5. At the end of September 1816, the sisters remaining at La Riedera were moved to

Notre-Dame-de-Toute-Consolation
Frenouville (Calvados), in the diocese of Bayeux

In May 1817, another transfer was made. The community settled at Lyon-Crois-Rousse, then in 1820 at

Notre-Dame-de-Toute-Consolation
Lyon-Vaise

In 1834–1837, they were obliged to transfer, then part of the community returned to Lyon, creating two communities.

Notre-Dame-de-Toute-Consolation
Lyon-Vaise

was transferred in 1904 to Canada as

Notre-Dame-de-l'Assomption
Rogersville (Acadie), in the diocese of Moncton

and

Notre-Dame-de-Bon-Secours
near Montélimar, in the diocese of Valence

6. The community of Our Lady of the Holy Cross

Holy Cross Abbey
Stapehill(Dorset)

remained in the same place after 1802, but in 1824 they underwent the great trial of being separated from the Reform of La Trappe through no choice of their own, at the request of the Vicar Apostolic of Plymouth. The community was reinstated into the Cistercian Order of the Strict Observance in 1915, and moved to Whitland, South Wales in 1990.

THE MEMBERS OF THESE COMMUNITIES

The following Table summarizes the number of persons who benefitted from their reception into the community of refugees called 'La Sainte-Volonté-de-Dieu', first at Sembrancher, then at the various places they stopped during their travels, and finally at the two foundations in Westphalia and England.

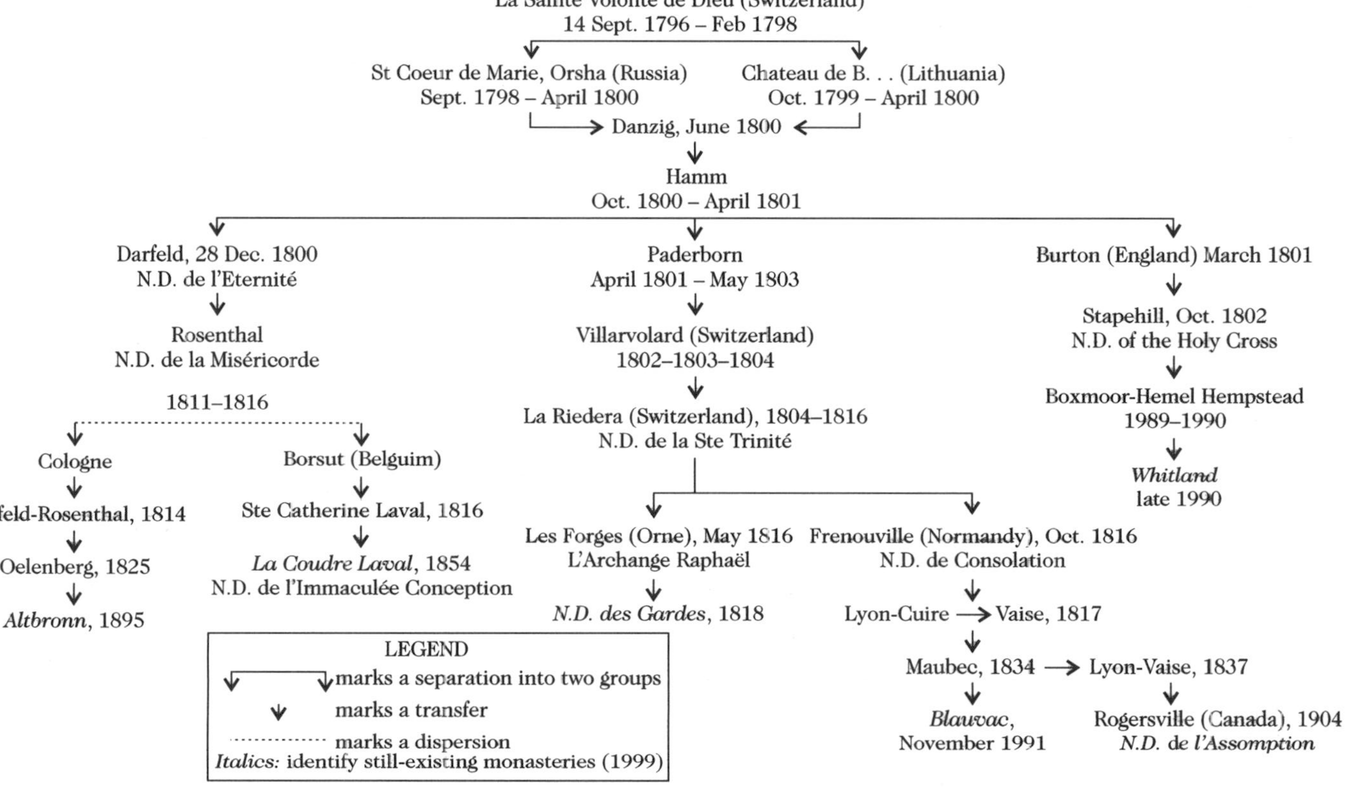

La Sainte Volonté de Dieu (Switzerland)
14 Sept. 1796 – Feb 1798
St Coeur de Marie, Orsha (Russia)
Sept. 1798 – April 1800
Chateau de B. . . (Lithuania)
Oct. 1799 – April 1800
Danzig, June 1800
Hamm
Oct. 1800 – April 1801
Darfeld, 28 Dec. 1800
N.D. de l'Eternité
Rosenthal
N.D. de la Miséricorde
1811–1816
Cologne
Darfeld-Rosenthal, 1814
Oelenberg, 1825
Altbronn, 1895
Borsut (Belguim)
Ste Catherine Laval, 1816
La Coudre Laval, 1854
N.D. de l'Immaculée Conception
Paderborn
April 1801 – May 1803
Villarvolard (Switzerland)
1802–1803–1804
La Riedera (Switzerland), 1804–1816
N.D. de la Ste Trinité
Les Forges (Orne), May 1816
L'Archange Raphaël
N.D. des Gardes, 1818
Frenouville (Normandy), Oct. 1816
N.D. de Consolation
Lyon-Cuire
Vaise, 1817
Maubec, 1834
Lyon-Vaise, 1837
Blauvac,
November 1991
Rogersville (Canada), 1904
N.D. de l'Assomption
Burton (England) March 1801
Stapehill, Oct. 1802
N.D. of the Holy Cross
Boxmoor-Hemel Hempstead
1989–1990
Whitland
late 1990
LEGEND
marks a separation into two groups
marks a transfer
marks a dispersion
Italics: identify still-existing monasteries (1999)

Table 11. Changes of personnel during the first twenty years

	Dates	*Admissions*	*Professions or deaths[1] in in the Order*	*or Departures*	*Destiny or Unknown*	*Deaths in these places*
Mother community Sembrancher	Sept. 1796 – Dec. 1797	63	31	31	1	2
↓ during travels	Feb. 1798 – Mar. 1801	36	14	21	1	14
↓ Paderborn	April 1801 – April 1803	25	11	14	0	7
↓ Villarvolard	Oct. 1802 – Aug. 1804	39	12	23	4	2
↓ La Riedera	Aug. 1804 – Oct. 1815	101	25	73	3	34
↙ Les Gardes ↘ Lyon-Vaise						
Total		264	93	162	9	59
First stable foundation						
↓ Darfeld	Oct.1800–1816	72	72[2]	?	?	49
↙ Altbronn ↘ Laval						
Second stable foundation ↓ Stapehill	April 1801–1816	46	29	9	8	7
The adopted community: Paris-Valenton-Mondaye	July 1798–1816	120	54	66		30
General total	1796–1816	502	248	237	17	145

[1] The first four columns represent the same people. The total of the last three columns equals the number of the first column. Though the column of the deaths are those of the period indicated.

[2] The records of Darfeld do not note the admissions and departures, but only the professions.

Table 11 shows approximately the number of persons, admissions, departures and deaths in the Order. I say 'approximately' because there are still some uncertainties in the Registers. This assessment can be considered accurate to within 1 or 2% over this period of twenty years, 1796–1816.

Of the forty-two nuns who set out along the roads of Europe, only four were still alive in 1816. Three of them were at La Riedera, and the fourth was in England at Stapehill.

— Mother Magdeleine Guyot, professed at Orsha, died at Lyon-Vaise in February 1825.
— Mother Marie du Saint-Esprit Allard, professed at Darfeld, died at Lyon on 1 January 1827.
— Mother Thaïs Bassignot, professed at Sembrancher, died at Gardes on 25 February 1836.
— Mother Augustin de Chabannes, professed at Sembrancher, died at Stapehill on 13 June 1844.

Twenty seven others died, either during their travels or in the various houses where they lived in community. Thus of the forty-two sisters thirty-one who left Sembrancher became Cistercian Trappistines; that is 73%, almost three quarters.

If we take all together the number of persons professed in the Order during the course of these twenty years, we note that at least eighty-two among them came from various other religious orders. It was this training that had prepared them to make the total gift of themselves until the end.

This diversity in itself could have been an obstacle to unity within the community, but they brought a wealth of humanity and spirituality which the Father Abbot well knew how to use for the common good. It was from among these religious that he chose the first superiors for the various groups. The following pages give a list of these Religious Orders and their members.

RELIGIOUS ORDERS WHOSE MEMBERS
BECAME TRAPPISTINES DURING THE PERIOD UNDER STUDY

ANNONCIADES
Mother House

Sister Jean-Baptiste (Marie Chassaignon), of Lyon
Sister Marie de la Résurrection (M. Claude de Montron), of Sens.
Sister Marie-Thérèse de la Miséricorde (Emilie Lamb), of Sens.
Sister Gabrielle (M. Gabrielle Lucottée), of Sens.
Sister Victoire (M. Victoire Chuffaut), of Lille.
+ plus three who left

Darfeld

Sister Marie du Sacré-Coeur (Anne-Thérèse Villart).
Sister Saint-Michel (Louise-Ursule Vermeire).

BENEDICTINES
Mother House

Mother Sainte-Marie I (Marie Laignier), Saint Sacrament of Charenton.
Mother Saint-Marie II (Marie-Françoise Bigaux), Saint Sacrament of Dreux.
Sister Bernard (Henriette-Françoise de Lestrange), Saint-Pierreles-Nonnains of Lyon.
Sister Marie-Toussaint (Anne Deschamps), of Beaumont-lès-Tours.
+ plus five who left

Stapehill

Sister Brigitte (Brigitte Le Brun), Abbey of Forest-en-Brabant.

Paris-Valenton-Mondaye

Sister Saint-Louis de Gonzague (Magdeleine-Julie Didier).

Sister Véronique (Marie-Jeanne Véronique de la Vierre). Sainte-Benoîte-d'Origny (Picardy).

Sister Philippine (Marie-Philippine Laurent), La Paix-Notre-Dame at Namur.

Sister Placide (Céleste-Marie-Anne-Morin), Abbey of Bellefond at Rouen.

Sister M.des Séraphins (M.-Anne de Chateaubriand), community Notre-Dame-de-la-Victoire, Saint-Malo.

Sister Humbeline (Catherine Gaudeau), Lay sister of Beaumontlès-Tours.

Sister Joséphine (Françoise-Michèle-Joséphine Bessirard La Touche), a nun of

Nazareth, Nogent-le-Rotrou.

Sister Geneviève (Françoise Mathivon), Abbey of Marsan (Puy-deDôme).

Sister Cécile de Saint-Augustin (Germaine Verpy).

Sister Marie-Bernard (Marie-Louise Le Caux).

Sister Saint-Michel (Jeanne-Marguerite Mercier), Abbey of Saintes.

BERNARDINES

Mother House

Sister Marie-Bernard (Marie-Barbe Guérin) of Colombey.

Sister Agnès (Marie-Anne Paelink).

CARMELITES

Mother House

Sister Marie-Joséphine (Marie-Anne-Pierrette de Montron), Carmel of Dole.

Sister Séraphique (Cornélie Van den Kerkhove), Carmel of Valenciennes.

Sister Placide (Sophie Parache), Carmel of Amiens.

+ four who left

Stapehill

Sister Augustin (Marie-Anne Hill), from Antwerp.

CAPUCHINES

Mother House

Sister Marie-Michel (Marie-Thérèse Ducourand), from Armentières.

Sister Marie du Saint Esprit (Dorothée Allard), monastery of Paris.

+ one who left

Darfeld

Sister Hélène (Cecile Thérèse Van den Broeck).

Sister Marie-Antoinette (Marie-Thérèse Daume).

CANNONESSES OF SAINT AUGUSTINE

Three sisters who entered the Mother House all left.

Stapehill:

Sister Magdeleine (Anne-Elisabeth Quatrelivres), from the convent in Cambrai.

CARTHUSIAN

Mother House:

Sister Pierre (Françoise-Claudine Rouph), Charterhouse of Savoy.

CISTERCIANS

Mother House:

Mother Augustin (Marie-Rosalie de Vergèzes de Chabannes), Saint Antoine- des-Champs-lès-Paris.

Mother Edmond-Paul (Marie-Antoinette de Barth), Koenigsbruck (Pont-du-Rois).

Sister Marie-Stanislaus (Marie-Jeanne-Thérèse Michel), of Sainte Catherine at Avignon.

Sister Euphrosine (Charlotte-Adélaïde-Joseph Mairesse), Abbey des Prés, Douai.

Sister Lutgarde, (Marie-Madeleine Zurkinden), of Feldbach (Switzerland).

Darfeld:

Sister Marie-Anne du Sacré-Coeur (Marie-Anne Boele).
Sister Robert (Agathe Poulman).
Sister Ida (Roseine Janssens).
Sister Catherine (Marie-Josèphe d'Erbaix).
Sister Marie-Etienne (Lucie Verkanteren).
Sister Albérique (Marie-Rose Cousine).
Sister Marie-Monique (Pétronille Van Spuyenbroeck).
Sister Agnès-Edmond (M. Agnès-Séraphine Thuilliez).
Sister Marie-Joseph (Marie-Joseph Casters).
Sister Philippine (Jeanne-Henriette Stas).

Paris-Valenton-Mondaye:

Sister Mélanie (Marie-Louise Sevestre), Abbey of Bival near to Neuchâtel-en-Bray.
Sister Benoît (Anne-Elisabeth Richeux), Abbey of Bival near to Neuchâtel-en-Bray.
Sister Marie-Angélique (Marie Le Rousseau de Saint-Dridan), Abbey of La Joie d'Hennebont.
+ plus two who left

Stapehill:

Sister Thérèse de Jésus Maria, Cistercian Collettine of Spain.

POOR CLARES:
Mother House:

Sister Marie-Rose (Marie-Thérèse Sergent), of Besançon.
Sister Scholastique (Marie-Anne-Claude Baron), of Polenis.
Sister Donat (Hélène Donis), of Auxonne in Burgundy.
Sister Marie-Madeleine (M. Madeleine Zacharie), of Auxonne in Burgundy.
Sister Pauline (Marie-Madeleine de Brye), of Lyon.
+ plus six who left

Darfeld:

Sister Angélique (Marie-Joseph Fruyt).
Sister Marie-Joseph (Bernardine-Josèphe Briesschiel).

DOMINICAN:

Sister M.-Augustin (Victoire-Josèphe Desjardins), of Arras.

FEUILLANTINE:
Mother House:

Sister Marie-Françoise Sempé, monastery of Toulouse.

FONTEVRISTE:
Paris-Valenton-Mondaye

one who left

FRANCISCANS:
Mother House:

Sister du Saint-Sacrement (Marie-Louise de Lassus).

Darfeld:

Sister Marie-Bernard (Isabelle-Claire Van Hems).

Paris-Valenton-Mondaye:

Marie-Françoise Thibault.

HOSPITALERS:
Mother House:

Sister Félicité (Anne Domino), Saint-Pierre-des-Corps.

Darfeld:

Sister Jean-Baptiste (Marie-Rose Piton).
Sister Humbeline (Catherine Barier), Sister of Charity, Paris.

Stapehill:

Sister Umbeline (Séraphine-Joseph Le Febvre), hosp. of Saint Augustin of Cambrai.
Sister Séraphique (Marie-Louise Huet), hosp. of Saint-Nicholas de Mons.

Paris-Valenton-Mondaye:

Daughters of Charity.
three who left

PROVIDENCE OF PORTIEUX:
Mother House:

Sister Scholastique (Françoise-Rose Methains), second Superior General, become a lay sister by her own request.

URSULINES:
Mother House:

Sister Albéric (Catherine-Cécile de Saint-Riquier), of Amiens.
Sister Thaïs de Jésus (Claudine Durdilly), tourière of Saint Symphorien-le-Château.
+ one who left

Darfeld:

Sister Colette (Cornélie Van Tièle).

VISITATION SISTERS:
Darfeld:

Sister Bernard (Marie-Jeanne Mollet).

Stapehill:

Sister Marie-Constance (Marie Clausie).

Paris-Valenton-Mondaye:

Sister Saint-Benoît (Elisabeth-Vincentine Gauchat), house of Langres.
Sister Marie-Cécile (Cécile Tarentière), of Semur.

Congregation unknown: Sister Julie-Joséphine (Julie Favot), entered during the travels, died at Stapehill.

THE LEADERSHIP

From the very first foundations, the superiors of the groups, whether monks or nuns, were appointed by the Father Abbot of La Valsainte, the Father Immediate of each group. As the years went by and the groups became established, the monks wanted full autonomy for their monasteries, as was the tradition of the Order. Dom Augustin still in fact held a universal authority, which he expressed in the emphasis of his signature: 'Abbot of the monks and of the nuns of La Trappe'. We had seen how this situation provoked the regrettable rupture at Darfeld.

With the nuns, the same uneasiness made itself felt; and this for at least two reasons: first, since they were enclosed contemplatives (even when travelling); the nuns had practically no opportunity for taking any personal initiative; in addition the Father Abbot chose, usually very well, the prioresses of the groups or established monasteries. They were generally remarkable women in various ways: in particular, the first superior, Mother Sainte-Marie Laignier, and the prioresses of the first two foundations, Mother Edmond-Paul de Barth at Darfeld and Mother Augustin de Chabannes at Stapehill. All three, before the Revolution, had lived under the Rule of Saint Benedict as Benedictines or Cistercians.

They had religious with real ability to assist them, like Mother Sainte-Marie Bigaux, Mother Stanislaus Michel, Mother Thaïs Bassignot and Mother Marie du Saint-Esprit

Allard, all of whom were part of the first community at La Sainte-Volonté-de-Dieu.

The second generation followed in their footsteps with the same spirit. Mother Elisabeth Piette, the foundress of Sainte-Catherine at Laval, was appointed by Dom Eugene de Laprade; she had been sub-prioress at Darfeld, and she knew how to give her community, very rapidly, a canonically stable foundation that soon led to her being elected Abbess for life. Mother Thérèse Malatesta, the foundress of Notre-Dame-des-Gardes, chosen by Dom Augustine, was a particularly gifted woman. An Irish priest, Father Coyne, wrote to Madame de Chabannes in September 1824, when he was travelling in France visiting cistercian monasteries. In this letter he called the abbess of Gardes 'very discerning, she is the most amiable woman that I have ever met . . . I think that if the Reverend Father had allowed her to use her own resourcefulness, she would have the best house in the Order'.[1]

THE MAN OF GOD

Augustin de Lestrange was and in the eyes of his sons and daughters of this period always remained an extraordinary man. Of his excellent intentions no one had any doubt. He was the providential man, the man of God. To conclude this chapter we call on two witnesses, one a monk and the other a nun; each sums up in his/her own way, the role, both human and spiritual, of this courageous founder:

The monk, Father François de Paule Dargnies, wrote:

> I do not believe that there has ever been a general in the army who could have employed more skill and industry, or left fewer stones unturned in leading and providing

[1] Letter XIII of Father Coyne to Mother de Chabannes, dated 24 September 1824, p. 45 of the collection.

> for his troops, than the Reverend Father Abbot for the maintenance of his community, composed of more than two hundred persons, who for nearly three years had no other resources than his industry to appeal for public aid . . . It is true and only fair that one must pay tribute to Dom Augustin. In all that he has done and undertaken he had no other principles than the desire to procure the glory of God. He made mistakes in the ways he took to achieve his purposes, but his aims have always been pure and disinterested.[2]

The nun, Mother Marie-Stanislaus Michel, at the end of her manuscript, enjoined her sisters to be encourged by the example of the Father Abbot:

> May this narrative, my dear Sisters, which I have written for you, make you think carefully. How powerful are faith and confidence in God and how they can work great things for those who possess them! If our Reverend Father had listened only to human wisdom and prudence, he would certainly have abandoned his projects, seeing that after all the difficulties he had to undergo to transfer the Order of La Trappe to Switzerland, he was obliged by the violence of the persecution to abandon La Valsainte and all the houses he had established in that country. He might have thought the task impossible, that he had done enough to prove his zeal. But divine love never says 'Enough', and it was this love for the glory of God which made him overcome so many obstacles, and during these unhappy times undertake the work of arranging for such a large number of monks and nuns to travel through foreign countries. Like another Abraham, faith was his torch, and he followed its light, believing against all hope; and like that Father of all who believe, he has been rewarded by a great posterity, because already there are six houses of monks and three of nuns.[3]

[2] *Mémoires en forme de lettres*, letter 5.

[3] Relation, *Cîteaux,* fasc. 3–4, 1984, p. 213.

Are we not entitled to think that the end of this text is 'prophetic'? The Spirit of God had been at work in what seemed to be chaos, guiding the first communities towards a stable and fruitful life. The epilogue will corroborate this. Should not the judgement of history rest on this?

EPILOGUE

THE EXPANSION OF MONASTERIES OF NUNS DURING THE NINETEENTH AND TWENTIETH CENTURIES

DURING THE YEARS which followed the relative stabilization of the six communities of nuns which had come into existence during the revolutionary persecutions, the Cistercian Trappist Order gradually made attempts to provide itself with some organisation. This was not without its difficulties.

It is not my intention to retrace here a detailed history of this expansion, which proceeded very slowly at first and then spread rapidly only during the second half of the twentieth century. I would like to point out briefly that Trappistine nuns have not only continued to survive, but have taken root in five continents, rediscovering their character as cistercian nuns without losing altogether the marks of strict observance inherited from the reforms of the seventeenth and eighteenth centuries.

Among the difficulties that had to be overcome from the very beginning, three in particular seem to me to have hindered the harmonious development of the Cistercian Order in its renewal. There was a poverty which bordered on destitution; there were Regulations whose austerity surpassed human strength; and there was a lack of juridical status recognized by the Church, together with General Chapters too long deferred.

Arising from the Revolution and the Empire, the poverty of various restored religious groups was widespread. The vast patrimony accumulated under the *Ancien Régime* had disappeared, and often the monks and nuns installed themselves in buildings that were in ruins. To re-build and provide for daily necessities, they had to have recourse to rich benefactors if and when they could be found. They had to receive young children to educate for a consideration. They had to receive state pensions, and very often they had to go begging. All this hardly favored an authentic monastic life for monks. In economic matters the nuns depended too closely on the monks, and owing to the strict enclosure of the time they could not exercise any initiatives or have any freedom in these matters.

What is more, the nuns had expressed a desire to follow in their entirety the Regulations of La Valsainte. The more austere they were, it seemed to them the better they could *conserver leur saint état*. This nurtured a spirituality of 'victimhood' in reparation for the 'sacrileges' of the Revolution. The result was a very high mortality rate which depleted the numbers of the community with a speed equalled only by the influx of new arrivals. There was an undeniable thirst for religious life lived in common, under various forms, something we know also from the great number of religious congregations founded or restored from the beginning of the nineteenth century. But there were also many young women, and some not so young, who had been hindered from marrying during twenty-five years of war or who had been victims of the Revolution. And on the other hand there was little anxiety about dying young.

The major difficulty for the Order in these years of new beginnings was the juridical confusion in which it found itself. The troubled events had given the abbot of La Valsainte a powerful reason for centering all authority in his own person—an authority he exercised devotedly, but also high-handedly—without any higher authority to whom to refer or have recourse. As early as 1808 the consequence of this was a rupture. In 1814, the breach was extended when the Regulations of de Rancé were once again accepted by one of the parties. This marked the beginning of what became known as 'the war of observances'. (*trans note*: Actually 'the war of observances' began in the seventeenth century). Stress was placed on one or another point of observance in which the two sets of Regulations differed, with the result that these means of fostering monastic life (observances) were turned into ends—with everyone forgetting that the true end is growth in charity. This deviation, which lasted far too long in spite of the efforts of the Holy See to reestablish the lost unity, had unfortunate effects on the vitality of the Trappist branch of the Cistercian Order, and especially on the feminine branch. Dom Vincent Hermans has thus summed up the events of this period and the different juridical situations which followed from it:

> It was not until 1834 that the Trappists again recovered their juridical union, thanks to a Decree of the Holy See of 3 October which re-united the two Observaces in France into a single Congregation called *Congregatio monachorum cisterciensium B. M. de Trappa* . . . . Alongside this Congregation another [was] erected in Belgium, with Westmalle at its head, juridically modelled on its elder in France . . . .
>
> The French Congregation which came into being in 1834 saw itself divided into two again by the Decree of 25 February 1847. Then there was 'The Congregation of the recent Reforms of La Trappe' with its motherhouse at La Trappe, and that of the 'The Old Reform' [of Rancé] generally called that of 'Sept-Fons'. This division was maintained until 1892 . . . .
>
> In that year of 1892, under the impetus of Léo XIII, the reunion of the 'Cistercians of the Strict Observance', with the election of an Abbot General took place'.[1]

The nuns, though they were not mentioned had simply followed their respective Fathers Immediate in the break. In 1816, four monasteries of nuns belonged to La Valsainte: Les

[1] *Actes des chapitres généraux des congrégations trappistes au XIXe siècle*, Introduction, p. [2].

Forges, Lyon-Vaise, Stapehill and Mondaye; two belonged to Darfeld, Darfeld-Rosenthal and Sainte-Catherine of Laval.

These difficulties notwithstanding, the monasteries of monks expanded during the nineteenth century. In 1816, there were five monasteries in France, one in Belgium, one in Germany and one in England. By 1900 they had increased to forty-five. By 1988 to ninety.

The nuns followed their brothers from afar, but they made seven new foundations and accepted one filiation during the nineteenth century. In the first half of the following century with its two long world wars, they made nine foundations and had four affiliations. In the second half of the century twenty-three foundations and eight affiliations.

The following pages contain a chronological Table of this expansion of the feminine branch of the Order. It seemed right also to add the help in personnel given to some foundations by other communities than the founding community; and also to note the foundations which existed only for a short time. Some communities no longer live at the place of their foundation. These transfers have been noted immediately afterwards, to make it easier to find their name now, which is better known, even if the transfer took place long years after the foundation.

For the affiliated communities, the date and the place of their foundation follows the indication of their affiliation.[2]

[2] Monastery names set in small capitals exist still today. Those set in bold are communities which have have transferred or are not autonomous. Those in italic no longer exist. Founding abbeys are identified by an asterisk.

FOUNDATIONS AND AFFILIATIONS DURING THE FIRST PERIOD OF THE UNION

1835–1847

1837. **Sainte-Catherine de Laval** sent a group of ten nuns to **Mondaye** to rehabilitate the disabled community of N.-D.-de-La Trappe (cf. the General Chapter of La Trappe, 1836).[3]

1841. **Sainte-Catherine de Laval** founded N. D. de Saint-Joseph at UBEXY*, in the diocese of Saint-Dié (Vosges), February-May 1841.[4]

THE YEARS OF SEPARATION, 1847 - 1892

A) *Congregation of the recent Reform of La Trappe*:

1852. N.-D.-de-Bon-Secours, Maubec* on 7 April made a foundation at **Blagnac**, in the diocese of Toulouse, approved by the General Chapter in the following September.[5] In 1939, the community of Blagnac was transferred to SAINTE-MARIE-DU-RIVET-AUROS, in the diocese of Bordeaux.

1852. **Lyon-Vaise** proposed a foundation in the diocese of Perpignan which was approved provisionally in September 1852 and definitively the following year. This

[3] *Actes des chapitres généraux* (see n. 1), p. [29].

[4] Ibid., pp. [39] and [61].

[5] Ibid., p. [259].

house, **Espira de l'Agly**,[6] transferred in 1904 to **Herrera** (Spain), and returned to France in 1921 to N.-D.-DE-BONNE-ESPERANCE, ECHOURGNAC, in the diocese of Périgueux.

1875. MAUBEC founded N. D.-DE-BONNEVAL* in the diocese of Rodez. The foundation was approved by the General Chapter of 1876.[7]

1876. **Lyon-Vaise** was invited to send some religious as part of a skeleton foundation made in 1875 and called **N. D de-Cîteaux at San Vito**, in the diocese of Turin, Italy (General Chapter of 1876). This impromptu foundation was in great peril.[8] It was transferred in 1898 to **Grottaferrata**, in the diocese of Frascati, then in 1957 to VITORCHIANO*, in the diocese of Viterbo.

1877. The Abbot President and the Abbot of Sainte-Marie-du-Désert allowed affiliation with the Congregation of La Trappe to a community of Cistercians of the Abbey of **Gomerfontaine** (Oise) before the Revolution, at the time reunited under diocesan authority at **Saint-Paul-aux-Bois** in the diocese of Soissons (Aisne) under the name 'Bernardines'. They sent twelve religious from Blagnac to '*rétablir les pratiques* . . .' in this monastery (General Chapter of 1878).[9] In 1884 another superior was sent from N. D. DES GARDES. The community was transferred in 1904 to **Fourbechies** in the diocese of Tournai, then in 1921 to N. D. DE-LA-PAIX, CHIMAY*, in the same diocese.

1880. MAUBEC founded *N. D. de-la-Nouvelle*, in the diocese of Nimes (Gard), approved by the General Chapter in 1879 'on condition that the conditions on which

[6] Ibid., pp. [259] and [264].
[7] Ibid., p. [423].
[8] Ibid., pp. [417] and [421].
[9] Ibid., p. [437].

it is founded are maintained'.[10] This did not happen and the house was suppressed in 1886.

B) *Congregation of Sept-Fons*:

1849. **Sainte-Catherine of Laval** attempted to make a foundation in the diocese of Vannes, *N. D. de-Nazareth*; it was refused by the General Chapter of La Trappe in 1849 and 1850, then by the General Chapter of Sept-Fons in 1850.[11]

1875. N. D. DE-L'IMMACULEE-CONCEPTION (Laval) founded **N. D.du Sacré-Coeur** at Mâcon (Saône-et-Loire), diocese of Autun. In 1908, the community was transferred to **Tremembe** (Brazil), then in 1929 to **Feluy** in Belgium, and finally on 15 June 1932 to N. D. DU-SACRE-COEUR, Chambarand, in the diocese of Grenoble, where a group of nuns from Maubec had preceded them.

ORDER OF CISTERCIANS OF THE STRICT OBSERVANCE, 1892

1893. LAVAL founded N. D. DE-BELVAL in the diocese of Arras, France.

1898. UBEXY (N. D. de-Saint-Joseph) founded N. D. DES-ANGES at Tenshien* in the diocese of Sapporo, Japan.

1902. BONNEVAL founded N. D. DU BON-CONSEIL at Saint-Romuald, in the archdiocese of Québec, Canada.

1902. LAVAL sent nuns to help Ubexy with the foundation of N. D. des-Anges. They sent more in 1908 and 1920.

1903. LAVAL founded an annex-refuge at *Blitteswijck*, Holland. The nuns returned to Laval in 1920.

1903. La Cour-Pétral founded an annex-refuge at Boxtel, in the diocese of Bois-le-Duc, Holland, closed in 1920.

[10] Ibid., p. [449].

[11] Ibid., pp. [76–77] and [245–255].

1905. Affiliation of the Abbey of Cistercians of LA FILLE-DIEU in the diocese of Lausanne, Switzerland, founded in 1268 and still in the same place.

1906. LES GARDES founded an annex-refuge at *Marnhull*, England. The nuns returned to Gardes in 1920.

1915. HOLY CROSS ABBEY, STAPEHILL* was again affiliated to the Cistercian Order S.O. from which it had been separated against its will in 1824.

1920. LAVAL founded **N. D. de Bonne-Garde** at Sainte-Anne of Auray (diocese of Vannes), transferred in 1953 to Campénéac (same diocese) under the name LA JOIE NOTRE-DAME.

1921. Affiliation of the **Bernardines de N. D. de-Consolation**, in the diocese of Besançon, issued from the **Abbey of Port-Royal of Paris**, dispersed in 1792, and transferred in 1925 to the Abbey of LA GRACE-DIEU, in the same diocese.

1922. Affiliation of the Cistercians of N. D. DE-SOLEILMONT*, near Charleroi (Belgium), in the diocese of Tournai, founded in 1237 and dispersed during the Revolution. In January 1797, they came back to Soleilmont and opened a boarding school; this was closed in 1914. The General Chapter of June 1919 voted for their adoption.

1923. Affiliation of the Bernardines of SANTA MARIA DE SAN JOSE ALLOZ*, founded in 1883 in the diocese of Pamplona, Spain.

1929. LAVAL founded N. D. D'IGNY* in the archdiocese of Reims, France.

1932. STAPEHILL founded SAINT MARY'S ABBEY, GLENCAIRN* in the diocese of Waterford, Ireland.

1935. TENSHIEN founded SEIBOEN, N. D. DE-LOURDES*, in the archdiocese of Osaka, Japan.

1935. CHIMAY founded KONINGSOORD-BERKEL* in the diocese of Bois-le-Duc, Holland.

1949. GLENCAIRN founded MOUNT SAINT MARY'S ABBEY, at

WRENTHAM* in the archdiocese of Boston, United States.

1950. SOLEILMONT founded O. L. VAN NAZARETH, BRECHT*, in the diocese of Antwerp, Belgium.

1951. Affiliation of the Bernardines of:
— N. D. du Saint-Esprit, of OLMEDO transferred in 1956 to **Arconada,** transferred in 1977 to N. S. DE VICO, in the diocese of Cartagena, Spain;
— monastery of SANTA MARIE LA REAL, AREVALO, in the diocese of Avila, Spain.

1953. BERKEL founded ABTEI MARIA FRIEDEN, in the diocese of Aachen, Germany.

1953. TENSHIEN founded N. D. DE-LA-SAINTE-FAMILLE at IMARI, in the diocese of Fukoka, Japan.

1954. Affiliation of the Bernardines of:
— S. ANNA DE AVILA, in the diocese of Avila, Spain;
— S. MARIA DE GRATIA DEI, BENAGUACIL, in the diocese of Valencia, Spain.

1954. SEIBOEN founded N. D. DE-NASU, in the diocese of Uravi, Japan.

1955. IGNY founded N. D. DE-LA-CLARTÉ-DIEU, in the diocese of Bukavu, Zaire.

1957. Affiliation of the Bernardines of:
— N. D. DE-L'ASSOMPTION, CARRIZO, in the diocese of Leon, Spain;
— N. D. DE-LA-CHARITÉ, TULEBRAS, in the diocese of Pamplona, Spain.

1960. LES GARDES founded L'ETOILE-NOTRE-DAME, in the diocese of Parakou, Benin.

1962. NAZARETH founded REDWOODS MONASTERY, in the diocese of Santa Rosa, California, United States.

1964. BERKEL founded O. L. OF PRAISE, BUTENDE, in the diocese of Masaka, Uganda.

1964. WRENTHAM founded O. L. OF MISSISSIPPI, in the diocese of Dubuque, Iowa, United States.

1968. VITORCHIANO founded N. D. DE VALSERENA, in the diocese of Volterra, Italy.

1968. LAVAL founded **N. D. de Grandselve**, in the diocese of M'Balmayo, Cameroon.
1970. LES GARDES founded LA PAIX-DIEU, CABANOULE, in the diocese of Nîmes, France.
1970. NAZARETH founded O. L. VR VAN KLAARLAND, in the diocese of Hasselt, Belgium.
1971. UBEXY founded LA MADRE DE DIOS, 'El Encuentro', in the diocese of Moreli, Mexico.
1972. WRENTHAM founded SANTA RITA ABBEY in the diocese of Tucson, Arizona, United States.
1973. VITORCHIANO founded LA MADRE DE CRISTO, HINOJO, in the diocese of Azul, Argentina.
1976. Affiliation of the Bernardine nuns of N. D. DE-BRIALMONT, in the diocese of Liège, founded in 1932.
1976. ALLOZ founded Nuestra Señora de LA PAZ, La Palma, in the diocese of Cartagena, Spain.
1981. VITORCHIANO founded Nuestra Señora de Quilvo, in the diocese of Talca, Chile.
1981. SEIBOEN founded **Miyako Shudoin**, in the diocese of Naha, Japan.
1982. GLENCAIRN founded **Saint Justina's Monastery**, in the diocese of Abakaliki, Anambra, Nigeria.
1982. VALSERENA took charge of the Angolan foundation of **Na Sa de Nasoma Y'Ombebwa**, in the diocese of Huambo, Angola begun 1978.
1985. VITORCHIANO took charge of **Humocaro** in Venezuela, founded in 1978.
1987. VITORCHIANO founded **Our Lady of Gedono** in the diocese of Semarang, Java, Indonesia.
1987. WRENTHAM founded **Our Lady of the Angels** at Crozet, Virginia, United States.
1987. TENSHEIN founded **Our Lady of Sujong** in the diocese of Masan, South Korea.
1989. ALLOZ founded **Armenteira** in the archdiocese of Compostella, Spain.
1991. L'ÉTOILE NOTRE-DAME founded **N. D. de Mvanda** in the diocese of Kikwit, Congo.

1992. TULEBRAS founded **Nuestra Señora d'Esperanza**, in Esmeraldas, Ecuador.
1993. LOURDES founded **Our Lady of the Rosary**, Japan.
1993. VITORCHIANO founded **Matútum** in the diocese of Marbel, Philippines.
1995. SOLEILMONT founded the **Ananda Matha Ashram** at Makkiyad in the diocese of Calcutta, India.
1996. CAMPÉNÉAC founded **Monastera Masina Maria** in the archdiocese of Fianarantsoa, Madagascar.

With René Habachi, we may draw the conclusion that 'Everything begins in the present, even the past . . . History is there to remind us . . . but history poses questions which each of us needs to answer.'[12]

[12] R. Habachi, *Commencement de la créature* (Paris 1965) pp. 149–150.

BIBLIOGRAPHY

Bibliography

1. MANUSCRIPT SOURCES

A) *Private Archives*

1. The Cistercian Abbeys of Aiguebelle, Altbronn, Bellefontaine, La Coudre-Laval, Les Gardes, Rogersville (Canada), Chambarand (Archives of Lyon-Vaise), Maubec, Melleray, Mondaye (archives preserved at Maubec), Oelenberg, Port-du-Salut, Sainte-Marie-du-Rivet, Stapehill, La Trappe.
2. The Monasteries of Saint-Martin of Mondaye (Premonstratensians), Göttweig (Benedictines).

B) *Public Archives*

— Avignon. Archives départmentales of Vaucluse.
— Fribourg. Archives cantonales and Archives diocésaines.
— Mende. Archives départmentales of the Lozère.
— Munich. Archdiocesan Archives.
— Münster. Archiepiscopal Archives.
— Paderborn. Archiepiscopal Archives.
— Paris. Archives nationales.
— Rome. Vatican Archives.
— Vienna (Austria). Österreichisches Staatsarchiv.
— Western District (Plymouth, England). Diocesan Archives.

C) *Registers*

1. Register of professions from the first house of La Sainte-Volonté-Dieu, in Valais 1796–1797, Lyon-Vaise (at Rogersville; photocopy at Maubec).
2. Registrum complectent acta professionum emissaerum in monasterio Sanctae Voluntatis Dei Beatae Mariae de

Trappa in Valesia, Lyon-Vaise, 1797 (preserved at Chambarand).

3. Register of the novices and professed of Notre-Dame-de-la-Sainte-Volonté-de-Dieu, near Sembrancher at Bas-Valais (1796–1806) (copy preserved at Sainte-Marie-du-Rivet). The original, thought to have been lost, was recently (15 September 1988) discovered in the library of the monks of Sainte-Marie-du-Désert, Levignac.
4. Register of professions made in danger of death during the journeys between 25 July 1798 and 29 April 1803, and a Register of deaths which occurred during the trip. Lyon-Vaise (preserved at Rogersville; photocopy at Maubec).
5. A list of Registers of the monastery of La Trappe-de-la-Miséricorde after the foundation of Darfeld in Westphalia on 28 December 1800 (preserved at Altbronn).
6. Register of the community (1806) (Villarvolard, La Riedera, Lyon-Vaise, Maubec; preserved and still in use at Maubec).
7. Register of deaths of the house of the Dames Trappistines at Darfeld (1802–1810) (preserved in the archives at Münster; photocopy at Altbronn).
8. Register of the religious sent to England on the foundation and some postulants who were received at Blythe House, Brook, near London, Burton House, Christchurch, 1803 (preserved at Stapehill and still in use).
9. Register of the acts of profession of the religious of the monastery of Sainte-Catherine of Laval, 1816 (preserved at La Coudre-Laval).
10. Register of professions of the lay sisters of the monastery of Sainte-Catherine of Laval, 1816 (preserved at La Coudre-Laval).
11. Register of the persons who entered the monastery of N. D. des Gardes near Chemillé (Maine-et-Loire), departures, clothings, professions and deaths after the foundation in 1818 (preserved at Les Gardes).

12. Register containing the name, age, profession, the place of birth of all those who entered this house of Notre-Dame-de-la-Trappe, with the date of their entry, their profession, their death or their departure (1798–1829) (Valenton-Mondaye; preserved at Maubec).
13. Necrology of the Trappistines of Mondaye (1815–1845) drawn up by one of the Norbertine Canons of the Abbey of Saint-Martin in 1935, copied from the Registers of the Parish and of the commune of Juaye (Abbey of Saint-Martin of Mondaye).

D) Schedules or Charts of Religious Professions

— made at La Sainte-Volenté-de-Dieu (1797): three preserved at Chambarand and two at Stapehill.
— made at Orsha in Russia (1799): four preserved at Chamabarand and one at Stapehill.
— made at Darfeld (Westphalia) (1802): two preserved at Chambarand.
— made at the monastery of La Sainte-Trinité, La Riedera (Switzerland) (1807–1810): nine preserved at Maubec and one at Chambarand.
— made at Grosbois, Valenton-Mondaye (1802–1829): twenty-eight preserved at Maubec and four at Stapehill.
— made at L'Archange-Raphaël (Les Forges) and N. D. des Gardes (without date): two preserved at Maubec.
— made at Lyon-Vaise (without date): fourteen preserved at Maubec.
— Some schedules of Cistercians or of Benedictines made before the Revolution, by some sisters who made their profession as Trappists. Cistercians: Saint-Antoine-des-Champs-lès-Paris, Bival (near Neuchâtel-en-Braye). Benedictines: N. D. de-Nazareth (Orne), N. D. de-Protection (Manche).

E) Various Manuscripts

— Narrative of the foundation of the monastery of N. D. de-La-Sainte-Trinité of the Reform of La Trappe on the property of La Riedera in the Canton of Fribourg (Switzerland): Trappe, ref. 55, piece 13 *bis*, not dated, between 1806–1813 (recital of Sister Stanislaus Michel, 1756-1813).

— Memoir in the form of letters (1809) written by Father François de Paule Dargnies, quoted according to the manuscript preserved at La Trappe (other manuscripts can be found at Timadeuc and at Tamie).

— Personal papers of Mother Augustin de Chabannes, foundress of Stapehill (archives of Stapehill).

— Manuscript lettrs of Father Urbain Guillet (archives of Bellefontaine).

— 'Relation des voyages de la vénerable Mère Saint-Maur, religieuse du Calvaire de Paris, pendant son émigration. 1829'. Manuscript of the Benedictines of Calvaire d'Angers (several manuscripts exist, there is one at the Benedictines of Limon).

II. PRINTED SOURCES

A) General Works

Bouton, Jean de la Croix. Fiches cisterciennes, *Histoire de l'Ordre*, série 6. Westmalle 1959-1960.

Canivez, J.-M. 'Cîteaux', in DHGE, 12:852–997.

Catherine de Bar—Mère Mechtilde du Saint-Sacrement, 1614–1698. En Pologne avec les Bénédictines de France. Documents originally collected and published by the Benedictines of Saint-Sacrement of Rouen. Paris 1984.

Cocheril, M. *Dictionnaire des monastères cisterciens*. Documentation cistercienne, 18. Rochefort (Belgium) 1979.

Gaillardin, C. *Histoire de La Trappe, les Trappistes ou l'Ordre de Cîteaux au XIX siècle*, vol. 2. Paris 1844.

Hermans, Vincent. *Actes des chapitres généraux des Congrégations trappistes au XIX siècle*. Rome 1975.

Lekai, Louis J. *The Cistercians, Ideals and Reality*. Kent, Ohio 1977.

Maire, E. *Les Cisterciens en France*, 2nd edition. Paris 1921.

Van der Meer, F. *Atlas de l'Ordre cistercien*. Brussels-Paris 1965.

Règlements de la Maison-Dieu de Notre-Dame-de-la-Trappe par Mr l'Abbé de Rancé, son digne réformateur, mis en nouvel ordre et augmentés des usages particuliers de la Maison-Dieu de La Valsainte de Notre-Dame-de-la-Trappe au Canton de Fribourg en Suisse, 2 volumes. Fribourg 1794.

(Anonymous). *L'Odyssée monastique. Dom A. de Lestrange et les Trappistes pendant la Révolution*. Grande-Trappe 1898.

Musée Carnavalet, *Les Cisterciens à Paris*. Catalogue of an exhibition held 21 January - 13 April 1986. Ed. Les Musées de la Ville de Paris 1986.

B) Biographies

Hermeland, F. M. *Vie du R. P. Dom Urbain Guillet, fondateur de La Trappe de Bellefontaine*. Montligeon 1899.

Loup, R. *Une grande abbesse de l'Ordre de Cîteaux, Mère Lutgarde Ménétrey, 1845–1919*. Fribourg 1942.

Rabory, Jean. *La vie de Louise de Bourbon, princess de Condé*. Solesmes 1888.

(Anonymous). *Vie de la Révérende Mère Pacifique, fondatrice et première supérieure des Trappistines de Lyon*. Bar-le-Duc 1891.

C) Monographs

Arnemann, C. *Les bienheureuses soeurs de Bollène, martyrisées à Orange* (adapted from the German by R. L. Oechslin, OP). Fribourg, 1965.

Bonnardot, H. *Abbaye Saint-Antoine (abbaye royale de Saint-Antoine-des-Champs)*. Paris 1882.

Bouton, Jean de la Croix. *Les moniales cisterciennes*, volumes 2 and 3. Abbaye d'Aiguebelle, 1987–1988.

De Marquette. *Dossier sur l'abbaye N. D. La Brayelle d'Annay* (typescript). Documents and texts collected by l'abbé Buquet. Arras 1982.

Daumont, O. *Soleilmont, abbaye cistercienne, 1237–1937*. Charleroi (Belgium) 1937.

Rabory, Jean. *Correspondance de la princesse Louise de Condé, fondatrice du monastère du Temple*. Paris 1889.

Anonymous:

— *La Trappe in England*. London: Burns and Oates 1935; 2nd edn. 1946.

— *Lettres de piété ou correspondance intime de la princesse Louise-Adélaïde de Bourbon-Condé*. Paris 1843.

— *Notes historiques sur l'abbaye cistercienne de Port-Royal ou N.–D.–de-Consolation, 1204–1915*. Besançon 1914.

D) Journal Articles

Collectanea Ordinis Cisterciensium Reformatum of 1934 to 1940. In particular:

'Aperçu historique sur la Congrégation des Bernardines d'Esquermes et sur les abbbayes dont elle est issue', COCS, 2 (1938) 96–106.

Cîteaux. Commentarii cistercienses, Achel (Belgium). In particular:

Baeckmund, N., O. Praem. 'Les Cisterciens français en Bavière', *Cîteaux* 32 (1981) 138–143.

Halgouët, Jérôme du: 1966/1–2:89–118; 1967/1:51–74 and 3:240–262; 1968/1–2:74–93; 1969/1:38–68; 1970/1:2361 and 3–4:279–289; 1971/1:61–92; 1975/1–2:57–81; 3:185–215, and 4:284–315; 1976/1–2:56–84; 1977/1–2:48–93, and 4:306–346.

Kervingant, M. T. 'Aux origines des Cisterciennes-Trappistines: Un document inédit', 1984/3–4:184–214.

———. 'Les registres des premières communautés', 1985/1–2:63–80.

———. 'La communauté mère: La Sainte-Volonté-de-Dieu', 1985/3–4:188–203.

Bouton, Jean de la Croix and P. Braun. 'Les Trappistes et les Trappistines en Suisse', *Helvetia Sacra* 1982:1066–1079.

Fux, I., OSB, 'Emigrierende Trappisten in Österreich', *Studien und Mitteilungen zur Geschichte des Benediktiner-Ordens und seiner Zweige*, 1987, Heft III/IV.

Hedouville, F. d'. 'La vie quotidienne d'un jeune trappiste à son arrivée à Sembrancher en 1797', *Etoile, reflets du Valais*, 4 (April 1982) 51–54.

Presse, A. 'Les moniales cisterciennes réformées', *Revue Mabillon* 24 (1934) 1–42.

Robert, A. 'L'Abbaye cistercienne de Mercoire en Gévaudan', *Revue du Vivarais* 4 (1973) 1- 19.

Robert, A., P. Savoie, F. Viallet. 'L'abbaye de Mercoire', *Revue du Gévaudan, des Causses et des Cévennes*, 4 (1981) 45–73.

III. BACKGROUND

A) General

Aubert, R., general editor. *Nouvelle histoire de l'Église*, 4. Paris 1966.

Baudrillart, A. *et al* . edd. *Dictionnaire d'histoire et de géographie ecclésiastiques*. Paris 1912-.

Marrou, H.-I. *De la connaissance historique*. Paris 1954.

Samaran, Charles (under the direction of). *L'histoire et ses méthodes*. La Pléiade 1961.

Veyne, Paul. *Comment on écrit l'histoire*. Paris 1979.

B) *Revolutionary Period and Restauration*

Bluche, F. *La vie quotidienne au temps de Louis XVI*. Paris 1980.

Burnat, J., G. H. Dumont, Wanty. *Le dossier Napoléon*. Bibliothèque Marabout Université, 17. Paris 1962.

Cholvy, G., Y.-M. Hilaire. *Histoire religieuse de la France contemporaine 1800–1880*. Toulouse 1985.

Droz, J. *De la Restauration à la Révolution: 1815–1848*, Collection U2. Paris 1971.

Furet, F., D. Richet. *La Révolution française*. Paris 1973.

La Gorce, P. de. *Histoire de la Révolution française*. Paris 1948.

Latreille, A. *L'Église catholique et la Révolution française*, volumes 1 (1775–1799), and 2 (1800–1815). Paris 1970.

Lefebvre, G. *La Révolution française*. 6th edn. Paris 1968.

———. *Napoléon*, 6th edn. Paris 1969.

Leflon, J. 'La crise révolutionnaire', *Histoire de l'Église*, under the direction of A. Fliche and V. Martin. Paris 1944.

Plongeron, B. *Théologie et politique au siècle des Lumières, 1770–1820*. Geneva 1973.

———. *La vie quotidienne du clergé française au XVIII siècle*. Paris 1974, 1988.

Raemy, Tobie de. *L'emigration française dans le canton de Fribourg*. Fribourg 1935.

Soboul, Albert. *La Révolution française*. 8th edn. Paris 1985.

Tackett, Timothy. *La Rèvolution, l'Église, la France*, trad. A. Spiess. Paris 1986 (Original title: *Religion, Revolution, and Regional Culture in Eighteenth-century France: The Ecclesiastical Oath of 1791*. Princeton: University Press 1986).

Vidalenc, J. *La Restauration*. 5th edn. Paris 1983.

Vigier, Ph. *La monarchie de Juillet*. 6th edn. Paris 1982.

Vovelle, M. *Religion et révolution. La déchristianisation de l'an II*. Paris 1976.

C) Studies on the Religious Life from the Seventeenth to the Nineteenth Century

Arnold, O. *Le corps et l'âme. La vie des religieuses au XIX siècle*. Paris 1984.

Hours, B. *Madame Louise, princesse au Carmel*. Paris 1987.

Langloss, Cl. *Le catholicisme français au féminin. Les Congrégations françaises à supérieure générale au XIX siècle*. Paris 1984.

———. 'Les effectifs des Congrégations féminines au XIX siècle. De l'enquête statistique à l'enquête quantitative'. *Revue de l'Histoire de l'Église de France* (1974) 39–64.

Reynes, G. *Couvents de femmes. La vie des religieuses cloîtrées dans la France des XVII et XVIII siècles*. Paris 1987.

Sonnet, M. *L'education des filles au temps des Lumières*. Paris 1987.

INDEX OF PERSONS

INDEX OF PLACES

CISTERCIAN TEXTS

Bernard of Clairvaux

- Apologia to Abbot William
- Five Books on Consideration: Advice to a Pope
- Homilies in Praise of the Blessed Virgin Mary
- Letters of Bernard of Clairvaux / by B.S. James
- Life and Death of Saint Malachy the Irishman
- Love without Measure: Extracts from the Writings of St Bernard / by Paul Dimier
- On Grace and Free Choice
- On Loving God / Analysis by Emero Stiegman
- Parables and Sentences
- Sermons for the Summer Season
- Sermons on Conversion
- Sermons on the Song of Songs I–IV
- The Steps of Humility and Pride

William of Saint Thierry

- The Enigma of Faith
- Exposition on the Epistle to the Romans
- Exposition on the Song of Songs
- The Golden Epistle
- The Mirror of Faith
- The Nature and Dignity of Love
- On Contemplating God: Prayer & Meditations

Aelred of Rievaulx

- Dialogue on the Soul
- Liturgical Sermons, I
- The Mirror of Charity
- Spiritual Friendship
- Treatises I: On Jesus at the Age of Twelve, Rule for a Recluse, The Pastoral Prayer
- Walter Daniel: The Life of Aelred of Rievaulx

John of Ford

- Sermons on the Final Verses of the Songs of Songs I–VII

Gilbert of Hoyland

- Sermons on the Songs of Songs I–III
- Treatises, Sermons and Epistles

Other Early Cistercian Writers

- Adam of Perseigne, Letters of
- Alan of Lille: The Art of Preaching
- Amadeus of Lausanne: Homilies in Praise of Blessed Mary
- Baldwin of Ford: Spiritual Tractates I–II
- Gertrud the Great: Spiritual Exercises
- Gertrud the Great: The Herald of God's Loving-Kindness (Books 1, 2)
- Gertrud the Great: The Herald of God's Loving-Kindness (Books 3)
- Guerric of Igny: Liturgical Sermons I
- Helinand of Froidmont: Verses on Death
- Idung of Prüfening: Cistercians and Cluniacs: The Case for Cîteaux
- Isaac of Stella: Sermons on the Christian Year, I–[II]
- The Life of Beatrice of Nazareth
- Serlo of Wilton & Serlo of Savigny: Seven Unpublished Works
- Stephen of Lexington: Letters from Ireland
- Stephen of Sawley: Treatises

MONASTIC TEXTS

Eastern Monastic Tradition

- Besa: The Life of Shenoute
- Cyril of Scythopolis: Lives of the Monks of Palestine
- Dorotheos of Gaza: Discourses and Sayings
- Evagrius Ponticus: Praktikos and Chapters on Prayer
- Handmaids of the Lord: Lives of Holy Women in Late Antiquity & the Early Middle Ages / by Joan Petersen
- Harlots of the Desert / by Benedicta Ward
- John Moschos: The Spiritual Meadow
- Lives of the Desert Fathers
- Lives of Simeon Stylites / by Robert Doran
- The Luminous Eye / by Sebastian Brock
- Mena of Nikiou: Isaac of Alexandra & St Macrobius
- Pachomian Koinonia I–III (Armand Veilleux)
- Paphnutius: Histories/Monks of Upper Egypt
- The Sayings of the Desert Fathers / by Benedicta Ward
- Spiritual Direction in the Early Christian East / by Irénée Hausherr
- The Spiritually Beneficial Tales of Paul, Bishop of Monembasia / by John Wortley
- Symeon the New Theologian: TheTheological and Practical Treatises & The Three Theological Discourses / by Paul McGuckin
- Theodoret of Cyrrhus: A History of the Monks of Syria
- The Syriac Fathers on Prayer and the Spiritual Life / by Sebastian Brock

CISTERCIAN PUBLICATIONS

TITLES LISTING

Western Monastic Tradition

- Anselm of Canterbury: Letters I–III / by Walter Fröhlich
- Bede: Commentary...Acts of the Apostles
- Bede: Commentary...Seven Catholic Epistles
- Bede: Homilies on the Gospels I–II
- Bede: Excerpts from the Works of St Augustine on the Lettrs of the Blessed Apostle Paul
- The Celtic Monk / by U. Ó Maidín
- Life of the Jura Fathers
- Maxims of Stephen of Muret
- Peter of Celle: Selected Works
- Letters of Rancé I–II
- Rule of the Master
- Rule of Saint Augustine

Christian Spirituality

- The Cloud of Witnesses: The Development of Christian Doctrine / by David N. Bell
- The Call of Wild Geese / by Matthew Kelty
- The Cistercian Way / by André Louf
- The Contemplative Path
- Drinking From the Hidden Fountain / by Thomas Špidlík
- Eros and Allegory: Medieval Exegesis of the Song of Songs / by Denys Turner
- Fathers Talking / by Aelred Squire
- Friendship and Community / by Brian McGuire
- Gregory the Great: Forty Gospel Homilies
- High King of Heaven / by Benedicta Word
- The Hermitage Within / by a Monk
- Life of St Mary Magdalene and of Her Sister St Martha / by David Mycoff
- Many Mansions / by David N. Bell
- Mercy in Weakness / by André Louf
- The Name of Jesus / by Irénée Hausherr
- No Moment Too Small / by Norvene Vest
- Penthos: The Doctrine of Compunction in the Christian East / by Irénée Hausherr
- Praying the Word / by Enzo Bianchi
- Rancé and the Trappist Legacy / by A. J. Krailsheimer
- Russian Mystics / by Sergius Bolshakoff
- Sermons in a Monastery / by Matthew Kelty
- Silent Herald of Unity: The Life of Maria Gabrielle Sagheddu / by Martha Driscoll
- The Spirituality of the Christian East / by Thomas Špidlík
- The Spirituality of the Medieval West / by André Vauchez
- Tuning In To Grace / by André Louf
- Wholly Animals: A Book of Beastly Tales / by David N. Bell

MONASTIC STUDIES

- Community and Abbot in the Rule of St Benedict I–II / by Adalbert de Vogüé
- The Finances of the Cistercian Order in the Fourteenth Century / by Peter King
- Fountains Abbey and Its Benefactors / by Joan Wardrop
- The Hermit Monks of Grandmont / by Carole A. Hutchison
- In the Unity of the Holy Spirit / by Sighard Kleiner
- The Joy of Learning & the Love of God: Essays in Honor of Jean Leclercq
- Monastic Odyssey / by Marie Kervingant
- Monastic Practices / by Charles Cummings
- The Occupation of Celtic Sites in Ireland / by Geraldine Carville
- Reading St Benedict / by Adalbert de Vogüé
- Rule of St Benedict: A Doctrinal and Spiritual Commentary / by Adalbert de Vogüé
- The Rule of St Benedict / by Br. Pinocchio
- St Hugh of Lincoln / by David H. Farmer
- The Venerable Bede / by Benedicta Ward
- What Nuns Read / by David N. Bell
- With Greater Liberty: A Short History of Christian Monasticism & Religious Orders / by Karl Frank

CISTERCIAN STUDIES

- Aelred of Rievaulx: A Study / by Aelred Squire
- Athirst for God: Spiritual Desire in Bernard of Clairvaux's Sermons on the Song of Songs / by Michael Casey
- Beatrice of Nazareth in Her Context / by Roger De Ganck
- Bernard of Clairvaux: Man, Monk, Mystic / by Michael Casey [tapes and readings]
- Bernardus Magister...Nonacentenary
- Catalogue of Manuscripts in the Obrecht Collection of the Institute of Cistercian Studies / by Anna Kirkwood
- Christ the Way: The Christology of Guerric of Igny / by John Morson
- The Cistercians in Denmark / by Brian McGuire
- The Cistercians in Scandinavia / by James France
- A Difficult Saint / by Brian McGuire
- A Gathering of Friends: Learning & Spirituality in John of Ford / by Costello and Holdsworth
- Image and Likeness: Augustinian Spirituality of William of St Thierry / by David Bell

- Index of Authors & Works in Cistercian Libraries in Great Britain I / by David Bell
- Index of Cistercian Authors and Works in Medieval Library Catalogues in Great Britian / by David Bell
- The Mystical Theology of St Bernard / by Étienne Gilson
- The New Monastery: Texts & Studies on the Earliest Cistercians
- Nicolas Cotheret's Annals of Cîteaux / by Louis J. Lekai
- Pater Bernhardus: Mentor of Martin Luther... / by Franz Posset
- A Second Look at Saint Bernard / by Jean Leclercq
- The Spiritual Teachings of St Bernard of Clairvaux / by John R. Sommerfeldt
- Studies in Medieval Cistercian History
- Studiosorum Speculum / by Louis J. Lekai
- Three Founders of Cîteaux / by Jean-Baptiste Van Damme
- Towards Unification with God (Beatrice of Nazareth in Her Context, 2)
- William, Abbot of St Thierry
- Women and St Bernard of Clairvaux / by Jean Leclercq

MEDIEVAL RELIGIOUS WOMEN

edited by Lillian Thomas Shank and John A. Nichols:

- Distant Echoes
- Hidden Springs: Cistercian Monastic Women (2 volumes)
- Peace Weavers

CARTHUSIAN TRADITION

- The Call of Silent Love / by A Carthusian
- The Freedom of Obedience / by A Carthusian
- Guigo II: The Ladder of Monks & Twelve Meditations / by Colledge & Walsh
- Halfway to Heaven / by R.B. Lockhart
- Interior Prayer / by A Carthusian
- Meditations of Guigo II / by A. Gordon Mursall
- Prayer of Love and Silence / by A Carthusian
- Poor, Therefore Rich / by A Carthusian
- They Speak by Silences / by A Carthusian
- The Way of Silent Love (A Carthusian Miscellany)
- Where Silence is Praise / by A Carthusian
- The Wound of Love (A Carthusian Miscellany)

CISTERCIAN ART, ARCHITECTURE & MUSIC

- Cistercian Abbeys of Britain
- Cistercians in Medieval Art / by James France
- Studies in Medieval Art and Architecture / edited by Meredith Parsons Lillich *(Volumes II–V are now available)*
- Stones Laid Before the Lord / by Anselme Dimier
- Treasures Old and New: Nine Centuries of Cistercian Music (compact disc)

THOMAS MERTON

- The Climate of Monastic Prayer / by T. Merton
- Legacy of Thomas Merton / by P. Hart
- Message of Thomas Merton / by P. Hart
- Monastic Journey of Thomas Merton / by P. Hart
- Thomas Merton/Monk / by P. Hart
- Thomas Merton on St Bernard
- Toward an Integrated Humanity / edited by M. Basil Pennington

CISTERCIAN LITURGICAL DOCUMENTS SERIES

- Cistercian Liturgical Documents Series / edited by Chrysogonus Waddell, ocso
- Hymn Collection of the…Paraclete
- *Institutiones nostrae:* The Paraclete Statutes
- Molesme Summer-Season Breviary (4 volumes)
- Old French Ordinary & Breviary of the Abbey of the Paraclete (2 volumes)
- Twelfth-century Cistercian Hymnal (2 volumes)
- The Twelfth-century Cistercian Psalter
- Two Early Cistercian *Libelli Missarum*

STUDIA PATRISTICA

- Studia Patristica XVIII, Volumes 1, 2 and 3

CISTERCIAN PUBLICATIONS

HOW TO CONTACT US

Editorial Queries

Editorial queries & advance book information should be directed to the Editorial Offices:

- Cistercian Publications
  WMU Station
  1201 Oliver Street
  Kalamazoo, Michigan 49008

- Telephone 616 387 8920
- Fax 616 387 8921

How to Order in the United States

Customers may order these books through booksellers or directly by contacting the warehouse at the address below:

- Cistercian Publications
  Saint Joseph's Abbey
  167 North Spencer Road
  Spencer, Massachusetts 01562-1233

- Telephone 508 885 8730
- Fax 508 885 4687
- e-mail cistpub@spencerabbey.org
- Web Site www.spencerabbey.org/cistpub

How to Order from Canada

- Novalis
  49 Front Street East, Second Floor
  Toronto, Ontario M5E 1B3

- Telephone 416 363 3303
  1 800 387 7164
- Fax 416 363 9409

How to Order from Europe

- Cistercian Publications
  Mount Saint Bernard Abbey
  Coalville, Leicester LE67 5UL

- Fax 44 1530 81 46 08

Cistercian Publications is a non-profit corporation. Its publishing program is restricted to monastic texts in translation and books on the monastic tradition.

A complete catalogue of texts in translation and studies on early, medieval, and modern monasticism is available, free of charge, from any of the addresses above.

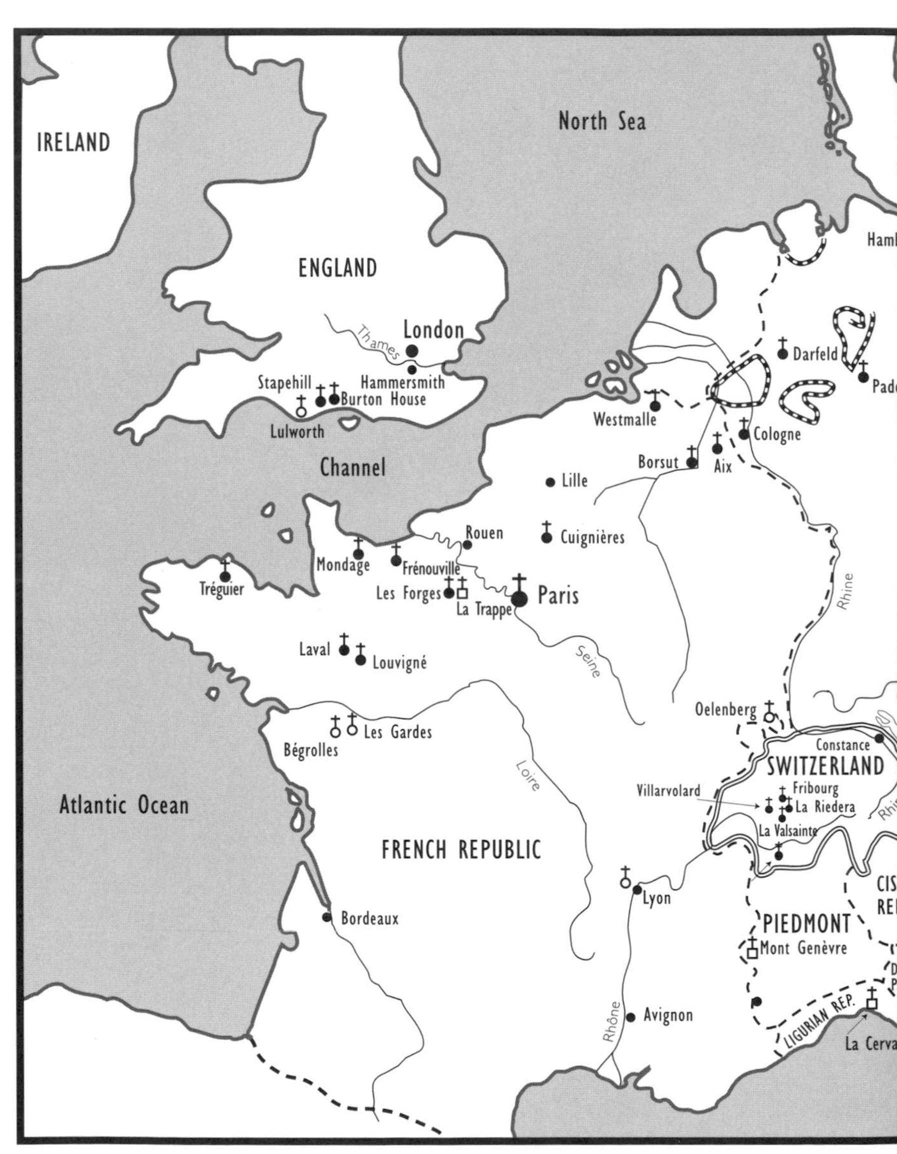
IRELAND
North Sea
ENGLAND
London
Thames
Hammersmith
Stapehill
Burton House
Lulworth
Channel
Westmalle
Darfeld
Cologne
Borsut
Aix
Lille
Rouen
Cuignières
Mondage
Frénouville
Tréguier
Les Forges
La Trappe
Paris
Rhine
Laval
Louvigné
Seine
Oelenberg
Les Gardes
Bégrolles
Constance
SWITZERLAND
Loire
Villarvolard
Fribourg
La Riedera
La Valsainte
Atlantic Ocean
FRENCH REPUBLIC
Lyon
Bordeaux
PIEDMONT
Mont Genèvre
Rhône
Avignon
LIGURIAN REP.

Baltic Sea
Danzig
PRUSSIAN POLAND
Orsha
RUSSIAN POLAND
Torun
PRUSSIA
Vistula
Warsaw
Terespol
Brest
Vistula
Bug
AUSTRIAN POLAND
Elbe
Cracow
Leopold (Lvov)
Château Buštĕrad
Prague
Brünn
Krems
Passau
Vienna
Munich
Linz
Danube
AUSTRIAN EMPIRE
OTTOMAN EMPIRE
ROMAN REPUBLIC
LEGEND
STATE FRONTIERS IN 1798
Switzerland
Austrian Empire
Russian Empire
Prussia
Other States
CISTERCIAN - TRAPPIST NUNS
Extended Stay 1796 to1816
Extended Stay 1816 to 1825
CISTERCIAN - TRAPPIST MONKS
...Some Monasteries
SCALE
50 Km
300 Km